Difficulties in Child Development

Originally published in 1928, *Difficulties in Child Development* was written, according to the author, as 'a response to many inquiries concerning a source of practical information relating to the development and upbringing of little children from a modern psychological standpoint. It also serves to put forward in a simple and direct manner, without unnecessary intricacies due to the unexplained use of the more specialized psycho-analytic terms, views and discoveries made by Freud and his followers, now scattered in many books that have been written upon this subject... and to condense those which especially touch the matter of child study into a more convenient form for parents, teachers, nurses, welfare workers, and others who are anxious to know what advances and contributions have been made towards the understanding and early education of young children during recent years.'
Today it can be read and enjoyed in its historical context.

I0084844

Difficulties in Child Development

Mary Chadwick

Routledge
Taylor & Francis Group

LONDON AND NEW YORK

First published in 1928
by George Allen & Unwin Ltd

This edition first published in 2025 by Routledge
4 Park Square, Milton Park, Abingdon, Oxon, OX14 4RN

and by Routledge
605 Third Avenue, New York, NY 10017

Routledge is an imprint of the Taylor & Francis Group, an informa business

© 1928 Mary Chadwick

Publisher's Note
The publisher has gone to great lengths to ensure the quality of this reprint but points out that some imperfections in the original copies may be apparent.

Disclaimer
The publisher has made every effort to trace copyright holders and welcomes correspondence from those they have been unable to contact.

ISBN: 978-1-032-90678-2 (hbk)
ISBN: 978-1-003-55920-7 (ebk)
ISBN: 978-1-032-90685-0 (pbk)

Book DOI 10.4324/9781003559207

DIFFICULTIES IN CHILD DEVELOPMENT

By

MARY CHADWICK

S.R.N., F.B.C.N.

*Member College of Nursing; British Psychological
Society; Associate Member International
Psycho-analytical Society*

LONDON
GEORGE ALLEN & UNWIN LTD
MUSEUM STREET

FOREWORD

THIS book is a response to many inquiries concerning a source of practical information relating to the development and upbringing of little children from a modern psychological standpoint.

It also serves to put forward in a simple and direct manner, without unnecessary intricacies due to the unexplained use of the more specialized psycho-analytic terms, views and discoveries made by Freud and his followers, now scattered in many books that have been written upon this subject, both in German and English, and to condense those which especially touch the matter of child study into a more convenient form for parents, teachers, nurses, welfare workers, and others who are anxious to know what advances and contributions have been made towards the understanding and early education of young children during recent years.

I should also be glad to make use of this opportunity to offer my most grateful thanks to all those who have given me valuable help in the compilation of this book; to the authors whose works have been used in reference, as well as to many who, by their ready advice, encouragement, and the placing of unique material at my disposal, have made it possible.

MARY CHADWICK

48, TAVISTOCK SQUARE, LONDON
July, 1928

CONTENTS

BIBLIOGRAPHY

ABBREVIATIONS USED IN BIBLIOGRAPHY

Int. Ps.-A. Verlag. Internationaler Psychoanalytischer Verlag. Vienna.
Int. Zeit. für Psa. Internationale Zeitschrift für Psychoanalyse.
Br. J. of Psychol. British Journal of Psychology.
Int. J. Ps.-A. International Journal of Psycho-analysis.

ABRAHAM, KARL, M.D. Coincident Phantasies in Mother and Son.
Int. J. Ps.-A. Jan. 1926.
Carakterbildung. Int. Ps.-A. Verlag. Vienna.
Selected Papers by Karl Abraham, M.D. Hogarth Press, London.
ADLER, ALFRED. Neurotic Constitution. Kegan Paul. Trans.
Über den Selbstmord inbesondere den Schülerselbstmord, with Freud
and others. Int. Ps.-A. Verlag.
AICHHORN, AUGUST. Über die Erziehung in Besserungsanstalten. Imago.
1923.
Verwahrlöste Jugend. Int. Ps.-A. Verlag. Vienna.

BACHOFEN, J. J. Das Mutterrecht. Benno Schwabe. Basel.
BALDWIN, B. T. Psychology of the Pre-School Child. New Era Library.
New York.
BALDWIN, J. M. Mental Development of the Child and the Race.
Macmillan.
BALLARD, P. B. The Changing School. Hodder & Stoughton.
BAZELEY, E. T. Homer Lane and the Little Commonwealth. George
Allen & Unwin.
BERNFELD, SIEGFRIED. Gemeinschaftsleben der Jugend. Int. Ps.-A. Verlag.
Heutige Psychologie der Pubertät. Imago. 1927.
Der Saugling.
Sisyphos. Int. Ps.-A. Verlag. Vienna.
BINNS, HENRY. Discrimination of Wool Fabrics by the Sense of Touch.
Br. J. of Psychol. Jan. 1926.
BRADBY, M. K. Psycho-analysis. Oxford Medical Publications.
BURT, CYRIL, M.A., D.Sc. The Young Delinquent. London University
Press.

CAMERON, H., M.D. The Nervous Child. Hodder & Stoughton.
CAMPBELL, HARRY. Differences in the Nervous Organization of Men and
Women. Lewis. London.
CHADWICK, MARY. Psychology for Nurses. Heinemann Medical Books.
Case of Kleptomania in a Child of Ten Years. Int. J. Ps.-A. 1925.
Notes in the Acquisition of Knowledge. Psychoanalytic Review. 1926.
Self-expression without Speech. Child Study Journal. 1925.

CHADWICK, MARY
  Six Months' Experiment in a Nursery School. Psychoanalytic Review.
    1928.
  Child's Early Discrimination between Sound and Speech. Psyche. 1928.
  Notes upon the Fear of Death. Int. J. Ps.-A. 1928.
CHILD'S GUARDIAN. Proceedings of the Society for the Prevention of
    Cruelty to Children.
COKKINIS, A. J., F.R.C.S., M.B., B.S. Reproduction of Life. Baillière,
    Tindall & Cox.
COLLINS, MARY, M.A. Experimental Psychology. Methuen.
COMENIUS. School of Infancy.
CORIAT, Dr. ISADOR H. Stammering. A Psychoanalytic Interpretation.
    Mental and Nervous Pub. Co.
COUÉ, EMILE. Self-mastery through Auto-suggestion. George Allen &
    Unwin.
CUMMY'S BOOK. Alison Cunningham. Preface, R. T. Skinner. Chatto &
    Windus.

DARWIN, CHARLES. The Origin of Species. Murray
  Biographical Sketch of an Infant. Mind. Vol. 2. 1877 (written thirty-
    seven years before).
DELACROIX, H. L'activité Linguistique de l'Enfant. Journal de Psychologie,
    normale et pathologique. XXI. Nos. 1–3.
DEUTSCH, HELENE. Psychoanalyse der Weibliche Sexualfunction. Int. Ps.-A.
    Verlag. Vienna.
  Über die Pathologische Lüge. Int. Zeit. für Psa. 1922. Vol. LVII. 2.
DRUMMOND, MARGARET. Five Years Old or Thereabouts. Edward Arnold.

EDGELL, F. Mental Life. Methuen.
EVANS, ELIDA. Problems of the Nervous Child. Kegan Paul.

FEHLINGER, H. Sexual Life of Primitive People. Black. London.
FELDMAN, W. M., M.D., B.S., M.R.C.P. (London), F.R.S. (Edin.). The
    Jewish Child. Baillière, Tindall & Cox.
  The Principles of Ante-Natal and Post-Natal Hygiene. John Bale,
    Sons & Danielsson.
FERENCZI, SANDOR, M.D. Some Contributions to Psycho-analysis. Badger.
  Further Contributions to the Theory and Technique of Psycho-
    analysis. Hogarth Press.
FLÜGEL, J. C., B.A. Psycho-analytic Study of the Family. Hogarth Press.
FORSYTH, DAVID, M.D., D.Sc., F.R.C.P. Children in Health and Disease.
    Murray.
  Mental Health of the Child, Public Health Report.
  The Psycho-analysis of an Early Case of Paranoid Dementia. Proc.
    Royal Society of Medicine. July 1920.
  Rudiments of Character. Psychoanalytic Review. 1921.
  The Infantile Psyche, with special reference to Visual Projection.
    Br. J. of Psychol. April 1921.

FRASER, SIR GEORGE. The Golden Bough. Abridged Version. Macmillan.
FREUD, ANNA. Einführung in die Technik der Kinderanalyse. Int. Ps.-A. Verlag. Vienna.
FREUD, SIGMUND. Interpretation of Dreams. George Allen & Unwin.
Psychopathology of Everyday Life. T. Fisher Unwin.
Three Contributions to the Sexual Theory. Nervous and Mental Pub. Co. Washington, D.C.
Introductory Lectures. George Allen & Unwin.
Collected Papers. Hogarth Press.
Group Psychology and the Analysis of the Ego. Hogarth Press.
The Ego and the Id. Hogarth Press.
Totem and Taboo. Kegan Paul.
Hemmung, Symptom und Angst. Int. Ps.-A. Verlag. Vienna.
Über den Selbstmord. Franz Deutike. Vienna.
Eine Kindheitserrinnerung aus "Dichtung und Wahrheit." Imago. V. 1917-19.
FRIEDMANN, DR. ALICE. Psychische Stummheit. Int. Zeitschrift fur Individual Psychologie. 1926.

GESELL, ARNOLD. The Pre-School Child. Macmillan.
GLOVER, DR. E. Notes on Oral Character-Formation. Int. J. Ps.-A. 1925.
GREEN, GEORGE H. The Day-Dream. University of London Press.
GREEN, HENRY. Blindness. Dent.
GROOS, KARL. The Play of Man. Heinemann.

HALL, STANLEY G. Adolescence. Parts I and II.
HALL, W. CLARKE. Children's Courts. George Allen & Unwin.
HAMBLY, W. D. Origins of Education among Primitive Peoples. Macmillan.
HARFORD, CHARLES. Squint and the Child Mind. The Child. Jan. 1924.
HARRISON, JANE. Ancient Art and Ritual. Williams & Norgate.
HARTLEY, GASQUOINE. Mother and Son. Eveleigh Nash. F. Grayson, Ltd.
HARTRIDGE, H. A Vindication of the Resonance Hypothesis of Audition. Br. J. of Psychol. April 1921.
HILL, J. C. Dreams and Education. Methuen.
HOBHOUSE, T. L. Mind in Evolution. Macmillan.
HOPKINS, PRYNCE. Fathers or Sons. A Study in Social Psychology. Kegan Paul.
HUG-HELLMUTH, DR. HERMINE VON. Study of the Mental Life of the Child. Nervous and Mental Pub. Co. Washington. D.C.
Von Mittlere Kinder. Imago. 1921.
Neue Wege zum Verständnis der Jugend. Franz Deutike. Vienna.
Young Girl's Diary. George Allen & Unwin.

INMAN, W. S. Emotion and Eye Symptoms. Br. J. of Psychol. 1921.

JAMES, WILLIAM. Principles of Psychology. Henry Holt.
Talks to Teachers on Psychology.
JONES, ERNEST, M.D. Papers on Psycho-analysis. Baillière, Tindall & Cox.
Treatment of the Neuroses. Baillière, Tindall & Cox.
Essays in Applied Psycho-analysis. Hogarth Press.
Social Aspects of Psycho-analysis. Williams & Norgate.
The Nature of Auto-suggestion. Br. J. of Psychol. Vol. III. 3. 1923.
Origin and Structure of the Super-Ego. Int. J. Ps.-A., Vol. VII. 3, 4. 1926.
Some Problems of Adolescence. Br. J. of Psychol. July 1926.
JUNG, C. G. Psychology of the Unconscious. Kegan Paul.
Die Bedeutung des Vaters für das Schicksal des Einzelnen. Franz Deutike. Vienna.

KELLER, HELEN. Story of My Life. Harrap.
KIDD, DUDLEY. Savage Childhood. A. & C. Black. 1906.
KIPLING, RUDYARD. The Five Nations. Macmillan.
KIMMINS, DR. C. W. The Child in the Changing Home. Herbert Jenkins.
Children's Dreams.
KLEIN, MELANIE. Frühstadien des Oedipus Confliktes. Int. Zeit. für Psa.
KÖHLER, PROF. W. Mentality of Apes. Kegan Paul.
KRAEPELIN, PROF. Dementia Praecox. Livingstone. Edinburgh.

LANE, HOMER. Talks to Parents and Teachers. George Allen & Unwin.
LANG, ANDREW. Custom and Myth. Longmans, Green & Co.
Myth, Ritual, and Religion. Longmans, Green & Co.
LAY, W. The Child's Unconscious Mind. Kegan Paul.
LEVINE, I. The Unconscious. George Allen & Unwin.
LIMA, AGNES DE. Our Enemy the Child. New Republic Press. New York.
LOW, BARBARA. The Unconscious in Action. University of London Press.

McDOUGALL, W. Group Psychology. Cambridge University Press.
McKAY, HERBERT. Educate Your Child. Oxford University Press.
McMILLAN, MARGARET. Education through the Imagination. George Allen & Unwin.
MACMUNN, NORMAN. The Child's Path to Freedom. Curwen.
MACNAMARA, N. C. Instinct and Intelligence. Hodder & Stoughton.
MAJOR, D. R. First Steps in Mental Growth.
MAYO, GERTRUDE. Coué for Children. George Allen & Unwin.
MENZIES, K. Auto-erotic Phenomena in Adolescence. Lewis. London.
MENG, HEINRICH, DR. Sonderheft über Onanie. Zeitschrift für Psychoanalytische Pädagogik. Int. Ps.-A. Verlag. Vienna.
MILLER, H. CRICHTON. The New Psychology and the Parent. Jarrolds.

NIETZSCHE. Jenseits von Gut und Böse.

PAGET, SIR RICHARD. Nature et Origine du Langage Humain. Bulletin de l'Institut Général Psychologique. 1925.

PFISTER, OSKAR. Love in Children and Its Aberrations. George Allen & Unwin.

PIAGET, PROF. JEAN. Language and Thought of the Child. Trans. Kegan Paul.

Judgment and Reasoning in the Child. Trans. Kegan Paul.

La Première Année de l'Enfant. Archives de Psychologie. Spring. 1927.

PRESSEY, PROF. SIDNEY L., PH.D. ⎱ Study of Mental Health. George
PRESSEY. LUELLA C., PH.D. ⎰ Allen & Unwin.

PREYER, W. Mental Development in the Child.

Development of the Intellect.

RANK, OTTO. Das Inzest-Motiv in Dichtung und Saga. Franz Deutike. Vienna.

RATTRAY, CAPT. R. C. Ashanti. Humphrey Milford.

Religion and Art in Ashanti. Humphrey Milford.

READ, C. STANFORD, M.D. The Struggles of Male Adolescence. George Allen & Unwin.

REANEY, JANE, D.Sc. The Place of Play in Education. Methuen.

REIK, THEODOR. Die Couvade. Pubertätsriten. Probleme der Religions-psychologie. Int. Ps.-A. Verlag. Vienna.

REVESZ, W. Psychology of a Musical Prodigy. Kegan Paul.

RICHMOND, WINIFRED, PH.D. The Adolescent Girl. Macmillan.

RICKLIN, F. Wish-Fulfilment and Symbolism in Fairy-Tales. Mental and Nervous Pub. Co. Washington. D.C.

ROHEIM, GEZA. Australian Totemism. George Allen & Unwin.

ROMANES. Mental Evolution in Man.

Mental Evolution in Animals.

ROWLAND, EDITH. Pedagogues' Commonplace Book. Dent.

RUSSELL, BERTRAND. On Education. George Allen & Unwin.

RUSSELL, DORA. The Right to be Happy. Routledge.

SACHS, DR. HANNS. Gemeinsame Tagträume. Int. Ps.-A. Verlag. Vienna.

SCHMIDT, VERA. Psychoanalytische Erziehung in Sowjetrussland. Int. Ps.-A. Verlag. Vienna.

SHINN, M. Biography of a Baby.

SIMMEL, DR. ERNST. Doktorspiel, Kranksein und Artzberuf. Int. Zeitschrift für Psychoanalyse. Vol. XII. 1926.

SLAUGHTER, T. W. The Adolescent. George Allen & Unwin.

SMITH, FRANK. Bilingualism and Mental Development. Br. J. of Psychol. Jan, 1923.

SMITH, HAMBLIN M., M.A., M.D. Juvenile and Adolescent Delinquency. The Child. July 1923

SPIELREIN SABINA, DR. Die Entstehung der Kindlichen Worte, Papa, Mama. Imago. VIII. 1922.

STERN, W. The Psychology of Early Childhood. George Allen & Unwin.

STILL, DR. G. F. Common Disorders of Childhood. Oxford University Press.

STOUT, G. F. Manual of Psychology. University Tutorial Press.
SULLY, JAMES. Studies of Childhood.

TOMB, WILLIAM. On the Intuitive Capacity of Children to Understand Spoken Language. Br. J. of Psychol. July 1925.

VINCENT, A. L. and CLARE BINNS. Gilles de Rais. A. M. Philpot.

WARD, IDA C. Some Speech Defects in Children. The Child. Jan. 1925.
WHITE, W. D., M.D. Mechanisms of Character-Formation. Macmillan.
WILLIS, GEORGE. Philosophy of Speech. George Allen & Unwin.

YEARSLEY, MACLEOD, F.R.C.S. Development of Speech in the Normal Child. Child Study Journal. 1926.
YERKES, ROBERT M. Almost Human. Jonathan Cape.

DIFFICULTIES IN CHILD DEVELOPMENT

CHAPTER I

INTRODUCTORY SURVEY OF THE CAUSES AND SYMPTOMS OF EARLY NERVOUS TROUBLE

THE fact that one considers it possible to devote an entire book to the subject of the Psychological Problems of Childhood, with the supposition that it may attract sympathetic interest in other readers, shows a hopeful belief that a more general appreciation of the value of recent psychological discovery has been awakened.

Formerly, the study of psychology was an academic subject that offered neither a wide appeal nor any distinct value outside the laboratory of the scientist, but recently the discoveries of its new "applied" forms have led those who have the welfare of children at heart, either from a curative or educational standpoint, to realize that with its help they may solve many of the intricate problems which have baffled them hitherto.

In the Annual Report of the Chief Officer of the Ministry of Health for the year 1925, published in London the following year (1926), Dr. David Forsyth, in an excellent article upon *The Mind of the Child*[1] drew attention to the discrepancy to be found between the highly efficient service which has been organized to combat the physical troubles of childhood and the lamentable ignorance that is generally prevalent where the psychological disturbances of early life are concerned, suggesting that this state of affairs showed a grave lack of appreciation of vital issues. He continued to point out that research upon the causes of these difficulties had now been taken far enough to indicate that treatment to effect cure is practicable, and expressed his belief that no institution working for the

---

[1] *On the State of the Public Health.* Annual Report of the Chief Officer of the Ministry of Health for the year 1925. Published by The Stationery Office, London, 1926. *The Mind of the Child*, p. 137, Dr. David Forsyth, Senior Physician Evelina Hospital.

care of children is better able to achieve this than the Welfare Centres, should it be possible to find and train suitable persons to carry it out.

It is most sincerely to be hoped that this great aim may become substantiated in reality before many years have passed, but in the meantime this book may help some who are seeking information based upon practical experience to lighten the task of trying alone to solve the many riddles offered by the complexities of the psychological development of children, and explain some of the more frequent and perhaps least understood of nervous disturbances of infancy and childhood.

It is proposed in this introductory chapter briefly to summarize the fundamental psychological problems of the earliest years of life, offering explanations of their origin and sketching their usual course of development, both normal and abnormal, so as to trace their subsequent result in adult life, before we come to deal with them in more detail in the separate sections. This plan has been adopted in order to be able to show more clearly the interrelation between the abnormalities of childhood and the incipient or manifest psychological instability of the adults around them. Although a good deal of attention has been focused of late years upon the early symptoms of nervous or backward children, very little notice or publicity has been given to the results of research that have been made upon the causes of such troubles and the close connection that exists between the psychological disturbances of parents and their children, or of infants and nurses, in whose care they are for the greater part of the day and night. Yet it is necessary to stress this point emphatically before it will be realized so fully that steps are taken to guard against its prevalence. Research carried out during recent years has, in fact, provided so much material touching upon the causes of child neuroses and their mental retardation that we may feel justified in using this ample testimony to point out the undesirable, but usually inadvertent, causes of the injurious conditions, in order that not only may they be remedied before their ill effects have had time to become more deeply rooted, but also in course of time they may be eliminated altogether and replaced by wiser methods of child education.

Not very long ago no particular heed was paid to the care

of children, even from the physiological point of view, with the inevitable consequence that infant and child mortality from preventable causes was extremely high. This has now been remedied. At a still more recent period no one attended to the question of the psychological difficulties in childhood, either from the point of view of cure or prophylaxis, and many, even to-day, consider that those who stress its cardinal importance exaggerate the necessity of taking steps to remedy the neglect. The problem formerly believed of greatest importance in the education of young children was to see that sufficiently stern measures were adopted to ensure perfect and instant obedience, and the high-water mark of child virtue was considered attained if he had caused no trouble to his elders. Nor is this ideal yet extinct, even at the present (*Pedagogue's Commonplace Book*, Edith Rowland. Dent).

The horizon has widened considerably during the last half-century, nevertheless, and each year opens up fresh vistas to those interested in the care of children, with all that this implies and includes, so as to require a large library in order to deal adequately with its problems. This has been due partly to the evolution of culture and, to a certain extent, to the revolution in ideas that has arisen as a reaction against the severe measures and lack of sympathy shown by the parents and pedagogues of the past towards the children of former generations.

Through an examination of the history of civilization and careful observation of the child's position in the primitive tribe and the family during different phases of the world's history we may gain a great deal of indirect information concerning the stage of culture which has been attained.[1] In some of the most primitive tribes or in remote times babies, especially the first-born, have been considered from an economic point of view as articles of adult diet, being eaten without hesitation in times of scarcity or famine and, at a later stage of cultural development, sacrificed for ritual or religious purposes, to bring luck to the tribe or to renew its vitality, or as propitiation to avert famine or any other tribal disaster.[2] This custom of

---

[1] (a) *Origins of Education among Primitive Peoples*, W. D. Hambly. Macmillan.
(b) *Psycho-analytic Study of the Family*, J. C. Flugel. Hogarth Press.
[2] *The Golden Bough*, abridged edition, Sir George Fraser.

infanticide connected with ritual and religious ceremonies, in the sacrifice of the first-born, has become familiar to us at a still later stage, that of the substitution of one ritual for another of milder character, which serves as a symbol of the more ancient, in the history of Jewish customs to be found in the Bible. Thus most of us are familiar with the Hebrew belief that it was necessary to redeem the first-born of every creature, since it was considered holy and the property of the Deity. The idea that the redemption was a substitute for sacrifice and death was clearly shown by the Mosaic Law, that if the first-born of a beast were not redeemed, its neck should be broken (Exodus 34, v. 20). Subsequently the custom of redemption became connected with the rite of circumcision.[1] Female infants were commonly destroyed in large numbers by most ancient peoples, and it is doubtful whether to this day they receive quite such a glad welcome as their brothers, even if they are not regarded as an absolute calamity and a sign of the anger of the gods.

Throughout the ages one idea has persisted, undergoing changes in presentation and interpretation, although not in essential values, which is, that primarily the purpose of the child is to be of use to its parents—as food, then to save them or the tribe from the consequences of displeasure on the part of angry supernatural beings; to propitiate forces of nature or as hostages given to a foe; as property, being sold if circumstances arose to make this necessary or convenient; to take their place in providing food and protection for the rest of the tribe as well as, finally, to support the failing powers of the parents in their old age. In addition to these services expected of the child towards the parents, expectation required then, as now, that the offspring should do credit to them and add lustre to the family in some way. Those who do not fulfil these many and varied functions have been and are regarded as failures and a cause of grave disappointment to parental pride, for which offence the parent in ancient times was allowed by law to take the life of the unsatisfactory child. Later, the same feeling was shown by a solemn gathering, during which the name of the miscreant was erased from the Family Bible, and

[1] *The Jewish Child*, W. M. Feldman, M.B., B.S. (Lond.). Ballière, Tindall & Cox.

probably still survives in the feelings of those who from time to time put an appeal in the papers for advice how best to punish refractory children.

With this end in view, to obtain from children the greatest possible amount of service or value, has been carried out the care of infants and children which has been practised at different periods of cultural development.[1] In early days, sickly or deformed infants were exposed soon after birth, since it was recognized that unhealthy offspring were of little value to the family or race, nor were superabundant infants permitted to live in times of food scarcity, since not only did they endanger the future strength of the tribe, but jeopardized the possibility of rapid migration in order to seek further supplies of food or to escape pursuit from an enemy.[2] The health of children in ancient times was maintained at as high a level as possible in conformity with the knowledge of hygiene and child care then in existence, because it was realized that the welfare of the tribe was contingent upon the health of the individuals who composed it. The value of the young men depended upon their strength in warfare or in hunting; that of the girls to carry on the work of the camp or the cultivation of the fields, as well as to bring wealth to the father from the future bridegroom, their market value being influenced by their health and beauty. In some ways it seems that ancient or primitive people were more attentive to the welfare of their children and understood their needs more deeply than those who, in much later civilizations, were more advanced in art, science, and luxury, when the children became useful chiefly as ornaments or social possessions, rather than for the maintenance of strength and hence the existence of the race. The focus of requirement was different, but the primitive peoples seem honestly to have attempted to do their utmost for the children's well-being, although their knowledge of their ailments and diseases, together with appropriate treatment, was then even more vague than that of adults. Hippocrates made many references to child hygiene in his writings, but we do not find many, if any, instructions for the treatment of

[1] *The Principles of Anti-Natal and Post-Natal Child Hygiene*, W. M. Feldman, M.D., B.S. (Lond.). John Bale, Sons & Danielsson.
[2] *Origins of Education among Primitive Peoples*, W. D. Hambly.

young children or infants in the works of Culpeper[1] or medical men of those days, although a few simple remedies for the whooping-cough or other childish complaints may sometimes appear in an old family recipe book.

The possibility that the parents should be of service to the child is a revolutionary idea of recent years, springing up from the realization that children are procreated for their parents' pleasure or benefit, rather than that of the child-to-be, and that the latter in consequence has a place within the family as a social unit, with rights, and not only privileges, in order that the parents may atone for bringing a child into the world without his or her consent, and therefore owe it adequate compensation.

Formerly this aspect was not considered; the child was considered the Gift of God, or it was represented that it owed the parents a deep debt of gratitude, which it should endeavour throughout life to repay with good behaviour and services rendered in exchange. With the growth of the idea that the child is an independent social unit, however, has developed a wider appreciation of the value of the child to the welfare of the race, not only physically, but also mentally, which brings the study of psychological problems of childhood into prominence together with those of the parents, who are influencing it in many ways, because of their opinions concerning mutual behaviour, expectations, and responsibilities. These old, new, and transitional beliefs of the values and duties of parents and children all play an important part in the psychological development of the family, in its entirety as well as amongst its individual components, not alone in ways that are realized, but through channels that are at present seldom, if ever, recognized in the home itself.

The traditional belief that children exist to be of value to their parents is one which the parents themselves frequently deny, and still more often disguise, even to themselves, imagining in many instances their honest opinion to be that they have no other ideal than to live for their children. But even were this to be the actual state of affairs, the child would still be of inestimable service to the home by providing such an unfailing focus of interest for its elders; without which

[1] *London Dispensatory, and Medicine for the Common People*, Nicholas Culpeper. 1653.

they would often have little else to occupy themselves. With many modern parents,[1] the education of their own children provides an absorbing hobby, into which as much time and energy are thrown as those of former generations bestowed upon the collection of bric-à-brac or the cultivation of roses; with this exception, that whereas the former collector or gardener realized that the main purpose of his occupation was to bring pleasure to himself, the parent who chooses child education to play the same part believes that it is carried out solely for the benefit of the children, and that he derives no great personal gratification from the recreation, nor looks for the gratitude of the children in return.

In our relations with children we all show a tendency to draw from them what we require for the building up of our own personality, rather than giving them full liberty to develop their own. From this remark it is not to be inferred that a doctrine of absolute licence is advocated for the child, nor that it is considered necessary for the young to ride rough-shod over their elders, but that freedom and *equal* rights to personal development of all should be the rule as much as possible, and that care should be taken not to allow one section of the community only the prerogative of having its own way and never to consider the requirements of any other. For the whole energy of a household to concentrate upon the development of one element in it is wrong, whatever that element may be, adult or child. It will injure the child as much to be focus-point as to be a nonentity, as we need even balance and a just sense of proportion to maintain mental health in the home.

Parents are fond of saying that their children are brought up in perfect freedom and have never been thwarted in any way during their lives. If this is true, we may rest assured that they will pay a heavy price for it later on. So will the parents. However, the remark is probably of more value as an interesting side-light upon the phantasies of the parent than as a statement of the facts of the case. If we were to examine the state of affairs very closely, we should probably find that the children were allowed liberty when convenient, and the reverse when this attitude coincided with the mood of the

[1] (a) *On Education*, Bertrand Russell. George Allen & Unwin. (b) *The Child in the Changing Home*, Dr. C. W. Kimmins. Herbert Jenkins.

adults; changes in treatment depending upon what was required from the children at that moment. When children fail to supply our needs we usually get impatient with them and consider their behaviour so eminently unsatisfactory that we urgently feel the need of some change *in them*. It never occurs to us that something may be amiss in ourselves or our treatment of the children.

Foremost amongst the difficulties that meet us in the care of children is that we do not really understand ourselves nor our wants and wishes where we and they are concerned. Secondly, we do not understand the children's point of view, but fancy it to be the same as our own, failing to recognize that their condition of immaturity and lack of knowledge form a barrier between them and ourselves which it is practically impossible to surmount. We may wonder why this lack of understanding should exist when we have all been through the same ordeal of childhood. A great number of us even say that we can remember it perfectly, although our actions often belie our words. Why, indeed, this should be so is a problem we will now endeavour to answer. (See Chapter II, "Psychological Differences between Adults and Children.")

If we, fully remembering our likes and dislikes, our fears and delights, persistently ignore them in our treatment of children, is it to be inferred that we are wilfully injuring them? We should prefer to believe our supposed memories to be less complete or accurate than we imagine, and that merely a few isolated incidents stand out like the peaks of a submerged mountain range. We have forgotten, that is, *hidden away*, the bulk of our childish experiences, so that for the time being they cease to have any effective value in our conscious lives or form an active part of our psychological equipment, which might be of real service to us, especially in our dealings with children. It has been discovered that the major part of our childhood has become extinguished in this way because it was unsatisfactory to us. We have forgotten or repressed it, and consequently believe that because we cannot recall past unpleasantness, it has never existed. The result of our dissatisfaction in the past seems to be that the greater part of our childhood is forgotten, or that we only remember odd scarps here and there. Therefore, we can still talk of our happy childhood and imagine we were happy. We actually believe it to be true. When people remark that they had such a happy childhood, one may ask as an experiment, "How much of it do you remember, and what incidents stand out most distinctly? " This is an unfailing test of the truth of the statement, but frequently little evidence is forthcoming, when one asks for proof of this kind. If we had been happy the recollection of it would have continued in our thoughts, and we should know what was wanted to make other children equally happy without being obliged to seek information about methods and theories from outside sources. We should, indeed, take this knowledge for granted and work upon it successfully and unconsciously, without any tendency to treat children as adults or vehicles through which our impulses may find satisfaction. (See Chapter V, "Forgetting and Remembering.")

Our next step is to inquire why childhood should be an unhappy time, if we agree that this may be inferred from the fact that it is so generally forgotten. We have already hinted at the cause in the introductory remarks about the primitive attitude towards children, their helpless condition, and the lack of consideration which was frequently shown them in the past. In a later chapter we will discuss the impressions left on the mind of the child by feeling helpless, its cry of anguish when it finds itself alone, and the relief when the return of the loved one puts an end to the intolerable suspense. As long as all our needs are satisfied we do not feel helpless ; it is a condition which we later designate as content or happiness. But growing-up and all that this entails must necessarily include a long series of alternating sensations of helplessness, cries for aid and relief, or disappointment when they are unheeded. Gradually as we develop a power of self-assistance, we learn to overcome our feeling of helplessness, and are thus able to relieve the tension by some action of our own. This, when accomplished, leads to happiness, just as failure to do so will add to the initial helpless agony. The aim of the adult should be freely to encourage the child to attempt independent action and teach it independence, but without allowing it to feel left to its fate or that no one wishes to come to its help. Yet important psychological mechanisms on the part of the adult frequently interfere with this course of development.

Once more let us return to the picture of life in the primitive tribe, which was always constructed upon the family system. The most powerful members of the tribe were those who could support their authority by physical violence, if necessary. Except among those races who regarded old age with almost superstitious reverence, men and women saw their power and position dwindle in importance when they became old and lost their physical supremacy, and in many cases they were actually assisted out of life. The rulers, the adults, used their physical strength to increase their own power and to destroy that of others in the tribe, especially in the case of the youthful members, taking active measures to keep them dependent and in subjection; the men exerting this influence upon the boys of the tribe and the women upon the growing girls.

Family feeling is equally strong to-day. Parents, elder children, and the younger ones all have their relative position, and we may see the older members of a family protesting if those younger than themselves are advanced to a premature sharing of privileges they have long waited to win, because the parents do not respect the rights of the individual children, but only exercise their supreme authority as did once the tyrannical Old Man of the Tribe in the treatment of favourites.[1] They wish to feel that there is some distinction between themselves and the new-comers to life; it adds to their feeling of self-esteem or success. There are many reasons of this sort why some of us may not wish to help the younger ones to catch us up too quickly, in case we may be overtaken and outstripped in the race of life. This is why we so often hear grown-up people say to children that they must wait before they can do, have, see, or know things, hinting all the time that themselves are quite familiar with them, and in this way trying to impress their superiority upon those younger than themselves. (See Chapter X, "Family Balance.")

In consequence of the adult love of power, we may find a certain satisfaction to be derived from artificially preserving a child's helplessness after the normal period. By force of comparison, it will add to the lustre of adult self-esteem and efficiency. It is a direct affront to this longing for power when

[1] *Psycho-analytical Study of the Family*, J. C. Flügel. Hogarth Press.

a child will not heed or hear our directions, or refuses to obey us without question, which often disturbs the equilibrium of usually mild persons, and causes us to take such firm measures with the offender. A child's will is not allowed to oppose that of an adult with impunity. If two persons wish to carry out different courses of action, the elder wins, no matter how strongly it is put before the child that it is a crime to want one's own way. We may often notice this insistence upon power and authority in those who, as children, were made to feel their weakness to a high degree and now seek every opportunity to reassure themselves that they are the superior force in comparison with one weaker than themselves. They do not consider that the puny might of the rival hardly makes the contest equal, or we should not have so many undignified squabbles taking place between adults and children when the former feel that they are bound to assert their superior power. It is this wish to feel strong in comparison with others which recruits so many helpers for children's institutions or Welfare Centres, where the adult may derive full gratification for his or her starved love of power and authority. Older children, or adults, even when they are ill, might prove more serious rivals or opponents whom we could not excel so easily or who might perchance beat us at our own game.

We find various people, for reasons such as these, sometimes trying to prove exaggerated differences between children and themselves, almost that they have no points in common, and others equally insistent that scarcely any differences exist at all, which shows us how greatly our faculty for observation or lack of it, where children are concerned, varies because of the trend of individual psychology and the action of personal impulses and instincts.

Very briefly we will survey some of the sensory differences between the child and the adult, for they will receive attention in detail later on, when we shall try to trace their physical basis and their psychological results. At birth, the first sense to receive stimulation is probably that of touch, the whole body of the child being a receiving organ, because the entire skin is covered with touch spots, sensitive severally to temperature, pain, or pressure. During the process of our entrance into the world, this receptor organ of touch is bombarded by violent stimulation of a kind which the infant has never before experienced. The squeezing, crushing process of birth, the subsequent contact with cold air, not to mention other stimuli that may be applied to establish the baby's respiration, all contribute to the record of *unpleasantness* to be stored up in the mind, which may be revived most acutely by cold or the pulsating headache experienced in some varieties of migraine. On the other hand, the restoration of quiet, darkness, and warmth will be felt correspondingly pleasant, and generally remains agreeable throughout life. (See Chapter III, "The Child Discovers the World Around.")

We know that sounds are heard in some degree by the newly born infant, that its eyes seem to be aware of a light, and that its taste can appreciate warm sugar and water between its lips; that it will move and sniff as though finding its way to its mother's breast by smell when only a few days or even hours old. But we should be scarcely bold enough to maintain that the psychological impressions left by these stimuli at or soon after birth bear any relation to those of the adult, or of the child at five, ten, or fifteen years old. The impressions made upon our minds by sensory stimulation are so much dependent upon experience, what we have learned or found out, that it is difficult to disentangle those of pure sensation from those of association, a state of affairs which we feel must always have been the same to some extent.

A few points, however, are worthy of notice. The child seems to have a greater auditory acuity for a familiar voice than that of a stranger, can recognize well-known objects at a greater distance than strange ones quite close, and usually enjoys most those flavours which are old and well-tried favourites. It is difficult, however, to test a child's sensory acuity, because we can never be quite sure of the amount of attention bestowed upon the matter in hand. The auditory apparatus may be perfectly in order, but if a child is not giving its attention, it will not hear. This is what happens in many cases of psychological deafness. In any case, however, the child does not attach the same meaning to things seen, heard, felt, tasted, or smelt as does the adult, and we frequently expect too great an appreciation of small differences and subtle distinctions from a child than is possible. Ways in which things and persons are alike are commonly grasped more readily than differences between them.

A child can always point out similar objects before it can distinguish dissimilar qualities in those which possess some characteristics in common. The problems of perspective, light and shade, the knowledge we obtain through our eyes, founded upon previous experiments on the properties of objects, appreciation of size and weight, cannot be accurately computed by a child, yet one often sees grown-up persons scolding or punishing a child for accidents which are the outcome of its lack of experience, and are results which only more mature knowledge could have foreseen.

Theoretically, perhaps, we could draw up charts describing the ways in which the young people and those of mature age differ, but in practice we forget or ignore what our intellect has appreciated. If not, we should not constantly force children, actually or metaphorically, to run to keep up with our longer stride, perhaps feeding them with spoonfuls so large that the little mouth must be stretched to its utmost to receive them, and then has no room to turn the food in the process of mastication, to mention only two of the most obvious and frequent lapses from common sense on the part of the educators.

This lack of understanding on the part of the grown-up person produces a feeling of helplessness in children equal to, or even more acute than, the physical helplessness we have already mentioned, even more *hopeless helplessness*, because cries are unavailing. The helper is at hand but will not come to the rescue, or may even be causing the suffering.

We may trace the stages by which the child tries to overcome this helplessness, first by cries, then by muscular efforts, wriggling to get away from the things that are unpleasant, finally by speech. It will try to use words to explain what is wanted, and here often meets with dire disaster.[1] The adult may try to help or understand, but often shows a particular incapacity to do so, partly through ignorance of the psychological tendencies which are seeking satisfaction and partly from failure to appreciate childish difficulties. Usually the adult believes children to be quite capable of saying what they mean, and meaning what they say ; also of fully comprehending

[1] *The One I Knew the Best of All*, p, 7, Mrs. F. H. Burnett. Frederick Warne & Co.

what is said to them, however complicated the words or the construction of sentences that are used, and no matter how fast or indistinctly the adult may speak. We may realize something of a child's difficulties in this respect through travelling in a foreign country with only a very limited knowledge of the language and noticing how bewildered we become by the rapidity and indistinctness with which the natives seem to us to speak.

These we may call the primary or sensory difficulties of the child, and we have explained some of the ways through which we increase them. Now let us study the secondary or affectual experiences and difficulties of the child in relation to the world around and the people in it, concerning the growth and development of its Ego, and discover what part we play there. (See Chapter IX, "Development of the Ego.") The baby is an egoist, but, then, so are we all for that matter; and if we complain that the baby always wants its own way, baby, if it could talk, would accuse us of the same propensity. The infant is sure of its power until it meets opposition and comes off the loser. Every adult is equally convinced that he or she can manage children better than anyone else, until some child proves itself unmanageable. Then, if that person be wise, a pause will be made and the question reconsidered whether all available information is possessed about the subject. If she or he be very wise, the matter will be thought over before such a crisis occurs.

The history of the personal development of the Ego is the history of the Ego in relation to the environment, how the child fits into the family, what measures are brought to bear to make it conform with home dictates, how it rebels, how it submits, and what happens then. In its own development the child repeats the history of the race, tracing after birth the well-worn track from the time when the human being was but little differentiated from the animal, until it reaches the intellectual standard of modern maturity. All along this line of development we find individuals drop out, unable or unwilling to keep pace with the struggle for intellectual attainment which the present day demands.

The family again repeats the conduct of the former tribe and the child has to learn to adjust to others as only child, the eldest, middle, or youngest one. All positions carry their own problems. In each the Ego finds opposition to development and lack of understanding by others, who are equally anxious for self-expansion and an opportunity to make use of it in the process. Adults will find among the children around them those whom they like and favour, those whom they dislike and consequently thwart, sometimes because of traits in the child resembling themselves or another known in the past, or because the child does not supply what is required to satisfy the adult need for flattery. (See Chapter X, "Family Balance.")

Few of us realize, or are willing to confess it if we do, how frequently we look for a particular sort of flattery from the child. For example, we take its love, its confiding little ways, its requests for help as a subtle tribute to ourselves, and feel that it is because the child realizes how lovable and helpful we are that it has selected us for these marks of favour, and that it will not behave in the same way to others. If it exhibits similar signs of love to another, we may often be jealous and feel a little less affection for that child afterwards, perhaps disappointed that it has done so, and we may even attempt to punish it by showing conspicuous preference for another child in revenge. Through this attitude and reaction of adults we may observe talion law once again taking a place in the practical events of daily life.

Children understand far more about the motives of our actions and behaviour towards them than we realize, and a child's judgment is usually reliable until it has been tampered with by adults, who deny the truth to them in order to disguise the real state of affairs. We constantly find difficulties arising from such behaviour during childhood itself or in the subsequent life of the child, because older people do not believe that it is in any way derogatory to themselves to lie or break faith with those much younger than themselves, although they may hold quite normal opinions about the ethics of such proceedings in their relationship with contemporaries.

A greater number of these difficulties than we realize are due to a fundamental lack of respect on the part of the adult towards the young human being as an individual. It is still thought to be of no importance, that it need not be given any protracted consideration and is of little consequence in education. We do not feel any need of the good opinion of the child where we or our ethical standards are concerned. That the child has a great sense of its own dignity we are ready to allow; it is most necessary that this should be preserved, but it may struggle in vain to do so should the adult constantly make fun of it, sharpen his or her wits upon it, make constant and unkind jokes at its expense, and fail to put into practice the precepts constantly taught, such as to tell the truth, not to take away other's possessions or good name, and to play fair. A very high percentage of people cannot help bullying directly they find one smaller than themselves who is defenceless or in their power, women particularly, possibly to pass on treatment which has been their portion from those larger and stronger than themselves in the past. It is like the office-boy kicking the cat after he has got into trouble with the clerk over him, who has been reprimanded by the boss. When it is only a cat it may not be of much consequence, but the treatment is decidedly more harmful for children, and we usually punish them severely if we find them copying ourselves in this respect where others are concerned. We tell them that it is cowardly to ill-treat someone smaller and weaker than themselves, probably adding point to our words by a smart slap to show them how it feels, but never remember that in our action we are doing the same as they, nor bear in mind the far-reaching influence of our example and the amount of satisfaction we are deriving from the whole situation.

The modern child observes these things and is beginning to notice the behaviour of adults without feeling bound to keep reverent silence about it as did earlier generations. Can we then be surprised should they not respect us, when we perpetually do what we forbid them, with reiteration that it is most reprehensible to act in such ways?

The attempt to find some solution to this problem of the discrepancy between adult precepts and actions is liable to cause serious conflict in the mind of a thinking child. To attribute the blame to the beloved adult is the safest course, although it will at the same time shatter the child's trust and confidence. To twist the blame round to rest upon the self, however, is a far more disastrous escape from the dilemma for the subsequent nervous health of the child, because it both destroys its sense of relative values and interferes with its acceptance of reality. To deny what we know to be true and to construct a personal reality more nearly approaching our ideal is in actuality always a perilous undertaking. Once we have successfully accomplished this in one instance, we may continue to do so and gradually forget that this new phantom world of ours is an invention of our own.

This is one of the most general routes by which several forms of child neuroses come into being. They are nearly all based upon the errors of those in charge of the children, although they at the same time may frequently pride themselves upon the excellence of their method of managing children. Our plans may, indeed, be excellent in themselves, but if they are not suited to the particular temperament of the child who is their focus, they will be worse than useless. It is easy to take our preconceived opinions with us when we observe children and interpret what we see as what we want to see, rather than go to them with an open mind and let them tell us their own story without any prompting. We are actually inclined only to see and hear the things with which we are familiar, like the children, or those things which remind us of our own childhood. We shut our eyes to all that is unfamiliar, to things we do not wish to recognize and which remind us of our past life in a way that reopens old sores of unhappiness.

The ways of children that annoy us greatly, including what we term "bad habits," such as nail-biting, accidents in want of cleanliness and such like, usually reflect conduct which was a source of trouble to us when we were young. Consequently we have erased the personal element from our minds and left in its place merely a shocked attitude respecting the habits or those who still practise them as a source of pleasure, deciding that they are intolerable and must be eradicated at all costs. We can learn a great deal of personal past history from the behaviour of the educationist in respect to these matters, as well as from methods adopted to deal with these lapses from convention and the accepted manners of grown-up persons. (See Chapter VII, "Childish Bad Habits.")

The happy-go-lucky person, the jealous, the sentimental, as well as the over-conscientious parent and the stern disciplinarian all produce a counter-reaction in children, like the seal and its impress. We have already discovered sufficient about the way in which the child's character develops through imitating those it loves, or those of whom it is afraid, to lead us seriously to consider whether the child will come to much harm by copying *us* too closely; if *we* have any characteristics which we should not like to see reproduced in the children, or which we would punish severely if we saw them emerging in those in our charge, although without recognition of the parentage of the behaviour. (See Chapter VIII, "Types of Those in Charge of Children.")

As a means of escape from the onus of training children, a new type of parent and teacher has arisen, who discard responsibility in order to avoid blame for anything that may happen later on which is undesirable. The results of psychological investigation proving the old methods of fear, shame, force, and blind obedience disastrous for the character-building of the young, a repudiation of authority has taken place. The adult simulates childishness, pretends to be a child among children, rather as an elder brother or big sister, a Peter Pan who refuses to grow up and accept the responsibility of others. If the theory be correct, that children develop by imitating those whom they love who have reached a higher stage of development than themselves, what will be the effect upon the younger generation if those who ought to be their model are themselves copying the children in order that they may not afterwards take them to task for spoiling their lives by playing the part of heavy parent? What may be expected to happen in the future according to the theory of development through imitation?

From all points of view it appears an unnatural state of affairs, and may well account for the modern child's attitude of camaraderie or hostility and nothing further towards its parents, or elders generally. The child expects to find differences in behaviour between contemporaries, children older and younger than itself and grown-up persons, in order to maintain the balance of the family and to provide a standard in life. It does not wish for an adult who behaves like a contemporary, nor for equals in age who order it about as though they were adults. The child has in many ways an acute sense of the fitness of things, and likes to know what type of behaviour may be expected from different people and for this to remain constant.

How eagerly and hopefully one looks forward to the day when at all Infant Welfare Centres and Children's Clinics, as well as in the Children's Departments of our Hospitals, will be found specially trained persons, well-informed upon this subject and competent to deal with children's psychological difficulties and abnormalities, just as there are physicians and surgeons who are able to diagnose and prescribe for their physical maladies. At present this aim is far from realization. It is exceedingly rare to find any who possess sufficient psychological knowledge or the necessary training for this delicate and intricate task. Should the matter be taken into consideration at all, it is frequently inclined to be of the most superficial character, although satisfying the owner of the knowledge.

When we begin to survey these difficulties in more detail, what do we find? What sort of children should be provided for at these clinics? Among them we may class backward and precocious children; those suffering from fears, bad dreams, and sleeplessness, temporary or permanent loss of appetite without physical cause; twitches, nose boring and picking, nail-biting, bed-wetting, and other lapses from habits of cleanliness after these have already been acquired; masturbation, irritability, rages, stammering, over-dependence, lying, and stealing, to mention only some of the most common types which are in desperate need of help.

It is not altogether easy when first brought into contact with a child or its parents to realize what is the matter; this can only be done by patiently listening first to all the parent has to tell, then to all the child confides. Frequently the two accounts differ enormously. It is of cardinal importance that each should tell his or her tale alone, without being hampered by the presence of any audience, or even a third person within sight or hearing distance. We can usually judge from the attitude of both parents towards the child who has been the principal cause of the child's neurosis, because most of the psychological difficulties in children are signs of incipient, if not actual, nervous trouble in some adult. It is possible that the best and most direct way of dealing with the child's trouble would be to give a course of treatment to the mother to steady her nerves and enable her to leave off influencing the child so as to make it her life-buoy, because this is a frequent occurrence.

In some cases, where the home environment seems particularly injurious, the wisest course to pursue would be to separate the child from its parents, at least for a time, a course which so many parents desire, but for their own sake rather than for the child's, because the neurotic child is frequently a problem in the home, and certainly does not reflect credit upon themselves. They do not want to be troubled with it any longer, now that it has become a nuisance to them. Contrarily, we find persons who refuse to allow the child to undergo any form of psychological treatment because they unconsciously feel that it will separate the child from them. This result will certainly occur, but of necessity, in order to make it free from the pernicious influence that is being exerted. One of the chief difficulties concerning the results of psychological treatment of children is that parents frequently expect the production of an inanimate doll, whilst the actual consequence is an independent creature, self-reliant and full of vitality and beauty. One usually finds that psychological treatment increases the good looks of the children who have it. Worry lines are smoothed away, fretful mouths are given an upward trend, curving into a smile, sometimes even a dimple will be discovered in some hiding-place, and, last but not least, complexions become much clearer, because the natural bodily functions, which have hitherto been under psychological arrest, are restored to their full activity.

Having once decided who is to be treated, parent or child, and settled that the child is of paramount importance—an opinion usually held by the parents, since they will scarcely ever entertain the idea that there is anything amiss with their own nerves, except that they are temporarily upset with the worry of the child—how does one proceed? The child comes to the psycho-analyst for one hour each day, if possible, and she or he, as the case may be, provides every available means by which the child may express the ideas that are filling its mind without being able to find any outlet or expression.

It is like exploring a deep wound for a foreign body with a telephone probe under X-rays. We continue to observe, but seldom take a hand in the proceedings except by giving explanations at times when they are asked for, although not unless; following the child's lead, but never going ahead, until we learn from him or her the secret of the trouble. Sooner or later we shall discover the cause, and then we must consider whether the child needs outside help to change injurious factors in its environment, as well as to alter its outlook on life, because in the case of child-analysis it is often necessary to lead the parents gently to see that other methods of child training would be more beneficial than those which have been adopted and which have acted as a real hindrance to the child's development or happiness.

Our hours with the children, however, will have other results. It should be remembered that neurotic children generally have either a superabundant or a deficient Ego-sense. If the former, they will find satisfaction in the opportunity for self-expression given by the treatment, and become more inclined to rest than were they always raging like wild beasts seeking food to satisfy their hunger and finding none. Should they be of the latter type, deficient in self-esteem, this need will also be fostered and developed, with the help and attention of a sympathetic person all to themselves for a time. But it is of the utmost importance than the adult carrying out the treatment really does know what he or she is doing, and has not merely gleaned a little superficial information from reading a few books or attending stray lectures, and is probably still deeply entangled in the meshes of personal unconscious impulses, or the second state of the child is worse than before.

Suppose we find a child with an over-developed sense of his own importance, snatching toys from little companions and always putting himself into a prominent position. Gradually in games we will find this child reconstructing the original situation of this lonely but magnificent state that he would prefer. By trying to creep into dolls'-houses, baskets, or boxes, an attempt is made once more to become the wee babe in the cradle, the babe unborn, in a world where he reigned supreme and where there were no rivals. Gradually we shall be able to show him that he does not want any other boys or girls around him. He wants a world all to himself, a mother all to himself, as he may have had when he was a tiny baby, and he will presently come to see that it is more satisfactory to be friends with his contemporaries and to be a *big boy* among other playmates than a baby who wants everything for himself and can therefore only play alone. We can encourage him to use his hands and make things, to create instead of destroying what others have made, and so foster his sense of pride in what he can do rather than in what he has; to be able to do rather than boast about imaginary achievements or possessions and trying always to get others to do things for him. This will mean a work of time and patience, but it is thoroughly worth while, because this type is a dangerous one for future development, as well as being extremely prevalent in these days of only children. It is often increased by parental pride in this child, and the parents' wish for him to have the best of everything.

This type which we have just described is likely to include the precocious children and those who tell lies; why this should be so we will explain later. Backward children are more usually found with a deficient Ego-sense, which needs encouragement in order that they may cultivate self-confidence and so help the child to take heart to struggle forward rather than slip out of the race because others go too fast, or because it has become hopeless about its own inferiority. One often finds children that are called backward because they do not reach the high standard of intellectual attainment seen among precocious children who are prevalent to-day, although their level would compare favourably enough with that of a less civilized nation or some ancient race.

When we come closely to examine lying in children, it is of the utmost importance to notice the kind of lie that is told, to determine how serious it may be; if it be told merely to save the child getting into trouble, thus whether it be pathological or not; but it may arise from a more complicated root. The first type can hardly be considered as a pathological lie. When, however, a child always caps the recital of another's possessions or achievements by saying he has a larger one at home, or she can do much better; that his mother is going to buy him an enormous engine, if someone tells him he cannot play with one that belongs to another, it is not difficult to see the underlying motive. These lies are wishes that are spoken aloud, perhaps in the belief that this may make them come true, certainly to impress the hearer, as well as because they will probably give the child a momentary feeling that the wish is realized. The chief intention without doubt is to provide a compensation for self-esteem which has in some way received a wound.

This is a very common form of lie, and may be extended to the proportions of a long romance, or end in a libel action, if the person adheres to this practice when grown up. It has another grave disadvantage, however, which provides an even more important reason why children with this propensity should receive skilled attention without delay. It represents failure to recognize reality or an attempt to avoid doing so, since the person may deceive him or herself with it almost or quite as much as others, imagining at the time or after long-repeated reiteration the tale to be an actual occurrence of daily life that has been experienced.

Slowly we must work towards the goal of trying to show the child how this fabrication resembles *what it would like* rather than *what is fact*, and point out that it will affect the attitude of others towards itself to make statements of this description. Just one word of warning, however, about dealing with the problem of these pathological lies, as they are called. If not on the alert, we may easily mistake an account of a dream for one of them. A child never says, "Last night I dreamed so and so." It narrates that such and such a thing *happened*. The dream has the full value of reality for the child. This is why anxiety dreams possess such terror for the child. The dreamers should always be treated gently in these cases and not scolded or punished for story-telling: neither should the child be treated harshly who is expressing phantasies in pathological lies, since that form of treatment would probably only make them more frequent instead of decreasing them.

Fears, bad dreams, sleeplessness, and bed-wetting are troubles of childhood that must be considered together, because they are more closely interwoven than we commonly believe. First, however, let us discuss briefly the question of fears, because we so often find adults estimating them as ridiculous and not giving them the sympathy nor attention they deserve.

They often consider it a good method to try to cure children by ridicule and put the little ones to shame about them before others. A fear on the part of a child tells us that something very serious indeed is the matter, which is in urgent need of readjustment rather than laughter.

What are the child's greatest fears? To be alone, of the dark, strangers, animals; dogs in the town and cows or bulls in the country; snakes, loud noises, things that may burst; fire; water in which they may be drowned; thunder, mice, little things, fur or feathers; being shut in anywhere, especially a dark cupboard; being lost or eaten, bogies, witches, ghosts, policemen, doctors, or hospitals may all be objects of excessive fear to a nervous child. Very often the root of a child's fear has been a threat, which may have been made in haste or anger, and then forgotten by the person making it, although not by the child. In the mind of the child it lives on as a terror by day and an evil dream by night. It is not uncommon for parents to say that they get so angry with a child that they do not know afterwards what they have said or done, and we may frequently trace the fears of the child back to the threats of its elders. These hasty threats, in fact, often correspond with a fleeting wish on the part of the parents at the moment and very often show a survival of what has actually been done to children by their parents in earlier stages of culture. What are some of the more usual threats from which fears spring? By reviewing them we may see how far we are justified in making this comparison.

We are all familiar with the following:—

"If you are not good, I will run away and leave you. I'll give you to the dustman, or throw you away. If you do that again, I'll kill you!"

The threat to boys found playing with themselves or having wet the bed: "I'll tell your father and he'll cut it off, or I'll take you to the hospital and get the doctor to take it away. The policeman will come and lock you up."

To the little girl: "Come along, Doggie, and bite a little girl who won't eat her pudding. Bogey will have you if you don't go to sleep. I'll lock you up in a dark cupboard and there you'll stay. I'll go away and be another little girl's mummy, or I'll get another little baby."

The child believes the adult who threatens these awful punishments implicitly and expects that they will happen. In dreams they do occur, so that the little one wakes up screaming and bathed in sweat. One usually finds that children who suffer from fear have been under the influence of someone with an irritable or uncontrollable temper, and subject to attacks of violent anger, which may or may not be directed against that child, but are witnessed by it: the actual results are often the same in both cases. Hence the consequences which follow—night terrors, incontinence, which is often a sign of fear in children as well as in animals, and general nervous instability or irritability—are the child's response to some neurotic element in one or both parents.

One violent or alcoholic parent's influence will unfortunately not be cancelled by that of one good-tempered, well-balanced one; the conflict between the parents that is typical in these divided households tells upon the children with calamitous results.

These may take the form of fear of sudden noises or loud voices, and the child's anxiety will be indicated by a constant searching of faces for signs of approaching danger, upon the first sign of which the child will go and hide rather than meet the impending storm. Fear habits such as these acquired in childhood leave scars that a lifetime cannot erase in the development of character and create barriers which separate the individual from any feeling of security or assured happiness.

Teasing may also be included under this section of adult treatment that causes such ill effects for later life. It will frequently cause far-reaching trouble when indulged in verbally, by way of horse-play from an adult towards a child, or when older children make systematic fun of a little one. Nevertheless it is a socially recognized method by which an adult can find discharge for his or her sadistic impulses and enjoy their release. The adult may, it is true, derive a certain satisfaction from this emotional outlet, but the other end of the joke falls upon the child with the full brunt of the cruelty which such jests contain, made even more poignant because it is actually a parent or close relative who is the torturer, yet at the same time seems so laughing and jolly about it, which causes an increased perplexity in the child's mind. Once more we are confronted with the factor that a difficulty in a child's mind about understanding a situation increases the child's feeling of pain and bewilderment that it experiences.

There is yet another foundation of fear in a child, and one that is often overlooked, or not mentioned for various reasons, yet nevertheless has the most evil consequences. This is the frequent custom for a small child to share the parents' bed-chamber, or to sleep in an adjoining room divided only by a party-wall, in which case everything that takes place in the one room may be heard in the other, even if it remain unseen. In this way children often overhear or are even eye-witnesses of intimacies on the part of their parents never intended for their participation, and which would probably be denied should the child venture to inquire next day about anything seen or heard in the night.

For this reason one would advocate that children should sleep away from their parents at a very early age, and yet, unless the financial circumstances of the parents are such that a night-nursery with a nurse in charge is practicable, it may be an ideal that is difficult to put into practice. Still, when it is known what serious consequences may arise from such causes, it would be worth while for parents seriously to consider the matter and make up their minds beforehand what they would tell their children to allay their fears when or if they should ask for an explanation of anything they may have seen or heard in this way. Very many fears that arise in childhood and persist into adult years have actually been traced at a later date to this cause without the parents having had the slightest idea that the child had been awake. It had probably been aroused by movements and voices, and had started listening, frightened and silent, not understanding what was happening, and thinking only that some deed of violence was taking place.

Some fears, as well as many serious maladjustments of child-hood, come into existence because the child's natural curiosity has been awakened, but not satisfied, about something taking place at home, such as the birth of a baby brother or sister, or those occurrences which we have just described. There is far less opposition now than there used to be, when a parent is advised to give a true and simple explanation to the child about the essentials of life instead of the silly fairy-tales which used to be and still are only too often handed on to them, if the whole subject is not treated as a mystery and put upon one side. The child's common sense easily sets aside sooner or later as impossible, or investigates and repudiates them after experiment, like two little girls who dug up row after row of newly planted cabbages in a doctor's garden to look for babies they had been told he distributed from this source. He was annoyed, and they disappointed at not finding one.

Not one type of result but many can be traced to this source: excessive curiosity, the asking of innumerable questions, or the exact opposite—entire apathy where learning is concerned, and even stealing. We have certainly investigated one case of kleptomania in which knowledge being withheld respecting the advent of a baby influenced a child's compulsion to take things which were wanted so much that he felt obliged to steal them rather than go without, in spite of knowing he would receive very severe punishment for so doing. This form of stealing, which we call *kleptomania*, is the compulsive taking and often hiding of small, almost worthless objects, which have an important associative value to the taker. The thing taken, some object, is usually a symbolic representation of what the child wishes to possess, rather than being actually the thing coveted, or it stands for the love of the person to whom it belongs. The precise articles taken and the person who owned them are the most important points to discover; then we may proceed to find out what was required from the person, and why it could not be obtained otherwise.

An irresistible desire to obtain something, or its representative, a substitute object that is more accessible, will give rise to this obsession. Cure takes place when the child or young adult realizes the unconscious motive that lies behind the action, and the idea that one object can take the place of another that is unattainable, as well as the important fact that, although these things were often wanted acutely in baby days, the need or even the desire for them is really past, and they would be of little service at the present stage of development, although the baby used to appreciate them and the unconscious mind still hopes to do so. When all these factors are worked through and made clear, we usually find the compulsion to take things belonging to other people disappears.

One more type of children's difficulties must be mentioned

before the close of the chapter. We referred to them when first giving a list of the childish manifestations which are called collectively "bad habits," namely, nail-biting, nose- or lip-picking, and masturbation.

Although, when regarded superficially, they may seem entirely disconnected, some points in common may be found amongst them, such as the following : They are all more likely to increase when severe measures are taken to control or prevent them, in which case the child is constantly having them brought to its mind. They will also appear more frequently when the child is nervously upset or worried from any other cause, and so becomes unduly interested in itself, because the world and persons in its environment prove so unsatisfactory or disappointing. Actually they do little harm in themselves, unless they assume very great proportions and absorb an unduly heavy percentage of the child's nervous energy, or because constant correction and punishment has increased the child's guilt where they are concerned to an overwhelming height.

The best methods of checking and preventing these habits from becoming dangerously fixed are to try to divert the child's mind from them altogether, but indirectly; to find out, if possible, the other causes of worry or unhappiness which so frequently have been their dynamic, and should these be due to a particular person or event, to deal with it in the most appropriate way. Several cases of nail-biting, which continued without intermission during the reign of a bullying or nervous governess, were found entirely to cease when the child was removed from her care. Nervous asthma and urticaria may also be produced by the same cause. Nose-picking may sometimes be a sign of defiance as well as a means of obtaining pleasure, or finding an occupation when everything else fails. These habits may be most persistent and may even continue, but in the altered form of a most punctilious and thorough method of using the pocket-handkerchief, which shows how a childish symptom and nervous gratification may be retained through finding some socially permitted channel that resembles it in which it can be continued without blame or guilt. In all these symptoms of unhappiness in child-life we may find some adult is usually responsible for their appearance.

In masturbation we have a still more complicated state of

affairs. Children may come to it by various paths, through seduction on the part of an elder child or grown-up person, through the suggestion being conveyed by watching animals, or, as we have already explained, the marital life of the parents. It may be exploratory, as are so many of the other investigations of the body. Whatever the cause of its origin, it will primarily serve the purpose of deriving pleasure, sometimes detected by parents or others in charge, sometimes so carefully hidden that it escapes remark altogether. Girls may often be unaware that they are doing anything that others might consider wrong in the stimulation of these parts of the body, and are therefore much puzzled when they are scolded about the habit. If discovered, it may be dealt with dangerously by means of threats or wisely turned into other channels, through providing other interests or attending to the children's general health or happiness, as well as by refraining from constantly reminding them about it by saying *"Don't."* Although adults would usually scold a little child who was found making use of the various methods common amongst girls and boys for providing this pleasure, they are by no means careful not to do so themselves in their games with the children. They will frequently give children, inadvertently, exactly the same stimulation by pick-a-back rides, or other games of a similar nature, which will be of equal value to the child and call up the same intense emotional pleasure.

It is certainly most perplexing to a child if we check a tendency one day and furnish encouragement to it the next by doing ourselves exactly what we have forbidden. Infants usually masturbate, or play with themselves at one time or another, and are generally checked with varying degrees of severity and roughness or threats, which, if too drastically put into force, may have extremely harmful results, to which we will refer again in the special chapter reserved for the consideration of this subject ("Childish Bad Habits," Chapter VII).

In this Introductory Chapter we have attempted to summarize the chief troubles and difficulties that beset the young child. We should be on a firm road out of the slough of despond presented by the state of ignorance which is now prevalent where children's nervous diseases are concerned, if only these few that have been mentioned could be accorded consideration and careful attention with the hope of leading to their cure; or, better still, if serious attempts could be made to bring up children so that the evil consequences of adult thoughtlessness might be prevented. When helpful treatment can also be provided for them when necessary, and all those who are in charge of children realize that they are probably playing an important part in causing these troubles, and consequently using these children in their neighbourhood as life-buoys for their neurotic character-traits, we shall have advanced still further.

BOOKS WHICH MAY BE READ IN CONNECTION WITH THIS CHAPTER.

Psychology. W. McDougall. Home University Library.
Introduction to Psychology. Susan S. Brierly, M.A. Methuen.
Mechanisms of Character-Formation. W. D. White, M.D. Macmillan.
The Unconscious. I. Levine. Leonard Parsons.
Love in Children and its Aberrations. Oskar Pfister. George Allen & Unwin.
Einführung in die Technik der Kinderanalyse. Anna Freud. *Int. Ps.-A.
Verlag, Wien.*
The Golden Bough (abridged edition). Sir George Fraser.
The Psycho-analytic Study of the Family. J. C. Flügel, B.A.
The Jewish Child. W. M. Feldman. M.D., B.S.(Lond.).
The Principles of Ante-Natal and Post-Natal Child Hygiene. W. M.
Feldman, M.D., B.S.(Lond.).

CHAPTER II

DIFFERENCES BETWEEN ADULTS AND CHILDREN

When I was a child, I spake as a child, I understood as a child, I thought
as a child: but when I became a man, I put away childish things.—
1 Cor. xiii. 11.

MANNERS and customs, peoples and knowledge, have undergone
many fundamental changes since the first book upon the
education of little children was written by Comenius, in the
Czech language, in the year 1628. It was called the *School of
Infancy*, and five years later a German translation appeared,
which shows that an interest in the education of children was
alive in that country before the days of Pestalozzi and Froebel.

Starting his survey from the earliest days, Comenius calls
the first section of the book, appropriately enough, "The
School of the Mother's Lap." One wonders for whom the book
was written, and whether it gained a large circulation at the
time; if so, it would be interesting to speculate upon whom
these readers may have been. One's first thought is that it was
probably compiled for some noble's household, or an ancient
burgher family of almost equal power, who had the interest
of their own children so much at heart that they were anxious
to provide better understanding for all children, as well as
the training that would enable them to live their lives more
fully and be of greater service to others.

In former days the children of the upper classes were
educated most seriously to play an important part in the
affairs of their country, and the list of subjects to be studied
and accomplishments that were then thought necessary to
acquire might, indeed, make the attainments of some of our
modern children seem deficient in comparison.

It is doubtful whether the education of children was at any
time in the past much neglected or as inadequate for contemporary conditions of life as we are inclined to believe. In the
past children were considered of great economic importance
as future workers, and therefore their training played an

extremely significant rôle in the thoughts and plans of their parents. Thus many in a bygone day may have been unable to read or write, unless they were destined for the priesthood, nor did they know anything about chemistry and physics, as do numbers of present-day children, but they as men and women of the future were instructed thoroughly to equip them for their position or future occupations. They were prepared for the life that was before them and were taught things that were esteemed necessary to make them self-supporting and able to play the part of fellow-citizens to the rest of the community. Book-learning is not everything in life, although it is an essential in our present state of civilization; yet it is more than likely that we lose a great deal of valuable knowledge by relying upon an education founded upon information gained from books alone.

Throughout the world's history there have always been some who could understand the child from the child's point of view, but they have always been comparatively few. There have always been some who boast that they cannot understand them at all; and the large mass between these two small sections, consisting of those who firmly believe that they can, and that their knowledge concerning the management and care of children cannot be surpassed, while all the time they know practically nothing about the real child, and their management is usually rough-shod tyranny or sentimentalism. The care of children is one of those arts in which most people cherish a belief that they excel, because they refuse to see any other point of view. It is very easy to force most children to obey us if we exert enough energy to do so and are equally remorseless about the methods we use. The process may be that of Procrustes, who boasted that all travellers would fit his bed. How many lost their lives in the process was not recorded; just as to-day we do not stop to investigate how many children forfeit their individuality through similar methods of education.

This system has been found in all periods of the world's history and in all quarters of the globe. A rigid educational pattern is laid down and all children are made to fit it. All overlapping portions will be squeezed in or cut off; if the child does not fill out the regulation size, stretching is applied until it does come up to standard. To conform to regulations, to do as others do, think as others think, and look like others, is generally the aim and object of education the world over.

There is also a real danger confronting us in this respect, when we work out a psychological theory of what children are, what they ought to like or dislike, what they think about things and persons, and how they will act under certain circumstances; because once we have formulated it, regardless of the source whence it has sprung, even though it may be our own imagination, we shut our eyes to the fact that it may not be correct in all cases. Neither are we prepared as a rule to relinquish our idea of its infallibility when experience gained from another child or a colleague is at variance with our previous conception. This is a danger which especially menaces us in the subject of child psychology. Through the study of psychology we are taught that certain senses are developed in a certain way, that the psychological make-up of children consists of certain elements, and consequently we are apt to believe that the children who reach certain stages of development must resemble each other minutely. However, when we come to deal with children in practice, and preserve an open mind about what we have read or thought, we are constantly finding contradictions in detail, or perhaps wide variations from what we have previously believed, although the outline may remain the same.

When dealing with children or the extremely intricate subject of psychology, we cannot afford to be too positive that our knowledge is complete, our judgment reliable, or that we are not confusing our own thoughts and ideas with those of the child. If this were so, we should then be seeing not those of the child in question, but only a reflection of ourselves.

Again, in our research upon children we must not forget to allow for the factor of our influence upon them. Should we watch a child very carefully in relation with several other persons, we shall find not one set of reactions only, but many, because of the influence of these several personalities in conjunction with that of the child. For this reason it is difficult to gain an accurate estimation of the actual behaviour of the child, when it may vary according to the stimulus provided by an adult. Because it is unsatisfactory to study reactions without their corresponding stimulus, and because we have human beings for our research material, whose behaviour is modified to a high degree by others in contact with them, it is therefore extremely difficult to make the conditions of our research constant and rule out what is known as *variation*. Furthermore, when both stimulus and influence come from ourselves, it is beyond all doubt a still more insuperable task to disentangle the identity of the child's actions from our influence in the investigations, especially if we are not on the alert watch for this factor. As a rule, we are profoundly ignorant concerning the characteristics of our own personality as well as the kind of reactions to be expected from the child in reply to our own psychological elements. To be thoroughly conversant with our personal tendencies and able to compute the amount of our influence should be considered a necessary groundwork to be acquired before we can pursue the investigation of children. Yet apparently it is usually both unconsidered and unappreciated, although results of its lack are often only too clearly shown in the published records of investigations which have been made, through the bias of the inquiry and its results in one direction or another, according to the tendencies of the person conducting the research.

When we say that those in charge of children should know themselves, it reminds us how often we find parents and teachers recommended to examine themselves by a process of *self-analysis*, while advising psycho-analysis for the children. This, however, is useless. It is as impossible to discover one's own repressions as one's own shortcomings, and our fundamental vanity will only perceive in the process of self-analysis a gratifying method of self-appreciation, a thanking of God that we are not as others, which is what we usually find when the exponents of this method give us samples of their discoveries in the books they have written. Sir Joshua Reynolds, in one of his note-books, once entered the pertinent phrase, "*The Eye sees no more than it knows.*" We are always more ready to accept corroboration of our own beliefs and apt to pass by evidence of distasteful possibilities, or views at variance with our own preferences. In this way we are apt to create a standard to which we may adhere in every case in order to save ourselves the trouble of continually thinking out a solution to fresh problems or as a defence against the evidence of facts.

From time to time the popular or traditional standards of education meet with criticism. Should the opposition come from a single person, unless he or she occupy an important social or public position, which in itself bears considerable weight, the reactionary is regarded as peculiar, a crank, and is ignored straightway. If others, gathering courage to express similar opinions which they have previously hidden, join the first, the group will extend, until it comprises all who have formerly held the same views, although without daring to show them until they were sure that others concurred, so that they should not run the risk of making themselves conspicuous with unique opinions. To the mind of most persons it is more comfortable to be one of the mass, the herd, to resemble the rest, to share their virtues as well as to be guilty of the same sins or vices, than to be original. They may console themselves then that even if they are no better than others, they are certainly no worse. But if the secret thoughts of many persons could be declared in this respect, we should find that almost invariably belief exists that *they* individually are a great improvement upon the rest of humanity in some way, usually in their management of children.

This, then, is one of the greatest difficulties in the training of children. We strive to bring them up to conform to standards —*our standards*—to resemble ourselves as closely as we may. If we feel a glow of satisfaction when some child excels others, its excellence will probably be along lines laid down by us, along which we have helped to push the little one towards some goal after which we may have fruitlessly yearned ourselves. As a rule, it will not be in any solitary or original direction, because most of us are afraid of being responsible for a *peculiar child*, even though it might show very great ability. Our attitude would remain unaltered whether the peculiarity were harmful in itself or excellent, as though it represented a form of mental deformity.

The usual aim of education in the past was to make the child a grown-up person in miniature, and to assume that there were no essential differences, except those of size and inexperience, an opinion which has found corroboration in the similarity between fashions for children's clothes and those of their elders through the centuries. Broadly speaking, it has been the custom to clothe small boys and girls in garments which were the exact replica of those of their parents. Yet, at times, there have been periods when children's clothes became entirely different from the adult type, which, of course, reflects the adult attitude towards the child and the realization that there is something so essentially different between them, that the same style of clothes is not suitable for both. (Compare, "Clothes: Habits.")

It was characteristic of the late nineteenth century and the increased interest that was awakened in the child as an individual that clothes should have been designed for them at that period which varied from those of their elders, although these clothes were strange and unsuitable for children's needs. Yet, in consequence of this revolution, an interesting phenomenon appeared; it became the fashion among some grown-up persons, mainly young and psychologically immature women, to imitate the children's styles in their turn, and also to wear them without special adaptation. Concurrently a somewhat childish ideal crept into the adult standard in other ways; a taste for baby language, diminutives, and juvenile games became fashionable. One refers, in the first place, to the Kate Greenaway fashions and the art of Walter Crane that created the Liberty styles of dress and also entirely changed the character of illustrations in children's books, which suddenly developed with the most startling rapidity from ill-drawn and badly coloured pictures into works of art, and, later, we may compare this fashion with that of the Peter Pan Cult: smocks and loosely hanging yoked frocks on the one hand, and boyish turned-down collars upon the other, in both cases showing the adult wishing to return to childhood.

From external indications such as these we can read the secrets that lie at their root, the wishes of these adults, and their ideal which seems most worthy of imitation apart from reality. Most grown-up people have slammed the door between themselves and their childhood; they have forgotten how things really were or how they have altered since then, and instead of reality have created a conventional picture of things as they fancy them, which conforms entirely to a conventional standard. They relate how happy they were as children; the games they liked, the lessons they hated, the books they read and what they thought about them. Some few years ago it was unusual to come across anyone who would admit hating a book that had been popular in their youth. Now this phase is out of date, and it is more usual to find those who represent themselves to have been rebels at heart in those days of childhood and systematically opposed to all teaching that was enforced. Yet although people frequently say they have forgotten first-hand details of their childhood, when expressly questioned about it, they may remember with extraordinary accuracy anything that they have been told about it. Nevertheless, in spite of these contradictory attitudes of knowledge and ignorance concerning childhood, we still find educators and parents of to-day assuming that modern children will like what they imagine they preferred as children, or what they favour now, without taking into consideration how time and changed conditions have altered opinions or taste in so many ways, so that present-day children have a quite different point of view from that which we possessed when we were young.

The changes that take place in our bodies since infancy, as well as in our minds, come about so slowly that they are almost imperceptible. We are scarcely aware of them until comparison brings them to our notice. We cannot sit on the floor and put our toes in our mouth, nor do we find crawling on all fours our most rapid means of locomotion, yet both are habitual to the baby. The infant finds it as alarming and objectionable to walk upright on the floor as we might were we obliged to try to walk along a mountain-path beside a precipice. The baby gains a different impression from ourselves about objects within its range of vision, and has no knowledge of the tricks and illusions played by perspective or light and shade. Only pure visual images, which at first do not even possess the stereoscopic factor, since optical co-ordination is incomplete, present themselves to the infant's gaze. What we see and how much we observe is largely a matter of what we know about the objects we perceive; yet this knowledge the infant does not possess.

Usually, however, we do not take this element into our

consideration. If a baby allows its eyes to rest upon us or upon any other object, we conclude that it sees everything exactly as we do ourselves. Nevertheless, it is thought by some authorities that infants have no accurate colour-vision established until they reach the third year, although some will apparently be attracted by some light colour, preferably a shade of red, or a glistening object at a quite early age—within the first year, that is to say.[1] Little children are pleased by the pure, bright colours that many adults repudiate in favour of more subdued shades, and will joyfully put all combinations of vivid hues together without showing any hesitation or æsthetic distaste for violent contrasts of colour.

During these early years of childhood we often try to exert our influence in order to modify what we consider the *crude tastes* of the children in our care, imposing our own preferences upon them instead, in the attempt to make them conform to the generally accepted standard or our own taste, by saying one thing is nicer than another, or prettier than another, when to eyes with incomplete colour vision no colour-difference may be visible at all, and the only variation discerned will be that of brightness. In this way we constantly try to influence children in ways that seem against their better judgment, should they surrender their choice for ours. Consequently the new preference bears no actual relation to their opinion nor preference, but merely represents that which we have taught them to think right or perhaps merely to say. Thus we may establish a dual standard, one which represents the true opinion of the child, while the other reflects a conventional attitude adopted in order to please or agree with the adult in charge.

With very few exceptions we find that adults will immediately like the child who shows similar preferences or distastes to themselves for food, sights or sounds and shares their mannerisms or tricks of pronunciation, saying with pride, "I was just like that; I could not bear that either. I used to do that," and show a marked dislike as well as a lack of understanding and sympathy for children who are different. When the child is a close blood relation, the astonishment is increased, as though sons and daughters must of necessity resemble their

[1] (a) *Children in Health and Disease*, Dr. David Forsyth; (b) *Experimental Psychology*, Mary Collins.

parents in every respect, each child each parent, although the parents themselves may be totally dissimilar.

Should a child not concur with our tastes or opinions, we immediately say, "How strange! What an odd child!" But is it reasonable to expect that a child should have grown-up preferences? Should we consider the question carefully, have we ourselves always liked or disliked the same things which to-day attract or repel us, or have not a large number of our tastes been acquired in order to conform with an accepted standard or in imitation of someone whom we loved or admired?

Having thus formed our inclinations originally upon the model of others in the past, we now do our best to hand them on to the next generation, without reviewing the matter and considering whether it is of real benefit or necessary that the child should follow our example in every respect. Still in order to continue this transmission of ideas, we will often force a child to eat some form of food that it dislikes keenly, in order that it may not grow up *faddy*, which means different from others, and withhold a favourite pudding because a piece of fat or tough meat has not been obediently swallowed. Again, we frequently hear a child scolded for not finishing a large helping of meat, with the precept, "If you can't eat meat you can't eat pudding." Now, no one really wants to eat gristle or more than is comfortable, although a very stringent standard of home behaviour may demand that we do not leave food on our plate. All children have not the presence of mind of the little girl who plucked up her courage to argue the point with her mother: "Well, you see, Mummy, my meat-box is quite full, but my pudding-box is empty!"

Is it possible that the adult sometimes wilfully misunderstands or forgets these differences on purpose, as well as memories which a moment's thought would recall, about what is "understood as a child and thought as a child." Have these things been deliberately put away now that man's estate has been reached? Did we slam-to that door on purpose and forget what lay behind because it was such a confused, bewildering time of being misunderstood ourselves and not understanding others, of knowing so little and constantly being scolded or punished because we did *not* know things that we had never learned, things altogether beyond our comprehension and experience at the time. "But I didn't know," wails the child. "Then you ought to have known; and anyway you could have asked," storms the grown-up when some accident occurs which a little forethought on the adult's part might have prevented, although impossible for the child to realize.

Adults frequently blame a child who is with them, rather than shoulder the responsibility of being in the wrong themselves, or having been clumsy and careless; but this is considered quite compatible with the adult standard of ethics.

From time to time in the world's history, children have been estimated as too mature or kept too long in a helpless state. Too much has been expected of them or too little; they have frequently been believed to be less capable of understanding or doing things for themselves than is really the case. We commonly find the supposition that children of the upper classes are more slow to develop than those who have no nurses and governesses to attend to them, so that the entire burden of the care and training of the young child falls upon the shoulders of an already overworked and harassed mother. But this is not invariably the case. We find the boys and girls of parents who could afford to keep them at home in dependent helplessness being sent away to fend for themselves at school, while the poorer children, when a little older, attend day-schools and have their mothers spoiling them the whole year round by waiting upon them always. Parents who wish to spoil their children do so because of psychological reasons and not solely because they are wealthy.

What lies at the root of our blindness where the well-being of children is concerned? We cannot learn from books to understand the child; mere rules to be observed by the adult or the children themselves are no manner of help where the real issues of life are concerned. What we think we require from the children in our charge, or what we feel we want to do for them, when put into practice will frequently be found to have a result the opposite of that for which we were striving. Why should that door between us and our children remain so obdurately fast, although we may beat upon it until our hands are bruised and bleeding?

It may be temporarily well for our peace of mind that we

have kept these secrets hidden deeply away. Perhaps, as children, we were too unhappy to dare to remember how things appeared to us then; perhaps, again, we may grudge these children of to-day more understanding and help than we ourselves received. We may feel, because of our old misery, that it is good for the child to bear the yoke in its youth, to learn life's lessons of discipline and experience at the price of tears and sorrow, as we ourselves, and rationalize this opinion to ourselves and others thus, that should things be made too easy for a child, it will not remember.

However, if we examine the recollections which we have preserved from childhood, it would seem that we forget the hard things and the difficulties with equal readiness. Yet these memories in the background of our minds are enough to prevent us from realizing how much little children suffer when we act in a tyrannical way towards them and harry them, simply for the reason that we are able to do so because of our superior strength or mental reserves, because they have no way of remonstrating that we are prepared to recognize, or of retaliating that we admit to be justified, and which we will not crush in time.

Only by means of repeating what was done to us in our youth can we contrive to identify ourselves with those grown-up persons we used to know, whom we formerly thought so powerful, and whom we longed to imitate. This is the dynamic which makes us unsparing and old-fashioned, trying to bring up children of this generation with the methods of our own or even earlier days which in many ways resemble our own childhood. Some people, however, also as a result of upbringing without much sympathy or understanding, may entirely repudiate their responsibility, allowing children to take their own way and give them absolute freedom without support or help of any kind from those who have a wider experience of life and things in general.[1]

In this way and for this reason our misunderstanding of children does not always err upon the side of over-severity; it may equally fall short on account of too much vagueness or sentimentalism, too much encouragement given to the child's inclination to continue as a helpless baby, who is always being

[1] *Child's Path to Freedom*, Norman Macmunn.

waited upon. This forgetting of essentials necessary for the upbringing of children is but another proof of some difficulty of our own in the past. We may also have forgotten that we used to take a pride in being trusted to do things for ourselves and to be independent; or perhaps we were one of the helpless ones, who viewed as deliberate unkindness any attempt to train us to be self-supporting. Most children like to be thought big and useful, and resent as a deep insult being called a baby, or being treated as one. How much energy is wasted because children are kept idle so that it cannot be turned to account would be difficult to compute, but the average child finds great pleasure in learning to master difficult feats and acquire new skill, especially of a manual or physical sort, connected with dexterity or balance. (See chapter on "The Kinæsthetic Sense.")

"I was never allowed to do such things at their age, and I do not approve of children being so precocious," we will often hear. We do not wish to be outstripped; that is to say, we do not want to think that little children can do more now than we could or were allowed to do at their age, and so we keep them back, because of our baby feelings or rivalry belonging to so many years ago.

Again and again we will hear an adult make some excuse if a child can do anything better or more quickly than he or she, even such things as running upstairs or creeping under the table, and beating them at draughts. The adult will always try to give a reason why this should have occurred, and will say anything rather than honestly admit the facts of the case and give the child the benefit of the merited triumph. Suppose we did underrate the child's ability and consequently played so carelessly that we were beaten. It is always a bad principle to think poorly of your opponent and too highly of yourself, so the victory and defeat were still more well-deserved, and should teach us a lesson into the bargain.

We may see in this instance of adult behaviour, where the child is concerned, another drawback to the understanding of the little one from its own point of view. It is difficult for a grown-up person ever to regard a junior except as in some way inferior. The greater the difference in age, the wider they believe to be the inequality. It is always hard to be just, except to an equal. Directly we regard another as an inferior, we feel that we are justified in behaving rather differently, and that no one has any right to call us in question for being high-handed and superior. The more we can extend this difference by thinking the child cannot or will not do things which are so easy for us, the greater seems to be our proficiency and skill. It seems also to heighten personal satisfaction for an adult to forget that the child has not had the opportunity to be so skilled or to know so much; because to recognize this would be inconvenient when we wish to enter into competition with the youngsters. If handicaps were distributed quite fairly, the children might not appear as inferior to ourselves as we should wish.

It is a curious and tangled situation, view it how we will, and anything but logical. We like to think the child has powers equal to our own, yet because of laziness or some other reason, is vastly inferior to ourselves. The child must be regarded as inferior, or we should not feel the urgency of teaching it all the time, and requiring that it should exchange its own ways and preferences for ours. If the child is such an apt pupil that it rivals ourselves, we are glad that the child learns well, because we feel that this reflects credit upon the teacher; but we do not like to be beaten at our own game, because we in turn must then admit that the tables are turned, and it is we who are inferior and that one younger than ourselves can surpass us. Well, indeed, may we ask, what do we want of the child? Do we know? It seems exceedingly doubtful.

It is a case of "thus far and no farther," in many directions where the child is concerned. It must understand us, but always follow at a respectful distance; humbly ask questions, but never present us with problems which we cannot solve. It must always take our cue, but never give us a lead. It must always be obedient and submissive to us, and yet at the same time have plenty of character and will of its own, not be too subservient to others, always know its own mind, and stick to its own opinion in respect to others. It must come to us with its difficulties and troubles, yet, should it ask too many questions which we cannot answer, we shall be vexed, and tell it to run away and not always be plaguing us with everlasting queries. We expect that the child shall make endless allowances for us, to know when we are not well or tired, worried, or wish to be left alone. On the other hand, we never imagine that the child may feel the same; we do not allow the child to claim mental sanctuary, but consider it bound to submit to any amount of teasing from grown-up people with imperturbable good-temper. When we take these things into account, it would seem that we are expecting of children an understanding and tolerance, wisdom and knowledge of the world or the peculiarities of human nature as great as, if not greater than those we possess. It will constantly be a matter of annoyance to adults that children do not instinctively know all about some things they could only learn through experience, and at the same time forget that they are quite capable of understanding other matters and learning to recognize our foibles and short-comings, which we never imagine they could observe.

The child mind used to be described as a blank sheet of paper, upon which it was represented we had the power of writing anything that we wished, and no one else. The only comment which seems applicable to such a contingency would be, "What fun for these privileged people, the parents and teachers!" But a most rudimentary study of Psychology has taught us that the child mind is more like that clever little device for writing upon which, with a swift movement, can erase everything that has been recorded upon it and make itself ready for a fresh consignment of notes. Yet with this exception: that in the case of the child mind, when the writing disappears from view, it does not vanish for ever, but is stored up somewhere else for all time, from whence it will subsequently reappear in many ways and for many purposes out of this wonderful storehouse of mental impressions and psychological experiences. Another difficulty is that all impressions which the child receives will be stored in the same way, and not only those which we intend to write upon that "blank page" of the child mind.

We are by no means the only persons who have the privilege of writing upon this magic tablet; all the past ages which have contributed their share in the structure of the human mind have traced precepts and prohibitions upon it also. We write, not only the things we wish to be remembered, but also words said in haste or in a moment of forgetfulness, which we would give much to be able to erase afterwards. Nor can we control the writing by others upon the minds of children in our care, different records that we consider most undesirable, which are impressed from all sources and remain, whatever course we take to prevent this misfortune. Everything with which the child comes into contact through all its sensory receptor organs has an equal right to be recorded there, in ways which may often be passed by unheeded.

BOOKS TO BE READ IN CONNECTION WITH THIS CHAPTER.

School of Infancy. Comenius.
Children in Health and Disease. David Forsyth, M.D., D.Sc. Murray.
The Pre-School Child. Arnold Gesell. Macmillan.
The Child's Path to Freedom. Norman Macmunn.
Educate Your Child. Herbert McKay. Oxford University Press.
The Changing School. P. B. Ballard. Hodder & Stoughton.

CHAPTER III

THE CHILD DISCOVERS THE WORLD AROUND

A. Touch. B. Smell. C. Taste. D. Sight. E. Hearing.
F. Speech. G. Kinæsthetic Sense.

THE first few years of the child's life are essentially years of exploration and adventure, sometimes pleasant, sometimes quite the reverse. It is very difficult for us all, who are now familiar with the common exigencies of daily life and the possessors of knowledge which we have taken years to acquire, to think ourselves back to this early stage of development, when we were not aware of all these things. Consequently we find it hard to understand the complexities which are constantly facing the little ones, who cannot have as much knowledge as ourselves about their surroundings.

When we consider this question of the comparison of adult and child knowledge, we are inclined to dismiss it as a foregone conclusion and to think that it is absurd to go farther into the matter, taking for granted that no one could be so dull of comprehension as to fail to realize the existence of differences, even should they be exceedingly vague about what precisely they might be, and could not enumerate them if called upon to do so. Therefore, granted that the mere existence of these differences is accepted, a question of still greater importance arises, which is, to what practical use do we put our knowledge, to help us understand the child, so that we may assist and not check natural development, or prevent us expecting behaviour from it which could be only the product of wider experience?

If we should take, as proof of this knowledge, behaviour and expectations where little children are concerned, we may then be justified in feeling more doubtful whether the adult does actually realize how slight a child's knowledge of persons and things can be when stripped of all supplementary information, which we have learned through experience and with which we now automatically enrich our slightest observations.

It has been the result of many years of research to find out even a little concerning the sensory and psychological impressions made upon the mind of the baby by its surroundings long before it can speak, and so give us even a fragmentary idea of what these may be. The investigation has had to be carried out by means of observation made upon babies and tiny children, and compared with the memories of these early days which have lingered on into later years in the case of older persons. The greatest handicap to direct research of this kind in which we observe little children is, of course, the impossibility for the children to add verbal corroboration to our findings, or to contradict them with denial, for many years to come, because, even when they have gained considerable proficiency in the use of speech, we cannot rely greatly upon their ability to describe abstract impressions and emotions, even when they can talk freely about concrete objects or events which have happened. The language factor is, therefore, one of the cardinal obstacles between us and children, because it often proves a barrier rather than a bridge between one human mind and another. The earliest apparatus through which the child makes discoveries about the world around it, as well as about itself, are its own sensory organs. At birth, few of these are highly developed, yet all have some rudimentary power for receiving stimuli or impressions from without and transmitting them to the brain, where some comment is made upon them almost from birth which results in a reaction of a sort, even if it should be of the simplest type, *withdrawal*, of the whole body or the part concerned, if the stimulus is unpleasant and the comment negative; *approach*, if the stimulus is pleasant and the comment favourable or affirmative.

Many descriptive names have been found for our senses, these pathways by which messages from the outside world are conducted to the brain. Once they were called, "Gateways of the Soul," which name opens up to us extensive vistas of the result of these messages which represent hunger and comfort, pain, as well as more complex pleasures and anxieties. We may study them from their two main aspects, *physiological* and *psychological*, as well as learning many interesting things about their development in the course of evolution and noticing what special contribution each makes to the life of the individual, where the chief and most primitive aims of existence are concerned; that is to say, the preservation of the individual and the race. Each of these gateways, our sense-organs, has an outpost upon the surface of the body, carefully shielded from dangers from without, and a nerve pathway running from it to connect it with that part of the brain which, like a department store, deals with that one section only. This in turn sends on messages to other sections which lead to muscular response and action, as well as preserving them in the storehouse Memory, where they are kept for future reference. In our later life, when anything of a similar nature comes before our notice, it will usually awaken an echo more or less clear from the former message, which has been put away so carefully.

In most of the higher animals we find practically the same five senses as our own, although in some one will preponderate, while in others a different sense will take the lead, according to the particular conditions of life for that creature and the special dangers which need to be guarded against by the high development of one sense rather than another. For instance, many of the mammals have a far more acute sense of smell than ourselves, and the eyes of birds of prey can detect a moving object at a great distance, when we should perceive nothing. Those whose lives depend upon the rapidity with which they can escape from an enemy have, in addition to keen scent, speed of limb and well-developed hearing, so that they may be aware of the approach of the foe before it springs. It has been left to mankind, nevertheless, to develop the sense of touch to a paramount degree which other creatures cannot rival. Taste is also a valuable asset in the lives of many wild creatures for the preservation of life, since by this means they are able to detect poisonous plants, living creatures, or substances which are in a state of decomposition. This instinct of taste discrimination is, however, entirely lacking in the young of the human race, who cram everything within reach into their mouths, regardless of taste, which to other creatures might give a clue to the poisonous properties of the object.

Speech, although not counted as one of the five senses, is, after all, one of the most important gateways of the soul, upon which civilized people rely almost exclusively for sending messages from one to the other. Common language has become one of the most significant bonds uniting different persons, so that those who have acquired this means of communicating with one another consider as their equals only those with whom they can thus exchange thoughts, and regard with more or less contempt other creatures, human and otherwise, with whom they cannot do so. Hence the prevalent idea that all foreigners are slightly inferior, especially if they cannot talk our language, but that one who has learned to do so has at least done his best to make up the deficiency of Nature in not including them in our own nationality.

After this brief general survey, let us turn our attention to the first of these gateways, pieces of apparatus. For the position of honour has been chosen Touch, and for the following reasons. Not only is the development of this sense one of great interest in mankind, but also in the history of the development of creatures far below the human level. It is one of the first to be developed from the rudimentary ability of animalculæ to move towards and away from objects, to avoid danger in this way as well as to pursue particles which are felt to be useful for food. When we continue up the ladder of development, we find the touch-spots of the sea-anemone and tentacles of other creatures until we reach the wonderful specialized adjustments found in the human hand as a vehicle of touch-sensations, by means of which delicate and varied operations can be carried out by skilled persons.

Books which may be Studied in connection with this Chapter.

Instinct and Intelligence. N. C. Macnamara. Oxford Press. Warehouse.
Mental Evolution of Man. Romanes.
Principles of Psychology. William James. Henry Holt & Co.
The Origin of Species. Charles Darwin.

A. TOUCH

To escape contact with something which is for some reason dangerous and to move towards and enfold fragments which may serve as food are the two movements which we have come to regard as characteristic of all creatures from the lowliest to the highest. What means these tiny organisms have of judging a harmful substance which causes the withdrawal or of discriminating the nutritional value of some small particle in their neighbourhood we do not know with certainty.

Some scientists have considered this movement a purely chemical process, somewhat similar to the heliotropism to be observed in plants, by which they move to the light; but whatever the origin of the process may be, it is certain that movement away from some things and towards others does take place, and that similar forms of activity are to be observed in living creatures at a higher stage of development. In organisms at a rather more complex phase of development than the animalculæ with tropic and anti-tropic response, we begin to find particular specialized spots on the skin, or rudimentary organs, which have but one purpose, that of receiving touch-stimuli. These may be at first sensitive areas on the skin, hairs or tentacles, which we know in the cat's whiskers, the feelers of the crustaceans and the antennæ of butterflies and moths. The touch-spots upon the skin, which in ourselves are connected with the sensory nerves, form our receptor organs for touch-stimuli or tactile impressions. These are situated over the entire surface of our skin and mucous membrane, which allows us to regard the whole surface of the body as a receiving organ for the sense of touch. Some parts, however, are more sensitive than others, such as the lips, tips of the fingers, soles of the feet, the fine skin of the groin and between the folding surfaces of the joints, as well as all surfaces covered with mucous membrane.

If we begin our examination of the touch-sense from birth, what do we find? Primarily, it is the first of the senses to receive stimulation, and usually far greater consequences are connected with this event in later life than we are generally aware. During the labour-pains of the mother and the passage of the child through the extremely restricted vaginal canal, the touch- and pain-spots upon the baby's skin are stimulated as they have never been during the nine months of intra-uterine life. These spots on the skin are small and invisible, but have been discovered to be of four kinds, each registering one variety of sensation only, namely, heat, cold, touch, and pain. The ante-natal state of the child cannot, we imagine, have provided any unpleasant touch-stimuli; it is only during labour and in the act of birth that these touch-spots receive their introduction to activity, and then in a most violent and unpleasant manner. First touch and then pain are experienced in the squeezing, crushing, downward contractions of the labour-pains of the mother, when the whole body of the child is caught in the grip of these paroxysms.

It is of some interest to note that the circle of pain around the head which is found in some types of migraine, and which the sufferer often describes as though some string drawn tightly around it were contracting and expanding, follows the line gripped at one time by the vaginal orifice, where the circumference of the head is the greatest and, therefore, where the pressure must consequently have been the most severe, which probably gave the child the same fluctuating impression of pain at that time. Once birth is accomplished, a third variety of touch-sensation of an unpleasant character assails the poor infant, that of cold, when the outside atmosphere of the room strikes its body for the first time. Should respiration not be established readily by the cold air, the baby may receive further unpleasant stimuli on the part of assistants at the birth to cause crying and thence respiration. Thus all the first stimuli have been those of touch, and all are of an unpleasant character. Later a few pleasant ones are received : warm water, warm blankets, and the contact of a soft bed; a dim light and, perhaps, the proximity of the mother's body. The presence of surrounding softness and warm contact gives the babe a feeling of security, well-being, happiness, love, in terms which will only be understood later, yet from the beginning a feeling of *something all round* means completeness, warmth, and pleasure to the baby—all that it needs at this stage to fulfil its wants; hunger and its gratification will come second.

The obvious discomfort of the newborn infant when for the first time it feels itself not surrounded is quite plain and analogous to that feeling to which the name "loneliness" will be attached later. We often say that the first movements of the baby are reflex and not voluntary. A physical movement takes place because a certain stimulus has brought into play the corresponding reaction, and some portion of the child's body moves without deliberate intention on its part. Thus it has been noticed that a newborn child will twine its fingers around a thin stick so tightly that it may be lifted off the ground, should the object be but lightly laid across the palm; or the lips will begin to move with a sucking movement if anything be placed between them. Good; in both these cases we find a touch reflex in action, the fundamental use of which is embedded deep in the history of development, the first to serve the purpose of nutrition, the second that of our personal safety, both nevertheless closely connected.

Some people even contend that the clutch reflex is a survival from the time when our ancestors lived in nests among the branches of trees, and the child developed this tendency in case it might fall out. This cannot be proved, but in some tribes we know that it was used as a test of vitality. If the child's grip were sufficiently strong to cling to the edge of the thatch of the hut, it was allowed to live; if it fell, it would be left to die or exposed upon some bleak hill-side.

As time passes, what more does the baby learn from this sense of touch? Hands and feet are at first of paramount interest to the gradually expanding mind, because they can be seen most easily and also are always there when wanted. The little fingers rove around exploring, and find infinite pleasure from rhythmic touching, allowing them to contract and then relax upon something soft which offers but slight resistance, or by using a stroking motion, particularly noticeable when the infant is being fed or when put down to go to sleep. Whilst being fed it will either touch the breast of the mother or nurse, even when not being suckled, or will frequently pull the lobe of its own ear or that of the nurse. This latter action may often be continued while waiting to go to sleep, or some other part of the child's own body may be used as a substitute for the breast of the mother which was stroked or patted during the feeding. We often find that some little children will not go to sleep unless they can hold somebody's hand, and, later on, may even clasp one of their own, doubtless to give themselves an hallucinatory impression that the protecting adult hand is still there. Cases have been known when children feel the right hand must protect the poor little left one, which is frightened and wants comforting. The source of this idea is plain to us from the context.

Not infrequently do we find that the hand of the infant will seek his or her genitals, and strive to play with them for a double reason—the pleasure derived by the fingers from touching the soft skin and the pleasure gained by the genitals through the gentle manipulation of the little fingers. It frequently seems that great sensitivity of touch may be a natural sequence of this early pleasure, which has been allowed to develop naturally without being checked by any great or sudden shock, such as tends to produce touch inhibition.

This possibility introduces us to a matter which is of the utmost importance, since it may affect the whole subsequent career of the child. This sense of touch, whether it be inhibited or allowed freedom in which to develop, may be the underlying cause why one profession is impossible to a child on account of the touch inhibition or deficiency of tactile discrimination, or chosen in another because it has been allowed to develop naturally. It is now recognized, by those engaged upon research relating to the psychological development of infants, that the tendency to infantile masturbation is practically universal, and that it is neither a certain sign of incipient idiocy nor the cause of subsequent mental derangement. It is a phase through which all go at one time or another, like teething, the matter of the greatest moment being whether the difficulty passes without complications or if the habit should become permanent; it may remain as it is, or increase in severity with the growth of the child.

In dealing with it, the wisest course to follow is not to be distressed or unduly anxious, and apparently not to take very much notice of it. Such manifestations will then usually be found to cease after a time. The hands may be gently removed from the genitals, but without giving the child reason to suppose that the adult who does so is angry or considers it guilty of misdemeanour, any more than if found scratching its face. Certainly it is most unwise to slap the hands or the genitals, or make use of threats or emphatic scoldings, because their use, even in the mildest forms, has been known to lead to the most serious consequences. The child should not be allowed to feel a wrong-doer for this action, which, after all, is common to all small children. Unless the habit be accentuated and fixed by measures intentionally preventive, but actually *causative* of still greater trouble, this will fade when the fingers have found something still more interesting to play with, and the novelty of the interest in the baby's own body begins to wane in favour of outside objects. The baby's own person is of first importance because it is always there and presents so many possibilities for wonder and discovery; also because it, of all objects, can provide a double share of pleasure, since we can never feel the dual pleasure of stimulus *and* reaction, unless we touch ourselves. In this way the child learns one of its first lessons in distinguishing between the self and the non-self, the world around, which is a problem, the solving of which will absorb the major part of its attention for many years to come, waning and being rediscovered from time to time.

After the child has learned something about itself by touching, it begins to explore the environment in the same way. It cannot discover many of the characteristic qualities of itself and others except by this means, through touching and comparing the sensations derived in this way with others and remembering the impressions so gained. Gradually it will learn, when a double sensory response is gained, the questing fingers have encountered a portion of itself; when there is but one, it has met an outside object, which needs exploration by every means at the baby's command, not only with the hands alone, but also with the mouth, which we must remember is equally a touch-receptor organ in the young child.

The child in its early years will use its mouth as well as its hands as an organ of touch to discover the properties of things, as well as to gain some notion of their size. Size, shape, and weight must all be learned partly through touch and feeling with the hands, as also the qualities of hard, soft, rough, smooth, the gloss of satin, the resistance of velvet. If we watch a baby as it passes tiny hands over various substances and notice the expression on its face, we shall realize the degree of pleasure or the reverse that it is deriving at that moment from the sense of touch. It is by no means uncommon to hear of a child who cries most bitterly whenever touched by the exceedingly rough hands of a housemaid who takes the place of a nurse upon her "evening out." The contact with her coarse, chapped fingers will be like a nutmeg-grater upon the extremely sensitive skin of the baby. Many small children will also protest most loudly when daddy kisses them before a shave. Again, we do not realize the extreme tenderness of a child's skin, or what exquisite torture a starched armhole or a coarse towel may cause a child, and that hasty and rough handling will often hurt its soft limbs as much as a blow would affect ourselves.

If we are constantly telling a child not to touch, either itself or some other object, we impress upon its mind an idea of guilt in connection with this action that may tend to limit or entirely inhibit this sense in later life. The slapping of hands, the tying on of gloves, or securing the hands outside the bedclothes, still more, the use of metal gauntlets, which are to be had for this purpose of hindering the child from touching itself, because it cannot then do so without causing itself considerable pain, are all methods calculated to have the most disastrous consequences. The sense of touch should be guarded as one of our most precious treasures. Many of the most important professions as well as skilled trades require the finest touch discriminations, and should this sense become blunted by injudicious treatment in childhood, it is exceedingly difficult to restore it.[1]

A note of warning, however, must be uttered in connection with the gain of pleasure through this sense of touch, because those in charge of children themselves frequently give too much stimulation of this kind quite unintentionally. We may be most anxious to check the baby, when we see it seeking pleasure from its own little body, and yet at the same time without thinking may do exactly the same ourselves, probably also

[1] *Discrimination of Wool Fabrics by the Sense of Touch*, Henry Binns. Br. J. of Psychol., January 1926.

for the pleasure our fingers derive from stroking or tickling its soft skin and rounded limbs. It is by no means rare to see an adult gaining very obvious sensory gratification by stroking, patting, or tickling the soft little body of a baby, especially when undressing or bathing it, kissing it continually, either in play or during the simple routine of washing, dressing, and toilet operations. These, if indulged in too often or with too great emotion on the part of the adult, may prove highly injurious to the infant later on, and lead to results which were both unforeseen and undesired by the persons responsible for the harm that has been done.

Tickling is also considered a very pleasant pastime by the active partner in the game, but many children suffer acutely when this intense touch stimulation is too long continued. It is not nearly so much fun, however, for the passive partner, even if he or she may laugh, because when tickled, or, in fact, during many other kinds of intense emotional excitement in children, the laugh does not by any means always denote pleasure. They may at the same time be trembling on the verge of tears.

The pleasure derived by the child through adult stimulation of the cutaneous touch-centres is far more powerful and injurious than when the stimulus has been self-applied, and may often rank in the child's mind as an act of violence or a *sexual aggression*; not, of course, that it is familiar with this term, but it realizes that unusual feelings have been aroused in it by another which are pleasant and at the same time alarming, especially when the adult concerned is one who is particularly beloved or one of the child's parents. Slapping or whipping may also be included in the list of touching sensations which are best avoided, as are the administration of soap suppositories, enemas, or the taking of a child's temperature per rectum, although this is a usual hospital routine. Many children also resent it most bitterly.

All these actions arouse emotions connected with the body and with a part of the body that are not wisely provoked in young children. Such forms of sensory stimulation will without doubt provide extreme pleasure in infancy, but they have been found to lead to the most undesirable consequences in later life. The chief danger connected with precocious emotional excitement is that when extreme pleasure of this kind has been experienced by a child too early and too often, it may want to continue the same process itself, with the result that not only will this form of pleasure usurp a too great importance in its life, to the exclusion of other pleasures which require a greater expenditure of mental energy to provide, but will also cause the child's interest to become focused upon these bodily possibilities and to exploit them whenever there is an opportunity of so doing, as well as seeking methods of procuring this stimulation.

In some children one part of the body may possess greater interest and possibilities for pleasure-gain than another. Knowing how easily this may arise, it is well to be on guard, when in charge of little children, not to supply them with unnecessary assistance for the establishment of an undue fondness for this form of pleasure as the only one which is of real value. One may also point out in this connection that the present fashion of extremely tight clothing for small children is equally injurious, for reasons which we have already mentioned. It may, in the opinion of some, look "smart" or pretty to see very much abbreviated skirts and skin-tight knickers, but in winter they will be very cold, and also provide a constant stimulation through pressure and dragging in moving upon just those parts of the child's body where stimulation of this kind is most injurious.

We have now sketched briefly the primary function of the touch-receptors for discovering the immediate surroundings of the infant and for gaining some knowledge of its own body. We have shown how important it is to preserve their function in childhood, so as to allow them to be of unrestricted value in adult life; but there are still three further aspects of the sense of touch which should not be neglected, since they present considerable interest for those in charge of children. These are, first, what can the child learn about its environment, and especially the persons in its vicinity, through touch? Second, are there any ways in which this sense may be trained? And third, what can the person in charge of children learn from observing how a child touches or handles objects?

1. *What can the child learn about the people around by means of touch, not only from touching them, but also from impressions gained*

from the way they handle itself? This may be a new point of view
to some, but it is nevertheless one of some considerable
importance. The child records sensory experiences through
memories of feelings. It gains impressions and knowledge of
the character and dispositions of people, as well as some idea
what may be expected from them, long before it acquires
speech, by means of which it may communicate discoveries of
this description to others. When we say that a child *instinctively*
knows what others are like, and is able to discriminate those
who are fond of children from those who are not, we should
probably be more accurate if we were to say that the child can
very readily make use of its sensory impressions to determine
what may be expected of other people, and remembers them
with certainty for reference in the future. We are led to believe
from several sources of evidence, from our observation of the
behaviour of infants, and their obvious preferences for different
persons that seem derived from their method of holding them,
as well as a few very early memories of feelings produced in
the infant from being touched or handled in a certain way,
that the infant's impressions of various persons are derived
from its sense of touch.

Thus amongst the memories of one adult remained an
impression of the comfort and happiness that was obtained as
a baby by having both her cold little feet held in one large
warm hand. From further evidence connected with this
experience, it seemed more than likely that the recollection
belonged to her first year of life, when in a most unhappy
condition caused by difficult teething.

The infant will learn very early to discriminate between
those whose sure, gentle handling gives them a sensation of
comfort and therefore security, in contrast with the rough or
uncertain handling of those who do not like children or who are
inexperienced in dealing with them; those who have a hasty
temper, or are undecided and floppy, so that the baby feels
all the time as though it were going to be dropped. The
infant always likes to be held in such a way that the feeling
of being surrounded is appreciable, added to which the touch
should furnish a certain amount of warmth and softness. It
must be quite easy for a baby to notice the changes in handling
as it passes from one person to another, or alterations of touch

in one person from time to time, corresponding with variations in that person's moods or feelings, from extremes of gentleness to those of roughness. In this way it will become aware of changes in the behaviour of persons or in one person, although without at first being able to account for the reason why this should be so. This variation nevertheless, if constant, very pronounced or rapid, cannot help being extremely injurious for the psychological well-being of the child.

It has been found that the helpless condition of the infant requires a certain amount of counterbalancing security to maintain its mental equilibrium, to prevent fear playing too great a part in early life, because the apprehensive fear of little children springs originally from this feeling of helplessness and want of security. Rapidly alternating moods, such as we have just described, must tend to arouse such fear and disturb the sense of security through establishing a feeling of uncertainty. Security is typified in the child's mind by contact with a loved and well-known person, as well as being warmly surrounded, which is admirably represented by the presence of loving arms which encircle it closely.

A remarkable proof of the beneficial effect of contact and active affection upon children who have hitherto suffered from a deficiency of these most necessary factors for a healthy childhood, may be gained from the experiences of those working amongst children brought up in institutions, or homes where there is only little or no individual care and affection given to the children. It has been found that when never nursed, petted, nor loved, or where the home environment contains an atmosphere of danger, violence, and uncertainty, due to the bad temper or drunken excesses of one or both parents, the children are nervous, suspicious, and do not thrive as do those who have a sufficiency of this necessary attention. Should these little ones be brought into a more congenial atmosphere, where someone has time to show them some personal attention and love, and where there is no harmful atmosphere of uncertainty brought about by the moods of those in charge, the children will be found to respond to the changed conditions in a remarkable way and improve rapidly, not only in their general mental health, but also in physical well-being. The results are as striking as those brought about by Sunlight Treatment for other troubles.

For the child, love is as necessary as sunlight, and it appears from these results that children need a certain amount of demonstrative affection and petting for their satisfactory development. One says "a certain amount" intentionally, however, because too much tenderness can be as harmful as too little. We may with advantage add cream to the feeds of some babies, but in a right proportion. We cannot safely work on the premise, with cream or love, that because a certain amount is beneficial, double or treble that quantity will do a proportionate amount of good.

2. In what ways may we provide training for this sense of touch?
This problem has been so admirably dealt with by Madame Montessori in her methods of teaching, as well as by those who preceded her with similar views, notably Froebel, who in these days has become undeservedly overshadowed, that there is little to add, except to point out that each child will require to find ways of fulfilling needs which the individual home environment does not supply at present. Perhaps the most important caution of all is to point out that we may far more easily baulk the child's natural ability and methods of development by hindering them with our well-meant but clumsy, ill-timed efforts, than actively train it. We can do far more harm in the early years by constantly saying "Don't touch," than years of kindergarten teaching may accomplish. We may provide the opportunity and material for exploration and adventure in this direction and then stand back and not interfere—that is, if we have sufficient self-control; but as a rule we are apt to get annoyed with the children if they show any inclination to use apparatus in the wrong way, or to carry out other experiments than those we have set before them.

During this process of exploration or adventure, as we have called the early educational efforts of childhood, the child may do more or less damage. This is unavoidable in some ways. We must be prepared for that by providing material which may be experimented upon fairly harmlessly, and allow the child to discover as soon as possible the properties of common things. For instance, the child must learn that fire does burn the fingers and consumes and spoils other things; that damage of this kind can frequently not be made good; that what is destroyed cannot be restored as though the damage had never been carried out; that water makes things and people wet, as well as injuring some objects, and that articles break if dropped or hammered too hard. The child, having satisfied itself upon these matters, will not be so likely to continue being destructive or wish so urgently to destroy things in order to see what happens as though it had never had a chance to make these discoveries under conditions where the harm done was as little as possible. Thus, if the child wishes to discover how hard you must hit china before you break it, the experiment is preferably carried out upon a jam-jar, value one penny, than a priceless china vase. The child, having satisfied itself upon these matters, will not continue to be so destructive, if the *only* motive is experiment, as one who is always trying to find out what happens under special circumstances and is prevented from doing so. A great deal of childish damage is the result of the wish to investigate the properties of objects, and is the result of ignorance, rather than malice, as people are often inclined to think. The impulse to destroy rather than to create will be discussed at length in a subsequent chapter, because it is a complicated and important subject which springs from several roots.

3. *How the child touches and what may be learned from these differences.*

We may learn a great deal about the mental development of the child from observing how it behaves in respect to this sense of touch, which includes, of course, its methods of handling persons and objects. At first the baby touches with the whole hand rather than with the fingers, and the thumb is held tightly pressed against them, side by side. The next step is for the thumb to gain its independence, to be opposed to them and yet used in alliance with the fingers for picking up objects and for grasping them still more closely than before. At the beginning the hand is used more as a scoop to move things towards it or to push them away. Once the child has discovered the art of finger-work, however, and the pleasure to be derived from picking up, it will spend hours in trying to manipulate small fragments of fluff or crumbs.

Some children, mentally retarded, show this infantile

position of hand, and the same tendency to use the fingers together rather than individually. They are also loath to handle objects or to do anything which requires careful manipulation, such as fastening buttons, doing up shoe-laces or the like. When this is long continued, into the fourth or fifth year, without other characteristic signs of backwardness or dullness of mentality being obvious, one is inclined to wonder whether the sense of touch has not been inhibited in these cases, just as in those where a definite fear seems to be connected with the touching of certain objects, or being touched by them. Sometimes this will be brought about through threats or punishments in connection with infantile masturbation. There may, however, be another cause of the unwillingness to do things for themselves, if, for instance, they derive such intense pleasure from being the helpless baby, for whom everything is done, that this gratification cannot be renounced. They see in the service of the loving mother a sure token of the love that is proof of their own value to her; so that the refusal of assistance becomes to them not only an equivalent of the withdrawal of love, but at the same time seems to lower themselves in their own estimation as much as in that of the person who has refused help. This symptom is seen most conspicuously in boys, and may be aggravated by the fact that the person who used to do things for the little boy so willingly, now suggests that he should do things for himself, or to help her: giving as a reason for so doing, *it is to please her.* This may make him refuse to do things for a double purpose, to try to force her to them as formerly, and to punish her for refusing, in the same way he feels hurt by her withdrawal of help.

BOOKS TO BE READ IN CONNECTION WITH THIS AND OTHER SECTIONS
OF CHAPTER III.

First Section.

First Steps in Mental Growth. D. R. Major.
Mental Development in the Child. W. Preyer.
Development of the Intellect. W. Preyer.
Mental Evolution in Man. Romanes.
Mental Evolution in Animals. Romanes.
Mental Development in the Child and the Race. J. M. Baldwin.
Biography of a Baby. Miss M. Shinn.
Studies of Childhood. James Sully.
Savage Childhood. Dudley Kidd.

B. SMELL

Smell is one of the Touchstones by which Nature trieth what is convenient for itself.—Nicholas Culpeper. London Dispensatory. 1653.

ONE is inclined to believe that the olfactory sense is brought into the baby's service next after touch, and that by this means the child also learns much about its surroundings. We find the sense of smell developed in living creatures at a very early stage, and in many it reaches a far higher degree of efficiency than that which it attains in mankind. In point of fact, it is remarkable that it plays such an exceedingly small part in the adult life of human beings. It has perhaps the smallest rôle of all the senses, and the one which is regarded with least esteem. If possible, we will try to find out why this should be the case.

Rather than employ their own sense of smell, men will breed special kinds of dogs whose scent is keen enough to trace the footsteps of any creature, and have, especially in England, raised the chase, in one aspect certainly, that of fox-hunting and coursing, to the level of national sports. Few, however, would be prepared to acknowledge that they themselves could even distinguish one person from another, their possessions or clothing, by the same means, even were they able to do so. The faculty of using the sense of smell seems to have fallen out of use in the adult years of the human race.

For this reason it was surprising to find the faculty to recognize persons by this sense mentioned in one well-known autobiography, that of Helen Keller,[1] written by the girl who was not only blind but also deaf and dumb. She states that she can and does often distinguish persons known to her in this way, by noting some characteristic smell about them, not only that of smoke, perfume which is used, clothing or the like, but declares that each person can be distinguished by a smell which is personal and typical of the character and disposition, temperament, and so on, as well as giving her some indication of the occupation or profession. One wonders how

[1] *The Story of My Life*, Helen Keller.

she has been able to achieve what seems to most of us so remarkable, whether she was always gifted with a particularly keen olfactory sense, or if it has been increased by way of compensation, to balance her deprivation of the other senses, sight and hearing, and that this acuity might be accentuated in all people if the cultivation of the other sensory organs did not prevent us feeling the need of this one.

As the result of observation and investigation of the senses in use in childhood, however, it would seem that the sense of smell is both active and highly prized by the child, yet for some reason it appears to become forced out of existence later on, or inhibited, in favour of the others. Not only does it seem more than likely that the olfactory sense plays an important part in childhood, but we believe that it is one of the two which accompany the infant into the world ready-for-use.

Why should we think this to be the case? Chiefly by observation of the infants themselves, what we can see by watching their behaviour during the first few days of life. We have only to study a baby, especially one that is breast-fed, to realize that the little questing nose is not moving hither and thither at random, but is definitely seeking something of value to it. The business-like action leads us to believe it to be instinctive and therefore a purposive activity, the heritage of the experience of the race, and that the smell which is perceived takes a message to the brain. This sets in motion the seeking of the breast to still the hunger which has been dimly perceived without the infant being consciously aware of the meaning of the series of movements that the smell has called up. In all probability the infant is particularly sensitive to this smell, which signifies the satisfying of hunger, when that smell is present.

This instinct has the characteristic of other instincts that may be seen in animals, birds, and fishes, the preservation of the self by the satisfaction of hunger, and it is carried out at first as an involuntary or reflex action. The child cannot be said to know what this smell signifies when it first seeks its source, the mother's breast, nor to have reasoned out this particular course of action. It is attracted there by the function of some ancient nerve pathway in the brain, arising from sensations of hunger, which make it more susceptible to smell, which then lead to muscular movement ending in sensory gratification of several sorts. This will soon establish new pathways in the child's mental processes, and from being at first an unconscious or involuntary act, will become one that is both conscious and voluntary, an outcome of the pleasure principle, carried out to gain the baby's first wish, the mother and her breast, which gives solace and satisfaction for these primary wants.

Originally in the history of the race, the sense of smell was of great importance to living creatures in the seeking of food and in ascertaining whether that which had been found was good for food or injurious. If it smelt in a way that was unusual or putrid, the creature decided that it was harmful and would not partake of it. Again, instinct was of service in this respect. All food odours would not have the same result upon different creatures. To some of the mammals, the slightest odour of taint will cause them to turn from food, although other creatures will prefer flesh in this state or vegetable matter that is in a state of decay. The smell of various substances will attract one living creature and repel another, according to whether that substance is wholesome or poisonous to that particular species. Scientists assure us that it is rare for animals in a wild state to partake of unwholesome or poisonous food, even the young of these species. It is not accidental by any means that our noses are placed just above our mouths. In a great many ways, smell and taste are closely allied, so that it becomes a difficult problem to discuss the one without the other. However, in this section we will attempt to keep the two senses as separate as possible and reserve the taste stimuli for a later section.

We have said that wild creatures will seldom attempt to eat anything that is injurious, and that warning is given them by some means of its poisonous character through the sense of smell; this sense and instinct is by no means operative in the young of the human species, however, because the baby will without hesitation put everything into its mouth which may be induced to enter this cavity, size being apparently the only deterring factor. The warning function of smell has apparently become obliterated in the process of civilization.

We have suggested, however, that the first use to which the infant puts its sense of smell is that of finding its way to the

F

source of food. In the case of children brought up upon a bottle with a rubber teat, the smell of warm rubber would become in time as much the smell equivalent of the pleasure *food* as that of the mother in the case of babies who are breast-fed. In early infancy the ideas food and mother or nurse are almost, if not quite inextricable, so that the smell which is sought in order to still the pangs of hunger will be registered as one of the most pleasant sensations or ideas that the infant's world has to offer.

This particular smell connected with *food-mother* will also include that of warmth, general body odour, and possibly contain a hint of blanket besides, which may possibly account for Rupert Brooke alluding to blankets among other things which are remembered because they have particularly endeared themselves for the sake of old associations. Many of the other objects in this poem are obviously chosen because of affection felt for them on account of a smell association, which has been retained in definite memories.

Without doubt the child learned to distinguish quite a number of intimately related persons and objects by their particular scent long before their names or other characteristics were discovered—the flannel bath-apron, the smell of a towel warming before the fire, the peculiar odour of hot water steaming from a painted can, that of the bath itself, and its accompanying pleasant scents of soap and powder. It is by no means uncommon to see a little baby never before accustomed to scented soap or powder sniff appreciatively when first introduced to these adjuncts of the bath, or for a child of about a year old to seem interested and appreciative at the approach of a visitor who is wearing flowers or has perfume upon her frock, showing curiosity and pleasure quite plainly by wrinkling up its nose and inhaling deeply, then breaking into a smile, or it will draw back with a grimace of disgust from a smell which it considers unpleasant.

Sometimes we shall find children turn away with evident dislike, the closing of the nostrils, which we have come to regard as typical of a personal aversion or a repugnant smell from something which in itself has no particular odour, or none which *we* can discern. In consequence of this action, we find ourselves wondering whether the child's olfactory sense may distinguish qualities of unpleasantness where we cannot do so; if it should have a different standard governing its likes and dislikes, or yet again, whether some quite different characteristic altogether has caused the displeasure, and the reaction of the grimace is one which has now already become a standard expression to denote anything nasty, which is no longer necessarily a smell, although at first it was this stimulus which produced it as an appropriate response. We are all familiar with this typical facial expression, which includes drawing down the nostrils, which has the effect of closing them so that the unpleasant smell is excluded. It seems probable that this was the origin of the expression we now associate with the idea *disgust*, and that it was connected with smell or taste, as the word itself denotes. Other similar expressions for the same thought present themselves to one's mind to denote unpopularity, such as, "to stink in one's nostrils" or to be "in bad odour"; these survivals tell their own tale, beyond need of further comment.

It is a theory of popular superstition that evil people had an unpleasant smell. In the seventeenth and eighteenth centuries it was a current euphemism to talk of witch-hunting as "smelling out witches." These folks, who were singularly ingenious in questioning the poor souls and making them incriminate themselves, were said to have a "wonderful keen nose for a witch." Only a few years ago, an echo of this idea was expressed by a little girl, who showed the greatest interest in witches. She had done her best to make friends with the idea that witches existed by inventing a story about one who had renounced all her evil practices and entered into an alliance with the fairies.

At first they had been suspicious of her offers to look after their babies or to do things to help them, but then, as a way out of their difficulty, they devised a method of detecting bad witches and distinguishing them from good ones. This was how they did it. The bad ones smelt nasty and the good ones nice. The bad witches were the cross ones that did horrid things and frightened you. From corresponding memories of what they thought and noticed as children, one finds recollections which may be correlated with this little girl's theories about the nasty-smelling witches. Other children are aware that their mothers or nurses have a peculiar and unpleasant odour about them at certain times and are curious about it, although their wondering meets with no response from the adult should they ask, nor are they able to find out the cause unaided. If we link together this curiosity and the child's rule for detecting witches—they smell nasty, they are cross, do horrid things and frighten you—we are probably justified in believing that the witch is the menstruating woman, who is more likely to be irritable with children at that time than when she is in a happier state of mind.

If we remember this discovery of the child and connect it with observations of their other interests, that bodily odours and those of the excretions do interest them, somethimes most profoundly, is it not some guide towards solving the riddle presented at the beginning of this section: why the sense of smell is not accorded an equal place of honour with the rest? The answer is this: because the smells which originally interested us most were those which were not tolerated by society, or about which we were not allowed to speak. (See Chapter IV, "The Great God-wish." Section B). If we follow up this theme, what do we find? What is the usual course of action adopted by a mother or nurse when she finds her baby taking extreme interest in, or being curious about, its own bodily products, and perhaps asking questions about them, or those of another? Is it not to show some sign of disapproval, to say "naughty" or "ga-ga," or something which gives the impression that this form of interest is illicit, even if she should not have recourse to stronger measures? What particular method is adopted by the adult to deal with such an eventuality will depend very largely upon her own training as a child. How this perfectly normal manifestation of inquisitiveness and desire for knowledge was treated then, will account for how complete has been the subsequent repression or forgetting of her own early interests as well as the consequent development of an equivalent reaction-formation, which has turned the original impulse of curiosity and interest into an opposite manifestation of disgust.

By means of too severe measures taken to banish them, the interest and pleasure found in these bodily products may be repressed and subsequently make a fresh appearance in an opposite tendency, either that no appreciation or interest is taken in any scent or perfume, or that an exaggerated disgust is shown for all bad smells and is allied with a pride in the fact that the person possesses an olfactory sense of the greatest acuity for detecting them, which is made doubly emphatic by a crude comment upon their unpleasantness.

This is another of the unwished-for consequences that unwise training may produce. An interest for these things is quite normal and represents merely one of the many subjects that the child meets upon the path of its development about which it wishes to find out. If curiosity connected with the topic is stamped out, the tendency may take the course we have mentioned, or continue in secret, until it becomes an obsession to smell every unpleasant odour obtainable, to seek and find in this form of curiosity the chief attraction in life. It may also appear later as an exaggerated love of scent, or of those who are in the habit of lavishly perfuming themselves, love of strongly scented or flavoured cheese, or the narration of risky stories, which are often called "highly-flavoured" or "high," and many other undesirable tendencies.

If we should accept this explanation it is not difficult to see why our sense of smell should have become so unpopular and so frequently inhibited, why so many of us have repressed our olfactory sense until it has faded almost out of existence and is but little use in daily life. Only in memories does it linger on with many of us, and the scents and smells with which we were familiar in childhood will bring back with startling vividness sights, sounds, persons, and events, about which or whom we have not thought for many years. *Scents* are all that our noses are allowed to appreciate, and to some extent the aroma of food. But even then we do not allow this sense as many opportunities for enjoyment as we permit our ears in music, or our eyes in the contemplation of a work of art or natural beauty. The person whose keenest pleasure is taken in finding gratification for his or her olfactory sense is not regarded in the same way as those whose chief ambition is to satisfy a craving of the senses connected with hearing and sight or what is regarded a trifle vaguely as the intellect.

The poets are allowed the greatest licence in their work; in a verbal gratification of love of scents and perfume, especially when surrounded by the halo of associative memories of a sentimental variety. Rupert Brooke and Kipling, for example, are perhaps more honest than most others, because at times both will remind us of many quite humble scents that still remain dear to us by means of links of association, although perhaps not all of us might be prepared to acknowledge how dear they are. Many other poets have, however, sublimated this interest, and turned it into the socially recognized and accepted channel of love and memory of fragrance, or perfume, instead of the original loves of our childhood, which were of such prime importance in the past. They sing of the fragrant memories that bring back the scenes of the past, as, for instance, Kipling in his well-known verses called "Lichtenberg," published in that little volume called *The Five Nations*, which came out at the end of the Boer War, in which he writes as follows :—

> Smells are dearer than sounds or sights
> To make your heart strings crack,
>
> .   .   .   .   .
>
> Like the smell of the wattle of Lichtenberg
> Riding in, in the rain.

C. TASTE

THOSE of us who have been concerned with the feeding of quite young infants have doubtless been surprised at times to find how early their sense of taste develops, and that it is by no means a matter of equal importance to them with what they satisfy their hunger. They will show their likes and dislikes quite plainly by changes of facial expression and movements of the head almost from the beginning of life.

At the commencement of this discussion of the influence of the senses upon the life of the child, we noted that the very lowliest creatures showed at least two reactions to outside objects: to move away from enemies and objects that were not liked, and to move towards anything that seemed to be good for food. The psychological terms for these movements, *appetition* and *aversion*, declare their connection with food from the outset.

We often find that a reaction of a higher organism survives in a movement of part of the body or a limb which at earlier stages of development involved the behaviour of the whole creature, in the same way as does now the part. This is a reaction of the baby confronted with a feed which is not liked because of taste or temperature. Its head will move this way and that, from side to side, doing its best to avoid some form or vehicle of food. At first, this may be the mother's nipple (although very rarely), afterwards the feeding-bottle, and later a spoon or cup. Food which is approved will be sought and the head will follow the receptacle of food, should anyone attempt to draw this away from the mouth of the infant.

It has, indeed, been thought by many investigators of childhood, who were also interested in the rudiments of language, that in these two movements we have the first idea of *gesture*, which later becomes allied to speech. Gesture has been defined as *an action in little*, by Captain Rattray, in an interesting chapter on "Drum Talk," occurring in his book on *Ashanti*, and our observation of the baby confirms this statement. Is not this same shaking of the head the most usual gesture of refusal in infancy or denial, which survives also throughout life, and the words in various languages which denote *NO* are inclined to close the mouth upon the final sound, as though to refuse admittance to unpopular food. Affirmation, however, is shown by an up and down movement of the head, a well-known sign of pleasure in the baby, and one that is frequently made when sucking with great appreciation.

The words in several countries signifying *YES*, moreover, do not close the mouth nearly so tightly as in the case of the negation, but tend to even leave the lips apart to receive the desired food. (See section on "Speech".)

If gesture may be taken as an equivalent of action, facial expression is a quite safe guide to the thoughts of the infant. Feelings of placid content, discomfort, blissful repletion, hunger, flatulence, disgust, may all be traced in the changes which pass over the little face, if we are at all familiar with this early equivalent of speech. Indeed, for many years, facial expression in small children may be a more sure indication of their thoughts and emotions than the words they use, but as yet understand very imperfectly. At the same stage of development, we notice that they will observe the faces of those around them very carefully for the same purpose, to be able to act upon what they see written there with a higher degree of certainty than is gained by listening merely to what they hear, and in this way they supplement the evidence of their ears.

When we take into consideration some of the most elementary facial expressions in use at the present day among civilized races, we may notice that quite a large number of them are to be found as frequently upon an infant's face in connection with food and the process of digestion and mal-digestion. The eagerness and pleasure represented by pursed-up lips, which is the baby compliment paid to something agreeable for the satisfying of hunger, will later on be given to a favourite person or toy. It will reappear in the kiss, and still later become visible upon the face of a scientist or artist when brought face to face with some long-sought proof of keenly contested theory, a rare specimen, or a work of art of great beauty, and again will be seen in the smoker enjoying a particularly satisfying blend of tobacco. The expression of disgust, however, with which the child will turn away its head, refusing unacceptable food, will be the sign of intense displeasure throughout life, whatever be the rejected object.

Not only does the infant show reactions of these two types, but a considerable amount of discrimination and power of deliberation or judgment also enters into the early mental life of the baby. If a feed be refused immediately or at first approach, we may assume, firstly, that the baby is not hungry, and secondly, that it does not like the smell or temperature of what is offered; that is, the touch-receptors are not satisfied. Sometimes, however, after the milk is tasted once or twice, it will be most obviously considered and afterwards quite intentionally rejected, which shows that gustatory discrimination leading to refusal has been at work.

If we are feeding the infant artificially when such a reaction occurs, we shall probably know exactly how we have changed the mixture of which the feed consists, and why it has met with disapproval—perhaps there was less sugar, more or less of some other constituent than the baby has been accustomed to, or because a dose of medicine has been slipped into the bottle, thinking that if administered thus it will not be detected. We are thus already beginning our tactics of deception where the baby is concerned. In this refusal the infant will show an attitude of resentment where it detects change, which is one of the outstanding characteristics of early life.

Should the baby be breast-fed, however, we are then faced with a different and harder problem, also one that will be by no means as readily solved. From very early times it has been a widespread belief that the milk of a nursing-mother is affected and changed in quality as well as quantity not only by her diet, but also by her state of mind. This is probably true beyond all doubt, since modern investigation of psychological problems has added proof to the old theories founded upon folklore and observation. If a baby is able to realize and resent any alteration in an artificially mixed diet, it must also be equally capable of appreciating changes in its natural food, should they occur from any emotional disturbance of the mother.

Food and emotions seem closely connected in many aspects. We may notice the exhibition of many emotions in the infant's attitude towards food, and that the adult does the same, although not always so openly, is a matter of everyday knowledge. Further proof that we have placed emotional values upon tastes may be shown from our habit of using the names of the four fundamental tastes, sweet, sour, acid, and bitter, as adjectives to describe and include many ideas beyond their original sense. We apply these daily to dispositions of people, situations, moods, and affects in general, as frequently as to the original percepts, which use of words shows us clearly what infinite importance is attached to our sense of taste, and the emotional experience we derive from it.

It may come as a great surprise to some that recent psychological research has demonstrated that several character-traits with which we are all familiar have arisen from the early experiences of the baby, where this question of nutrition is concerned. The baby who was always satisfied at its mother's breast, without stint, decrease in nutritional value, or disturbed by early or too sudden weaning, will go through life a happy *optimist*, always expecting and generally finding the world to be a "promised land, flowing with milk and honey." But the infant who suffered disappointment over quality or quantity, perhaps in some cases both, who was weaned too early or too suddenly, through an illness of the mother or for any other serious reason, will grow up a *pessimist*, always feeling deprived of lawful rights, and that the world in general is a disappointing place, which never satisfies according to promise or expectation.

In our dealings with infants we become acquainted with a great many food idiosyncrasies, all of which have now been found to possess a definite bearing upon subsequent character-formation, besides those which we have just mentioned. Chief amongst these may be reckoned the steady refusal of food, or continued disagreement of some special kinds, when no particular physiological cause for it can be discovered. This, however, may be a reflection of the mother's state of mind and not arise from the baby itself. Where the child is concerned, it is but a secondary reaction. Thus we have often found that the mother of an unwanted baby was not able to feed it herself, or only inadequately, so that it did not thrive.

Some medical men who have specialized in the study of infant troubles are most emphatic in pointing out that diet is of paramount importance for good health, and that it influences the mind as well as the body. Psychology, however, has shown us ways in which this occurs still more profoundly in the reversed order, that the mind has a powerful effect upon the digestive function, and in ways which are more significant and widely diffused than many are aware.

We may gain valuable help in understanding how this state of affairs may come about from the popular belief, to which we have already called attention, that the condition of the mother's mental health, her content or anxiety, will produce changes in the quality, that is, nutritive value, as well as the quantity of her milk; that the baby is aware of these changes and is influenced by them, not only physically, but also psychologically, or emotionally. We, who have worked among infants and have thus had opportunities of watching the reactions of not merely a few children of our own, but many babies who are in no way emotionally connected with us, so that we are more likely to regard them without bias of any kind, have noticed that an emotional upset in a baby regularly affects its digestion, as well as the reverse—that vagaries of digestion react upon its "temper."

To determine with certainty which condition has actually been the cause and which the effect—whether or not something happened to disturb the emotional equilibrium of the baby in the first instance that consequently threw the digestive apparatus out of order, or if the intestinal trouble were the origin of the baby's psychological upset—is a difficult problem to solve. Research of this kind requires the most accurate and open-minded investigation, which is hard to obtain for the following reason. If the origin be an emotional disturbance, it must probably have been caused by the action of some person in relation to that baby, probably ourselves, and we may be unwilling to admit that we have been the intentional or unintentional cause of the trouble. We prefer to attribute the cause to an outside or independent stimulus, or the baby's innate disposition to bad temper or digestive trouble.

A case of this kind is on record where a probationer, feeding a small baby, remarked one morning how bad-tempered and difficult he was to feed, because generally that infant enjoyed his bottle. It transpired, however, that *she* had mixed that feed with *disinfectant*, put ready for cleaning the baby tray, instead of the customary *barley-water*. Her olfactory and other senses had not been so much on the alert as those of the baby, but his warning that something was amiss, recorded by his reaction to an unusual and unpleasant taste, which was trying to tell her that he was in pain, went unheeded. He was scolded for bad temper into the bargain. This lack of observation on the part of the probationer cost the baby his life, due to the fact that the girl took for granted that the baby was at fault rather than herself.

The question of the refusal of food from psychological causes is really of essential importance, particularly as regards possible influences upon later life. We will often find that a baby will refuse food when an accustomed person is absent who has been in the habit of feeding it. Should it be the case of a nurse who is away on holiday or has been dismissed, she may be recalled, in order that the baby's life may be saved. This successful carrying out of a hunger-strike will establish a precedent, the value of which the baby will appreciate only too readily, and it will continue to use this method of terrorizing the parents and getting its own way. Indeed, we have even found the system serving the purpose of a struggle in the cause of politics, and for the same reasons.

We must not ignore the emotional side of this reaction of the baby, however. We say it is carried out to enable the little one to terrorize the adults in charge and for the purpose of getting its own way. This is the *unconscious* aim as well as the *result* that was striven for. The process is most probably set in motion on the one hand by the emotion *sorrow*, and on the other by the strong influence of *habit* upon the mind and consequent behaviour of a small child. To feel no appetite is a classical symptom of sorrow, especially when connected with missing a familiar and well-beloved person. It is one of the strands out of which the fabric we call loneliness or helplessness is woven. But, in addition to this motive, another must be taken into consideration.

The child, very early in life, learns to connect one person with a particular function or action, and the strong influence exerted by habit in the infantile life makes it almost impossible for an infant to accept a substitute in this particular rôle. Either or both of these mechanisms, grief or habit, come into action in response to the stimulus of the absence of the customary and beloved person. They produce the familiar symptom of anorexia, i.e. loss of appetite, or something will arouse anger in the baby, which is another emotion which furnishes the same result, namely, that food is refused. All strong emotions have an equal tendency to suppress hunger at any age throughout life, probably because of the original situation of cause and effect in babyhood. The ultimate consequence of the refusal of food is practically always a disturbance of the household, and that efforts are made to restore the condition desired by the baby to produce once more the wonted tranquillity. This means that the baby receives extra attention and perhaps the intense satisfaction of the return of the missing person or food before the former state of content is fully reinstated. This train of incidents which brings about the eminently desirable termination may have been carried out accidentally in the first instance, but it will nevertheless leave traces in the baby's memory, which creates a tendency for these tactics to be repeated whenever a subsequent occasion suggests the first link in the sequence of events. The more often this series of actions is carried out successfully, the more thoroughly will it become established, until, when a definite habit is formed, it will be difficult to divert it from its course or change it into another chain of reactions.

Weaning is the commencement of a great many psychological troubles. Some of those arising from a sudden or too hasty break from one mode of feeding to another have already been described. We not uncommonly discover that to the child's mind this process seems to represent an act of unmitigated and intentional cruelty, or an entirely unnecessary and spiteful thwarting on the part of the grown-up person, for which it will be always seeking some method of revenge.

This idea of weaning being such a grievous process may, of course, be accentuated by the fact that it usually coincides with teething, which is generally a more or less painful event. Children commonly have a tendency to connect synchronized circumstances or events, and often regard them as having some intimate relationship with one another, such as cause and effect, although actually this is not the case. Sometimes the child will reverse this sequence and fancy later on that the pain in its gums was caused by this unpleasant change in the food, rather than the opposite state of affairs, the eruption of the teeth, calling for the alteration of diet. Sorrow and resentment on account of a transition from a pleasant and familiar process to one that is unfamiliar, and thus, to a young mind, essentially unpleasant, will, as we have said, be aggravated by the incessant even if *slight* pain stimulation in the mouth. But can we be certain that the pain which a child suffers during the cutting of teeth, about which we ourselves should no doubt complain most bitterly, is trivial? Were we suffering from acute toothache, we should probably resent its being attended with a forced change in diet, especially if this necessitated mastication upon inflamed gums.

The mouth, because of its alliance with food and taste as well as emotions stirred through them connected with a beloved person, will become of intense importance to the little child, and continue to hold a deep significance for those persons who, as children, may have had very frequent or violent emotions, such as love or anger, disappointment or pain, connected with their mouths. One also believes that these people to whom weaning presented a serious trauma find it difficult to bring themselves to accept a substitute. Rather than content themselves with anything which nearly represents or resembles what they feel they need, they will prefer to go without altogether, and persist in striving for the original gratification, however hopeless its attainment seems, or continually grieve over their sad and bitter disappointment, feeling that they are fully justified in believing that the world and the people around them have betrayed their cause.

Once a child begins to advance to a diet which consists of substances other than milk, it is obliged to encounter a whole series of substitutes and constantly receives annoying additions to its diet, which by some children are resented equally acutely. The addition of any fresh taste to the menu calls forth a new struggle, often merely because it is new, and the baby quickly ejects it from its lips for this reason, not waiting to find out whether it likes it or not. This, in point of fact, may be the only survival in the child of the ability we find in animals and birds of distinguishing poisonous food-stuffs and so leaving them untouched. The strange taste, to the baby, may perhaps awaken some primeval echo that what is unknown may also be injurious and therefore best avoided. But yet this is constantly contradicted by the baby's habit of stuffing painted toys that *are* injurious into its mouth and wanting to suck bright, pretty pennies covered with verdigris, which shows that if this instinct does survive at all in our time, it is also most unreliable.

It is, however, interesting in this connection to find that children may often be induced to experiment with food they do not like because it is a novelty, by seeing other children eating it, or if they are told that mummy and daddy like it. This may be proof that it cannot be so bad after all and worthy of a trial, at any rate, which will be increased by the imitativeness of little children, especially of those a little older than themselves or of parents.

Children's palates, which heretofore have been accustomed exclusively to the taste of milk or foods made with and consequently tasting of milk, must find other flavours very conflicting and probably unpleasant. It is no unusual occurrence to find children disliking eggs, fish, or meat, when first introduced to them, all of which have a very distinct and rather strong flavour when compared with that of milk, so that they will often avoid them if possible, or, should they have been forced into taking a spoonful into their mouths, will make use of various expedients to find a way of expelling it again sooner or later. They will, especially with meat which is inclined to be fibrous, or gelatinous milk puddings, such as tapioca and large sago, roll them round and round in their mouths, refusing to swallow the nauseating bolus they have thus formed, and trying to spit it out should they have a chance to do so. Some children will also persistently vomit after any foods they do not like. To force a child to eat substances for which it has really a great repugnance is by no means wise, and it is also quite unnecessary cruelty. It is perfectly simple to make gradual transitions in diet, and at first, when introducing new or unpopular ingredients, to mix them with something which has a flavour that is liked, so that the new taste may be allied to an old one and thus not seem entirely strange.

As a child gets older, the force of example set it by others will come into play. It is extremely difficult to try to impress upon a child that good manners require everything upon a plate to be eaten, while at the same time hiding unappetizing morsels under our own knife and fork, or behind a tea-cup. If we say in the hearing of a child that we are not surprised it cannot eat so and so, we never liked it, or could not digest it either, we give it a model to follow, because the fact represented by the old proverb, "Actions speak louder than words," is one of the strongest incentives to child behaviour.

The child, forced to take something into its mouth which it dislikes, will keep it there sometimes literally for hours, and then spit it out when one's back is turned or when it thinks one has forgotten about it. Forced to swallow it, the hated food may be vomited afterwards, to show us that whereas we can compel obedience in the letter, we cannot do so in the spirit, or the child may also insist upon doing as it wishes about accepting these disliked substances into its body in ways we are powerless to prevent.

Digestive troubles and special dislikes and likes, ideas concerning what agrees with a person's health or otherwise, usually have their origin in early years. Sometimes they may spring from some unwise remark or action on the part of an adult, "That such and such foods are nasty, they do not like them," or "They are not good for anybody," the idea in the adult mind which gives rise to such a statement being because they are tiresome to prepare or the child makes itself or its clothes in a mess eating them; for such reasons they will be struck off the menu. Again, perhaps the child may once have had some digestive disturbance after eating some special thing, which may actually have been caused by excitement.

The over-anxious adult in charge may put, nevertheless, an incorrect causative value upon it, which will deprive the child of an article of food. Sometimes it happens that the little one, encountering some other unpleasant event whilst eating some special dainty, or having acquired it in a way which caused humiliation or trouble, may take a dislike to it henceforward through the associative link.

A very intense distaste for the little bitter oranges usually to be found in boxes of dried fruits was once traced to the following cause. A little girl had been particularly fond of the glacé apricots to be found in these same boxes. It was pointed out to her that it was greedy always to seek out these delicacies and to gobble them up without giving anyone else a chance to have some too. In addition to the scolding, on one memorable occasion one of these oranges was substituted for the greatly desired apricot. She set her teeth into it and was horrified at the taste, now so bitter, instead of the sweetness she had been expecting. She wanted to spit it out but was ashamed to do so, because of the former scolding she had received on account of her greediness and because she also thought that it was really an apricot all the time, which was now tasting like this to punish her. Mortified and sick at heart, she choked it down somehow, and subsequently renounced *all* crystallized fruits as dangerous. For ever afterwards the expression "Dead Sea fruit, turning to ashes in one's mouth," seemed to possess this special significance for her. She could not clear her mind of the notion that, however nice things looked on the outside, there was sure to be an unpleasant disappointment somewhere when you got to know more about them. "All is not gold that glisters" became registered in her unconscious mind thus, "All yellow and rotund things that shine are not apricots." After all these connections had become clear to her, she tried the little oranges again, and found them rather enjoyable than otherwise.

In the last section, devoted to Smell, we said that a great many smells and tastes are inextricably interwoven, so that one may never think of the one without the other. These two companion senses are responsible for a great many preferences and antipathies, especially in food. If a thing should resemble in taste the smell of a favourite substance, whether it be edible or not, it will be popular. The reverse also holds good, for a scent to remind us of some food over which we were worsted in a struggle of wills with an adult as a child is enough to cause us to put that particular one, and all others remotely resembling it, upon our mental black-list for ever. Children usually regard any resemblance between objects as a sign they are identical, or at least equivalent. A painted top, which for some reason the child fancies smells like the taste of Sunday's sugar-cake, will be called the Sugar-cake top, and both will be thought of together, and the child may have pleasant dreams of eating it. A frock the colour of the roses on the pergola will call forth a comment of this kind: "You do look like the roses over there, Mummy; do let me smell you." The same reasoning applies to things that have other similarities, which our æsthetic views might not estimate so highly.

We have pointed out that little children are deeply interested in their bodily products or those of other people or animals. It has been discovered that a large number of antipathies to special kinds of food in children, as well as in adults, are derived from the resemblance, real or fancied, between them and some form of excretion—to name but a few, spinach, prunes, eggs (thought perhaps to be the fowl's excretion), sago pudding, or thin cornflour, producing vomiting because it may remind the child of mucus from the nose or phlegm. Curry and chocolate pudding, from obvious reasons, are frequently disliked; but, on the other hand, sausages will often offer irresistible attraction to children on account of several associations, one of them certainly being their resemblance to bodily products.

We must bear in mind, however, these parts of oneself have not yet become invested in the child's mind with the disgust and horror which many adults feel for them, which makes the idea of liking to eat a substance because it reminds us of such things positively loathsome. The baby has none of these prejudices; nor have some of the primitive races of mankind. The baby will cheerfully dabble its fingers in its excretions and proceed to put them into its mouth without the slightest feeling of repulsion. Nor should we take too serious a view of this or too vigorous steps to prevent such a thing ever happening again, should we find it occurring in any child of whom we have the care. It is more easy to awaken fear and guilt about any action than to allay it afterwards, just as we can more quickly inhibit healthy development, which prevents one stage from passing over into the next, than we may encourage it to do so.

Each of these stages of development requires time and opportunities for its fulfilment, so that the lessons belonging to each, and the experience which only they can give, may be fully assimilated before passing on to the next. Should we hurry the child too fast or prevent it finding out all that one stage should provide for development as a whole, the experience belonging to that stage will always provide a tendency to try to get back to this gap and make good the deficiency, but at an age when the carrying out of the impulse will probably be most inappropriate. Another result that may be produced in the same way is that all interest in this particular matter will be erased from the mind as though it had never been, unless it undergo the transformation we have already described as reaction-formation, the change into the opposite manifestation, hating what we formerly loved and ignoring that in which we originally took such interest in the past.

We have already quite unavoidably mentioned the appearance of objects which lead to their confusion with the taste or smell of others which they resemble, which is another proof of the interrelation of the five senses. They cannot be kept apart in description any more than they are able to be separated in reality or function; but since we have found this sense, *Sight,* as the next link in the chain, let us continue to examine it in further detail, in order to find out what we may from this sense, what are the main sensory differences that exist between us and children, by discovering how the child receives impressions as things of themselves, shorn of all the associative values with which we cannot help adorning them, and also what the child learns of the world through the medium of vision.

D. SIGHT

An experiment was once made with students in a psychology class. They were asked to write a short description of some object from the South Seas, which none of them had ever seen before, the name and use of which they did not know. It was held up before the class, well in sight of all, for a minute and a half, and then hidden until the descriptions were written. None of these students were particularly short-sighted, yet many of them excused their inability to give any detailed description of the object on this account—they could not see clearly what it was—or that they did not know its name nor for what it was used. The few who were more successful described it by comparison with other articles with which they were familiar, and it is doubtful if any gave a description of their pure visual perceptions without the addition of other matters or speculations as to the use of the object.

This shows us rather plainly to what a very great extent we are apt to confuse our visual impressions with those derived from other sources, and our tendency to help the faulty action of one sense by the aid of another, almost without being aware of the transference of the interest-focus from what we can see to what we know about it, which are the associated ideas. If we were able to banish entirely from our minds all associated ideas, all knowledge that we have acquired since childhood through various sources, and look at objects, receiving only the mental impression gained from the visual image, their shape, colour, texture, and not supply other details which we add automatically from other sources, we should then be able to estimate in some small degree how and what the baby sees during the first few months and years of its life.

The difficulty of ascertaining correctly what these impressions may be is immense, but several people have gallantly attempted to do so and have written accounts of their researches in books, a list of which will be found at the end of the first section of this chapter. They represent, of course, records of observations made upon the acquisition of visual ability in children, as well as the development of the other senses, and do not in any way set out to show what secondary impressions arise in the mind of the child from these visual percepts, nor the results that may follow misunderstanding of the child's difficulties where this sense is concerned, nor how fears and similar undesirable consequences may arise from childish perplexities stimulated by sight, more perhaps than from some of the other senses we have already examined. We shall endeavour to bring forward these problems after a brief survey of some physiological data connected with the acquisition of normal vision.

All who have investigated the subject agree that soon after birth the infant's eyes have some visual ability, but they have no power of co-ordination, and that their function is exceedingly limited. The eyes will follow a light at a few days; the child will blink and appear to show discomfort in a strong glare, obviously preferring subdued twilight. By and by, however, it becomes plain that the baby can distinguish moving objects, but only within a most restricted field, because they will immediately vanish if raised above or below the infant's line of vision, or moved far to the right or left. Shining things made of metal will attract as much attention at this early stage as moving objects, and far before stationary articles of a sombre colour. The baby will survey with the greatest interest parts of its own body, but without realizing that they are in any way different from other interesting sights in the near neighbourhood. Feet are some of the best playthings and provide excellent material for visual research, as they do for tactile manipulation, primarily because they are at a convenient distance from the eyes.

During the first year of life—some extend this period to two years—it is to be presumed that colour-sense is weak, and degrees of brightness only will be noticed, the whole world appearing in light and dark shades of drab, resembling the world as seen by a person who suffers from total colour-blindness. But the evidence of research upon the baby's increasing abilities seems to show that a gradual appreciation of colour begins to make an appearance after the seventh or eighth month, at the earliest computation, and that it can then not only distinguish one shade of brightness from another, but that some tints will give a higher degree of pleasure than others—for example, red and its derivatives, pink and scarlet.[1]

By the end of the first year, while the visual acuity is developing, co-ordination of the eyes becomes established and colour-vision grows in intensity, keeping pace with other mental processes which are taking place and gaining power at the same time. As we suggested before, in order to gain some idea of the infant's visual percepts, an attempt should be made to banish from the mind all that has been learned about objects through sight in alliance with other senses. We believe that we are justified in stating that associative links begin to form at a very early age, and that through them, in connection with sight, we gain information about things and their function, which far exceeds pure visual perception, that by itself would only teach us to recognize the appearance of the object, without being able to deduce its other qualities from what we see.

It is believed that, by the time a child has completed its first year, vision is well developed. It is difficult, nevertheless, to be sure how far the child's range extends, but we may be certain that this will be greater in the case of familiar than of unfamiliar objects, although it is always hard to ascertain with certainty to what extent the factor of attention will influence actual sight. It would seem to be very great. At the end of twelve months, co-ordination should also be established, unless some permanent condition of squint be present. This power of co-ordination of the eyes will be frequently found to lapse through fear or at times of severe physical exhaustion.

The next step to be taken by the infant is the correlation of visual percepts and their related mental processes, and from these will be derived the lessons that can be learned about the baby's extent of observation, which includes knowledge of the function of the object as well as its mere appearance.

We have already mentioned the baby's first and greatest object of interest is itself. Throughout this first year, and perhaps for a still longer period, it will be content to lie for hours looking at and playing with fingers and toes, the latter being, of course, raised and allowed to wave conveniently before its eyes. Their capacity for providing copious pleasurable

[1] *Children in Health and Disease*, David Forsyth, M.D., D.Sc. Murray.

sensations when grasped by the hands or touched with the other foot has also been explained, and this serves to make them doubly alluring as a plaything and eventually leads the child to distinguish between the self and the non-self. Impressions gained from touch or taste will have to be re-tested by sight, and the whole welded together into the mass of the child's sensory experience. We may realize from the baby's look of surprise, when it encounters hand or foot in the course of aimless movement and feels the pleasant response which flows from it, that it was not expected. A few months, however, will show a difference in the baby's reactions in this respect, and we shall notice that it will deliberately seek something that it cannot see but which it remembers should be somewhere in that neighbourhood, and will hail with joy when found, which shows how much happy expectation has provoked the seeking.

The first year also establishes a fair ability in the exercise of judgment connected with appreciation of distance and direction, based upon the infant's visual impressions, which have been developing steadily. At first the child has no sense of direction or distance, and we notice that it will grasp indiscriminately anywhere in order to reach anything that takes its fancy. Later, it still cannot distinguish between a small object close to its eyes and a large thing far off. For this reason the baby tries to seize the moon, and the little boy implores his father to climb up on the top of the summer-house in the garden, because he feels certain that from this vantage-point the combined height of his father plus the arbour will be able to procure it for him. Originally the child's hands will grope vaguely after the desired object, without any appreciation of distance; but presently we will see this hit-or-miss reaction gradually giving place to a more definite aim, and the child of a year old ought to be fairly proficient in gaining what it wants at the first attempt, showing that it realizes without the aid of experiment whether the thing can be reached by the hand alone, by stretching out an arm, if it must enlist the help of the body, or whether some means of locomotion is necessary.

We have derived this capacity for gauging position and distance through sight, combined with experiments involving touch and the muscular sense; in all, a complicated process for an infant mind, yet one we take for granted that a child should acquire without trouble. We may complain bitterly when errors of judgment of this kind result in what we call clumsiness and accidents by which objects are knocked over, or should the child relinquish its grasp of a thing before a table is reached, because it cannot accurately estimate where the edge begins. Sight also contributes not a little to our power of computing size and weight, in addition to other evidence, although the baby will always require to verify the ocular proof by touch, as well as to strive to find out the relationship between itself and other things. This is to discover whether they are larger or smaller than itself, and if it can lift them.

This ability to appreciate the size of objects is one that has a curious development. Children who seem so precocious and clever in other ways will sometimes show a most remarkable lack of appreciation of size. Visual observation does not always seem to help them in this respect for many years. It is by no means uncommon to find children of four, or six, even eight and ten, doing their utmost to fit a much larger object into a smaller one, or even to creep into a doll's cradle or a doll's-house, where there is only room for their head or their feet alone. One attempt will never suffice to prove to them the impossibility of their task, but they will try over and over again, becoming increasingly sad or angry at each failure, and in the end frequently bursting into tears and blaming the objects, as though they had been purposely thwarting them. One of the roots of this difficulty is the failure of the child to realize the fact of its own bodily growth; because at one time it could sit in the doll's perambulator, it cannot understand why this should be impossible later on. One little girl vigorously repudiated the idea of her own change in size and persisted in believing that her bed was getting smaller.

With our eyes also we learn to recognize and appreciate shape, to observe similarities and differences. The evidence of the eyes once more will not serve unaided, and tactile sense will again be requisitioned. In the use of the *form-board*, which contains so many differently shaped holes for the child to fill with pieces of thin wood or cardboard out to the same pattern, we can see how difficult the child finds it to put the correct two together. Very seldom will it do this only by visual comparison of which two are alike; they are usually tried one after another haphazard until one fits. We may say that observation of shape is slow in developing in children, but it is uncommon to find the same difficulty in the adult. Some few years ago, when jig-saw puzzles were at the height of their popularity, it was more usual to find people putting them together through looking for a piece of the suitable colour, or by going by the missing part of the picture, than by observing the requisite *shape*, and one would constantly see them trying to fit a section of quite the wrong shape into an empty space if the colour were right.

We, who have gained some sense of appreciation of position, size, weight, colour, shape, and other attributes of objects by means of experience, in addition to our visual perception, find it very hard to realize, unless we specially consider it, that the small child is really ignorant about these things, and is not merely being stupid or obstinate in order to annoy us. It all seems so extremely simple to us that we are misled into expecting ability from them which they cannot possibly have had time to acquire.

Their recognition of objects develops irregularly and in some ways surprisingly—here a tract, where the observation and comprehension of the child are extraordinarily precocious; there some area, where one is amazed at the dullness of its perception, and where all our help seems unavailing. If this irregularity be remarked in the case of the recognition of inanimate objects, how do they behave when the subject of the investigation becomes the recognition of persons? We know that infants in the first few months of life, even if not in the first weeks, *can* and *do* distinguish persons who are constantly around them. The chief problem presented to us is by which sense do they do this? Some scientists claim that it is by touch, as does Baldwin in his book, *Mental Development of the Child and the Race*. He states that his boy was able to distinguish in the dark between the touch of the mother and the nurse at the age of two months. It has also been suggested that the infant can recognize persons by characteristic odours, and certainly by their voices. There are many reasons why we can be sure that sight does not play a prominent part in this earliest recognition by infants.

At first the baby's vision is not so far advanced as are the other senses which we have mentioned. It can as yet trace only broad outlines and mass contours; and if adults were to judge only by these, which are at the same time still rather vague, we also should certainly not readily be able to recognize one person from another. It is only when visual capacity and mental capacity have advanced to the extent of being able to appreciate details and differences that the child can distinguish people by sight. Hence we find the baby calls every man Daddy in the distance, and many women Mummy, and then looks woefully disappointed when the person speaks to it or comes closer, because it then realizes the presence of a stranger. There was a little girl who could remember this sort of disappointment from her perambulator days. People would play tricks upon her by saying they were Mummy or Daddy, but she could always tell by their voices if they were right.

It is also interesting in this connection to note how very seldom children have any distinct recollection of the appearance of the face of a relative who died or went away when they were quite little. They may remember the sound of a voice, the touch of their hands, perhaps the look of a frock or a smell of tobacco, but not the features or expression of these persons, whom they may often have loved tenderly. Again, there are others who say, even in adult years, that they cannot visualize the faces of people they know—that is, see them in their mind's eye; nor do they ever see the face of any person in a dream. We call these people lacking in visual memory.

If we watch a baby when introduced to a mirror in the company of another, at first it does not recognize either itself or the companion. By degrees, and in course of time, it will realize the person who is holding it is familiar, but still with difficulty, although it may have reached the stage of being able to pick that person out of a group of strangers and to call her or him by name. The child is baffled with the problem of position, which is afterwards proved, because it constantly turns round to look if the person is really both behind it and in front at the same time. How can one person be in two places?

This problem will puzzle a baby at a later stage when looking at a picture-book, when two pictures of the same series, representing the same persons or animals, but drawn doing different things, appear on the same page or upon opposite pages. If the doggie is here, how can it be there? If we find it on this page, has it moved from the other? The child will look back to see if it is still there, and from the one to the other, by no means sure that the dog is not moving quickly from one page to the next, because it cannot see both at the same moment. It is a task of years before the child can immediately and with complete certainty recognize itself in a looking-glass, because it has no means whereby it can recognize itself, since it is unfamiliar with its most distinctive part, the head and features. But we will return again to this problem of the child and the mirror in the chapter on the Self.

The childish characteristic of seeing only the largest or most brightly coloured objects, or those to which its attention is called by the names of these being spoken, appears in a particularly marked way; when it advances to the stage of looking at picture-books. It will now in turn play showman to us, and point out and name the objects represented in the pictures, but at first only the central figures, those that are most brightly coloured and which have already been pointed out to itself. It would seem that the others remain unnoticed and unseen, even if the objects represented are familiar enough in other pictures. This habit of seeing and naming is a curious and long-lived one, and survives in the strange propensity of some people at a play, who constantly tell one another what is happening on the stage at the moment, although both are equally capable of noticing these things for themselves.

At the same time, this idea of drawing a child's attention to anything by saying the name introduces another mental process which develops in connection with vision. We point out some object and say its name, thereupon drawing the child's attention to that thing. It will seem to the child as though when we speak the object appears, because attention has been focused upon it simultaneously with vision. Therefore, as far as the child is aware, the word has produced the object, like the magic words of the sorcerer in the fairy-tale. The child has also a strongly marked tendency to give an equally concrete value to the word, as to the thing that it represents, which is increased when it finds that by using this same word it can itself often produce the same result and cause the object named to appear before its eyes. This represents a wonderful sense of power to the child, which will be fully discussed when we come to investigate the child's development of speech. The aspect of the question that concerns us most at present is the idea in the mind of the child that things seen may be created by words, that they have an equal value with words, and that it may control the *appearance* of things as well as people by this means.

Another related idea frequently present in the mind of the child is that everything seen may be and probably is connected with itself, and ceases to exist should the attention of the eyes be diverted. In this way the focus of attention becomes identical with seeing and the calling into existence of the objects which are thus marshalled before us; and here we have one of the greatest riddles which the child is required to solve in some fashion during the early years.

The converse of this theme, objects may be created by looking, presents us with the theory that they can be made to vanish or cease to exist, if one should leave off looking, by shutting one's eyes, or going away and leaving them. All children go through this stage of belief, but in some persons it survives throughout life in a more or less disguised form.

For the young child "out of sight" is actually "out of mind," so easily does it forget what is not within the field of attention and vision at the time. It will also frequently ask if the Zoo is still there, when it is not visiting the animals, or where the Zoo goes at night. In an excellent book upon the physical and psychological problems of childhood,[1] the author quotes the instance of the easy distraction of a child's attention, when a fountain-pen cap which had been happily played with for several minutes was dropped and instantly forgotten. It had vanished from sight, and the memory of it was as though entirely and instantly obliterated from the child's mind. It had ceased to exist until it reappeared a few moments later, when the play was resumed as enthusiastically as ever. Sometimes, however, the child will retain a memory of a visual

[1] *Children in Health and Disease*, p. 75, David Forsyth, M.D., D.Sc.

object and look to see where it can be, although at the same time it may be clasping it in its hand or sitting on the lap of the person for whom it is looking. More evidence of this sort is to be found in the fact that the child, learning to play hide-and-seek, will be perfectly satisfied that it is invisible if it shuts its own eyes or puts its head under a sofa-cushion. Slowly, by dint of many experiments and failures, these problems will at last find their elucidation.

Children, having discovered that they can make a person or thing disappear by shutting their eyes or turning away the head, will sometimes deliberately shut their eyes when persons or objects that displease them come into view, for the express purpose of banishing them from sight and mind. Survivals of this childish tendency to eliminate from our sight those who have offended us appear frequently in the punishments meted out to little children—to be sent from the room, to stand in the corner with one's face to the wall; all in fact representing banishment, a ceasing to exist for the time being, and understood as such by the child, which is the reason why it becomes such a terrible punishment to say to the child, "You are so naughty, I don't want to look at you; you must go away till you are good again."

One very interesting remnant of this purposeful shutting of the eyes, probably also in imitation of the adult punishment, came to light among the symptoms of an adolescent girl who was suffering from pseudo-epileptic attacks. They would occur when she was deeply upset by those against whom she could do nothing by way of retaliation. When this feeling was not quite so intense as to provoke an attack, she would shut her eyes tightly, so that they felt, she would say, "as though they were going back into my head." At the same time she would tell the person who had annoyed her, "I don't see you!" and would, of course, be intensely disappointed if her action were not observed and received as an insult or punishment, as she intended, for what had been done to incur her displeasure; it also included the idea of the permanent extinction of that person. In the one instance, she would eliminate the single person by refusing to look at him or her; in the other, the fit occurring when the provocation had been still more intense, she closed her own eyes and obliterated thereby not only herself but the whole world by becoming unconscious for a time. These attacks would always be heralded by the words, "Mother, I'm lost," which further explained the situation.

As the logical sequence of this childish idea we have already mentioned, we find belief that things seen are the outcome of personal vision, rather than having an independent existence, which same impression frequently appears as a serious symptom of acute nervous trouble both in childhood and adult years. The young child, as we have already explained, will habitually look to see if persons and things have disappeared altogether because they are not within the field of vision at the moment. It will also, upon occasions, take for granted that persons who have gone from the room temporarily will never return, and that it has been abandoned for ever, crying when they go and being delighted when they come back, as though they had arrived from the dead by a miracle. This problem is seldom solved quickly by the little one, and may continue to grow more puzzling the more intense is the consideration given to it. The child will be constantly confronted with the dual problem that whereas it can sometimes make persons and things vanish by not looking at them, or bring them back again at will by opening its eyes when it wants them, this is by no means constant. There are occasions when it is impossible to influence objects or people in this way, however much it longs to be able to do so. Then again, persons may be present and able to see us when we cannot see them, which may also be inconvenient at times ; and there are things that the children can see which adults deny, which is the hardest problem of all, and the most perplexing, perhaps, of any to them.

These problems of vision have been found to give rise to some of the most serious fears of childhood, upon which we will now try to shed some light. It is difficult to lead many people to understand the poignancy of fear in the young child, because if ever they lived through terror of this sort themselves, it has now become so completely forgotten or so remote that the whole idea seems to them overdriven and absurd that children can suffer so acutely from their own imagination.

In the Introduction we showed that one of the fundamental fears of childhood was to be alone, since it induces the condition of utter helplessness with the greatest intensity. This feeling of loneliness and helplessness springs up more or less acutely in all children when they realize no one is near them. The fear it provokes may be mitigated to some extent by the simple expedient of the children's game of peep-bo, which has always been popular in the nursery, although why this should have been so has never been given much consideration until now. Like many other children's games, it presents in a modified form some of the stern necessities of life in vogue now or in bygone days. Freud has pointed out in his book, *Hemmung, Symptom und Angst*, how the grief and apprehension felt at the disappearance of the mother may be diminished by the relief caused through her habitual return in this game. The child learns under less painful circumstances than in reality to regard her absence as the prelude of a joyful reunion and to expect this as the inevitable sequel, which will beneficially influence the baby's attitude to the disappearance of the mother upon other occasions.

If the child imagines that persons and things exist as long as they are kept in sight and disappear because it shuts its eyes, an equally conflicting state of affairs meets the child in *visual imagery*, when, accentuated by fatigue, excitement, and frequently by the darkness, it will see the visual projection of its own thoughts, of scenes and toys, which seem to belong to the past or which have been left in another place.[1] These creations of its own imagination will bear the stamp of reality for the child as much as the incidents that occur in day-dreams, and especially night-dreams. The expedient of shutting the eyes to drive them away in this case will, however, not have the desired effect, but rather the reverse, since it may make them appear with greater vividness. Adults to whom the child may appeal for help against these weird visions, not being able to see them, and often not understanding the mechanism of their appearance, add to the confusion of the child with a scolding for being "silly," and perhaps reiterating, "but there's nothing there or I should see it."

Dr. Forsyth, in the article referred to above, mentions this capacity of the child for projecting vivid mental images, especially in the dark and when alone, as one of the most

[1] "The Infantile Psyche, with special Reference to Visual Protection," David Forsyth, M.D. *Br. J. of Psychol.* General Section. April 1921.

important reasons for the almost universal childish fear of the dark. We gain an overwhelming mass of corroboration of the strength of these early fears from children as well as from childhood memories preserved with great clearness by those who are now adult. Fears of being alone, of the night, of blindness and death, appear all to belong to this group. Francis Bacon demonstrated this connection between the fear of the dark and that of death in his *Essay on Death*. There he says, "Men fear death as children fear to go in the dark."

Let us try to see why children should so universally "fear to go in the dark." We have supposed the child's worst fear at an early age to be loneliness. Now, in the dark, it is impossible to see if anyone is there or not. In this way one is always alone or lost, doubly *lost*, because anyone coming to find you could not see where you were either. These two reasons are weighty enough to produce fear in the infant, but there are others besides. In the dark one cannot see the familiar shapes of day nor the well-known sights which are as reassuring as the friendly faces of beloved persons. If it is quite dark these will be blotted out and imaginary figures from story or threat may invade the darkness. If, on the other hand, there be a dim light, such as that given by a night-light which flickers, this will lend strange deformities to familiar contours and cause them to take on fantastic characters, which will be almost as alarming as the creatures of our imagination—in fact, they will merge and we shall not be able to tell one from the other.

These sights cannot be seen by others, nor can they be made to vanish, as can realities, by closing our eyes. They are therefore altogether beyond our control. If we wish to do so we can turn day into night by the simple expedient of closing our eyes, but we cannot perform the opposite miracle, turn darkness into daylight. Such conditions of extreme anxiety, known as *Night-terrors*, are frequently due to experiences of this kind. Usually they do not meet with the sympathy they deserve from the adult. It is the accepted custom to ridicule fear in children, and to believe the correct treatment is to laugh them out of it, or at any rate to show the child that it has fallen in our estimation by proving itself not so brave as we had imagined;

that is, we make matters infinitely worse through our efforts to improve them.

People used to attempt to stem the tide of night-terrors by attention to diet, from the conjecture that they had been caused by unsuitable suppers. But psychological investigation has shown that they arise, as a rule, from other sources, chief among which are the fears of the child which have sprung from visual images, dreams, threats, too exciting stories read before bedtime, realistic games with adults, who in the guise of a bear may pretend to gobble up the frightened child, and so on. Teasing and the like are all made infinitely worse, because the adult sees only the amusement which he or she derives from it and insists upon believing that it must be equally funny for the child, quite forgetting that to the child all these things carry the aspect of reality far more than make-believe, and that it firmly believes the adult does mean what is said. How much meaning does lie unconsciously behind the adult's words and action we will try to discover later.

All these fears of the child are made infinitely worse because it has been taught that no sign of fear must be shown or it will incur this worst of all reproaches, to be called "baby" or "coward." Moreover, if it is bound to disguise its fears, this does not allow of asking questions about what is worrying it or what it does not understand, nor can any explanation be given of these problems that weigh so heavily upon it, mainly because adults do not take the trouble to find out anything about the little one's point of view. They continue to work upon the assumption that it never thinks, and so cannot worry, without considering the possibility that children have thoughts and worries they keep to themselves because they are still more afraid of being laughed at.

There is one very important cause of night-terrors in children which we have not yet discussed. When housing or other difficulties do not allow them to occupy a separate bedroom from that of the elders, it is more than possible for them to receive very harmful and terrifying impressions from witnessing incidents in the intimate life of their parents which were never intended for their notice, and which, if considered at all, would probably be thought unable to claim any attention from a child, especially at a very tender age. Investigation of children and adults, however, has proved the opposite. The idea of terrible deeds of violence that happen in the dark, apprehension aroused by people moving about the room like shadows and doing strange things which the children cannot understand, or upon which they put some other construction, fill them with alarm. The worst horror of all occurs should these children cry out in their fear and be scolded afterwards, or attempt next day to ask what was happening and be told "nothing," or that "They must have been dreaming!"

They detect the lie and are therefore faced with the complex problem of forcing themselves to believe one of two things, both of which they know to be false and both of them harmful to the child. They may believe the lie and learn thereby to doubt the evidence of their own eyes and better judgment, or believe themselves and doubt the veracity of their parents. In this way their idea of reality, truth, and their own judgment become hopelessly confused.

As children grow older they will think more persistently about these conflicting ideas, and will refuse to be content until they have either wrested some information from a reluctant adult or found some solution which seems plausible to themselves. Once they have found some solution, however, although it may be far remote from the actual facts of the case, they will generally be quite satisfied with it, and will promptly dismiss any contradictory, even if accurate, evidence which may be encountered later rather than forsake the old, self-found reasons of childhood. It is by no means uncommon to find adults still cherishing at the back of their minds some of these queer myths of infancy, although the reasoning part of them knows they are in no way connected with the facts. They will be preserved, as some folks hide away toys and picture-books belonging to the same period.

Sooner or later, children realize that things are not as they appear, and that evidence of the eyes requires to be helped out by further knowledge obtained from other sources. Things may not only be present when they are not looking at them, but they can apparently see things that have no existence outside their own thoughts. Furthermore, large and solid things like trees and houses may occasionally quite unaccountably change their position, and be seen in one place one day and in quite another the next, because the little person has not taken into account the curious optical illusions brought about by the observer's change of position, perspective, and the effects of light and shade. These things offer the most bewildering problems to children, because they resemble so closely the magic which is gravely presented to them in the Bible and in fairy-stories, which they are supposed to believe without question, and, on the other hand, their own accounts of wonderful dream happenings that they will tell the grown-ups and for which they will receive a scolding, because they are accused of telling lies.

Adults seldom stop to listen very carefully when the child is groping uncertainly with words, trying to explain some trouble that is far from being clear even to itself, but jump to some conclusion concerning what the child wants to know that is often wide of the mark. It does not occur to them that the child can be puzzled in this way about things which *they* take for granted and which they feel the child ought to know by using its common sense. In fact, it is sheer stupidity not to know that streets do not go together in a point at the end, that the gratings in the pavement will not let you through if you walk on them, and that trees do not touch the sky.

So the child has to work through these labyrinths of difficulties alone, solving some of them perhaps to its satisfaction with the real answer, discovering some mythical answer for others, repressing or forgetting a great many, by relegating them to the limbo of such things, the Unconscious, whence they may reappear at some future date as obsessions, bad dreams, or some form or other of neurotic symptom.

Books which may be Read in connection with this Section; those which have been mentioned before will not be listed again.

The Infantile Psyche, with special Reference to Visual Projection. David Forsyth, M.D., D.Sc., F.R.C.S. *Br. J. of Psychol.* April 1921.
Emotion and Eye Symptoms. W. S. Inman. *Br. J. of Psychol.* October 1921.
Squint and the Child Mind. Charles Harford. *The Child.* January 1924.
Experimental Psychology. Mary Collins, M.A.
Hemmung, Symptom und Angst. Sigmund Freud. Int. Psychoanalytischer Verlag. Vienna.

E. HEARING

Oh! canst thou sew cushions and canst thou sew sheets,
And canst thou sing balaloo, while the bairnie greets?
                                        Hebridean Cradle-song.

     From ghoulies an' ghaisties,
     An' lang-leggetty baisties,
     An' things that go *bump* in the night,
       Good Lord, deliver us!
                                        Cornish Prayer.

How soon after birth an infant can distinguish definite aural stimuli seems to be a point upon which scientists cannot agree. Dr. G. F. Still, in *Common Disorders of Childhood*, tells us that "hearing is supposed to be absent during the first two or three days, but I doubt if this is so," and adds records of cases in which no response and some response was shown to loud noises at ten and twenty hours after birth to prove his own opinion as well as that of other authorities. He also states that in normal children hearing is established beyond doubt at the end of the first month, and that the most reliable test of an infant's auditory capacity is for a familiar voice, preferably that of the mother, to call to it from an adjoining room.

Further interesting information upon this same question of the baby's early hearing ability is to be found in Dr. David Forsyth's book, *Children in Health and Disease*, from which we have previously quoted. In the chapter entitled "Progress in the First Month," part of the section devoted to "The Psychology of Children," we find this significant addition to what others have written on the subject:—

The new-born infant has been held incapable of seeing and hearing. This statement is true to the extent that no sign is made to show that a stimulus from either source has been appreciated, yet it is probable that the deficiency lies rather in expression than in sensation. The anatomical and histological characteristics of the organs concerned are not known to change in the first week, yet both light and noise are appreciated before the end of this period.

One wonders, perhaps, whether there may not be some simple explanation of this phenomenon. When one considers that practically sound-proof chamber in which the babe has lived during the pre-natal months, and compares its silence with the sudden introduction to an immense number of different sounds at birth, does it not seem possible that one sound will not attract more attention than another at first? It is with special intent that one uses the expression *sound-proof* in reference to the pre-natal condition of the infant. But we must also remember in this connection that before birth the child has probably been aware of many rhythms and vibrations which will in later life become associated with sounds in the outside world. Thus the vibrations and rhythms originating from maternal respiration and circulation are no doubt familiar to the infant and will become equivalents of appreciated sounds in subsequent life. Thus Helen Keller, the blind and deaf American girl whose autobiography (*The Story of My Life*) we have already quoted, stated that she derived intense pleasure from the music of a piano which she heard by placing her hand upon the case—in this way receiving the vibrations, which she translated mentally into sounds, without apparently requiring the service of her auditory apparatus as the receptor organ.

The result of the total accumulation of conflicting stimuli will be deafening to the babe, so that each separate noise will pass unheeded. If we in adult years go into a factory where a large number of machines are at work, we cannot at first distinguish any one sound from another, or from the whole : the result is aural stunning; but gradually our ears adjust themselves to this unaccustomed over-stimulation and we are able once more to appreciate separate sounds of which we were at first quite oblivious.

Again, when under the influence of an anæsthetic, especially nitrous-oxide gas, we are often aware of stupendous noise, which, we are told, is occasioned by our own blood-pressure. If this be the case, it is more than likely that the infant, whose circulation has had so recently to undergo complete reorganization, may be suffering for some time to come from this same noise which originates from blood-pressure. It seems likely that the baby may be aware of physical processes through sensation at first to which we, in later life, become so much accustomed that we do not notice them as long as they maintain their habitual function. We become aware of them only when they undergo some change, and then this change is recorded by our mental apparatus as pain or discomfort. To the infant, however, all physical processes are new, and it may be at first they all give an impression of pain, which subsequently becomes obliterated when the infant is accustomed to the functions of its own body, muscular sense, sensory stimulation and the like.

This may be the case or it may not, and it is difficult to find exact means whereby it can be proved. Let us, therefore, continue the examination of the child's hearing at a later stage, where response is both certain and more readily available for observation. It has been ascertained that after the first week the infant is capable of showing reactions of two kinds to auditory stimulation—*displeasure*, through crying, wrinkling the face at loud noises, or by spasmodic movements of the entire body; *pleasure* through satisfied, wriggling body action, when it hears the tones of a quiet voice which it knows or some sound that it has already associated with the preparation of food.

It has been recognized since the twilight of humanity that a soft speaking or singing voice is a sound which, before all others, brings satisfaction to small children from the earliest days of infancy. There are few countries, if any at all, where we do not find some sort of lullaby or cradle-song in use and where the mother does not croon or hush her infant by soothing sounds in the language best known to her. A sudden noise or a loud, harsh voice, however, will cause the baby to start and show signs of fear long before we should have thought that it would have possessed any associative ideas connecting a loud voice with anger, and therefore danger. Some may suggest that in this fear reaction we may find traces of atavism or ancestral memory, by which the infant knows that injury might be expected from persons with this characteristic. Again, one wonders whether the unpleasant impression caused by a loud noise may not be merely a revival of the chaotic tempest of sound that attended the baby's first introduction into the world—because Freud, as well as many others, have seen in the act of birth, the first fear situation of the child—or if it be derived from some other early experience.

It is, however, possible that even an extremely young baby

may have known feelings of fear and uncertainty to arise from loud noises, from the quarrelling of parents or others around it, or by living in an extremely noisy neighbourhood. Welfare workers and health visitors will agree that a young baby needs quiet surroundings and will not thrive in noise or in an atmosphere of strife. One person, to whom angry voices and loud noises were particularly disturbing, had a very early introduction to an unpleasant situation of this sort in which a sudden loud noise played an important part and surely caused great alarm to her as a baby in her first month. Her monthly nurse was inclined to an over-fondness for stimulants and was sitting dozing over the fire in this condition one evening, with the baby's long clothes on her lap and its head in the fender. The child's father came into the room unexpectedly, grasped the cause of what he saw and awoke the woman, told her in no uncertain way what he thought of the manner in which she was discharging her duties, and sent her away there and then. It is to be presumed that the baby was suddenly aroused by the noise of angry, expostulating voices, one of which may have set the pattern for the dislike the baby retained even when grown-up for any voice which was loud, angry, and especially drunken. The nurse had been in the habit of singing her to sleep at other times with a particularly soft and plaintive air, to which these lugubrious words were set :—

> Mrs. Carter, here you may see
> All that remains of your Sallee!

To distinguish voices and to derive great pleasure as well as discomfort from them has been characteristic of this woman, who also, as a child of eleven, became almost entirely deaf, presumably from adenoids, but there was, in addition, full evidence of many other psychological causes, which probably contributed their share.

As the months pass by the infant gradually links up the sounds it hears around with people and things, as well as imitating these. Far more attention has been given to the aspect of hearing that gives rise to imitation, which is the basis of speech and language, than to the subject of pure auditory sensation, most probably because it is more easy to conduct investigation upon the sounds uttered by the child than to compute the sounds heard by the child and their result. At first it has few means of communicating these effects except by body movement or crying, which, after all, are vague, except to persons initiated into the secrets of baby ways; and one is never quite sure in these cases how much of the supposed prowess of the infant is not the result of projected thoughts and wishes on the part of the adult.

The self-feeling of persons in charge of infants is an interesting matter for research. All those interested in an infant and anxious to exhibit its merits invariably find the most reliable test or conclusive proof of its ability, intelligence, and attainments in something connected with *themselves*. Men conducting investigations of this kind regard the supreme demonstration of a child's auditory acuity to be a look of intelligence and pleasure when they whistle, or for the baby to look or point in the right direction should they say "Where's Daddy?" Conversely, the baby is thought to be incapable of real intelligence until it can pay attention to the sounds they are making to please it, and show greater interest than in watching the approach of mother or nurse with the feeding-bottle.[1] Dr. Still is exceptional in his candour when he remarks that the most reliable test is the voice of the mother.

The mother knows full well that the baby will recognize her by sight or voice long before the father, if she be in constant attendance upon it; or should a nurse take the first place in the infant's life, as do so many, it will then be the nurse to whom the infant will turn as its greatest ally and confidante and who will be the recipient of the most subtle signs of early developing mental powers. Fear of the stranger always sends the baby backward by several weeks or even months in expressions of intellect. But, strange as it may seem, the best-known investigations of infant life have been made by fathers and not mothers. Darwin, Preyer, Baldwin, Romanes, Sully, and Piaget have made the most detailed studies of their own children; those women who have carried out similar research and published the results, Miss Shinn, Frau Dr. Hug-Helmuth, and Miss Margaret Drummond, were all aunts working upon materials supplied by nieces and nephews.

[1] "Development of Speech in the Normal Child," Macleod Yearsley, F.R.C.S. *Child Study Journal*. 1926.

At first all sounds are of undifferentiated value to the baby, but very soon it learns to distinguish those that are familiar and those with which pleasant or unpleasant ideas are connected. The sound alone, apart from knowing why or in what way it is an integral part of what is in preparation, will arouse in the baby a state of expectancy long before the first year is out. The tinkle of a spoon, the sound of splashing water, herald the delights of food and the bath, which will set many babies bouncing with joy. But to an infant who is opposed to spoon-feeding, or knows that medicine only is administered in this way, or who is afraid of water, these two preparatory, warning noises will be a signal for discomfort that quite often ends in tears. In such cases, beyond all doubt, we are presented with a sound that has obviously been heard, with which an associated idea is already connected, which meets with a response giving us a clue to the corresponding mental attitude of the baby, who shows like or dislike, pleasure or pain, in all quite an elaborate mental process, although one of which infants are capable at an early age.

The power of correctly associating ideas and sounds increases with the development of the child and embraces many of the other senses—sight, touch, smell, taste. Gradually, by means of the associative ideas, bridges will be formed between the various sensory stimuli. This means that the child is beginning to learn what to expect from objects; in other words, it is acquiring knowledge of the properties and functions of things from sounds that they make.

Very early in the child's range of knowledge derived from observations may be found the capacity of discovering the characteristic sound made by an object or person, and thinking of that thing or person in this way, which is shown by the fact that so many of the baby names for familiar things in its neighbourhood show a connection with the function, and especially the sound which it makes—a habit also to be found among the primitive races. We have, in fact, many *onomatopœic* words that survive in our own to this day, although many, of course, have undergone some change in form, so that the sound value is not quite as plain as it was at first. To the child, however, the train is always a puff-puff, the dog a bow-wow or a wow-wow, and the rooster a cock-a-doodle-doo or something that means the same, the world over. Some of these ideas will doubtless be suggested, if not actually taught, to the baby by well-meaning adults; but we frequently meet with children who have found their own names for persons and things which also represent the noise made by them or by some sound by which they have been remembered or distinguished from all others. Such a name is Unkie Tick-tock for the uncle who showed the little boy his watch, and Auntie Baa-baa, not because her name was Barbara, as might be supposed, but because she first made her appearance and impression upon her small niece wearing a white, fluffy fur tie, and the similarity was clear.

Here we trespass on material which should belong to the section Speech. But in order to understand the child's ability to hear, it is almost impossible to refrain from doing so, because only in its early attempts to reproduce sounds can we find some certain proofs of its hearing and how it comes to recognize objects by some auditory association. We have already suggested that adults and those who have already mastered the idea of language are inclined to place a barrier of inferiority between themselves and those who have not done so. The child in all probability knows few barriers of this sort and regards itself upon an equality with everything else around it, since it clearly shows the propensity which it shares with primitive peoples of endowing inanimate objects and animals with exactly the same kind of life and the same powers of sensation, thought, and speech.

This stage of thought has been given the name of *Animism*. To the child the noise made by the singing kettle, the rattling of the hail upon the window, the mother's voice, the barking dog, and the creaking chair are all equal. The noise made by anything is its voice and its speech, the sign that it is alive and the way in which a child will think of it to itself; but in this labelling faculty of the child it will find many difficulties that tend to destroy the earliest landmarks and distinguishing features. For instance, everything that makes a noise like a dog will be called a bow-wow, no matter what its appearance, and at the same time a black sheep running among a number of white ones may also be called a *bow-wow*, although it makes a noise like a *baa-baa*. According to the sound classification, objects will appear to be one kind of thing; from visual evidence they are clearly of another sort, and it takes some time for the baby to sort out what kind of thing an object may be when it possesses characteristics typical of several quite distinct and often conflicting species.

The early academic psychologists used to show that people were mainly of two types, *Visual* and *Auditory*. The first, those to whom visual stimuli were the more important and the more lasting; *auditory*, those to whom hearing was the more significant. According to this method also the young child will become aware of the objects about it. Should the visual centres be predominant, the appearance of an object will be the deciding factor; if the auditory receptor be of more importance, hearing will strike the keynote for the child's impressions.[1]

But whence comes it that persons can be divided into these two types? Are they always and only caused by the physiological structure of the organs, or can they not also be influenced by attention to some psychological process? Let us see what evidence we can find upon the second account, attention or psychological bias or inhibition, for both may play their part. How focus of attention or withdrawal, psychological bias or inhibition, may cause the person to belong to either the visual or auditory type will be the next question we shall try to solve.

We often remark in quite tiny babies that they show a marked preference for sounds and listening to them than for looking at objects. At a later stage they will show more enjoyment at being sung or read to than being shown picture-books, long before they can understand the tale, because they appreciate the rhythm and modulations of the voice. They may, however, derive so much pleasure from listening to another making these delightful sounds, or when another plays some musical instrument and sings, that the passive attitude becomes theirs for life, whereby the executive of their personality will become the poorer. We are more likely to *strive* to get something if we cannot obtain it in any other way than if it is always at hand without any effort to ourselves. But this is a statement of tendencies which may be observed in the child; what has contributed to the bias towards this auditory preference? It may be a native endowment. Yet if we carefully investigate these cases

[1] *Manual of Psychology*, Stout.

where a baby shows such keen enjoyment of sounds we will usually find that they are in some way connected with the actions of another, and that this person is particularly dear to the baby.

The initial love for this person has made the characteristic action preferred. The musical adult will usually amuse a baby by singing to it or reciting verses in a pleasant way. The artist will draw pictures or show it those in a book. Almost without being aware of what we are doing we will influence the children who cross our path in many little ways. Such occurrences will set the bias in one direction or another, because of the gain of pleasure which has accompanied it at first. But, again, the child may have some psychological shock in which some sound played an important part. For many years afterwards this may ring in the ears and be heard in imagination connected with other sounds, although they may have only the slightest resemblance to that originally heard. Or it may make that person particularly sensitive to all sounds and find them extremely painful, as well as sometimes having the reverse affect of dulling all auditory percepts, which will make the person to some extent *psychologically* deaf.

There are other reasons besides these, however, for psychological deafness. That we may find a man becomes deaf to avoid the constant nagging of his wife does not seem in the least surprising to many people who do not give equal credence to the fact that a child may do the same to escape from the perpetual scolding of a mother. There have been known such cases, nevertheless, when quite small children have apparently become deaf. They have not taken any notice when people speak to them, and seem unaware of the sounds around them. In order to find out the reason for this state of affairs, when physiological examination can give no clue as to the cause of the trouble, it is necessary carefully to observe the people or special conditions present when the child's deafness is most apparent, because in these cases it is often found that the disability is variable. There may be a special person whom the child never seems to hear, or one particular member of the family, perhaps a friend. Or the child may hear members of the family perfectly and yet be apparently deaf to the voices of strangers. It is usual for quite young children to have a difficulty sometimes in recognizing even familiar words pronounced by strangers with an unfamiliar accent, which will be explained fully in the next section; but there are also some children peculiarly fixated to their own families who refuse to have contact of any sort with the stranger or an unrelated person.

When the deafness takes the form of not hearing anything said by even a well-known person, or never certain things, we must inquire a little more closely into the circumstances and functions of the person, the attitude of the child towards this person or that of the person towards the child. It will probably be found that the child wishes to remain oblivious of something this person says or does, or wishes to banish him or her from its mind for ever, and feels that just cause has been given for taking this decisive step. Suppose mother or nurse speaks, saying that it is high time that the toys were put away, because the hour has struck when all good children go to bed. There is an excellent reason why the little one should remain deaf to this suggestion; it may even have heard some adult make an excuse about "not hearing hints."

Invitations to get ready to go for hated walks, instructions from a governess over unpopular lessons, may all bring on this special kind of deafness. One little girl always became deaf whenever anyone asked her to run errands, when her mother was angry and preached at her or scolded. Another boy developed the same symptom soon after the birth of a baby brother, whose advent disturbed him a great deal. He hated to hear the baby cry or his mother's voice singing or talking to it, because it seemed to him that she never had time to do these things for him now, and so in order to remain unaware of these disagreeable reminders about the baby, he became deaf for a time, so that he did escape from them to some extent.

Little children also do not take very long to find out that to remain deaf to orders or anything else that adults say to them is an unfailing way of making them annoyed. They will use this weapon systematically too, should they feel inclined to tease them or inflict punishment for some act of aggression. The juvenile sense of justice is acute and does not see why the prerogative of punishment should be kept entirely on one side.

"Sending to Coventry," therefore, is to be found in operation from both camps in the nursery. The difference is this: the adult considers it an excellent educative principle when carrying it out upon a child, but refers to it as "the sulks" when the child is actively putting it into force. For a child to take no notice when an adult speaks will generally make the latter show some signs of temper, which amuses the child, unless there be fear of bodily injury arising from it, because adults in a rage appear to the child as such a contrast from their usual dignified behaviour, because they are now doing themselves what they point out to the child is "acting like a baby."

We have already enumerated some of the first sounds heard by the infant, what it may learn from them and by associating sounds with functions, and functions with particular objects, all of which are things, persons, fragments of reality belonging to the outside world; but since we pointed out in the last section on Sight that the child suffers considerably from things seen which have no separate existence from itself, we may now repeat this same question in relation to auditory perception. Is it possible for the wishes and imagination of the child also to produce sound hallucinations and phantom noises which will lend still more terror to being alone and in the dark? Our answer will be that it is only too certain to happen.

As our eyes are capable of receiving subsequent impressions of things once seen, delayed or recurrent *after-images,* so do our ears hear echoes of sounds which have been silenced for some time. The child will often believe that it hears the voice of some person of whom it is either very fond or frightened, and look round expecting to see the person to whom the voice belongs, but without success. According to the special circumstances, this is a relief or a disappointment. Usually it is a voice to which the little one would gladly listen, and it looks particularly pleased to hear the words spoken, usually its own name. But to the child in whom a sense of guilt has been early aroused, and who has many fears in consequence, the voices will be connected with wrong-doing and retribution, because it will have been threatened with the Voice of God warning the wicked, and told about the still, small voice of conscience.

Darkness and silence will fill the house with strange terrors derived from sounds. There are many adults who suffer untold agony when they are obliged to spend a night by themselves in a house. The various noises that are to be heard in the dark fill them with vague alarm. They may go to seek the cause or hide their heads under the bed-clothes, according to type, but still the terror persists, although they know very well that the noises do not represent anything that could really do them any harm. They retain the feelings of the child shivering in its bed and hearing a leaf flicking the window-pane, conjuring up from a rapidly working brain perhaps a ghostly hand tapping the glass, or some other horror peculiar to the fancy of that little one. All these old ideas and fancies will flow back into the mind of the adult without clearly knowing to what extent they are connected with fear experienced in very early childhood, and about which it was much too alarming to talk, or which could not be mentioned even to ask for an explanation, in case the adults of those days should have laughed or scolded.

> From things that go *bump* in the night,
> Good Lord, deliver us.

After a child has gone to bed, the house is still full of sounds made by the adults downstairs, upstairs, and in the house next door, which will all sound so very different when one is half asleep, that even quite familiar noises, which are easily recognized in the daytime, will seem mysterious and sinister in the dark. The child always imagines that if it has been to sleep and then wakes up again, it must be the middle of the night, and that the sounds now heard must be made by the bogies. Children's stories, fairy-tales, and those about ghosts, all contribute their share in finding interpretations for sounds heard at night. It is a general tendency to be unable to hear a sound without trying to imagine what has caused it, especially at night. When natural causes are dismissed, the realm of supernatural beings will be open to our imagination, and then nothing will be impossible, because, though we can find no evidence that we are right in our conjectures, we can seldom prove that our fancy was wrong.

Children, however, need no proofs of this sort; for them their thoughts are weighty enough without test, and they will never, or only in exceptional cases, dispute the veracirity of the guesses. A water-pipe outside the window that gurgles and makes sinister, hollow noises is terrifying enough, even if the child does not imagine the form of its inhabitant or conjure up what this particular monster might do if it were to get into the room. The *unknown* and the *unexpected* are far more alarming to contemplate than what is known, for which one can be prepared, so that to be able to call up some distorted shape as the author of the noise or imagine the penalty to be received from it would partake of the nature of a lesser trouble, and be a relief to the incessant pondering what unimagined or unimaginable creature could be in ambush at such unpleasantly close quarters.

Sounds made by the child's own quickly beating heart will seem to come from some panting animal ready to spring. The plea to the parents, summoned at the last by a scream, or sought when panic has become unbearable, "I heard a funny noise," receives as little understanding and sympathy, as a rule, as flurried explanations of "nasty faces" that have been seen in the shadows. The adults may say, without paying much attention to what the child has been saying, "Nonsense, there's nothing there; you've been dreaming," and send it back again without taking any trouble to go and see what the difficulty has been. Even if they do, they generally cannot hear what has frightened the child, or say they do not, thinking this will be the most reassuring thing to say, and seldom understanding how menacing a cistern can sound or that the creaking of bed-springs can be a due cause of alarm.

When we were explaining the origin of some of the fears connected with things vaguely seen in half-light or at night, it was suggested that children sleeping in the bedroom of their parents might be alarmed at what they may witness without the knowledge of their elders. A near sleeping apartment to that of the father and mother may also be the cause of similar fears arising from frightening noises of an unknown origin that are heard in the night. Children frequently sleep in a dressing-room or small room adjoining that of the parents, where everything that happens in the other room may be distinctly heard. All noises heard by a sleepy child in the silence of the night will be magnified. Fear and lack of understanding will render them still more terrifying, and the little one imagines that something awful is happening, and gets ideas so frequently of deeds of violence taking place, murder or someone hurting someone else, fighting and bloodshed—ideas that weave themselves in with all the other bogy-tales the child has ever heard or imagined.

Not knowing the reason of a noise and seeking to find the cause in the agency of some supernatural and malignant spirit is exactly the same process that was evolved by the primitive races. All the natural phenomena were explained by them as the actions of malign and terrifying spirits, the thunder, the boring beetle, and the death-watch, exactly in the same way as the frightened child of to-day will find some explanation to account for all that it has heard that it does not understand, and to which it reacts with the same awestruck dread.[1] A cave through which the wind moaned was left strictly alone by our forefathers, who said that it was inhabited by some monster or devil who would tear intruders to pieces; and the modern child who is frightened by the noise made by the lavatory cistern will make all manner of excuses rather than visit this alarming apartment, except when it cannot possibly be avoided, and will do anything rather than shut the door, which would be closing oneself in with the monster, or pull the chain, which apparently lets loose its fury.

This fear of the noise of rushing water and clamorous pipes is very common among children and leads to many difficulties connected with the discharge of physical functions, a cause and effect sequence which adults often fail to realize because they have forgotten how real and compelling that fear can be. Again, fear of the creatures inhabiting the dark, who may make themselves either audible or visible should we have the temerity to move out of bed, is a frequent cause of bed-wetting in children. The fear of braving these things, and putting oneself at their mercy by getting up and feeling under the bed, which is sure to be their lurking-place as well as the home of what the child wants, and then sitting down in their midst, so that for a while one is absolutely prevented from escaping should they take advantage of one's temporary helplessness to attack, is so great that the boy or girl puts off the evil moment until it is too late—children are infinitely less afraid of the real

[1] *Myth, Ritual, and Religion*, Andrew Lang.

I

scolding and subsequent punishment than of the unreal but still more terrible creature that may moan from the corner, patter across the floor, or hide under the bed.

BOOKS THAT MAY BE READ IN CONNECTION WITH THIS SECTION.

Common Disorders of Childhood. G. F. Still, M.A., M.D., F.R.C.P.
Development of Speech in the Normal Child. Macleod Yearsley, F.R.C.S. Child Study Journal. 1926.
Five Years Old or Thereabouts. Margaret Drummond.
A Study of the Mental Life of the Child. Dr. Hermine Hug-Hellmuth.
Myth, Ritual, and Religion. Andrew Lang. Longmans, Green & Co.

F. SPEECH

Romanes, in his interesting book, *Mental Evolution in Man,* most emphatically states that the discoveries of philology show that during the development of speech in the individual child the same stages are followed in the same sequence as in the course of cultural progress amongst various races, or the same race, during the process of civilization. It is often stated that Man is the only living species which has obtained mastery of speech or language, but upon examination it seems doubtful whether we are really justified in making this assertion, for the following reasons.

Should we define speech as "any declaration of thoughts," as do some dictionaries, or a means of communicating ideas, we cannot limit this power to human beings alone, since it is certain that a very large number of the higher mammals and birds have some means of communicating thoughts and passing on information, warning and the like, from one to another. We observe that the transmitter uses special sounds with purpose and intent, the meaning of which is correctly interpreted by others hearing them, that signify their understanding by making use of appropriate actions without delay. These several processes perfectly fulfil the conditions of rudimentary speech, and to deny their language function would seem analogous to asserting that we may class as language only those verbal means of expression the significance of which we understand, which we ourselves are able to use and which represent to our minds a suitable vehicle of our thoughts.

Should we study the habits of animals and birds, we find that they possess quite a wide range of distinct sounds, which they emit upon special occasions, that these appear constant in meaning, and are certainly understood by others of the same species. These may be love-calls, those of warning, cries of pain and fear, as well as low sounds indicative that hunting has been successful. Beasts and birds of prey do not make any sound prior to the kill, because that would alarm the prey. One frequently reads of animals or birds—owls, for instance—

giving special hunting calls when in pursuit, but this is probably the result of faulty observation: the kill has already taken place and the mate or young are being called to share the spoil. The mother creature will always use special calls to summon her young to food or return to the open when a danger is past, to escape from which she previously warned them to take cover.

Small differences in inflection or intonation can be discovered in these sounds upon occasion, which are without doubt intentional and indicate some special meaning. It seems obvious that these sounds have an equal speech-value with the *clicks* made by the Kaffir, that are an integral part of that language, which, however, few Europeans can imitate accurately or understand with exactness. It is no criterion of language that it must possess grammatical rules or various parts of speech, because many primitive methods of thought communication are composed of nothing but strings of sounds representing the names of objects or persons, without any indication of their relation to one another except that supplied by the inference of the hearer. Language became a necessity when one creature wished to communicate with another in a less cumbrous method than by action or gesture, or when out of sight but still within hearing; just as signal language, whistling, drum-talk were evolved, or forms of making signs by smoke, marks on the ground, bent twigs and writing when men found it necessary to transmit ideas at a distance or without sound. The more elaborate became the thoughts to be communicated, the more intricate necessarily grew the vehicles of transmission. Words have also had the purpose of helping us to formulate thoughts. Geiger, a German scientist, has postulated that Speech created Reason, by which he undoubtedly means conceptual or abstract thought, *reasoning*. Others, who have carried out research on the subject of the probable methods by which man discovered the way to make verbal sounds and then attached meanings to them, all try to prove that the discovery of words has served the purpose of helping us to think and crystallizing our ideas, which would certainly have been more difficult, if not impossible, without some such medium.[1]

[1] "Nature et Origine du Langage Humain," Sir Richard Paget, *Bulletin de l'Institut Général Psychologique.* No. 25. Parts 1–3. 1925.

It is true that language was evolved as a medium of conveying thoughts from one person to another, but we, as human beings, do not necessarily always use language to clothe all the thoughts within the compass of our minds. This presents us with another problem. Those people who have lived in different parts of the world at various times of their lives, especially if they started upon their travels during early childhood, will use all the several languages with which the particular incidents are connected, about which they happen to be thinking at the moment. Should their thoughts carry them back to stages when they thought and expressed themselves in pre-speech forms, by which may be understood stages of expression before the adult speech current around them was used, they will consequently continue to think with the corresponding forms of gesture, sign, cry, croon, and gurgle of delight, or shriek of rage to express memories which are little more than revived emotions, representing pleasure or pain, comfort or discomfort, that are essentially akin to the pre-human methods, and which possibly refer to thoughts that are also common to all living creatures, including those of pre-human stages of development. Romanes, in his survey of philological discoveries which have been made in different parts of the world, shows how and where we may trace in human races the stages of the child's development of speech.

If we turn aside for the present from the subject of advanced human speech, that is, the stage of words which undergo inflection and which are submitted to laws governing grammar and syntax, to devote a few moments to the early forms of expression of ideas, news, emotions, warning, rivalry, and love that are to be found in men as well as in animals and birds, and which are afterwards superseded by word equivalents, what do we find in the first instance; and then, as a second consideration, may we believe ourselves justified in comparing them with the earliest pre-linguistic efforts of the modern human child?

The lowest stage of all in the use of sounds is that of the simple CRY, which primarily is a reflex action, denoting discomfort and acting as an emotional discharge. This is to be found in the young of every mammalian species directly after birth. It is not possible, however, to state whether this cry represents any corresponding mental process at this stage. It is generally considered that it does not, but partakes more of the nature of a reflex action occurring as motor response to an unpleasant stimulus, nor does it seem probable that any intention or purpose may be connected with its early use. Only when the child finds out through constant repetition and unvarying experiment that one action produces certain results, and that the noise which it hears comes from itself, will mental processes connected with it be possible. We may then say that intention and motives assert themselves.

Those who spend much time with any living creatures and become really intimate with them learn how to interpret the sounds that they make, whether they are human or not. As one day follows another, very soon after birth differences are discernible in the cry. This will be agreed by all experts in Cry Language, which was the name given to it by a little girl, who could not only remember using it herself, but believed she could understand any other baby. The cry of hunger is not to be confused with that of pain or rage, and experts will, if possible, supply the need that this sign denotes, and thus help to register in the baby's mind a rudimentary idea of language, which is, that special sounds can produce certain results, and that to gain these results it is necessary to make one particular noise.

As we have mentioned before, when describing the process of gaining information by means of touch, sight, smell, and hearing, so also with this most complicated method of all, the acquisition of speech, the baby by degrees becomes more proficient in its ways of gaining knowledge of the outside world, and with its use of the Cry Language discovers that it can gain all that is necessary at first by this means. Gradually, nevertheless, it learns the use of other methods of communication, finds out fresh activities which are still more interesting, and that it can make other sounds with its mouth besides crying, which give equally pleasant sensations, if not even more delightful. All these new experiences and new activities of tongue and lips belonging to this early stage that the baby acquires, some apparently by means of spontaneous discovery, many more through imitation of other children or adults, are to be found also among the primitive races, and the most simple of all among animals and birds.

It is interesting to remark to what a great extent it is possible to hasten speech development, and concurrently with this, the awakening intelligence of the child, by loving attention and by giving it a model from which to copy. M. Delacroix, in a paper written upon "Speech Activity in Children," in a special number of the *Journal de Psychologie*, published in Paris[1] points out that a child's linguistic precocity depends almost entirely upon the amount of attention bestowed upon it by the parents, and that, conversely, those children who are thrown almost entirely into the society of contemporaries or the illiterate will show a greater tendency to cling to pre-speech methods of communication or to baby-talk. This means that given the stimulus of hearing others speaking to them in adult speech, they will try to imitate the sounds they hear, and perhaps wonder about them, wishing to be able to do the same, whereas, should the baby's companion be almost entirely silent or converse with it exclusively in baby language, the child still continues to imitate the sounds heard, and will in that case have no ambition to strive towards a more complicated means of self-expression, nor will it have the complicated thoughts which this means of language cannot entirely satisfy. We should remember that Delacroix stated that the child's linguistic activity kept pace with that of its intellect.

The state of affairs to be found among creatures or a primitive tribe, where all stages of development communicate with one another in such a simple way that all practically use the same means, and where we find little developmental change between the young and adult of the species, will be rare, but it will simplify the task of the young. The human child is confronted with a problem which shows the opposite pole of complexity. It is surrounded with beings which use every known means of communication at one time or another, except perhaps some of those that are only found in foreign lands or peoples of another race. The human child, however, shows a remarkable ability to acquire new methods of thought communication, and by this facility to learn fresh methods marks one of the greatest differences between the human race and the inability to do so of animals or birds.

[1] "L'activité Linguistique de l'Enfant," H. Delacroix. *Journal de Psychologie, normale et pathologique*. XXI. Nos. 1-3.

All human beings, however primitive, unless imbecile, have some ability to learn other forms of thought expression, and few have but one natural means. It is usual to find all those varieties through which they have passed to reach the ultimate stage will be requisitioned at times, should occasion require their use. Some of these may still be used to communicate with persons within sight but out of hearing; others, when in the dark; if talking to children, or with those who speak another language which they can neither talk nor understand, when they will have recourse to a primitive sign language. Human beings can also with more or less ease acquire the speech of another race or people, using it with intelligence as well as accuracy, and not automatically, as though merely repeating a sound to which no meaning is attached, as birds will do. Some birds have certainly been taught to imitate word sounds, in the same way that they will learn to whistle airs, but it is doubtful to what extent even parrots attach meaning to the words or phrases they utter, although at times, either by design or accident, they use them more or less appropriately. Yet, despite the most patient and long-continued efforts, animals have not been able to acquire human speech at all satisfactorily, nor to use it intelligently to any great extent.[1]

In an exceedingly interesting book brought out recently by Professor W. Köhler, *The Mentality of Apes*, we read a description of the efforts that were made to induce these most intelligent creatures to acquire human speech. However, beyond a very few instances of isolated words being imitated by them and sometimes used aptly, as though with intention and understanding of their meaning, not much was achieved by way of result, in spite of unremitting patience on the part of the investigators, who had also been their instructors. Still in the same book, we find a very full account of the natural language of these larger apes; and in another, *Chimpanzee Intelligence*, by the same author, written in conjunction with Mrs. Learned, we find a most complete account of their own language, showing that it is complex, adequate for expressing their emotions, thoughts, and ideas, as well as constant, and understood without hesitation by others of their species and can be readily interpreted by their human observers.

[1] *Mind in Evolution*, L. T. Hobhouse, D.Litt. Appendix, "The Elberfeld Horses,"

Testimony of the same kind is to be found in Romanes's *Mental Evolution in Man,* a book which appeared now many years ago—1888, to be precise. There we are given several instances of gorillas communicating with white hunters to express their pain and surprise at being wounded, or to beg the body of a slain comrade. They used sounds which unmistakably represented their intention, and also gestures, which were entirely adequate to express their meaning and to serve as a method of communicating their thoughts for this specific purpose.

Children who have not the incentive to strive for a means of thought communication by the companionship and example of a loved person, who shows them ways of doing so, as well as cultivating in them the thoughts and feelings they will wish to impart, remain retarded at the cry stage, or that of almost complete silence and inanimation, until very late. We learn that Clara Schumann, who, in her infancy and early childhood, was left almost entirely alone, with only the company of an old servant, did not talk freely until she was several years old.[1]

It is quite possible, however, for individual children to refrain from advancing to other stages because of definite reasons which hold them fixated to the one they have already reached, either because they lack incentive to advance—the stratum at which they have arrived giving them complete satisfaction, expressing adequately all their thoughts—or because they have a great objection to making any advance and acquiring any new activity, since it entails more effort than the corresponding gain seems to be worth. It will frequently happen that the child who adopts a reaction of this kind, and shows a reluctance to speak or to acquire an adult form of speech, is not very strong. The robust child usually finds pleasure in making sounds as an outlet for surplus energy from the very first day. Not only is the weakly child inclined to conserve energy by refraining from making any unnecessary efforts, but often shows an intense dislike for all loud noises and will be extremely quiet in its ways. The loudness and resonance of the voice throughout life will always be a sure index of the health of the person.

The Cry Language admirably expresses the needs of the

[1] "Psychische Stummheit," Dr. Alice Friedmann. *Internationale Zeitschrift für Individual Psychologie.*

very young infant and serves the purpose of summoning assistance for its helplessness, although it may not be made with that intention from the first. It asks that the pangs of hunger may be stilled, gives warning that it is suffering pain, and can even denote rage and defiance. Little sounds of pleasure, comfort, and appreciation, which may be called *love*, perhaps, can also be made at this same level, but the love is probably *self-love*, which becomes projected upon another, as provider of the comfort and happiness that is consequent upon hunger satisfied and a feeling of warmth and protection.

All these needs are found surely enough in the young of every species, in both young and adult animals and birds, as well as human beings, however primitive. But there are a few sounds which belong to this stage of cries or calls which are used by adult creatures only, and never by the young of that species. These are the calls characteristic of giving warning of danger from an outside source, made by male and female alike, love-calls connected with mating, and the cries of rage and challenge that are used to provoke similar displays of vocal or other ability on the part of others that hear. These last are to be found generally among male animals, although it is stated that in many parts of Switzerland, before the village herd takes up the summer quarters upon the high Alpine pastures, a series of combats take place among the cows for the position of Queen of the Pasture. The younger cows challenge with characteristic cries the last year's Queen to single combat, and the vanquished cow shows every manifestation of humiliation and shame at her defeat.[1] We are also familiar with the sorrowful cries uttered by the female animal that has lost her offspring and seeks them, and some females will also give love-calls to attract their mates; but, except for the account of the cows in Swiss herds, who call each other to combat, it is unusual for them to give voice to challenge rivals to vocal displays.

The second stage of pre-speech equivalents is that of *Gesture*, which is of utmost importance in the life of all creatures alike. Captain R. S. Rattray, of the Gold Coast Political Service, in his book on *Ashanti*, gives us much new information about

[1] "Stories of Animal Life in Switzerland," Clement Heaton. *Parent and Child.* Spring, 1927.

Drum Language, which seems to represent all stages in one, and may be said to occupy a transitional position between speech proper, music, gesture, and imitative actions and sounds. He tells us that "the African is a past-master in the art of gesticulation," adding that "gesture is abbreviated action" and speech the interpretation of both. Therefore in speech we may find a still more convenient form of abbreviation to save both effort and time. We also read that among the Ashanti "the drums are not used as a means of signalling in the sense that we should infer—that is, by rapping out the words by means of a prearranged code—but (to the African mind) are used to *sound or speak the actual words*. . . . To a people who know nothing of grammar, a word *per se*, cut from its sound group, seems almost to cease being an intelligible sound."

Drum-talk may, therefore, be classed as a *holophrastic* language, the drummer and those who listen to him being acquainted with the combinations of sounds that are made on the male and female drums respectively, as well as knowing the significance of these sounds—that is, the gestures which were used to make them. In just this same way a person who is familiar with the Leitmotif system used by Wagner in his operas may learn by means of these musical phrases the corresponding thoughts or ideas, which have been thus symbolized, as they are introduced in the actions of the characters or recalled in the course of subsequent events.

Should we carry this theme still further, we find that not only will artificial instruments of percussion be found among the earliest musical instruments, but that some of the higher mammals use a similar method of conveying messages. For instance, a male gorilla will beat his own chest to proclaim a challenge of mortal combat to another within hearing distance. The stallion neighs to the mares and stamps with his forefeet until the ground reverberates. But the gorilla's habit of beating his chest is by no means confined to his own species; it is also practised by the young human males in the pride of their manhood, who, when stripped after the morning bath, go to draw deep draughts of air into their lungs before the open window, and one supposes that the position taken up before the action commences is not without some significance. Neither is a baby so pleased with any other occupation as that of making a rhythmic drumming noise with an old tin or spoon. It will continue this play for hours, if allowed, even though the reverberation may actually cause it to wince and blink at every stroke.

If gesture is but action in little, which nevertheless contains the germ of speech, we may also place in this section various forms of Sign Language in use among so many primitive peoples, chief amongst whom should be mentioned the Red Indians.[1] These forms will adequately express thought of all descriptions, the communication of news, warning of danger, a judgment delivered upon a prisoner, and a business transaction by barter. Included among the most highly developed forms of gesture or action language, however, must also be the large section comprising all the imitative dances, showing war, hunting, and love-making, as well as the Fertility Rites, many of which activities find their echo in children's games at a much later stage of development or survive among the religious celebrations or rituals of civilized peoples. The Gesture or Abbreviated-action Language is the natural sequence following the Cry Language, the next step in the individual speech development of the child that carries it still farther towards the adult goal of using a word symbol for the representation of an action or the presentation of a thought.

The baby uses both gesture and grimace, which are practically the same, except that a different part of the body is used as the agent in each. We have already mentioned the infant's earliest use of both in that it opens its mouth to take in welcome food and turns away its head with an expression of disgust from that which it does not like, to which we referred in the section on Taste. These two gestures, the nodding head and the shaking head, the open mouth and the shut mouth, have become world-wide signs to signify affirmation and negation, yes and no, which many philologists have viewed as the rudiments of speech as we know it. The baby adopts Sign Language with conspicuous assiduity, gesture and pantomimic actions being freely used to signify to others what is wanted. Thus it will open its mouth when hungry, shut its eyes when sleepy—although this is partly involuntary, of course—rock itself to and fro and hold up its arms to be taken on a lap or

[1] *Mental Evolution of Man*, Romanes.

in a person's arms, which are all gestures or actions intimating what it wants others to do for it or to it, just as an Australian aborigine pours water on to the ground in order to make rain fall, so as to intimate to the Deity through action that rain is needed. This is known as Imitative Magic.

This magic ritual on the part of the child has still more constant success than the rites of the primitives. The adults in charge usually pay attention to these signs, and the child generally finds that its gestures are understood. For this reason a baby will show both surprise and disappointment should someone be left in charge who does not understand its own particular Sign Language, and consequently fails to give the right response. It has, moreover, not the least hesitation in showing its dissatisfaction with the offender quite openly.

This is probably one of the most weighty reasons why a little child prefers to be amongst those who are well-known—those, in fact, who understand its language and will not make mistakes over interpreting its signs or giving the necessary response. Being able to give some sign and to obtain what it desires bestows upon the little person a wonderful sense of power and importance.[1] The baby never tires of repeating an action of this kind, as we know to our cost should we have ever started the game of picking up something that will be dropped on the ground again at once for this very reason.

Before long, however, a new idea becomes incorporated with the baby's notions concerning the use of magic gestures, which are its first signs of power. It learns that it may make its wants known and sway others to a still greater extent by making sounds with the mouth, by which means the infant discovers the use of words. We have already mentioned that the baby derives particularly keen pleasure or discomfort from the stimulation of its skin, particularly those surfaces which are covered with mucous membrane, and how active are its touch receptors in the lips and mouth from the moment of birth in connection with the sucking reflex. The supreme importance of the oral zone is usually retained throughout life, unless it should become repressed by some traumatic incident which inhibits it from taking its habitual significant part in human life.

[1] *On Obscene Words*, Dr. S. Ferenczi. Some Contributions to Psycho-analysis. Trans. Dr. Ernest Jones.

Very early does the baby begin to derive pleasure in feeling its breath being slowly inspired and expired, with an accompanying sound, to which name "lalling" has been given. Each sound will be repeated for hours together, when it has been discovered for the first time, before it is once more dropped in favour of the next newest achievement. The passage of air over the lips, the slight tickling sensation apparent as they are first approximated and then separated, the vibrations in oral and nasal cavities, will give the baby untold delight. To check and control these sounds, to play with the intake and expulsion of the breath, has been shown by Dr. David Forsyth[1] to be connected with the habit found in some children of holding or playing with the breath, allowing it to escape by degrees, or again, by holding their breath occasionally until the stage of cyanosis is reached. The former, however, is usually a sign of pleasure, the latter of anger and obstinacy, and may be compared with the child's habit of voluntarily checking the passage of urine and fæces from the bladder or rectum by the contraction of the sphincter muscles of urethra and anus. The pleasure lies in the conscious control of its own activity, in the child's possession and demonstration of power, the anger and obstinacy being shown in satisfaction at being able to thwart the adult and deprive her of the pleasure of gaining her wishes, while at the same time the child gains its own way in refusing to obey the dictates of another.

This love of acquiring and exercising power is probably an important factor behind the incentive which drove the child on up the ladder of Speech from the rungs of the Cry Language and Gesture Language to Word Language. The child feels that it gains power and importance whenever, through some action of its own, it may produce something, some person or state, that it requires. It comes to feel in time that the smaller its own effort and the greater the result obtained, the more successful it has been and the stronger this magic influence. It discovers that many of the objects round about make sounds; it learns, too, to recognize them by the sounds they make, and to imitate them; by which action it notices it can often produce the effect of making them appear. Thus it is beginning

[1] "Rudiments of Character-Formation," Dr. David Forsyth. *Psychoanalytic Review*, May 1921.

to make use of words, names taken from the function of the object and the sound which it makes. At first the infant uses simple words to express any and every meaning, or doubled simple sounds, such as gee-gee, bye-bye, which will generally be sounds that it has heard made by an object, or in connection with things or actions, by those in charge.

Of course, these words or names are by no means always self-invented, because adults will deliberately teach infants to use baby words instead of the real ones, which in many cases would be just as easy. Why should it be any better for a child to learn that an engine is a puff-puff, and then, later, to be obliged to connect a second idea, or word, with this object? Again, is not duck quite as easy to say as *quack*? Yet the grown-up person teaches the child to call this thing quack, in a picture-book or a toy of this shape, when it will not be able to hear the noise that is made by it and so find any connection for itself. The adult may teach the baby to take its first step, but not the second; this the child takes of its own accord, which is to call other objects which seem to resemble the original one by the same name. Thus Darwin tells of a child who, having been taught that a duck was called a quack, in time not only called all other birds quack, but also the water upon which the duck swam, and money as well, because he had been introduced to coins in the form of French francs which bore the imprint of an eagle.[1]

Romanes points out that primitive races show a similar preference for onomatopœic words derived from the function of the object for which they stand; that they use nouns only, or verbal nouns, taken from these sounds, representing the function of the object, and will employ the equivalent of a sentence by making a series of many words without any verbs, prepositions, or pronouns to explain the relation of one to the other. It is thus that a child of a year to eighteen months will talk in civilized countries. However, it is extremely difficult to assign any precise age to the acquisition of speech, since individual children vary so widely in the speed at which they pass from one stage to another, because of various reasons—incentive, models, practice, ambition, wish for power, health, and many others. Whereas one child will begin to say a few

[1] "Biological Sketch of an Infant," *Mind.* Vol. ii. 1877.

words with certainty at the age of eight and a half months, as did Romanes's infant, another investigator, Preyer, records that his little son was more than a year old before he first attempted to repeat any word.

Once a child begins to initiate words, close observation will give us exceedingly interesting material for research. We may discover which sounds are the most easy for one particular baby to produce and those that present peculiar phonetic difficulties, or notice a tendency to mispronounce, lisp, or that trouble arises in sounding R, th, or a labial; for example, a final *le* sometimes proves quite unmanageable and is replaced by *un*. These are easy to detect, because a young child will always eliminate a difficult sound from a word and immediately replace it with one that is easier, or will invent an entirely new word to take its place, which is the typical reaction on the part of those children who will not admit failure. If they find they cannot do what they want, they will quickly change their first intention and make up something new, which they can do with ease, and pretend this is what they meant from the beginning.

When children habitually mispronounce, we are led to wonder upon occasions whether the defect does not lie in auditory acuity rather than in their power of reproduction, especially when the mispronunciation is general or extensive. It is well, then, to test the keenness of hearing for sounds other than words—with a watch, for instance; and also to remember that a child's apparent deafness or incapacity to imitate sounds correctly may arise from inattention in listening as well as in reproduction. To discover where the trouble lies is sometimes quite a complicated business, but it can generally be detected by one who knows the usual disposition of the child, and whether inattention or undue hurry is a characteristic of this particular child.

Some children, always in a hurry, will produce the first letter or syllable correctly and then cease to take any interest in the remainder. They have never listened to the whole word, and therefore cannot reproduce it. This may sometimes be done for fun by adults, or children who are rather older, when they will use the first half of words only, asking others to "pass the butt" and whether they ',want any marm"; others seem more interested in the end of a word and confuse those with similar terminations, never seeming to know for certain how a word commences or what is its initial letter; sometimes they will begin every word in a sentence with the same letter, usually D or T. This may sometimes be found persisting in adults, when it is extremely difficult to understand what is meant until one has grasped that no notice must be taken of this first letter, and that one must recognize the word from its subsequent portions.

We usually find that a child's verbal expression corresponds with its general reactions in other departments of life. If a child is careless in speech and pronunciation, too much in a hurry to listen to and carefully imitate what it hears, we find the same hurry throughout. Speech is an indication of character to a most remarkable extent, which has been proved by the more recent developments of psycho-analysis. The child's character is at the most formative period during the acquisition of speech. The baby learning to talk will also, in all likelihood, closely imitate the speech and voice of those who have the most to do with it and whom it most deeply loves, so it is well to consider this factor of imitation when choosing those who are to be the most intimate companions of infants.

As the child becomes more proficient in the use of words and imitation of sounds it is faced with increasingly complicated problems. At first the baby makes sounds and imitates all it hears without discrimination, purely for the pleasure to be derived from the concomitant stimulation of lips and tongue, oral vibration and so forth, but without purpose or meaning. To connect meaning with a sound shows that a much higher stage has been reached, that of an associated idea. "Mummy" and "Daddy" at first signify visible objects of a certain shape; then a man and a woman who are familiar. There comes later a tendency to take these words as representing the class and to apply it to all men and women. Only later on does it dawn upon the mind of the child that the name has a significance of relationship, and that the word is connected with special people, and yet may be applied to other people in relation to their little friends. It is a gradual process for the child to recognize the names for its parents, Mummy and Daddy, mean special people, of whom certain behaviour can be expected, and who will equally be known by touch, active and passive, smell, hearing, perhaps also taste, and possibly in other ways of which the baby alone is aware and has no means of communicating. One small word, therefore, has to do duty as a symbol, which represents all these associated ideas and is a simple expedient by which can be understood this vast number of attributes and characteristics.

We suggested at the commencement of this section that the child's difficulty was increased in comparison with those of other young creatures, because it was being brought up in a stage of society where so many other varieties of thought-communication methods are in operation simultaneously, and it is necessary for the infant to learn to use any one which appears the most suitable or convenient to obtain the particular result required. But when the stage is reached of learning to recognize and distinguish sounds, as well as to imitate them; to attach an exact significance to each, as well as to grasp the peculiar meaning of words which may not describe a sound or function, not even an object which is visible, but one that has an abstract meaning, the child is confronted with a still more perplexing problem. When we consider its difficulty we may sometimes wonder how it is accomplished by such a tiny creature as the human baby, and yet the miracle takes place more frequently than not.

The infant is surrounded by sounds upon all sides, which at first have but two characteristics only, pleasantness and unpleasantness; otherwise they are of equal importance, and as yet quite devoid of meaning or associative value. The impression they produce upon the child's auditory receptor may probably best be illustrated as a sound pattern, consisting of long and short vibrations, sound-waves, that is all. Sentences and long-continued sounds will be represented by a long pattern or series of vibrations, short sounds, by a streak, or quite abrupt pattern. It is also probable that children are as much more acutely aware of the auditory impression which is caused by a sudden cessation of sound as by a sound itself, which has been demonstrated by experiments with resonators and tuning-forks in psychological laboratories.[1]

[1] "A Vindication of the Resonance Hypothesis of Audition," H. Hartridge. *Br. J. of Psychol*. April 1921.

The average adult is scarcely aware of these auditory phenomena, unless special attention is called to them for scientific
purposes, because through constant habit they have become
daily commonplaces beyond interest or attention. Here, then,
is the child's problem, to associate these sound patterns with
their correct value and meaning as wholes, just as we are told
the African native does in connection with the sounds made in
Drum-talk, one isolated portion of which, like one word to
the child, will probably be devoid of meaning. More than this.
Among the sounds which are familiar to the child there are
those which have many kinds of origin, that in time teach the
child not only what can be learned about the sound and the
way it is made, but also about the thing that makes it, and what
response it is necessary to make to this stimulus should one be
desirable, or what to expect as a consequence of that sound.

For instance, when the baby hears a spoon rattling in a cup,
it knows that food is coming and prepares to welcome or resist
it. It will hear water being drawn for a bath and know also
what to expect; or a kettle singing on the fire, the rain splashing
down, the voice of father and mother, and learn what they are
saying, whether it is praise, blame, or a command; whether this
must be obeyed, or if it can be safely ignored. These sounds have
different meanings from people singing a song or playing a game
to amuse themselves or itself. All these varieties of sound will
gradually become heaped up with meaning, and will stand out
from the others in the former pattern of sounds that surround
the child. The child will now be able to distinguish not only
similarities in sound patterns but also differences in them, and
will learn in time to attach meaning and a response to each.
It will know a considerable amount about the world around
it from understanding what is to be expected as a consequence
of the sounds that it hears, and how it should act when it
notices any one of them. All these things will be acquired with
time; they are not innate in the baby.

Put in this way, one might well feel appalled were it our lot
to start over again to unravel a riddle of such vast dimensions,
even with the experience of the world that lies at our disposal;
and yet one realizes that this great task confronts the infant
during the first year or so of its existence in order that it may
acquire the necessary knowledge to live its life. To acquire

power over the objects in its environment and the companion-ship of people who may come in its path, to make use of circumstances and rise superior to the handicap of ignorance, this colossal work must be accomplished. How, then, let us ask, is the baby able to achieve it?

Other senses beyond that of hearing come to its rescue, as well as the understanding adult. The child will see the thing that makes the noise, see what it does to make it, and so learn what is to be expected to follow as a consequence or con-comitant. Somebody, perhaps, makes a special sound when this thing comes into sight or makes this noise, or when the baby sees it and looks at it attentively. Then it will try to make the same noise itself, and the thing may be brought nearer. The sound has been found to have an effect. The next step in the sequence of discovery is that often if the sound is made when the corresponding object is not in sight, it will appear as though from nowhere. Thus gradually the infant learns that this parti-cular sound is intimately connected with an object, and that making the sound seems to control it in some way, even to produce it at times. If the child discovers that by uttering a special sound it can acquire such a remarkable power over persons, objects, or animals exterior to itself, is it not easy to understand that a child will attach to the words or sounds themselves a very real and concrete value, almost equivalent to that of the things for which they stand, and that they are magic words indeed, attached to which is a creative function, which in later life may sometimes take on almost terrifying aspects, lest a word said may always have the power of pro-ducing that to which it refers? This will become of paramount importance in some of the symptoms of obsessional neurosis in children, to which we shall be referring again later in this chapter. We may find a similar belief in the many superstitions connected with calling up the Devil or the Dead by saying their names, or bringing bad luck through boasting, and such-like remnants of faith in magic power connected with the use of certain words.

The child finds assistance in learning to talk through the observation made by its other senses and through linking together these special sounds with the objects that seem to have made them. Further help is derived from the people around, who will gradually guide it to make associative links between all these factors, as well as making free use of the earlier pre-speech methods of communication to supplement the newly acquired means of verbal expression, or, when this fails, a combination of both, so that the new and unfamiliar will gain assistance from the old and well-tried. The infant was presumably fairly proficient in one mode of expression before it ventured upon the next step, just as we find a baby is usually an adept at crawling as a means of locomotion before it tries to get on its feet, and falls back upon the earlier way when tired or in too much of a hurry to struggle with the new and less rapid means of transit.

We shall find the same process repeating itself over the verbal difficulties. It will again regress to the former means of making itself understood and establishing *rapport* with those around, should it fail to make them understand what is wanted by the one that is in process of acquisition: an adult might have recourse to gesture or sign language in a foreign country, the language of which was almost unknown, so that words at command were totally inadequate to deal with a complicated crisis that needed much explanation, although simple phrases could be understood and spoken. The child, in a crisis, like the adult, or faced with a difficult situation, when unhappy, angry, ill, or in any way emotionally disturbed, will generally fall back upon some previous form of language in order to make him- or herself understood. The person, no matter what the age, who cannot find any other means to establish communication with others and is absolutely baffled in the attempt to be intelligible, exhibits every sign of helplessness shown by the baby in a similar predicament, and often as a last resource will use the most rudimentary gestures, the tears being not far distant, even if he or she should not actually break down and cry.

Not only will the child use the simplest of gestures, grimaces, cries, or other sounds, when words fail to express ideas and needs, in order to make the adult understand the thought that is struggling to find expression, but adults will frequently in their dealings with children who have only a rudimentary grasp of language tend to make use of the same double method, when ordinary words do not convey the right meaning to a child. For instance, we find that in speaking to quite young children we will often make use of gesture far more freely than when talking to our contemporaries, so that our meaning may be clearer, the underlying motive being, of course, that the gesture, or perhaps our facial expression, will convey our intention, even should our words find no response. In the English Language, particularly, we find many examples of a similar kind, where pairs of words of identical meaning but different derivation are used together, such as "let or hindrance," "beg and beseech," the origin of which curious custom was that one word was of Anglo-Saxon origin and the other of Norman-French; both were spoken together, so that people who could not understand one would know the other. The English Language has been built up very largely through the superimposition of one language upon another, the older tongues being those of the conquered races, who were made to perform the menial tasks, to attend to the beasts or the land. We therefore find words connected with these duties belonging to the older stocks, while those connected with chivalry, the chase, and politics, which were the occupations of the ruling classes—that is, the conquerors—would be in the new language which they understood and spoke, having brought the terms with them into the land.

In an article appearing lately in the *British Journal of Psychology*, " On the Intuitive Capacity of Children to Understand Spoken Language," the author, J. W. Tomb, postulates that children have an intuitive understanding of the meaning of words in any language, whether they are familiar with it or not. But it seems more likely that the basis of this faculty is their instinctive power of interpretation of gesture and facial expression which will accompany the words spoken. The child knows that the gesture, the facial expression, the accompanying touch are all indicative of the underlying intention, and are practically the same in all countries. We must also remember that in foreign lands gesture and facial expression are far more used than in our own, which would help the child still more to understand the meaning of the words that were spoken at the same time. It is always a difficult problem to know by what means the child grasps the sense of what is said; we can only gather it to some extent by noticing how much will be imitated in the child's own methods of communicating with others. If the child does not learn until late the use of the verbal predicate, or adverb, to indicate action or feeling, it may be because it so inadequately understands their significance by the observation method, through gesture, facial expression, or touch.

The child, unless inhibited in its capacity to do so, is, as a rule, exceedingly accurate in its power of associating ideas, and is very particular to keep all the links already forged quite separate from one another. For instance, someone may have said, in answer to a child's question, "What is Pussy saying when she mews?" that Pussy is asking for her dinner. But the little one will not mix up the two ideas and *mew* next time it is hungry, unless it is definitely pretending to be a pussy. To mew is what pussy does when she wants her dinner ; to mew would, therefore, be to expect a pussy dinner. Everything must be in keeping to satisfy a child, once it has arrived at this stage of understanding. It knows the difference between a pussy dinner and a little child's dinner. The child who mewed for a dinner in fun would expect the adult to understand this and carry on with the game to the extent of supplying a saucer of milk under the table, and would try to lap it up like pussy. It would be offended at being given a mug of milk in a high chair.

If we realize that the child originally hears all sounds as patterns, we will understand more readily that people who talk with a slightly different accent or intonation from that with which the child is familiar must be entirely unintelligible, as though they were talking in a foreign language, unless the child upon these occasions also reads the meaning of the stranger from general tone of voice, gesture, expression of face, and not from the words uttered. Small differences in pronunciation of words such as we know them must make large variations in vibration patterns, which are what the child has learnt to recognize as a whole, and the result is that the little one, having no ability to allow for variations of this sort, cannot understand what is being said.

When we think of the sound of words separate from their meaning, which is familiar to us, it is not difficult to understand that the variation in pronunciation of the same sentence spoken by a Scot, a Welshman, a Cockney, or a native of Devon, would cause it to sound quite unrecognizable to the child; but yet this is a difficulty which the baby has to face with nearly each new person it meets, and maybe recognizes just as clearly that the adult is equally bewildered by any little verbal peculiarities of its own speech that the home people understand so well. This is why the baby who is just beginning to talk often has a fresh relapse into shyness because it cannot understand others, and knows that others cannot understand itself, unless the services of an interpreter are ready at hand, in the person of Mother or Nurse, who restores all to a friendly footing once more by translating the language of both parties into sounds understood by the other. Nothing makes us so suspicious of another person as not to be able to make out what he is saying. It is an expression we may frequently discern upon the baby's face, or sometimes upon that of an intelligent dog, and works the same amount of havoc as the feeling of being laughed at.

It has been found that children who are brought up in countries where two languages are in constant use are generally more backward than those where only one is current. One wonders whether this may not be in some way connected with the fact that one of these is usually the language spoken in the home and the other in the school,[1] or in the case of a territory which has been conquered by another race, which forces its language upon the defeated people, hence there is a certain degree of rivalry or emotional conflict in the learning of the two, which may also be found in a household where the parents are of different nationalities and languages. Both parents not only try to teach the children their own language simultaneously, but feel a particular urge to do so, which produces an emotional conflict in the children, who know unconsciously that each parent is trying to establish a prior right over themselves, and they are consequently drawn both ways, because of the love they feel towards the two. Finally, the best loved parent will probably succeed in establishing the firmest grip of their language, which the two, parent and child, will talk together, and through which means will be formed a still stronger bond of love between them.

[1] "Bilingualism and Mental Development," Frank Smith. *Br. J. of Psychol.*, General Section. January 1923.

Language will frequently represent and include a very great emotional value. At one time common speech practically denoted kinship, and the teaching of a language to a stranger was almost equivalent to making him a blood-brother. We always speak of our mother-tongue, but our country can be either fatherland or motherland; with this distinction, whichever form is customary will be significant. Among certain nations it will be the one, with others the reverse; to the German his country is and always will be the *Vaterland*, but he still speaks of the *Muttersprache*. We who live at home and those English-speaking peoples scattered over the world in our Colonies all talk of our Motherland, although we sometimes refer to our speech as King's English, which probably comes from the fact that the translation of the Bible made in the reign of James I is supposed to have established the form of our language to a considerable extent. This may be so, but if one looks deeper one will probably find that there is a psychological reason which is still more far-reaching, to which we will refer later.

The acquisition of language is essentially part of the mother's teaching, transmitted first by lullabies and all the countless little intimacies and play between mother and child. This seems generally recognized, since we find several expressions in use denoting the idea, thus: "Learned at our mother's knee"; "Imbibed with our mother's milk." The subject of lullabies is often of the utmost importance. They often tell of days when the women who sang them were almost, if not quite, slaves, prisoners of war, or captives far from their own country where their language was spoken. This emotional setting would tend to make the tender bond to the babe the stronger, as well as to create a desire to transmit mother-tongue and perhaps also love of their own mother-country to the next generation, in opposition to the speech and country of the father. In connection with the idea of King's English we may remark that this is the term used to express educated speech and not colloquialisms, which might have been learned in the nursery.

The psychology of the woman originating from the old days of her slavery has yet to be deciphered. When this work is taken in hand, much will be discovered from the study of lullabies and folk-songs crooned by mothers over generation after generation of babies. A common characteristic of cradle-songs is that they are generally sad. If they do not represent the absence of the mother from her native land, they will show an absent father. He is dead, an outlaw, or in some dangerous situation whence it is probable he will never return. The infant is, therefore, frequently bewailed as fatherless in prospect or retrospect, and all that remains as a channel for the mother's love and a link with happier days. This, of course, is the echo of the deepest notes of woman's psychology, and also that of her child, who grows up in this atmosphere, but which cannot be explained here in its entirety. It is certainly worthy of remark, however, that the cradle-song, the most intimate of all speech communications between the mother and her child, bears out the teaching of Freud. It corroborates one of the chief tenets of his teaching, which has been so hotly disputed, nevertheless, the Œdipus Complex, which explains the intimacy between mother and son, their bond of love, and the wish to exclude the father.

Nearly all lullabies, of course, represent the babe as a *boy*. Ancient lore has once more endorsed the discovery of psychoanalysis that mothers prefer their sons. The cradle-song about Mrs. Carter, quoted earlier in this chapter, mentions the child specifically as a daughter, but one who is obviously in a most unflourishing condition, the exact opposite to the eulogies which are poured out in rapture as a rule over the bonny little son. "All that remains of your Sallee" rather suggests the marasmus baby, and recalls the incident mentioned by Dr. Forsyth in *Children in Health and Disease*, of the mother who, preparing her infant for examination in the out-patients department of a London hospital, exclaimed in horror, "Why the last time I undressed her she was a beautiful baby." The only cheerful ditty about a hunting father or a daughter is that of Baby Bunting, who is generally represented as a baby girl, which is quite in accordance with the usual fathers' preference for their little daughters. Some people, however, feel certain that this infant is also a boy.

Amongst primitive races a great many superstitions are to be found connected with the naming of children, what names are lucky and which are the reverse. In some parts a baby's name must never be uttered or evil will befall it, a nickname of a derogatory sort being used instead to avert the jealousy of the gods. This tendency we may still find surviving, although probably unconsciously, in the choice of the pet-name.[1] Magic connected with names is plentiful. One may destroy an enemy by seething a piece of bark on which his name is written in a pot of boiling water. A man must never mention the name of his mother-in-law. In some parts men and women have separate languages in use amongst themselves, and one in common as a means of communication with one another. Even should a man know the woman's language, he would not use it, as beneath his dignity, and for a woman to learn the man's speech would lead to her death. These men's languages are taught to the boys of the tribe during the Initiation ceremonies or Puberty Rites,[2] as well as secret or magic languages, spells, and incantations. This reminds us of the joy that boys and girls take in their own secret languages: how one generation after another of schoolboys and girls will evolve or learn from one another exactly the same forms, derived by making certain repetitions of syllables in words or by the addition of prefixes or suffixes, which will be used by them, fully under the impression that their elders do not know what they are saying and have never done anything of that nature themselves.

The idea of magic words and words of power may not only be present in the minds of children connected with pleasant things, however. We have already drawn attention to the superstition that to mention things or people in a certain way is dangerous, owing to the belief that to do so might make them appear. Nervous children particularly will become afflicted with troubles of this kind. Words have a very real value indeed to them, and consequently to put into words anything of which they are afraid becomes a possibility, because it may bring it to pass or make it once more visible. For this reason it is extremely difficult to gain any accurate knowledge of children's fears simply because they are too terrified to speak of them or give them utterance, especially when dreams or goblins that lurk around in the darkness are concerned. Having spoken about them to others may in some way bring one under their power and enable them to seize their little victims more easily. This

---

[1] *The Golden Bough*, Sir George Fraser.
[2] *Origins and Education among Primitive Peoples*, W. D. Hambly, B.Sc.

may seem ridiculous to the grown-up person, who has forgotten how alarming it was to speak of uncanny things, especially after nightfall, but it is a most serious matter for nervous children, and not one we can afford to treat lightly.

Children who begin to suffer from definite nervous trouble in early childhood will often declare their condition by some abnormal attitude towards words or things said, either by themselves or others. In this form of psychological trouble we find one of the symptoms of Obsessional Neurosis. We see the characteristic mark of obsession in the child's ideas, a "mustness" which will cause extreme anxiety should it not be possible to carry out the compulsive act. Doubts will also assail the child whether this or that has been said, and said correctly. We will hear him repeating unceasingly some special sentence or group of words, perhaps worrying others to say something for him over and over again, to tell him what to do, or what must not be done, or that what he has done does not matter; that he could not help it; they are not angry with him; he will not die! He insists upon special words being used for this purpose—no other phrase will pacify him; and he must reiterate them many times before he can gain any satisfaction. He (for we find these cases more frequently among boys than girls) may think that someone will be injured or may die because of something he has said, or he must carry out some special action to prevent harm coming to himself or others. This idea is an equivalent in the reversed form of the Death Wish of the Primitives, the power of the word to cause death in another, or to bring him harm, which did promptly have the effect of killing the adversary through the power of suggestion, unless still more mighty spells could be used to counteract it. They feel guilty about a wish to get rid of somebody, even that somebody might die, that they have had in their minds for some time, and expect that retribution will come upon them in consequence of their evil thoughts or wishes, so that they are obliged to invent some second form of words to cancel the first and make it as though they had never been spoken or wished.[1]

To invent rituals or spells in which special words play a prominent part, in order to ward off some disaster or undo

[1] *Hemmung, Symptom und Angst*, Sig. Freud.

what has already been done, will occupy a large part of the time and attention as well as the energy of such children. They may occasionally go to the length of trying to obtain punishment for something they have not done, in order to relieve the tension in their minds upon the score of this imaginary guilt, felt on account of wishes represented by thoughts or words, but which have never been carried through in action. The child then feels absolved by the outwardly *unmerited punishment* from the secret sense of guilt which oppresses him and which he finds still more hard to bear for this reason.

Obscene and childish or vulgar words occupy an important place in the growing vocabulary of the little boy and girl. When they are taught that there are certain words that they must not use, but which their elders may mention apparently with impunity, conflict arises. The child finds it hard to understand this double code, and thinks at the same time that it is very grown-up to say them upon every possible occasion, to the annoyance and perhaps also the humiliation of the adults present at the time, especially those who are responsible for the manners of the culprit. There are many children, especially little boys about four years old, who are very keen upon showing off their manliness, pretending to be thoroughly grown-up and making a scene. They like the commotion of being scolded, if it does not bring with it any severe punishment; they like the surprised and shocked titter or giggle and obvious embarrassment that usually follows the utterance of some word which the child knows full well that it is not allowed to say. To take no notice at all is generally one of the most speedy ways to stop the outburst on the part of the child, who will then generally leave off because it does not arouse the excitement for which the action was carried out.

Before closing this chapter, it may be well to mention briefly some of the principal speech defects and inhibitions that arise from psychological causes. They are fairly numerous, should we take into consideration all the various forms of lisping and lalling, as the retention of baby-talk in the older child is called.[1]

We usually find that it is not in language alone that the

[1] "Some Speech Defects in Children," Miss Ida C. Ward. *The Child.* January 1925.

baby ways persist. The child does not want to grow up. He or she wishes to continue in the position of somebody's, if not everybody's, baby, and the lisp or other peculiarity will become more emphatic when talking to or of this person whose baby he or she most wishes to remain. This adult may at the same time foster the symptom by treating the child in a babyish way and talk in baby language too, so that the factor of imitation of the loved one will join with habit to play its part of making the fixation still stronger. A bond which is too close and emotional between an adult and a child, be they blood-relations or nurse and nursling, is always a very grave matter. Usually it will have the effect of sapping too much of the child's vitality and retarding its development. In this way the adult is using the child as an outlet for emotions which are not suited for one of such immature years, but which cannot find another escape through a more fitting channel. This process may act as a life-buoy for the grown-up person, it is true, but will be a millstone around the neck of the child's future independence.

The normal tendency of a healthy child is to grow increasingly independent as it gets older, and not to rely so much upon the adults in its immediate neighbourhood for support in a help-less baby way. But there are many parents, nurses, and other persons who strive to keep their children young (which often means helpless and needing them) as long as possible, and they do all in their power to check the spirit of independence, because they think it will separate the coming generation from themselves. One may nearly always find such process has been at work when a baby habit has been retained in later life. It was probably encouraged and treated as though a mark of distinction, the sign of the family ewe-lamb.

The reverse situation, too drastic treatment or ridicule of a baby's early efforts at talking, will frequently have the result of making a silent person, who has the very greatest difficulty to speak in the presence of others, strangers especially, unless absolutely certain of not being laughed at. One child who could not say any word ending in *le*, and who used to say *appun* and *tabun* for apple and table, once announced to her family, who had been joining in a general laugh at her expense, "Well, if you laugh at everything I say, I won't talk at all." She did not quite literally keep this promise, but became a person of few words, particularly in the way of general conversation, and preserved the attitude of silent, critical listener, who never allowed to pass unnoticed, as she grew older, one of the many little slips and inaccuracies of her mother and elder sister, who were both exceedingly incorrect speakers. She later developed a certain ability for writing and a great fondness for words, which she herself endeavoured to use with great precision.

It is by no means uncommon for adults to ridicule children for a weakness they share, as did the mother of the little girl just mentioned. Once again, it gives the adults a feeling of superiority to find someone still worse than themselves in some particular respect, and to be able to triumph over another is sweet, even though the other may be but a small child. Adults are rather fond of practising minor cruelties upon children over words and mispronunciation, mocking them and repeating after them what has been said, but with gross exaggeration. The child knows that it is exaggerated, and knows, too, that it is being mocked, that it did not say the word really like that in the least, and hates and fears the persons for their mockery of its helplessness. At first it is most improbable that a young child can distinguish the finer shades of difference between consonants of allied sound, and it ought not to be punished or even scolded and laughed at for mistakes of this kind.

We may remember, perhaps, the beating that little Ernest got from his father for his supposed obstinacy when he continued to mispronounce a word in his Sunday evening hymn, in Samuel Butler's "Way of all Flesh." Another characteristic of the adult with regard to the child who cannot reproduce any word is to say it again very loud, to shout it, making such a cataclysm of sound by this means that the child will be stunned by it and can therefore hear nothing. A child's organ of hearing is exceedingly delicate at this age, and will be able to appreciate fine differences in tone far more readily when they are repeated softly than when shouted. On the contrary, when the child becomes always accustomed to hear loud voices, or when it lives in a noisy street, it does not seem able to realize any sound which does not come up to a certain standard of loudness, as, for instance, the London street child, who always talks at the pitch of its voice, shouts all it has to say, and only pays attention when others yell at it.

One often discovers in the same connection that there are certain children who never attempt to obey others or to carry out instructions unless they are said in an extremely loud voice. This shows the usual habit at home, if the child only associates doing what it is told with being shouted at, or if it believes that people only mean what they say when they raise their voices angrily. The child, in such cases, will also imitate the same manner and shout whenever it wishes to become emphatic or wants something done most particularly and urgently, in order to make itself heard above the general noise.

Unless children are used to an environment and people that are noisy, and so learn that they are not particularly harmful just because of that reason, a loud voice, with its ample vibrations, will alarm a child, just as we have pointed out in the section on Hearing that noise apparently will cause fear in quite a young child who has not previously been considered at all nervous. The child who is frightened of a loud, angry voice becomes at once psychologically and morally disintegrated, and will say or do anything that it believes necessary in order to escape from the voice of anger. The children in households where there is an irritable, loud-voiced parent may often go and hide as long as that voice is audible, the fear being like that instilled into the Children of Israel by the voice of God. Many people to this day are afraid of thunderstorms because they connect them with the voice of God, and also of an angry-voiced grown-up person. Some adults, however, only feel the joy of power when their wrath has made a child tremble and cower or reduced it to tears.

Another common speech defect, *stammering*, is generally acknowledged to be connected with fear and guilt. It is recognized that there are more boys than girls who stammer, and possibly because boys come into open conflict with their fathers more than girls. Large numbers of stammering men have had impatient, angry fathers who punished them severely when they were little, before whom they were afraid to speak, and who, if questioned about some misdemeanour, were never allowed time or opportunity to explain the circumstances or the event which had brought about the trouble. Fear is by far the most common origin of stammering, but there are often others besides. We have already referred to a baby's habit of playing with its breath, drawing it in and blowing it out again in bubbles, holding its breath in obstinacy, anger, and defiance. If we think of these baby ways and compare them with the idiosyncrasies of the stammerer's varieties of verbal hold-up, we may see a number of similarities. Some will go through agonies of shame and discomfort over their impediment—these are probably they in whom the defect originated with fear and guilt—while others are quite cheerful or even seem rather to enjoy keeping everyone waiting until they have finished what they want to say. These will never hurry, never curtail their sentences, or avoid the particular sounds which they know they can never accomplish successfully, but hurl defiance at their listeners with the final explosive utterance of the word, rigorously denying any suggestions and repudiating all help. This playing with words, as the baby plays with its breath or the child will amuse itself with checking and then expelling urine and fæces, may be revived in the peculiarities of the stammerer.

Again, it is possible for the stammer to appear in the form of a masturbation substitute. The breath will then be inspired in rhythmic gasps, higher and higher, until a climax is reached. A look of intense pleasure is to be seen upon the child's face, the word is then spoken with an explosive sound or a sudden jerk, and, excitement being at an end, the rest of the sentence may be proceeded with without further difficulty. Of course, many children find that they can attract a great deal of attention in this way, and will feel that they are more interesting and unique with than without it. Without this peculiarity they will be just the same as all the other boys in the school and will not have this easy means of making the others laugh. To make others laugh is a frequent ambition among many little boys, who, not being clever enough to achieve this by their wit, work to accomplish the same result by whatever means lies in their power. One little boy with a stammer, who was rather proud of it than otherwise, wept bitterly at the idea that he should be helped to get rid of it.

We have just said that children can play with their words

as they do sometimes over the production or restraint of their bodily excretions. It is fairly common for the two to become connected in the child mind. This may be caused by the two processes undergoing training at the same time, as well as the fact that both words and fæces are produced from similar mouth-like apertures, the resemblance of which the child cannot help observing. Moreover, it is by no means exceptional to find persons behaving over the matter of oral expression in the same way that they do with regard to their excretory functions. Those who are free-talkers will seldom suffer from constipation, and will also be generous in disposition. Whereas the people of few words will usually be the thrifty, economical souls, who are martyrs to constipation, and never talk if they can reasonably avoid doing so, nor pay for anything if they can evade the expense, as well as being constantly obliged to have recourse to aperients. These similarities have been found coincident in so many children and adults that it has been considered probable that the connection in the same person is not altogether accidental.

Furthermore, the physical functions will frequently be allied in the child's thoughts with the idea of magic production and magic words or sounds, because the mother or nurse will repeatedly make use of some onomatopœic sound or phrase to induce the child to pass water or fæces. Childish words for these functions later on will become connected in its mind with other obscene and vulgar expressions, and may indeed become material for obsessions and compulsions. They will be words to which great affect is attached; that is to say, when they have been left behind among the rest of our infantile possessions, we try to think that they have never had any particular interest for us, and that we had nothing to do with them. We try to forget them and experience great horror at hearing another use them. It is no uncommon occurrence to find people who have this intense dislike to these childish words, and take the greatest precautions to avoid mentioning them in any connection whatever.

BOOKS WHICH CAN BE READ IN CONNECTION WITH THIS CHAPTER.

Problems of the Nervous Child. Elida Evans.
Philosophy of Speech. George Willis.
Language and Thought of the Child. Jean Piaget.

Judgment and Reasoning in the Child. Jean Piaget.

Mentality of Apes. Prof. W. Köhler.

Papers on Psycho-analysis. Ernest Jones, M.D.

Some Contributions to Psycho-analysis. Dr. S. Ferenczi (especially the Chapter on Obscene Words).

Rudiments of Character. David Forsyth, M.D., D.Sc., F.R.C.P. *The Psychoanalytic Review.* April 1921.

Self-expression without Speech. Mary Chadwick. *Child Study Journal.* 1925.

L'Activité Linguistique de l'Enfant. H. Delacroix. *Journal de Psychologie, normale et pathologique.* XXI. Nos. 1–3.

On the Intuitive Capacity of Children to Understand Spoken Language. J. W. Tomb. *Br. J. of Psychol.* General Section. July 1925.

Bilingualism and Mental Development. Frank Smith. *Br. J. of Psychol.* General Section. January 1923.

Some Speech Defects in Children. Miss Ida C. Ward. *Child.* January 1925.

Nature et Origine du Langage Humain. Sir Richard Paget. *Bulletin de l'Institut Général Psychologique.* No. 25. Parts 1–3. 1925.

Psychische Stummheit. Dr. Alice Friedmann. *Internationale Zeitschrift für Individual Psychologie.*

A Vindication of the Resonance Hypothesis of Audition. H. Hartridge. *Br. J. of Psychol.* General Section. April 1921.

Biological Sketch of an Infant. Charles Darwin. *Mind.* Vol. ii. 1877 (written 37 years previously).

Mind in Evolution. L. T. Hobhouse, D.Litt. Macmillan.

The Child's Early Discrimination between Sound and Speech. Mary Chadwick. *Psyche.* April 1928.

Stammering. A Psychoanalytic Interpretation. Dr. Isador H. Coriat. Mental and Nervous Pub. Co., Washington. D.C.

G. THE KINÆSTHETIC SENSE

OUR Kinæsthetic Sense is, perhaps, one of the most important for our daily life, and yet one about which least is known generally, and concerning the functions of which the average person realizes but little. Should one put the question to half a dozen people representing as many different occupations or professions and different standards of education, we might find to our astonishment that most of them had not the least idea what we were talking about, unless we meant their appreciation of the Cinema and the magic of Film-land. Still, those preferences or antipathies are not the basis of this discussion, but the *secret of movement*, the reason why we use our muscles and know in what area of our body the movement is taking place and its direction, keep our balance, realize the position of our limbs, even should we not be able to see them, and judge the amount of muscular effort that must be applied to carry out any given action.

More than this. When we begin to investigate the subject thoroughly, we find that it is one of the very earliest of the infant's sensations, a contemporary of Touch. It bears strange, vague memories, and carries with it a high percentage of pleasure connected with muscular movement, that plays a particularly significant part as a determinant of some of the actions of the child that are usually ascribed to naughtiness, such as biting, kicking, destruction of different kinds; hating and fearing being held still and struggling against another person either stronger or weaker than itself, as well as various fears connected with balance and movement within or without the self.

The sense differs in many particulars from those with which we are so familiar in the usually recognized *five senses*, all of which have their receptor organs upon the periphery of the body. The kinæsthetic sense is situated in nerve centres called *proprioceptors* within the muscles of the body, out of sight, therefore largely out of mind, except for the most valuable contribution that they make to the information we have about ourselves and the world around us. Whenever we make any movement this sense is affected, and in several ways. It will come into action to help us to make up our minds exactly how much muscular power must be exerted upon each occasion; to inhibit contrary actions which might annul the success of the first. It may stimulate pleasurable or unpleasant muscular sensations while the movement is in progress, and will be capable of registering a memory of the process, so that it may in future be recalled as a feeling-image. Again, as we have seen to be the case in the vicissitudes of the impulses connected with the other senses, they depend predominantly upon their earliest treatment in the nursery days whether they develop freely or become inhibited or fixated at an early level of manifestation.

We may trace similar difficulties in alliance with the kinæsthetic sense, and as the results of various infantile experiences we may find reflected many childish traits and troubles with which we are unfortunately only too familiar, both in childhood as well as later years.

Let us follow the same plan which we have used in the case of the other senses and discuss the development of the kinæsthetic sense step by step. Naturally, we shall find that many of those characteristics which we discovered in connection with Touch will be equally true concerning the muscle and movement sense, because in many ways it may be regarded as a deeper touch awareness, and a susceptibility of personal touch among the deeper tissues rather than the superficial areas. This sense will probably coincide with the development of movement, particularly of those types which in themselves will be found to give intense pleasure or provide a soothing comfort to the infant in the early days of life. To what extent this sense may be active before birth we cannot establish with any certain proofs, but we know that the infant has movements of several kinds before birth. Mothers will tell us that the motile habits of their several children differ very considerably *in utero*, and that they are usually characteristic of the child's typical reactions in later life. The tempo and rhythm of life seems already established—the calm, placid child will be slow moving; the restless, impatient infant will kick and move in a much more definite manner, and have more speed and power in movement.

With the commencement of the labour-pains of the mother the pre-natal calm and steady rhythms of the maternal heart-beat and respiration are torn across by the convulsive but mighty rhythms of parturition. The stupendous power which thus seizes the infant and forces it from its earliest home, finally expels the little creature in a state more dead than alive, with a heart that beats but feebly, without respiration, and at first with no muscular movements. Gradually these are established, the babe breathes, moves, cries, and the heart's action becomes stronger and more rhythmical; then, again, the movements cease, when sleep claims the infant and charms it back to the old state of bliss.

At first muscular movements occur to gratify some wish, to gain satisfaction to still the pangs of hunger, or to escape from discomfort. But very early we may also observe that the baby shows signs of pleasure through muscular movement, pleased wriggling and heaving of trunk muscles, that both denote pleasure and probably give pleasure. With the development of the child we see muscular pleasure extending its range of possibility until we find the infant delighting in pushing against some resistance with feet or hands, later trying to pull itself up and indulging in all kinds of self-found gymnastics and rhythmical exercises, by means of which pleasant feelings are radiated throughout the body from the muscles in trunk and limbs, especially when these have full play without the hindering constriction of clothing, which is one of the reasons why babies love to get rid of clothes and kick in perfect freedom.

This muscle pleasure encourages the child to further efforts of movement, towards locomotion, and the making of noises for the sake of the vibrations or movements in the musculature of the speech apparatus. We find later on still more clearly that the child will derive pleasure from activities of several types; rhythmical movement that is continuous, soothing, interesting, and, we might term, *occupational;* or the mastery of muscular activity, i.e., muscular control, in being able to reach distant objects, to judge distances and the output of energy, as well as in sudden jerky movements, that give a syncopated pleasure to the muscle mass, which has a pleasure premium distinctly its own. We notice then that muscular tension alternating with muscular relaxation gives the child intense pleasure in whatever part of the body it may take place.

This alternation of tension and relaxation of the muscles will occur in many regions of the baby's body—in mouth zones connected with the making of noises, in respiration, checking and expelling the breath,[1] as well as in movements of the hands, clutching and dropping. Many people can remember the joy derived in early years from holding some object tightly and then suddenly letting go, or throwing things down or away, because of the pleasant muscular movement occasioned thereby, which sheds some light upon the baby's delight in throwing things out of its cot or perambulator, that to some seems so purposeless and obscure in origin.

Bladder and bowel control, which, of course, is another form of muscular tension and release, comes next, and plays an important part, to which also we have previously drawn attention ; and no one to whom babies are familiar need be reminded of the joy to be found in kicking and pushing with legs and feet, pretending to climb up the grown-up person, which are exercises preparatory to walking and many forms of adult athletics.

Freedom of movement, a good carriage, easy walking, balance, fearlessness of movement, climbing, running, dancing, will be the heritage of those children who come through these days with the kinæsthetic sense uninhibited and unimpaired. Freedom, a swinging rhythm, means perfect muscular control of a higher degree than the rigidity which we may often find in those people who were either punished or seriously scolded for fidgeting, made to walk before they were ready, or led to believe that to move energetically was unbecoming and a rather guilty pleasure. The habit of teaching little girls of a past generation that it was a crime of great magnitude to move freely, unladylike to swing their arms or kick with their legs, and that a graceful deportment had to be learned, which was sometimes graceful in a mincing fashion, and far more often stiff and entirely lacking in grace or graciousness, was responsible for much loss of pleasure in muscular movement on the part of women in the past, as were also the hampering long skirts and tightly laced corsets.

[1] "Rudiments of Character," David Forsyth, M.D., D.Sc., F.R.C.P. *Psychoanalytic Review*. April 1921.

We have seen in the case of the other senses that it has frequently been deemed wrong for the child manifestly to gain pleasure from its senses, although the adult may try to cultivate them from an æsthetic point of view later on. For the child to find these pleasures unaided seems to be considered reprehensible or guilty; and through the adult limiting this gain of pleasure, the sense will become inhibited and to a greater or lesser extent the finer development is lost. (See Sections "Smell" and "Touch.") We find a similar hampered development occur in relation to muscular movements, its expression then taking the form of rigid, awkward gait, bad posture or difficulty in balance, dislike for games requiring free muscular movement or rhythm. It may equally extend to movements of any kind, dexterity for skilled manipulation of tools or good instrumentation in music being impossible.

In place of the advantages that spring from well-developed muscular control and pleasure taken in its highest forms, we may find that the sense slips away into devious paths and pleasure will be taken in ways that may be disadvantageous, destructive, or show inhibition, as well as finding expression in nervous symptoms which are quite familiar, although their origin in impaired muscular control or the gain of pleasure by kinæsthetic activity of various kinds is generally overlooked.

Many forms of childish actions which are usually ascribed to naughtiness may thus be traced to the pleasure to be derived from them through this kinæsthetic sense. Biting, scratching, kicking, are the most direct forms, and the adult's firm grasp in order to prevent the continuance of the action is heartily resented by the little one It may even lead to panic and the fear on the part of the child that the adult wishes to kill it, because its movement or freedom is thus limited. Movement will become identified with life in the mind of many children who have noticed the stiffness of dead mice or birds they may happen to have found. Destruction, in the form of breaking or tearing, may be easily recognized as connected with this same impulse and pleasure. We may often notice the pleasure or triumph depicted on the face of a child seized with an irresistible desire to break off a flower or branch of a tree, or to tear paper off a wall, after this action has been carried out. A stalk that is fat and juicy, that offers a certain resistance, will be selected, because it offers the highest muscular pleasure from the action.

The over-investment of pleasure in muscular movement will lead to these actions on the part of the child, but will also originate many forms of nervous movement also, and those compulsive actions, twitches and the like that are often, but erroneously, believed to be the symptoms of chorea or St. Vitus's dance. A few of these may be of the rhythmical variety, a gentle waving of hands, arms, or legs, such as are seen both in the infant and in the mentally deficient, but most characteristic are the jerky, spasmodic movements associated with muscular tension and alternating release. This will account for numerous habit-spasms which are often considered of such obscure origin. They will frequently be the continuation of baby gestures, and will be continued and practised especially often at times of mental stress without their possessor being aware that they are being carried out. Any groups of muscles may be affected in this manner and in various ways, according to the particular persons who make use of the symptom, possibly, as we shall presently show in the chapter on Childish Bad Habits, to express some thought that cannot easily be put into words. But the pleasure will remain a conscious pleasure, sometimes indulged with increased effect because it is found to annoy others at the same time.

This muscular tension that may be used as a pleasure gratification may also in some persons reappear in subsequent life as a form of self-punishment, because we often find that those people who in the past derived pleasure from any special source or organ, which has been shown to them later in the light of a guilty pleasure, subsequently make of this tendency a continuing gratification, but with the addition of pain as a means of disguise and self-punishment, and as a method of atonement for the indulgence in the pleasure which cannot be renounced.

These people who gained pleasure through the play of alternating muscular tension and relaxation may by this means often cause themselves acute pain. The tension of the muscles is increased to such an extent as to press upon some neighbouring nerve ganglia and produce what those persons will call *neuralgia* or *rheumatism*. Medical men consulted on account of the trouble can find no adequate predisposing cause, but the pain continues, and may be found from psychological research to occur at some emotional crisis, when annoyed or the like, and that in childhood some corresponding muscle play may have taken place in the same region when the child was angry.

Anger will frequently set in motion muscle innervation without the conscious volition of the person. Thus one woman, known to the writer, when being verbally attacked in hospital by a superior to whom she could not justify herself because of professional etiquette, found her upper lip twitching like that of an angry dog snarling and about to bite. Twitching and clenching hands, the restlessly tapping foot, are all familiar signs of anger and gestures which are the remnant of the impulsive movement, the action in little, that provides muscular discharge of pent-up emotion.

Thus nervous twitches, cramps, stiff joints, and contractures tell some tale of disturbance affecting the kinæsthetic sense, which has resulted in an absence of free movement. Limitation occurs of the muscle sense, with its high investment of pleasure derived from activity and rhythm. Such will be found in those patients who suffer from contractures and paralyses, which have been called hysterical and are due to functional rather than organic trouble. In these cases no lesion can be found in nerve or muscle; the response to an electrical or faradic current is normal and the limb may be moved freely under an anæsthetic.

The child learns many lessons about the outside world and the properties and functions of the objects in its environment from the kinæsthetic sense. It learns to control the output of energy. When we experiment for the first time upon any muscular action that requires skill, we find that we expend too much or too little energy and are obliged to readjust our computation of the amount of dynamic force required. Balancing, carrying and lifting weights, in conjunction with eye judgments, are largely a matter of experience gained through experiment of the amount of energy that will be required to do so. We must prearrange in our minds the exact force needed to overcome a certain resistance confronting us before we commence action. We are all familiar with the feeling of extreme discomfort that may be produced by disappointed muscular expectation, which at times almost amounts to physical pain, such as when we pick up a small article that we believe to be extremely light and find it the reverse, or, contrarily, take up a large object which we are prepared to exert all our strength to lift and find that it is quite light. Still worse will be the muscular jar when, in coming up or down a staircase, we make a false calculation of the number of stairs, and find one more or less than we thought; motion then ends in a sudden jerk, setting up vibrations that tingle over our entire body.

We know without looking how to move our limbs and put them into any position we desire, without being compelled to have recourse to the evidence of our eyes. Again, should we be blindfolded and another move the position of our limbs or body, we are fully aware what part has been moved and the new position it has taken up, whether it has been raised or lowered and moved to left or right, without seeing. We can feel what is happening. Not so the young child, however; it appears obliged to look in order to know these things, and needs the experience of its other senses to learn to know the meaning of these familiar feelings which are present by testing them by other proofs.

Fears connected with balance and movement are very common. We are told that another factor which affects balance, movement, and giddiness on account of rapid movement, or swiftly changing position in space, is connected with the presence and amount of fluid contained in the semicircular canals of the ear. This is interesting and should provide material for investigation, especially since Dr. Kimmins, in his book upon *Children's Dreams*,[1] remarks that kinæsthetic dreams are practically non-existent among deaf children. Yet the examples he gives to prove what kind of dreams are most commonly to be found among them show those of adventure and bravery, including feats of physical skill and daring, as well as those that involve movement in plenty, which we are told are especially prevalent among deaf girls—he supposes by way of compensation. It is difficult to know what he means by these two statements, because the two ideas are directly opposed.

[1] *Children's Dreams*, C. W. Kimmins, M.A., D.Sc. Longmans, Green & Co.

More light is shed upon the subject of the important factors of pleasure in muscular control and muscular activity by the old idea that to dance cured some diseases and the popular name for chorea, St. Vitus's dance. It becomes especially evident in connection with the dance and rhythm that are known as the Tarantella, from the belief that people bitten by the tarantula spider escaped the muscular rigidity and convulsions that generally followed the injury if they kept on dancing. Modern experience and therapeutics have returned to the dance, and exercises for flat-foot and sciatica are performed to the strains of the gramophone in the out-patients' departments of our hospitals. Thus music is again used as an aid to the cure of muscular inaction, providing, of course, an additional pleasure connected with the activity which has been lost. Miss Shires, head of the Massage Department of Charing Cross Hospital, describes wonderful cures of patients suffering from muscular atrophy after meningitis which occurred during infancy, with exercises that are carried out to the singing of nursery rhymes, and refers to other forms of re-educative treatment of muscles in those suffering from the results of infantile paralysis, carried out to appropriate tunes on the gramophone. These helped to gain the co-operation of the little patients in trying to push against a graduated resistance, thus forming a restoration of the baby pleasure in pushing and kicking.[1]

In this way, when we come to recognize the part played by the pleasure factor of the kinæsthetic sense, we may be better able to make use of it in the cure or prevention of disease, rather than to continue to hinder its free development by needless commands to the child to sit still and not to fidget. A child's imperfect muscular control, shown in learning to write, clumsiness or jerky movements annoys us, and we feel that this is evidence of naughtiness or obstinacy, the wish to be in the limelight or rebellion, and we scold or use force in consequence, rather than have our orders disobeyed by the child. This inability to control its movements may be due to many causes, but muscular efficiency is still far from perfect in the little one, and we are often requiring it to be proficient in the use of tools which, in comparison with itself, are enormous.

[1] *Advanced Methods of Massage and Medical Gymnastics*, Shires and Woods. Faber & Gwyer.

For instance, a full-sized pencil is about the same length as a child's forearm, and thick in proportion—should we find it easy to control a pencil about eighteen inches long and equally thick and heavy? The same thing applies to the difficulty confronting the child who tries to feed itself with a spoon out of all proportion to itself, or swallow enormous mouthfuls which inconsiderate adults force into the small mouth to shorten for themselves the tedious task of feeding the infant. Should we find muscular ability deficient in young children, we should do well to increase the pleasure premium connected with it, rather than to decrease it with scoldings and punishment. It will need more encouragement to lead it on, or enable it to surrender the jerky movements which will give pleasure in themselves, but which are a hindrance to useful activity. They must be replaced by different actions which will make the writing or other handwork more satisfactory. We cannot afford to ignore the pleasure premium in the education of young children.

Should we increase the child's pleasure in its muscular activity by the use of rhythmical movements allied to music that are to be found in the singing and action-songs which children love so much, a need evidently recognized in the past by the proof of their antiquity and widespread prevalence, the difficulty will be met and the child's balance of mind and body restored to a very great extent. We would also in this way be able to counteract the fear that is often seen in little children who are beginning to walk and who fall about in the process. Fears are often connected with the kinæsthetic sense, and it would be worth our while to examine whether our present lack of recognition of the part it plays in the child's early life may not account for their prevalence, and in this way discover how best they may be avoided.

We may also in this section call attention to another problem of child-life which has recently attracted considerable attention from medical men from a purely physiological aspect. This is the discomfort experienced by many children during the first ten years of life to which the name of *Growing-pains* has been given, half in ridicule, by parents and nurses. Modern medical science, however, has declared these to be first signs of rheumatism occurring in the child, which, they believe, need to be extremely carefully watched, since they may be either a forerunner of *rheumatism*, or even a slight form of acute rheumatism, or rheumatic fever—which is at present unrecognized by the parent. Medical advice and not parental or educational ridicule, therefore, is a more fitting way of dealing with the trouble, since the results may be grave.

The most frequently affected parts of the body in this painful malady will be the joints of the lower limbs, i.e. the knees and ankles. It may also be pointed out that St. Vitus's dance or chorea, to which we have already referred in this section, may be the accompaniment, or is usually the aftermath, of acute rheumatism, which in many cases lays the foundation of chronic heart trouble. (See also chapter on Childish Bad Habits.)

Parents in the past used not to take as much heed of these manifestations as they ought to have done, and at present they have heard that growing-pains are a form of rheumatism, but still treat them without differentiation, never pausing to consider whether there can be an immediate cause of these pains other than rheumatism, nor do they realize that their location is of the utmost importance for diagnosis.

Should the predisposing activity that gives rise to the pain be studied, yet another cause of growing-pains may be discovered, in this instance an emotional or affectual reason for the pain in the deeper muscles. It is by no means unusual to see little children being hurried along by an adult, with whom they are obliged to keep pace. Eventually, they may cry for mercy, and beg for a slower pace, a shorter stride, or to be carried because their legs are hurting. This pain comes on as a result of the parent's lack of consideration, and disappears frequently as soon as relief occurs. Sometimes the children realize that their unhappiness has been caused by the action of the parents. It is exceedingly painful to be forced to walk faster than is comfortable and in accordance with the child's length of limb, and becomes distressing when those in whose company it is will not understand this, nor give it the help that it needs. In these cases the pain usually may be found along the front of the shin-bone and in the thigh, joint-pains apparently being found among the symptoms of rheumatic persons. Thus it seems that we might be safe in postulating that the growing-pains that occur in joints are of a rheumatic character, while those causing the child suffering in the long bones, or their superficial tissue layers, arise from an emotional cause. The child is both annoyed and pained by the thoughtless and ignorant parents who are causing it so much pain and distress. When the child tries to put its case and win respite from the remorseless pace, the adult will frequently not listen, will often answer at random, and quite possibly hurry the child still faster, adding, to spur its pride, that it is not a baby now, to get tired or to sit in the perambulator and be pushed.

The emotional conflict brought about by the child's unsuccessful efforts to keep pace with those taller and older than itself thus creates these pains when this stimulus appears. They may therefore be treated by eliminating the cause rather than by a period of rest in bed, which is frequently prescribed as though for rheumatic joint growing-pains.

CHAPTER IV

THE GREAT GOD-WISH

THE IMPORTANCE OF THE IMPULSE IN THE LIFE OF THE CHILD

THE ORAL IMPULSES. THE IMPULSES CONNECTED WITH THE EXCRETIONS. THE IMPULSE TO LOOK AND THE WISH TO BE LOOKED AT (including the manifestations of Love and Hate, Sadism and Masochism, which are all to be counted among the Impulses).

A. THE ORAL IMPULSES

IN a paper read before the Child Study Society in London, 1916, and subsequently published in his book, *Papers on Psychoanalysis*, Dr. Ernest Jones writes as follows:—

According to Freud, there exist from the very beginning of life two separate systems of mental activity which constitute the precursors of what later would be called conscious and unconscious thinking respectively. One conceives the mind, to start with, as an apparatus or machine which can be stirred into activity by any stimulus, emanating either from without or within the individual, and maintains that the object of the resulting activity is always to restore the original condition of rest by bringing about a state of affairs in which the effect of the disturbing stimulus is nullified. The result of setting the primary system in action is to create a condition of diffuse restlessness and excitation, which radiates widely throughout the mind, and which seeks in every direction for an outflow of the accompanying energy. The tendency to replace this state of excitation, which is experienced as pain or "displeasure" (Unlust), by the relief of satisfaction, which is experienced as pleasure (Lust), constitutes what we call a wish.

It has already been hinted that out of the wishes of the infant spring the impulses, which sooner or later meet with some kind of limitation from those in charge: that this limitation may lead to repression or some other vicissitude of the impulse, each process having a marked and different effect upon the character of the child in later years. We may, perhaps, most easily review these several impulses separately, and investigate what may be learned concerning the results of the correct or normal development of each and the consequences of faulty training. This will give us some idea of the effects which stern repression may produce in such cases and in what ways the impulse may struggle for readmittance or readjustment in the conscious mind and life of the child during early years, as well as in the character-traits or nervous symptoms which make their appearance later on as the result of incomplete or unsuccessful repression, reaction-formation, or sublimation. Those of us who have the care of little children meet problems such as these, which need our attention, among the affairs of daily life, and it is hoped that the following explanation may offer some solution to them.

As we should expect, the infant's first wishes or impulses are connected with the nutritional instinct, the acquisition of food, and the most powerful and enduring of all wishes are to be found at this stage, those for the mother and her breast. The desire for food is always an impulse of paramount importance and will leave some of the deepest and most indelible marks upon the character of the individual, based upon the amount of gratification that was given to these wishes at the commencement of life.[1]

It has already been shown in the section on Taste how soon the baby may discern differences in the taste and composition of milk and mixed artificial foods, showing distinct approbation or disapproval as the result of its discovery. Research has gone still further upon this question, however, and has enabled us to ascertain with some degree of certainty that strongly marked character-traits may also be traced to their origin in the early feelings of the infant representing complete satisfaction on the one hand, partial or even great deprivation on the other.

Those infants who were breast-fed full time, for whom the supply of milk never failed either in quantity or quality, grow up contented optimists, always expecting, and usually not disappointed in their expectation, that the necessaries of life will come easily and duly within their grasp. They always wait hopefully to be supplied by a beneficent Providence, who they believe will bestow blessings without fail or stint, and are in nowise anxious to exert much personal energy or hard work to obtain these same benefits. They will frequently give as

[1] "Rudiments of Character," Dr. David Forsyth, M.D., D.Sc., F.R.C.P. (Lond.). *Psychoanalytic Review.* April 1921.

generously as they expect to be given; and if perhaps they may be apt to be wasteful of ability and careless of property, it is because the possibility of want does not shadow their mental horizon.

Quite different is the character developed by the unsatisfied child, or the one who suffered from unequal, unsystematic, or unpunctual feeding in babyhood. Here we shall find other characteristics—impatience, suspicion, anger at being kept waiting, at being disappointed, and inclination to indulge to excess when any opportunity to do so occurs, which may end in sickness in the child or other digestive troubles in the adult. Any monotonous and constant occupation or employment will prove irksome and laborious, and a gambling existence of alternating affluence and poverty will offer a stronger appeal, as being more exciting than a steady competence of regular but rather unadventurous occupation.[1]

The children who suffered great deprivation, as well as those who for some reason were weaned suddenly or very early, will show still deeper pessimism. A constant expectation of the worst life has to offer, that he or she will have to go without while others have a generous supply of this world's benefits, are character-traits that are to be found in the later life of the baby who was orally not satisfied with a sufficient quantity or quality of food. A constant grudge will be felt against those in authority that they are not fulfilling their obligations, and a tendency will often be seen to pay them out in some way of counter-deprivation, withholding something wanted from them instead, which will frequently be discharged in anal hate, to be discussed later in this chapter. These persons may afterwards long even for the most meagre supply of this world's goods by way of consolation, and believe that if only they could feel certain of a little, upon which they were able absolutely to rely, they would be happy and contented for life. They will be found among the most ardent supporters of the "Safety First" maxim, and are often troubled with a morbid dread of poverty or starvation ahead of them, although their actual circumstances are such that make this eventuality extremely improbable. They will, in consequence of this fear, show a parsimonious and mean attitude towards life, grudging

[1] "Notes on Oral Character," E. Glover. *Int. J. Ps.-A.* April 1925.

to part with any of their possessions, especially money, because of the idea that it cannot be replaced, which will be further explained in the next section.

Another characteristic which usually accompanies those already described is a strong feeling of hostility towards rivals, and the conscious or unconscious belief that some person has been the cause of their deprivation, perhaps the father or elder brothers and sisters; sometimes those younger than the person in question may be blamed for drinking up all the milk and leaving none, or the feeling is that the mother abandoned this child in favour of the new-comer. Among children such as these, where deprivation has played a weighty part in the construction of subsequent character-traits, we find wishes persisting in later years connected more or less remotely with the original subject of food, and afterwards transferred to allied ideas, such as benefits, favours to be bestowed upon them by another, or their "rights," which they feel have been withheld or forfeited. These things that they feel "done out of" are also influential in effecting the persons' reactions to reality. They are not prepared to accept facts, preferring the phantasy wish-fulfilment, which has been called the *hallucinatory gratification* of the need. This, however, needs further explanation.

The baby who cannot gain immediate satisfaction of its hunger will suck a thumb or even its own lip, a corner of the pillow, or anything else which may easily be within reach, finding in this substitute a means of "nullifying the wish" for the time being. Should this hallucination gratification occur without disturbing sleep, we call this the infant's first dream.[1]

In this way the baby gains satisfaction which prevents the necessity of waking, in which we may see a clear example of that function of the dream to preserve sleep.[2] The child who had recourse to these same means of temporarily appeasing hunger or gaining sensory pleasure will find in this habit a long-standing means of gratification whenever life offers difficulties or deprivations of whatever sort. Habitual finger or thumb-suckers as children will tend once more to find satisfaction in this old form of consolation or self-gained relief of tension at other moments of mental stress and conflict throughout life.

[1] *Rudiments of Character*, Dr. David Forsyth.
[2] *Interpretation of Dreams*, Sigmund Freud. Trans.

The reactions of adults to these childish attempts to restore the balance and supply means of self-gratification will be explained in a subsequent chapter on Childish Bad Habits. Usually the methods used to suppress them are both summary and severe, out of all proportion to the offence, arising from the unresolved conflict of the adult in question, where this subject is concerned. This thwarting of the attempt to regain a substitute for deprivation without supplying the child with a more satisfactory outlet will be likely to lead to serious trouble in the mental economy of the child, since life is not endurable after a certain amount of deprivation has been exceeded without some corresponding compensation to restore the balance. This requires consideration before any self-found consolation is taken from the child, and the reason for the need should be found, so that it may be dealt with at its source. Deprivation in the child's emotional life has consequences that are as serious as those which have lately been demonstrated in connection with the diet for the healthy development of the child.

When we consider that the natural principle of the baby is to shun pain and seek pleasure, to strive to gain its wish with every power at its disposal, we may grasp that our demand for sacrifice and deprivation made too early or too insistently is not only against nature but will have a relatively injurious result, whether it is immediately accepted by the child or persistently refused. Both may lead to abnormal conditions later on, or even at the time. Suppose the mother or nurse to be a woman of inflexible will, who has the strictest theories that no baby requires more than a certain amount of food, administered at stated intervals, and that under no circumstance should this regimen be modified in any way. Some baby in her care protests that this is insufficient; it is not satisfied with the amount which has been prescribed or found suitable for others, but the person in charge remains staunch to her creed. The baby may put up a long and sustained fight to gain the gratification it really needs for adequate nourishment and ultimately fail: what results may occur as the sequel?

The whole *oral libido*, as it is called, which we may call, roughly, interest in food and the mouth zone generally, will become repressed, owing to this early trauma of deprivation, and an unconscious hatred of the mother, or depriving agent, will take its place. The hatred may appear as defiance, pessimism, or the belief that it is doomed to failure in spite of every effort to the contrary, besides the simple reaction of hatred towards all persons in authority, which will sometimes be accompanied by the physical appearance of malnutrition throughout life. Worry of any kind in later life will be the signal for digestive troubles to make an appearance, and without provocation from external circumstances of a distressing nature, anxiety concerning the maintenance of life, such as we have already described, will disturb the peace of mind of that person.

What symptoms, however, shall we find in place of these if the situation is reversed, and instead of the struggle being continued, the baby accepts the privation in a willing spirit of martyrdom? In this event we find the germ of the character type which we call *masochist*, the boy or girl, man or woman, who unconsciously, and sometimes also *consciously*, seeks misfortune and suffering, urges others to deprive him or her of rights or benefits, and whose pleasure in food is inhibited or conspicuously absent. This type is a difficult problem in the life of the community, and may have an effect upon others equal or worse than that of the thoroughgoing pessimist, who is always girding at Fate. He or she will certainly have a most demoralizing effect upon other people in the environment, because this unconscious invitation offered upon all sides for acts of deprivation and cruelty or injustice will most assuredly find eager response from the opposite type, the origin of which we may also trace back to the infantile oral impulses.

This is the *sadistic impulse* of those who take as much pleasure in inflicting pain as do their psychological opposites in suffering it, and it may usually be found in those who, as babies, tried to bite, or actually did bite, the nipple of the mother, sometimes in frustrated anger at deprivation of the food they were seeking, at others from a sense of, or a desire for, mastery over the object within their oral grasp. It is a sign of fierce and possessive love. Love-bites are by no means uncommon in older children or in adults. Sometimes the impulse will arise from pleasure gained from the muscular action in the act of biting, and at a later stage of suckling it may tend to relieve the painful tension of the gums caused by the eruption of the deciduous teeth. An early memory of a woman, from the age of ten months, discovered by means of hypnosis, was of a smart slap on the cheek, administered by her mother for biting her nipple.

These biters of infancy will grow up children of a distinctly sadistic or cruel nature, frequently biting playfellows should they be annoyed with them. They are destructive, spiteful, and revengeful, as a rule, although occasionally genial and good-tempered between their paroxysms of rage, or, in the cases where the bite is a sign of great affection, the attempt signifies a wish to incorporate the love-object. Should hate, however, be the chief stimulus, these persons appear always seeking anew to avenge the old injury, which they feel was experienced over the sudden or hasty weaning, or some insufficiency they suffered in early babyhood connected with food. It sometimes happens that the biting of the mother's nipple has been the cause of the weaning. In some cases, children with this tendency may invert the cruel impulse against themselves, so producing a combination of the two impulses, that of *causing pain* now practised upon themselves, and of *suffering pain*, emanating from the self in this instance. It is by no means uncommon in such cases to find children inflicting quite severe bites upon themselves in temper or from the morbid pleasure to be gained from pain derived from their own action. Other children have been known to hit themselves or scratch their own limbs or faces because they could not go to sleep. We imagine that this occurs before complete realization has occurred of differentiation between the self and the outer world.

We may divide persons according to these oral characteristics into biters and suckers. The biters have already received sufficient description in this necessarily short explanation; how may we summarize the suckers? Primarily, they will fall under two headings, the contented suckers, and the discontented or never satisfied ones. These are the vampires of life, who suck until their victim is exhausted and then turn away disgusted at the failure of the supply; perhaps trying to destroy the withholder of the former source of gratification or withdraw with abuse and vituperation. The contented sucker, on the other hand, lives and loves, is devoted to the mother-source of benefits and naturally turns to all other women as those from whom favours are to be expected. These benefits will be received without question or hesitation, but the recipient at the same time will often be as generous in gratitude and thanks as the deprived child is grudging in acknowledgment of a favour, even when one has been bestowed. These persons who find such complete gratification in oral pleasures of later life are usually men, to whom food and drink and tobacco and all other good things of life come as a matter of course.

B. THE IMPULSES CONNECTED WITH THE EXCRETIONS

It is not only the oral impulses which are important in the early training of the infant. The alimentary tract is of vast significance throughout its entire course. Digestive troubles will disintegrate the mental and emotional life of the baby, giving rise to outbursts of temper or melancholy, in precisely the same way that we will frequently discover that an emotional disturbance will throw the digestive process out of equilibrium in a small child. It is difficult to say which is of the greater importance, or, in many instances, which state acted as the inciting cause of the other.

During the first few days after birth, discharge of urine and fæces occurs automatically in the infant as the result of alternating tension and relief of tension. It is to be presumed that the release of tension will cause pleasure, which afterwards becomes accentuated in older babies and young children, who may frequently be found to withhold their excretions so as to increase this tension and hence the consequent pleasure through ultimate relief in evacuation. In early life it is a process performed without effort and during sleep, entirely involuntary; then it becomes a voluntary process with a pleasure premium, but sooner or later the training adult begins to interfere with the baby's liberty and wishes in respect of this voluntary action.

Once more let us ask, what may be learned from experience about the effect upon the infant that arises from this enforced limitation of the exercise of its wishes connected with the comfort and pleasure of its own body, and what types or type of response may be shown where it is concerned? It is usually found that early and consistent measures, but not too urgent, emotional, or stern training is the wisest course that can be followed. Where this presumably has occurred we find little later evidence by way of trouble to give us any clue to what exactly did happen. "Happy the country that has no history," runs the proverb, and the same may be said of the training of the child. "Happy the child who has no outstanding neurotic character-traits to be accounted for by injudicious or even cruel early treatment."

We may frequently find it repeated that neurosis is based on phantasy and represents the child's reactions to unreal situations, or an imaginary idea in a child's mind concerning the attitude towards itself of one or both parents. But actual experience has shown, when attempting to sift the history of any case down to bed-rock, that the causes of the symptom of the child have been predominantly due to a *real situation*, some injurious method of training, an uncontrollable temper, or some other neurotic manifestation on the part of a grownup person, discharged upon the child, which has had this extremely unfortunate result.

The question of bowel and bladder prerogative, whether it should belong to the child itself or some adult, is frequently a matter of great and bitter strife, as well as much preoccupation on both sides. It becomes a complex for both, a battle-ground upon which both fight equally stubbornly to gain their own way. What characteristics are developed in connection with the urethral and anal impulses we will now inquire. Especially in this connection do we find that normal attitudes to the physical functions on the part of adults seem to leave behind no undesirable residue in the character of the child. These are usually most emphatic after a severe struggle with those in authority.

Where the gain of pleasure is concerned in connection with the contents of bladder and bowel and their evacuation, the interest and gratification is self-centred. The child in this case is dependent upon no other person for satisfaction, as it is when the gratification is connected with the oral zone. Therefore, when a second person enters the field at all, it is in the unpleasant character of a disturber of pleasure, who will incur proportionate hatred for this reason, with perhaps an increasing determination on the part of a strong-willed child to preserve the prerogative to itself. The weak-willed child, however, will naturally be more easily trained ; so also will be the one who is very much dependent upon the love of the person in charge, since children often feel that the bodily product is a love-offering, something given up to please the beloved person, who, nevertheless, will be required to receive it with corresponding words of approbation and praise. Should these have once been plentifully forthcoming, and be omitted upon occasions of haste or from some other reason, the child will feel injured and wonder what it has done wrong upon this account. The extreme dislike shown by some persons to do what they are told often arises from this source. The obstinate child is one who is fighting the adult upon this anal level, and will often be found to suffer from extreme constipation, which may be often due to the refusal to give in or to give up its wishes for those of the adult.

The children whose prime interest is concentrated upon urethral activity are usually those of an ambitious nature, anxious to master the function for their own purpose of allowing it to express their wishes or to feel thoroughly grown-up. They will frequently hold back the urine stream when desired by an adult to micturate at a suitable time and in a vessel destined for the purpose, and show their personal freedom in the matter by performing the function afterwards how they please, when and where they please. Should the training on the part of the adult become more stringent, the greater persistence will be shown by the child. It is one of the few ways in which the child discovers that it can disappoint or thwart grown-up persons, and it will sometimes take extreme pleasure in spiting them in this way. Adults will often respond in a fashion that must be gratifying to the child of this temperament by showing the most childish reactions when thwarted by a small infant, and not infrequently take their revenge in a most undignified way, when one considers the comparative ages of the combatants and that the elder is supposed to set an example to the young.

It is only through the child's own change of attitude towards control of the function that an alteration in its habits may be effected. If it gains an idea that it will be a more important person and increase its social status by doing what is wanted, or by observing times and seasons, as well as places for this purpose, than by retaining the promiscuous habits of the baby, and changes its views upon the question of the attractions of uncleanly ways, it will eventually identify its wishes with those of the person in charge, and so gain both points. It will obey the will of the other and itself at the same time. But upon this question many children hate to give in to another; they consider this the cardinal point of having their own way. They will believe that conformity, giving in to another, means weakness, strength being shown only by refusal to obey. Character-traits so formed in childhood may be easily recognized in many adults without having undergone much radical change.

The child who, because of too much fear of losing love or through too much pain in the process, is unusually quickly "broken in" to habits of cleanliness, will be the suggestible, easily led, and readily influenced child of the future, always ready to adopt every suggestion made by another for fear of displeasing that person when present, or ready to surrender to the lightest bodily stimulus in order to relieve its feelings in any way. It has no power of holding back, no firm resolution; an effort of will is almost impossible, or only made at the insistence of another; and although this may be considered a lovable child, whose docility is the admiration and joy of parents and nurses, those with wider issues in mind may have cause to fear that its lack of strength of character may influence its subsequent development undesirably.

The impatience shown by urethral children is familiar to us all. They will not wait for anything else, as they cannot or will not wait to relieve the bladder until a suitable time or place is found. Should they be called upon to do so, there may be an accident, attended with feelings of injured innocence and spite on the part of the child against those in charge, as if to say, "It's all your fault, see what you have made me do." On the other hand, too great severity, a too intense sense of shame and humiliation aroused in children by reproaches of an adult over these childish lapses, may destroy self-confidence and lead them to believe that they will always be as incapable of carrying out any enterprise throughout life as they have been with regard to the present childish propensity. This will only too often be the fate of the unfortunate child who suffers from bedwetting, from whatever cause this may arise ; but we will discuss this habit at length in a later chapter. For the present we may only point out that scorn or contempt poured out upon the child will do far greater harm than good. A cure may be intended, but it can seldom or never be achieved by this means.

Playing with the urine stream, competitions of skill in checking and starting it at will, directing it at a certain mark, are common enough among children of a rather older age, and should be dealt with cautiously, because unwise, hasty, or angry threats, or, still more, severe punishment, may do untold damage. These last-mentioned urethral activities will naturally be found more frequently in the boy than in the girl. The most important factor for her in connection with this matter is that the possibilities for convenience and pleasure where micturition is concerned are so far inferior to those enjoyed by her brother that she cannot help being affected by it. It is a natural disappointment to her, as well as a problem attracting the greatest curiosity and wonder, why this discrepancy between the sexes should leave her so conspicuously upon the minus side. Parents and others who have charge of young children would be well advised to realize this childish disappointment from the beginning, and to take all possible care not to increase the little girl's sense of inferiority in this respect. Once established, it will rapidly be transferred from the one subject to all others. One should also guard against exaggerating the little boy's usually highly developed feeling of superiority, occasioned by his possession of what his sister lacks. This double-sided pride and envy, which may each contribute to the other, is largely responsible for the conscious and unconscious feelings of hostility between the two sexes.

The power, which we have pointed out in another chapter, which adults love to exercise where children are concerned can find no more characteristic outlet than in this battle over anal and urethral prerogatives. For them it is the second phase of the struggle waged in their own infancy against a superior force. Then, no doubt, they were finally compelled to yield, but with a secret determination to fight this battle again, should fate allow, and this time to come off victorious.

It is an unequal battle at best, with opponents of such disproportionate sizes and resources, but it is easy to see that children who are forced to "do their durndest" to the challenge of the educator's vow to "break them of the habit," or "to break them in, break their will," are fighting for the preservation of their rights and personality. They put up a very plucky fight for the liberty of their own person, which at a later stage of development is taught to be the most worthy cause in which an English person may justly fight. But English law, which claims that one may protect oneself and one's possessions from the hands of a foe, finds little representation in the nursery, nor is there often any strong sense of justice in nursery administration, although the small child who suffers from its lack usually has a keen instinctive sense of its want of logic. "What is sauce for the goose is sauce for the gander" sums up the earliest recognition of this claim, until taught by the axiom of adult principles that this by no means holds good in their eyes, and that there is one standard for adult morality and another for children.

Lying, deceit, protracted obstinacy, and hate are the consequences of this unequal struggle between adults and children. The hatred which a child will show at being interrupted or interfered with in the performance of any action in later years frequently arises from this source. A loathing of arithmetic may be caused from the association of numbers with the nursery names for the acts of defecation and urination, Number One and Number Two. Anal hate is allied to obstinacy, as we have already suggested, and the wish to withhold and refuse any demand made upon the person, or a repugnance felt towards "duty," sometimes even of "doing things," may arise because of the early meanings of these words implanted in the mind of the child. Whereas *oral hate* throws down, expels, or destroys, *anal hate* withholds and drives back into the self, although pain may be caused through the action. Therefore the oral hater is more likely to wish to injure another as a means of revenge, and the anal hater will tend to injure the self in rage originally felt regarding another. *Anal love will be ready to surrender* for the sake of love, the surrender taking the form of the love-gift, whereas *oral love will show love by accepting* and wanting still more as a token of affection. We may see in this way the main differences in the disposition of children and adults in their reactions of love and hate, reactions which remain typical throughout the whole course of life, as a rule.[1]

The action of the pleasure-pain principle may be seen to a very high degree in bowel evacuation, both in the child and the adult. What we have already mentioned, relative to sensations of pleasure derived by the child through discharge from the bladder, is still more conspicuous in childish habits of bowel motion. One of the chief differences between these two types is the *tempo* habitual to these children. The urethral child acts and thinks with far greater speed, with flashing inspiration, while the anal child meditates and "works it out," slowly and deliberately. We see in each case the process of evacuation transferred to the method of the other activities, especially those of thought and speech. An additional reason why similarity is apparent in thought and speech processes is that the child learns control of its sphincters at the same time as it begins to learn means of self-expression in speech, so that the two become interwoven in the child's mind with many intricate and collateral meanings, all of which cannot be dealt with in the compass of this elementary work.

Voluntary control over the anal sphincter is acquired readily by those children who find a keen source of pleasure in self-control and mastery, and it will become for them a topic of the deepest concentration and preoccupation. These children will develop into persons who pride themselves upon their self-control and self-mastery, which they bring to such a point of perfection that they cannot understand how others fail to do so without being mortally ashamed of themselves for being so deficient of this power. The pride in their achievement, and the belief that others ought to experience as much shame for the absence of self-control, is strongly characteristic of the child who has acquired cleanly habits and his or her attitude towards those who have not. We may also notice, in connection with the self-inflicted pain gained either by retarding the stool or forcing its passage when solid, or even hard after several days' constipation, which may sometimes lead to the tearing of the anus, an idea of bravery through self-torture, and find a continuation

[1] "Rudiments of Character," Dr. David Forsyth. *Psychoanalytic Review.* April 1921.

of these same children a few years later, when they will be revelling in the phantasy of tortures of the Indian Braves, of the Martyrs, Inquisition victims, or any other histories of pain bravely borne, in which we may clearly see the outcrop of the sadistic and masochistic components just described.

The same play of backwards and forwards movement, release from check and then fresh withdrawal of the fæces within the rectum, is similarly indulged when the infant plays with its breath and the urine stream. Developed from the breathing play, we find the child who will take pleasure in holding its breath, or who does so in temper, sometimes until it becomes black in the face (to be described more fully later), or it will begin to practise this method when afraid. After talking has commenced, it is by no means uncommon for this same tendency to give rise to a stammer.

The anally inclined child shows deeper resentment of interference than the urethral child, and will take the most elaborate precautions to outwit unwelcome surveillance by the most carefully premeditated secrecy. Nearly all children discover that the lavatory is the one place in which they are able, permitted, and, in fact, encouraged to lock the door between themselves and the grown-up world, and take full advantage of this fact to escape there whenever they wish to be alone and unobserved. This idea of secrecy becomes attached to the function of defecation for several reasons. This product appears so mysteriously, to the child's way of thinking, how and whence it does not know. It is usually not allowed to ask questions about it, to look at it, or examine it. It is generally spoken about in a hushed voice, and should the child wish to signify to an elder that it needs attention of this kind, it must ask for it in a roundabout way, so that others can only guess what is wanted. It is then removed from the present company for the purpose with stealth, which all contributes to give the child the notion that it is some secret function, which will in itself add an additional pleasure premium for some children. But to the idea of secrecy is also likely to become attached the feeling of *guilt*, which shall be explained at length presently.

The child may also occasionally feel cheated by the training adult. It will be encouraged to defecate, to yield up the contents of its bowel as though these were precious, much wanted by this person, and that the *goodness* of the child would be materially increased by the correct and timely performance of the act, to which so much ritual becomes attached at all times in life. Then, once it is produced, the adult attitude undergoes complete change. The product is no longer regarded as precious; it is treated with aversion, even signs of disgust; it is called *dirty*, or the child itself *rude*, if it shows too much interest in what has appeared, which increases both the air of mystery and secrecy, as well as giving the child a clue to adult hypocrisy and the amount of disgust which bodily products may provoke in them.

In this connection we may discuss the effect of the various means adopted by the training adults to bring about the wished-for change in the child's manners, where the anal function is concerned. Some may persuade or offer bribes, flattery, or some material gain in the shape of sugar-plums. Others believe in fear or threats that they cannot love the child who is dirty or does not do as it is told; they will go away and leave it, will give it to the dustman, or use a mixture of fear and pain when the threat suggests a coming punishment. The child may be smacked, told it will be ill, or will have an enema or something of the sort.

What now do we find in the way of results in the subsequent life of the child who has been trained by these methods? First the love and kisses method. The worst possible consequences are to be found when the promised rewards are not forthcoming or forgotten after the desired end has been achieved. This is by no means uncommon, although it is not a pretty sample of adult ethics. But even when this does not happen, it is not a good precedent to establish as a life-maxim that nothing can be done except for hope of reward, yet this will most assuredly be the case if we train our children by these means. Neither are the pain and fear, threat and punishment, methods any more sound as life-principles. It is, in fact, silly to make use of threats which will not or cannot be carried out, such as giving the child to the dustman. It only proves to the child sooner than is necessary that adults are not nearly as truthful as they pretend to be, and to be able to train a child only through making it afraid we shall hurt it if it is not obedient is a poor expedient. The little one who cannot be made to conform to adult wishes in any way unless forced to do so, and at the last possible moment, after the pattern of its habit of bowel evacuation, will grow up a person who finds it exceedingly difficult to find happiness in life through its relations with other people.

The child who regards this self-made product with corresponding pride, a feeling shared by the adult in connection with derivative interests, predominantly collections of all kinds, the heaping up of wealth, often called *making one's pile*, will generally repeat, with respect to money matters, the same behaviour which, as a child, attended the movement of its bowels. Some will regularly and punctually discharge small debts, or make it their habit to pay ready money always; whereas others allow bills to accumulate, and only at the last moment will send a cheque after a second and a third reminder that money is still owing, and that unless the debt is immediately discharged more stringent steps will be taken. Sometimes even then it will be dispatched unsigned, which causes a further delay in parting with the money, and then, of course, not as money itself, but as a cheque, a piece of paper. This putting off until the last moment is the typical reaction of the child who suffered from constipation, when the habitual procrastination was finally relieved violently by desperate relatives or medical advisers, through the use of enemas, suppositories, or that once-favourite nursery medium, which one still finds recommended in astonishing places by unexpected persons, the *soap-stick*.

Such children will always put off any unpleasant course of action until some circumstance outside themselves compels them to take the final step or commit themselves so that there is no drawing back. They will be thrifty to meanness, grudging, sparing, and saving; keeping what they have, rather than exert themselves to gain more by their own efforts. The spendthrifts, however, are the children who in the past were more troubled with relaxed sphincters (usually urethral) and undeveloped control, who can never hold back. Those persons are also frequently incontinent verbally; they cannot keep any news or information to themselves, but run round immediately telling all they meet all they know; writing books, or spreading the little knowledge they have collected about the world in the superficial paper-smearing of the daily Press.

Children's anal impulses too early and severely repressed

find their return to consciousness through discharge of this kind in undesirable character-traits. It is a wiser course to drain off their superfluous energy and the interest which is attached to these impulses by safe and socially preferable channels, such as playing with sand, mud-pies, chalks, clay-modelling, plasticene. In this way we may give the child an opportunity to indulge its natural love of making a mess at an age when it is comparatively harmless. The conditions being then easily supplied and controlled, very little damage to itself or other people's property can happen. The children will out-grow the wish in time, and this stage being complete, are free to advance to higher levels of the same manifestation, progressing from sand to clay, colour-work, modelling of a more elaborate kind, building, construction of all descriptions; handicrafts, art, literature, or music may all be heirs of the childish anal impulses which have found a sublimation.

The last addition to this list of derivatives of anal interests, music, may need some explanation before its inclusion in this category will seem justified. Two factors must be taken into account, if not more. It has been remarked that a small child will show intense interest in listening to the sounds made by urine falling into the waiting vessel. This will often be carried out in response to some encouraging sound made by mother or nurse; and the child itself will also make noises to indicate that it has wants which require attention, all assisting materially to fix the connection in the child's mind of the magic property of sound with the power to produce it. Besides considering the infant's pleasure in sounds caused by the ejection of products from its own body, we must also include with these flatus sounds, as possessing an almost equal fascination for the baby. From these the small child will transfer its interest to water-pipes, cisterns, lavatories, pumps, as well as to musical pipes, whistles, and flutes, which is usually derived from urethral curiosity. Singing will denote an oral sound derivative, and the larger wind instruments, trumpets, bassoons, drums, as well as all resonant musical instruments, represent anal impulses and flatus sounds. Thence comes the desire to be the "big noise," meaning a very important person, like the parents, whose power of passing flatus the child believes to be in proportion to their bodily size.

N

Control of the breath should, perhaps, be mentioned in this connection before passing on to give a short account of the conjunction of sadism and masochism with anal interests and impulses. Dr. Forsyth, in his paper upon "Rudiments of Character," from which we have already quoted upon several occasions, points out that it is to the respiratory impulse (oral), and control of this function, that we must look for the origin of fits and convulsions in childhood which arise from a *psychogenic source*. This may be frequently overlooked when considering this important question in early as well as later childhood, and examining the possibility of epilepsy. He says:—

Psychogenic epilepsy thus represents a deep and inveterate unwillingness to face life, even the most elementary, and serves as the fulfilment of that wish which, as was indicated earlier, must be the first wish of every newborn child.

Then as a footnote we find as follows:—

It is only necessary to watch the infant work itself into a fit to realize how completely this explanation meets the facts. As its annoyance grows into overpowering anger, it drops the rattle in its hand (renouncement of the pleasures of the world), turns from the mother or pushes the bottle from its lips (disavowal of alimentary wants), holds its breath until black in the face (repudiation of the lowliest function under its control), and finally, becoming unconscious (return to vegetive state), wins the only haven that gives shelter from every vexation.

Thus in all the simplest actions which make up the baby's daily routine we may find ample opportunity for the exercise of its love and hate impulses, the interference of the adult motivated by desire for power, the resistance of the infant which moulds the character and strengthens the will or leaves the flaccid amiability of the docile child beloved by the masterful adult, except when this characteristic appears in relation to another in the child's environment. In this instance a remarkable phenomenon is shown. The masterful adult wishes the little one to exhibit absolute docility where she is concerned, yet an iron will, equal to her own, self-assertiveness and determination, in relation with the world in general. Now this cannot happen. The character-traits that we develop or destroy must be developed or destroyed generally, not in relation to one person only. Yet this is an essential in the principles of child-training which the educator cannot be induced to see or understand, nor to make use of as an educative principle, because the unquestioning and immediately obedient child is to her a *sine qua non* of existence. These folk do not stop to consider what has happened in the character-formation of the child and in its mental economy to make such obedience possible. We may well ask, Is it love, fear, or extreme suggestibility which has caused it, and what will be the effect in the adult life when this unquestioning surrender at the first demand is always in practice? (See Chapter, Dangers of Suggestion.)

Anal masochism turned in upon itself finds its opportunity for satisfaction in the cultivation of constipation, because of the pleasurable pain or painful pleasure experienced in the passage of the hard fæcal mass through the stretched sphincter. It may be achieved even more thoroughly by the pain and surrender to an overwhelming force when caught and submitted to the indignity and sometimes even physical torture which can be administered to a child by an angry adult with a roughly or unskilfully given enema, suppository, or soap-stick, especially when composed of soap with a large admixture of irritating ingredient such as soda, to the delicate mucous lining of the rectum, or by the introduction of air bubbles into the anal passage. Yet, if the child struggles or protests at such treatment, it is probably further punished for its bad temper, and if it submits, it finds a morbid and dangerous pleasure in the subjugation and surrender of its body to the pain and humiliation. This will probably lay the foundation of grave psychological trouble in the future; certainly it will fixate the energy attached to these impulses at a lowly phase and prevent them developing to higher levels of sublimatory discharge in creative effort or social service.

Anxiety and fear will generally be found connected with these primary childish impulses, fear belonging to the conscious level and dependent upon the threats and punishments which have been used in order to train them, but anxiety of a much deeper origin. Throughout life, any arrest that occurs in connection with the bodily functions connected with the oral impulse, the respiratory function, an urgent desire to relieve bladder or bowel which cannot be immediately gratified, will be accompanied by anxiety, sweating, the feeling of suffocation, sometimes acute hunger or thirst, dryness of the mouth, and the urgent desire to micturate, defecate, or vomit.

One feels that the basis of all acute and fundamental fear, that is, *anxiety*, is to be found in the fear of death, the non-continuance of life, and that it is bound up in these two ways, working backwards and forwards. We know, moreover, that if any prolonged hindrance should occur in connection with any of the primary impulses, oral, urethral, or anal, on the part of a child, or of the adult, death will occur. All are equally essential to life. The respiratory function is absolutely necessary to our life to-day; we must satisfy our nutritional impulse to some extent. The calls of nature to relieve bowel and bladder must not go unheeded; their failure to function after a certain time would cause death. Yet there was a stage of existence when we were alive, but when these functions as we know them were unnecessary to our continuance—that is to say, before our birth.

Thus we live in anxiety and a constant fear of death; but the dissatisfied child, at times, voluntarily retreats to the comatose state, which most closely resembles both death and the pre-natal state. In this problem of humanity is to be found the profound Freudian doctrine of the Impulses of Life and Death, which, however, are too intricate to trace out to their sources in this little summary.

C. THE IMPULSE TO LOOK AND THE DESIRE TO BE LOOKED AT

In the case of the impulses already mentioned, we have seen how first one zone of the body and then another will usurp the whole interest of children, and become the vehicles of emotions connected with the self in regard to the outer world, as well as a means whereby the child may express its own reactions to the stimulus of others. It has been pointed out that a marked prominence of one zone in infancy will probably lead to the primacy of that zone throughout life, as the organ which is most easily affected by way of physical derangement, possibly caused by psychological or emotional origin. The greatest degree of pleasure and its reverse, the most acute suffering, will also be derived through the same channel, so that it will become the leading zone in the life of that person.[1]

The problem which arises from this state of affairs and which cries aloud for solution is, what are the predisposing causes of this condition? Why should one zone bear the cardinal emphasis; what factor gives the bias of selection to one rather than another; or why, if all children equally undergo deprivation and interference, where the impulses are concerned, should not all be equally important in their life? Why should they not follow one another in some regular sequence, first one and then another; and is it possible to find reactions characteristic of all the impulses in the life of one person? Experience tends to show the orientation of personal characteristics gives a distinct prominence in the direction of one impulse rather than a sequence of several of mixed type.

Our next problem may be as follows: are we justified in supposing these differences to be due to heredity or to environment? It would seem doubtful whether either of these alternatives would answer the question with any degree of satisfaction. In the first instance, should heredity be the prime factor in the determination of a leading zone, might we not expect to find all children of the same parents with the same paramount impulse, or, in the second case, that all the inmates of one school or institution, where the children were under the same influence, should show but one tendency? Yet, in point of fact, this does not occur. It has been thought that in many cases the determination has been caused by some quite trivial and accidental occurrence, such as a forced weaning, sudden deprivation or a chance mishap, some trauma, which has set the whole current of the child's emotional life and its impulses flowing in one channel rather than another. This may be the case to some great extent in instances which have been proved. We must also take into account that in some infants there may be a constitutional predisposing cause to organ hyper-sensitivity, through which one zone or organ of the body will predominate in importance over the others, or be unusually in advance of the rest in development. Therefore, because of the precocious development, it will require more gratification, or one of a

[1] *The Vicissitudes of the Impulses.* Collected Papers by Sigmund Freud. Trans. Hogarth Press.

different kind from that required by another child of the same age. The greater the desire connected with one particular zone, the more difficult will it be for this to obtain sufficient gratification, so that deprivation should be estimated from the point of view of the precocity or backwardness of the child. Continuing this line of reasoning, it may be true to say we are *as old as our emotions*. In every case it is the emotions that are actually present, seeking the gratification they need, which suffer or cause trouble when they cannot obtain it, rather than those we suppose ought to require gratification, or that correspond with the actual age of the child.

To assist us in the determination of zone predominance, we must first inquire whether the child has ever suffered *deprivation* in connection with one of these major impulses, and not permit ourselves to ignore any because they seem insignificant, since a deprivation which would be almost or nearly imperceptible to an adult may be stupendous to an infant. We may also inquire whether any surplus *gratification* has been afforded to one rather than another, since this will make an equal bias in the selection of the predominance of the leading zone. This bias may easily be the outcome of the same or an exactly opposite tendency on the part of an adult, parent, or nurse, since an unresolved complex on the adults' side will tend to become reflected in the production of difficulties and emotional barriers in the children with whom they come in contact.

For example, should the mouth be a predominant zone in the psychology of the father, mother, or nurse, leading to constant playing with the mouth of the baby, pretending to gobble him up, the invention of endless baby games and fairy-stories in which the mouth plays an important part, if rewards and punishments are all made through the mouth, we will find one of two things occurring. Either the child will develop the same tendency to oral gratification or will develop oral inhibition, a horror of the oral cavity, its own and that of others, which may easily extend to everything connected with the mouth, kissing and eating, and therefore produce fear or anxiety corresponding with it. Why this should be so is because the person or persons in question will have carried the games too far, possibly because of exaggerated emotional discharge, which has been poured out upon the child, although possibly unrecognized by the adult. From this the child instinctively shrinks, as we may sometimes see a little boy or girl turn aside from passionate kisses or caresses from an adult, which will have the effect of making her or him avoid being kissed by other people in the future.

We may see, then, that the fixation to or predominance of one zone may be caused by acute deprivation, over-gratification, or precocious gratification, due to the same tendency in an adult, which might be regarded as a case of heredity were it not just as frequently passed on from nurse to nursling as from parents to children; some super-sensitivity of a special physical organ,[1] some traumatic incident, somatic or psychological, which contributed its part towards the stress laid upon one particular zone, and lastly, but by no means least in importance, the amount of guilt which has become attached to the trend.

This whole subject of Guilt is of the utmost significance where the training of children is concerned, and as an educative principle one of the most harmful. It certainly leads to widely diffused as well as deeply injurious results. In a previous section of this chapter we suggested that the air of mystery and secrecy with which the bodily functions are invested may possibly give rise to an additional pleasure premium in the case of some children, but certainly give an appearance of wrongdoing, which brings the child under the shadow of guilt.

We no longer burden the child with the shackles of Original Sin, as did our ancestors, but we cannot yet relinquish the use of guilt, fear, and threats from our category of educative principles. We make a child feel *guilty* for a lapse from cleanliness —we intend that it shall so do, and frequently scold until it cries, says it is sorry, and promises not to do so again. Which, of course, it does, when peristaltic action takes the sphincters unawares. Little children have very imperfect knowledge of all the premonitory feelings that the adult knows should be regarded in this respect. Again, we are expecting in the child knowledge of cause and effect equal to our own and blaming it for want of extensive experience, which in many instances is quite beyond its stage of development.

A too great emphasis of Guilt placed upon any subject will

[1] *Introductory Lectures on Psycho-analysis.* Fixation to Childish Experience. Sigmund Freud.

teach many children to use deceit and to lie, to spare themselves the humiliation of the scolding of the adult. Not only this, they know that a still greater grief may follow, their fall in the estimation of this beloved person or the consequent deprivation of his love. In fact, this threat is actually often put into words, and they are told, "If you do that, I shan't love you any more. I can't love dirty little children"; or someone else, perhaps the father, or even God, may be held up as an avenger of nursery peccadilloes. Then, in order to spare itself sorrow caused by this disgrace and loss of love, which to the child is really acute pain, it will lie or deceive the adult; perhaps, even worse, deceive *itself* about what it has or has *not* done, in this way tampering with its conception of reality rather than lose the love which is so essential to its happiness or its very hold upon existence. A child who feels deprived of love is hopelessly adrift without any anchor in the storms that buffet it, whether the waves be real or imaginary. The latter case, although always with some strand of truth running through the phantasies, may be worse than the first. We may find proof of a real thing, but it is more difficult to find evidence to assure us of unreality. This is almost impossible, because any proof that comes our way seems to show that what we feared is only too true.

Let us suppose that the anal and urethral impulses become invested with guilt, what, then, arises in consequence? Secrecy, lying and deceit, loss of reality. The whole subject will become surrounded with shame and false modesty. Denial of truth occurs, which gradually spreads until its far-reaching tentacles grip all other subjects which in any conceivable way may be regarded as connected with the first, while anything that may bear any resemblance to the original object of interest, in shape, colour, consistency, or in odour, all that might be called dirty, rude, or be a waste product, will be equally abhorred. The possibilities of transference attached to this sense of guilt are as endless as the sands of the desert and have been traced as the basis of many early fears, such as, for example, the child's usual fear of black or dark things. They are dark, that is, dirty or rude, and, one step farther, seem as though covered with this forbidden material, fæces, which is dirty. The idea of guilt and fear has done its work. The child has been kept from touching the *forbidden thing*, but the inhibition works so effectively that it will also feel disgust at touching any other dark-coloured or black substance, because this will remind it of the original fear attached to fæces.

A little boy in whom this fear of black was very strong gave evidence of an origin of this fear in the same source, which was also responsible for his fear of bogies, dark fur, and dark hair. It led to a strange preference for calling all colours *pink*, even black or dark green at times, because, as was discovered later, black was considered dirty or rude. Grass also he did not like, because grass sometimes had mud on it, and mud was dirty. If sheep ate grass they were dirty. *He* could only eat bread and butter; there was nothing else to eat. Did one ever have to eat anything dirty?

Life for him was surrounded with things that were unpleasant, that could not be touched, could not be eaten, played with or enjoyed, because they were or might be dirty, or had some black mark on them. He called a black hoe in a picture dirty, and seemed surprised that such a repulsive thing could ever have been introduced into the drawing. He tried to hide it away and pretend he had not seen it, in a hasty, furtive way.

This is a consequence of too much guilt having been brought to bear upon the natural impulses of a child by those who trained it, without due regard for the fact than in childhood everything is of interest, everything is good, and especially, when itself is the creator of these products, does it naturally esteem them as "good." The child estimates them as equal with the rare achievements of mature men, all equally possessing an idea of value as personal creations. In training we shall do well to consider the future and ponder as to the results of our working methods, whether the consequences will be in the main constructive or destructive; whether by rooting out this and eliminating that tendency we may not remove or too deeply repress some necessity for activity in years to come that would have been more wisely redirected.

Of all these zones that of the mouth has the mildest fate. The childish sin of greediness, or the infantile love of putting everything in the mouth, may connect it with guilt especially reserved for censure under the heading "dirty," but certainly of all the impulses the oral is allowed the greatest amount of gratification in childhood as well as in later life. Eating, drinking, smoking, to mention but three most usual gratifications which come under little restraint, are satisfied without incurring much guilt in a way not possible for others, unless in a disguised and indirect manner.

The Impulse to Look and the *Desire to be Looked At*, which have not yet been described, nor traced to their origin, may, although checked during childhood, find subsequent gratification. The active form, *looking at*, appears in scientific research, art, the theatre, or cinema; the passive form, *being looked at*, in the theatre from the stage, in the church, as well as in the duties of the professional athlete, artist's model, mannequin, etc. : all these are permitted socially without much change in their course of development from the prohibited to the permitted form.

We see in these last-mentioned impulses that few alterations are necessary before they can once more be enjoyed in the life of the adult, although they came under the ban of the adult prohibition in nursery days. But what of the others? Sadism cannot find satisfaction quite so directly, without a curious change taking place, the alteration in motive, although the act itself may be the same. To be socially allowed there must be some accepted altruistic or traditional motive instead of a social or personal one providing interest or pleasure to one person only. Thus many kinds of cruelty are countenanced under the name of war or sport, but we call Gilles de Rais,[1] the one-time companion-in-arms of Joan of Arc, who, in his retirement from war, found interest and gratification of the most intense kind in the murder of children, a pervert and a sadist, because his aim was personal pleasure or devil worship, which resulted in the death of the children. The successful surgeon may perform the same actions as Gilles de Rais, and find equal interest in watching their result, derived probably from the same unconscious motive, but his *conscious* aim is the improvement of the little ones' health or his own knowledge. For this reason he is called a social benefactor, yet the impulse to be interested in pain and in those who suffer it will have the same dynamic in both cases. Some modern sadists become educationists, and find ingenious new methods of controlling

[1] *Gilles de Rais*, A. L. Vincent and Claire Binns. A. M. Philpot.

or punishing children and forcing them to be immediately obedient. Some of these forms we shall have occasion to mention when we come to discuss the impulse of looking and the wish to be looked at with more detail. But unfortunately sadism gains only too frequent discharge in the training of children.

The masochist finds direct gratification in any persecution, and therefore is apt to espouse lost causes and unpopular parties. Physical pain of a direct kind is not so easily attained nowadays in this way, and so they adopt, as its substitute, being a martyr to some complaint or another, not of a very serious or painful nature as a rule. Moral or mental pain more frequently takes its place and may always be produced by an enlarged conscience over imagined wrong-doings of the self or others, or the opinion may be held that one's lot in life is harder than that of others, that everybody has but the one intention, to make things harder for that particular person. Self-torture of this kind may provide the masochist with stimulation as keen as the hair-shirt or penitentiary lash of any ancient saint.

But we must not confine our investigation of these trends only to zones that are allowed direct channels by which they may represent a vehicle for emotions derived from or expended upon others, a means of self-mastery and self-expression, in which may be seen possibilities for later interests, choice of profession or life occupation, as well as a danger-zone for subsequent disturbances or diseases. The impulses and interests attached to both bladder and anus are equally highly charged with emotional possibilities, and become still more strongly loaded with repressed effects, because they have so little means of direct gratification. They are matters which have become so heavily dealt with through generations of child-training that they are always obliged to find some disguise or altered form before they can make any satisfactory appearance in the social world or derive any gratification there.

The nursery taboos have been most stringent in this respect. The whole topic has been excluded from polite notice as "rude" or "dirty" and not nice, becoming shrouded in secrecy, so that many children are obliged to suffer agonies of physical distress as well as shame because they feel it rude to allude to such dreadful things and ask for attention to some of the little affairs of nature. They believe that it is only *they* who are so dirty and horrible as to need to do any such thing ; "grown-ups," of course, never being afflicted with such humiliating necessities.

We may gauge the depths of repression which have taken place in the lives of most people from the amount of embarrassment discernible in them should subjects of this sort come up for discussion. In the hasty turning away of the eyes, the painful blush, the anxiety to give swift assurance that nothing of the sort has ever entered their minds before, although they profess simultaneously that it is a subject about which they feel absolutely no false shame, they declare the influence it has had upon their lives. Or, contrarily, they may say that it is quite unnecessary to be constantly referring to it, but nevertheless it needs the strictest discipline in children. In such ways they give evidence through the energy with which they endeavour to hide the emotional investment which the subject has for them, the struggle that the initial repression must have cost. We are never so eager to deny anything unless it is of peculiar importance to us. It would not be worth while. We deny it because we are afraid that others may believe this subject does possess some interest for us. We may, indeed, believe it to have shifted round entirely into an absence of interest or even a hatred of the subject. Its negative aspect rather than the positive appears to disguise the opposite state of affairs. These people resemble those who will point out "filth" in the roads in order to explain that other people might be morbidly attracted by it, and then expatiate upon its horror, pretending that it has no fascination at all for them. If it were devoid of all interest, of course, they would not have noticed it; their attention would have been turned upon something else; still less would they have commented upon it to others as of no interest or with so much emphasis.

It is exceedingly necessary to study this attempt to escape from believing that, as a child, one behaved like a child oneself, and did all the childish, dirty, silly, greedy things that are common to practically every human being in infancy. The general tendency is to realize that it is both probable and possible in the case of other people, but to admit that one really did the same oneself is a plunge which few will take ; and yet, if only our repression or vanity were not so strong, it would only be reasonable to suppose that if all children are alike in these ways—and we have all passed through these same stages of childhood—we, since we were once children, must by this token have done, liked, and disliked the same things; behaved, in fact, like children and not like adults seen through the wrong end of a telescope.

In the oral, urethral, and anal impulses we have found a connection and attachment to particular zones of the body; we have described the impulses of sadism and masochism in operation where the other major tendencies are concerned; what may be now learnt with regard to the other pair of impulses which we have already mentioned, although as yet merely in passing—that is to say, the impulse to look and the desire to be looked at? We may trace these through an almost infinite maze of complexities, regarding them first with reference to the child, who wishes to look at all persons and things in the near neighbourhood indiscriminately. The other aspect of looking is that of an *emotionally toned impulse*, such as we have seen in the case of gratification of the oral zone, when some other factor enters into the simple process of nutritional value, *pleasure*, which at once places it far removed from actual sensory perception or a mere desire to see. Curiosity has in some way become reinforced with the additional trend, which is often closely allied to the obsession "the feeling of mustness,"[1] described as felt by persons suffering from this form of neurosis. The child must look, must see, in this case, however clearly it remembers that this has been forbidden.

The most simple manifestation of the impulse will be shown by the baby's *primary curiosity*, its wish to see, to watch everything that moves or has colour in its neighbourhood, by which means it will learn about the objects and their properties. This form of the impulse has already been described in the normal visual development of the child, but that which we may term the *secondary stage of this impulse* develops at a rather later stage of mental growth, and is very closely connected with the psychological aspect of what is seen and the impressions so made rather than pure sensory perceptions registered by the organ of vision.

This pair of impulses comes into play, in the special sense,

[1] "Treatment of the Neuroses," chapter vi, *Obsessional Neurosis*, Dr. Ernest Jones.

later than the others and develops in correlation with the growth of the ego-sense, since so much of the desire which impels *looking* works in conjunction with the wish for comparison of the self with others, to observe them and see in what respect they vary or resemble the self. Particularly is this the case when the child begins to seek for knowledge concerning the differences between adults and children, boys and girls, which, nevertheless, takes place at a far earlier age than is usually supposed. (See chapters on Dawn and Growth of Personality.)

This lack of realization concerning what is taking place in the mind of the child from the evidence supplied by its actions and questions is but another proof of the repression which is at work in adults, that not only prevents them from observing much that seems clear to others, but which also leads to misunderstanding the gist of questions and interests on the part of small children, which therefore appear aimless and silly. We often hear it stated that "children ask so many silly questions." If we had a clearer understanding of their real meaning, however, and were consequently able to discover what the child really wants as the answer to its questions, we should be able to clear up our own doubts in this respect, as well as those of the child. So many of these "whys" of children which grown-up people find so irritating represent natural questionings, such as, "Why are you bigger than me?" "Why should some folks be grown up and do as they like, while others are children and have to do as they are told?" "Why am I a boy and Susie a girl?" "What is a boy?" "What is a girl?" "What is a so-and-so, or why is a so-and-so?" form questions most frequently heard upon the lips of children, and they may sound so ridiculous that we may be inclined to reply, "Because they are!" in an annoyed tone. But could the child express more clearly what it wants to know, it would ask, "What is the nature and what are the properties of a so-and-so; and wherefore do we call it that?" The question thus formulated would be more distinct, but then our knowledge would often be found sadly inadequate in proportion to the knowledge required by the child, to answer the queries concerning the nature and causes of everything around.

The child needs to look and learn, and to ask in order to understand, and so to have its wonderings corroborated. We thwart this looking impulse very often, especially when it becomes linked up with any of the other impulses which we have already described as having fallen under a heavy ban of prohibition. The bodily functions nevertheless are one important section of life upon which the child's curiosity is focused, especially significant for the fate of this looking impulse because so strictly forbidden, and for this reason it will be correspondingly invested with guilt.

It is easy to tell by a child's stealthy, furtive glances whether guilt has already been connected with looking, and has thus been made an immense factor in its life—if it has played, or is still playing, an important rôle. If we inhibit curiosity, inhibit looking, we may also hinder the child's power of observation, or even impair the function of vision. It is possible, through guilt, to become *psychologically blind*. We all know the story of Peeping Tom, and at one time this tale was an educative principle, along with many others of the same sort, devised to frighten little children into doing what they were told.

The story of Peeping Tom at once touches two significant factors of childhood, the link between nakedness and guilt. The guilt connected with nakedness, or rather with seeing nakedness, is never experienced by a child until it has been taught to feel ashamed about it, a factor introduced with this connection into the story of the Fall in the Bible. The child probably experiences greater pleasure from this impulse, when the passive form is reached, *being looked at*, because of the underlying wish to attract admiration. This aspect of looking, being looked at, exhibiting its beautiful naked body, is a source of great pleasure. It loves to do so, as much as it loves the beauty of that body itself. It knows that it is beautiful and anticipates the admiration of those upon whom it bestows the favour of this view. Shame and guilt enter the child's mind only when the adult says "rude," "shocking," in this way giving the child the idea that to be without clothes is wrong, or that "looking" and "being looked at" are forms of wickedness.

One of the chief drawbacks connected with the establishment of Guilt as an educative principle is that it will frequently make this forbidden thing imperative for some children. They will feel that they must put it to the test and prove whether what they have been told is true. The feeling becomes so strong that it amounts to an obsession, and the child is caught in the grip between desire to look and the fear and guilt connected with looking.

Peeping Tom and the story of Perseus and the Gorgon's Head both give colour to the web woven by imagination around the idea that one may see sights that are so full of terror that one may be terrified into immobility. What some of these are have been explained in the section on Sight. Adults in anger, a face seen by the flicker of a candle or night-light, between waking and sleeping, bending over a child, distorted and out of proportion, due to the angle of vision and the sleep-filled eyes of the child, may easily cause alarm and give rise to attacks of crying and night-terrors. Yet we increase the ways in which fear may be bred in young children by taking them to cinemas, where they see in "close-ups" the faces of adults distorted by fear, rage, and other emotions and passions, which, besides not being suitable study for the young, will cause great fear and remain indelibly fixed in the memory long after the accompanying adult has forgotten the same picture. A young boy, now about thirteen, gave advice to an adult friend, a short time ago, not to go and see the film *The Black Pirate*, "if you don't like ugly faces," he added. One may conclude from this comment that the faces of the pirates had spoilt the entertainment for him, and that the meaning behind them went too deep to be borne with equanimity.

Many children suffer acute fear through being *looked at* in an angry way, and are afraid of the eyes of adults, or even other children. They regard the steady look or the fixing of the eyes as a potential injury, possibly because they read in them the unconscious thoughts of the person gazing at them, reminding one of the saying, "If looks would kill," and recalling the fear of the evil eye, which was a grave menace, i.e. the belief that a witch or wizard might overlook a person or animal with the most disastrous results, so that it fell ill or died. A great many people, generally considered well-intentioned, deliberately use this fear in children to awe them into goodness or passive obedience. They will gaze steadily at them with a stern or angry expression and refuse to look away or allow the child to do so, but wait until the fear has increased so much in the child that it will do what is wanted to escape at last from those torturing eyes. Sometimes they will make use of the threat that it is no use for the child to try and disguise some misdeed committed, because they can read its thoughts through its eyes, or look into its mind or heart, taking over in this way the divine properties attributed to the Almighty, a tendency we often find in grown-up persons in their dealings with children.

This doubtless is one of the many ways in which adult sadism discharges itself in a more or less accepted way upon children, and is a present-day socialized form of one of the perversions of Gilles de Rais, whom we have already mentioned. He used to take a keen interest and pleasure in watching the sufferings of little children. The child feels the gratification of the adult in this looking and reacts to the taking of pleasure in its misery, when it is powerless to escape or to retaliate. In fact, some children develop a habit of staring yet not seeing, blinking or shutting their eyes, when they look at people they do not like, as though to blot them out of existence. Sometimes when they stare it may be in imitation of the adult, hoping to alarm others as much as they have been frightened by the same act themselves.

We frequently find that children resent being watched while performing their physical functions, possibly because the adult will never allow the child to satisfy its own curiosity in this respect afterwards. Also, because they have been taught to believe it is rude and shameful, a process for which a scolding may be forthcoming at any moment, as well as for the reason that their elders may have laughed at the grimaces they have made during the process, or at their look of intense pre-occupation when passing a constipated motion. They feel that looking on is participating in their action and they do not want to share any pleasure that it may involve with another. Some children will object to others looking on while they eat, with the animal tendency to turn away and eat privately, or they will get others to turn away while they pretend to do "magic," and hope that the grown-up will show intense surprise at what has happened when he or she at last is given permission to look.

There are several roots to the child's dislike of being watched, but one is probably the simple explanation that few adults can look on at a child's occupations and activities without a ceaseless running commentary or remarks of this kind, "Don't do it like that," "No, that is wrong," "You have put that crooked," "You have too much paste." They feel bound to interfere and find fault all the time, so that it is not surprising if the child learns to dread anyone watching, because it will mean that correction for something is not far off.

It is also correspondingly true that many grown-up persons hold the opinion about children that unless they are constantly watched they will get into mischief, and that their prime object in life is to "go and see what Willy's doing and tell him not to." One can nearly always distinguish a teacher from amongst a number of others by this hall-mark of finding fault, especially when children come upon the scene. Directly they see a child, whether that one is under their jurisdiction or not, they will tell it that its hat is on back to front, or that it is a bad girl for getting a pimple on its nose, as though the little unfortunate had done it for malice prepense. The child colours painfully and looks exceedingly embarrassed, edging away as soon as possible, while the teacher remains blissfully content that she is carrying on her mission in life or unaware that she has worked this havoc, because her action has become too automatic to receive attention; and she goes on her way to find fault with somebody else. Probably adults are quite unaware that their chief subject of conversation with children is what they ought not to do, or what they should alter straight away; and that whatever a child tells them, they correct in some fashion, in accent, pronunciation, or sentiment, and then they wonder that children are not always as spontaneous with them as they might be.

For example, there was once a rather shy little girl who had a very fierce governess of whom she was much afraid. During one holiday the father of this lady died and the little girl did her best to write a letter of condolence. She had honestly done what she could to say the right thing. When term began again, to the child's chagrin, she was confronted with this same letter, with all possible corrections marked in red ink and all her childish attempts of offering sympathy criticized for their lapses from orthodox grammar. The child was covered with confusion and hated that governess from the bottom of her heart, also feeling ashamed that the teacher should make an opportunity for finding fault out of a family grief.

In all probability these fault-finding teachers were children who were always being found fault with, who even then identified with their elders and set to work to keep their younger brothers and sisters in order. Now they have found out a means of deriving gratification from their profession, which is the wonderful way that impulses have of finding some socialized form in which to carry on in later life, with the sanction of the community, what they were prevented from doing as children, because the conscious aim has been shifted. They believe that they are now finding fault, not to satisfy their own craving to show superiority, but because it is good for others to be put right and to be given a good example. Still, whatever the conscious idea may be which has become attached to this impulse to set an example, it may be reckoned all the same among the derivatives of the looking impulse in that form of being looked at called exhibitionism or *showing-off*.

To study the fate of all the impulses in the infinite array of variations that may be found would occupy a volume to itself. We must, however, content ourselves here with this brief summary of a few of the forms that are most commonly seen in childhood and later years. Those impulses which in childhood suffer most severely and become repressed, sink away into the unconscious and apparently vanish there, and become forgotten, although they will constantly be seeking to find some means of escape in a suitable disguise. They may escape this fate, nevertheless, by adopting a socially permitted form of disguise through changing their interest focus into the opposite manifestation, or giving it a strong, apparent altruistic colour. To the first of these forms has been given the name *reaction-formation*. Thus the child who was anxious to peep and pry, to exhibit its naked little body to all who pleased it, will become over-modest and a prude, or take a pride in the fact that other people's affairs possess no interest for her or him and all the time engaged, perhaps, in some form of social work that necessitates going into and inquiring into the most intimate details of other folk's private affairs. The cruelty that once wanted to destroy everything that was possessed by another, or to hurt all around, may be changed into some *sublimated form* which saves pain and bestows benefits upon the community instead of organizing world-wide deprivation, or shrinks from pain and becomes an ardent supporter of the Society for the Prevention of Cruelty to Animals or Children, or an eager Anti-Vivisectionist.

In the games of children we may often see the route that these impulses will probably take in the course of their development. For instance, this last-mentioned desire to look and be looked at, besides influencing the tendency to act and perform feats of skill or even naughtiness on purpose to attract the attention of others, becomes the foundation of many definite children's games, not only those such as "I spy," but those to which the name of "Doctors" has been given, which will be explained later more fully in the chapter on Children's Games and Phantasies. It is frequently stimulated by a visit to a hospital, a doctors' consultation, or a school inspection. One child will take the place of the doctor, while others in turn are the patients. When adults discover the existence of this game, punishments are meted out plentifully as a rule, leaving the children wondering why it is right for Dr. So-and-so to look them all over and not for them to do the same. When the wish is strong to do this, the game continues, but with the precaution that it is carried out with strictest secrecy, which is still more injurious, because it will thus be connected with guilt and occasionally some self-seeking of punishment, apparently for another less important action, by which to cancel the guilt caused by the game.

BOOKS WHICH MAY BE STUDIED IN CONNECTION WITH THIS CHAPTER.

Papers on Psycho-analysis. Dr. Ernest Jones.
Notes on Oral Character-Formation. E. Glover. *Int. J. Ps.-A.* April 1925.
Interpretation of Dreams. Trans. Sigmund Freud.
The Instincts and their Vicissitudes. Collected Papers. Vol. IV. Sigmund Freud.
Introductory Lectures on Psycho-analysis. Chapter viii. Fixation to Childish Experiences. Sigmund Freud.
Treatment of the Neuroses. Dr. Ernest Jones.
Further Contributions to the Theory and Technique of Psycho-analysis. Dr. Sandor Ferenczi.
Three Contributions to the Sexual Theory. Sigmund Freud. Mental and Nervous Monograph Series. Washington, D.C.

CHAPTER V

FORGETTING AND REMEMBERING

THE words "I don't know; I forget," are so often to be heard upon the lips of little children that one is forced to wonder sometimes whether they have not some further significance beyond that which we usually attach to them. It is not only in connection with events or persons encountered by the child several years ago, or even a few months previously, that the phrases are used, but the child will frequently appear to be equally oblivious of happenings of the previous day or of persons whom it has seen quite recently and knows intimately.

We may, of course, ask ourselves at the commencement of our investigation what is the span of the child's memory, how early may we expect to find it in existence at all, and what are the circumstances or events most likely to be long retained by it. But to all these questions the answer must of necessity be indefinite, to allow of the wide range shown by individual children in this respect.

In all probability we are correct in assuming that the baby is at first quite devoid of memory such as we know it. Through constant repetition, sights, sounds, smells, tastes, and touch sensations will become registered as impressions, so that they may be thought about when not present, which is the dawn of memory. We may be sure that memory is established when we see a child look around for an object or person who is out of sight, and hail such a one with a welcoming smile or a crow of delight. When, later, it will name anything or ask for a person or thing not in view, this shows that an image which can be recalled, expected, or anticipated has been formed in the child's mind, derived from the memory of previous experience.

The pleasure-pain principle, to which we have already referred, plays the chief part in the formation of memory. It will be the most beloved person, the favourite toys, which are looked for first, inquired after, and recognized. Those persons or things about which the baby is indifferent, or, still more, which it dislikes, will be retained with difficulty in recollection or even actively excluded from it. In this way we might almost consider that the infant's memory serves as a register of its affections, and we should be by no means incorrect in our assumption should we do so. This being the case, we might then find the next step far more intricate, to ascertain what had been the deciding factor for the affection, and we might possibly deduce that it was the result of some baby preference for one sense gratification beyond all others which had escaped unrecognized by our observation. The extremely early memories of persons or things connected with the first few years of life are usually *sensory memories*, and those which are pleasant will usually predominate.

With the growth of the child, memory becomes relatively more firmly established, more certain, so that it presents us with still more interesting problems of duration, vividness, and accuracy. At first one impression will fade quickly when a fresh incident or object crosses the infant's field of vision, which gives rise to the belief that children live only in the present and for the moment. For this reason it is, therefore, unnecessary to concern ourselves deeply with their joys or sorrows, since they are so fleeting. That this is not strictly true, however, may be proved by the fact that there are some memories of childhood which endure throughout the whole of life, both of happiness and of grief, shame and humiliation. Certainly there is always a tendency for the happy memories to be retained in consciousness, remaining ready and available for use, while those concerning sorrow or guilt suffer extinction by repression, so that they subsequently disappear and enable the child, when asked anything about them, to reply truthfully enough, "I do not know; I have forgotten."

This is the action of the pleasure-pain principle, to accept, that is *to remember, the pleasant things*, those that are compatible with our ideals of what we want and life as we wish it; to deny, *to forget, the unpleasant things*, which we strive to thrust out of our lives and to repudiate them. When children, therefore, tell us what they remember and what they forget, we may gain an insight into their likes and dislikes. "I don't know; I forget," may thus through interpretation come to signify, "I don't want to remember or know anything about that; I would rather not talk about it—the person or incident exists no longer for me. I wish to obliterate them from my mind, and should like by some form of magic to make it as though it had never happened."

The force and prevalence of this wish on the part of the child has been demonstrated in one of Freud's most recent works, *Hemmung, Symptom und Angst*. In this book such wishes are shown to be the cause of many hitherto unrecognized motives of child behaviour, which have generally been considered incomprehensible, and certainly explains what we have previously regarded as proofs of the unreliability of child memory.

Children who experience some incident which is unpleasant or shameful, who feel that they are not understood, try to wipe this out by forgetfulness, as we might sweep a slate clean with a damp sponge. It may, however, not have this result altogether —the incidents cannot be so easily eliminated—and they may attempt the alternative method of repeating these events over and over in the mind, and obliterating only those special features which are unpleasant, altering them into the opposite, changing them into the action of another rather than those of themselves, or arranging some transfiguring sequel which changes the recollection into one that is more flattering or pleasant for some reason. This we may call *Falsification of Memory*, and it is carried out to work the miracle so much desired by the child, to undo the painful past and to make it *as though it had never happened*.

We may prove this to be true if we should take the trouble to examine cases in which the memory of children appears to be extremely uncertain, and find that it is governed consciously or unconsciously almost entirely by the child's preference or wishes. A promised treat, for instance, is seldom forgotten, whereas a child will frequently forget to perform an irksome task that it has been told to carry out. Forgetting in this case is an easy way to escape from unpleasantness, and the child who discovers that the words "I forgot" are permitted as an excuse, when "I didn't want to do it" would meet with a scolding or punishment, naturally chooses forgetfulness as a tactful *façon de parler*, although its memory may be actually perfect where the instructions are concerned. Many children discover the diplomatic value of convenient forgetting. They may also use the method to avoid the tedium of being asked constantly to run errands or to give messages. The continued forgetting in the life of the child will in time serve the purpose of establishing the opinion that it is no use to ask that child, because he or she is so forgetful, and consequently the burden devolves upon another, and so leaves the first in peace.

Another general use of the expression "I forgot" is a sensitive child's final refuge from the persistent questioning of the grown-up person, an appeal for sanctuary from the pursuit of the adult's merciless refusal to let it alone. Many children feel this to be acute torture and rebel against the fact that a grown-up person can and does shut the door to any intrusion into his or her thoughts on the part of the child, just as the adult will have possessions kept beyond the child's reach or out of sight, under lock and key, yet denies all such rights to the child. The younger generation must have no secrets, no possessions or treasures safe from the violation of adults or beyond reach of their prying eyes or mocking laughter.

This is a question which seldom appears under discussion because the adult usually fails to realize it is worthy of dispute, but takes for granted that the rights of mental sanctuary should belong to adults alone—and that the power to probe the mind of a child, to wring secrets from reluctant lips, to force it to open hidden treasures for the gaze of our often unsympathetic eyes, is only right and proper. In this way the adult will find an outlet for sadistic impulses. The child is terrified and yields, or resists to the utmost, shattered with indignation that there is no escape, no preventing the attack, except, perhaps, by this attempted subterfuge, "I forgot."

Children's reactions to questions usually give us a great deal of information as to the habits of the adults who are training them. The child who shows resentment to all questions, and extreme reluctance about answering them or telling the truth, proves that most unpleasant consequences have been experienced as a sequel to giving correct answers, that it has discovered that it is extremely unwise to give information, because this usually proves to its disadvantage sooner or later. To question a child continuously as to its actions, or those of others, and then to deal out punishments, will have several harmful results besides that of destroying the child's memory in self-defence through the action of the pleasure principle. At first this takes place consciously, but afterwards it is carried out unconsciously, because we have also taught the child that it is wicked to lie, so that the forgetting happens automatically when escape offers in this direction. Another alternative to the results of forgetting will occur when we have made it feel that it acquires merit through suffering and gains absolution by punishment. For this purpose it will sometimes forget those facts which might serve to exonerate it from blame, and its already developed masochistic tendency will cause it to provoke punishment by its forgetfulness or to confess an imaginary crime, though a falsification of memory, so as to derive a feeling of justification by this means. In this way, also, the magic so often required by the child to reverse a situation or make it appear as though it had never happened may be achieved by the punishment, whether it had been actually merited or not.

Some children, when being questioned, are anxious to cut short this inquisition, which to them is more unpleasant than the punishment they know will follow, and accordingly answer "yes" to everything; or because they feel that it is the reply that is wanted, so that in this way it is an *attempt to please*, to avert disaster. Some, on the contrary, will deny everything, seeking by this means the same end. We are usually correct in assuming that the untruthful child has been mishandled, just as the forgetful one, these two character-traits being old scars which show the site of former wounds.

There was once a Headmaster of an English Public School who refused to allow any boy in his school to say "I don't know." This seems an excellent method of promoting lying, but he probably thought it would have some more beneficial result. A governess who taught a little girl, who later came under psycho-analytical treatment—the same, in fact, about whom the incident of the corrected letter of condolence was recorded in the last chapter—read of this plan and tried the same experiment upon her little pupil, with the result that the girl's memory responded by becoming suddenly swept bare. She felt that she knew nothing or was not sure of a single fact, if one did by chance escape more complete destruction. The terror aroused by the presence of an angry person, who shouted at her and asked questions which she could not answer in any way, led to the persistence of the utter blank in her mind, which acted like a safety-curtain, an unconscious barrier raised in opposition and defence against the anger and tyranny of the governess, who stormed while the child wept. The woman insisted that lessons learned one day *must* be remembered the next. The child would guess wildly in her misery and said the first thing that occurred to her, hoping to extricate herself from this predicament, but the blank remained. Should it lift in the night or during the week-end, it would come back directly lessons were resumed and the teacher began to raise her voice and shout at her.

The girl's tears and this impenetrable blank instead of the memory she had set out to cultivate goaded the governess beyond endurance. She saw only conscious obstinacy in the girl's actions instead of unconscious resistance caused through fear, and determined to break it somehow. Her sadism was discharged full upon the girl, and she sought by every possible means at her disposal to make her learn so that she could not forget. Lessons had to be gone over and over again, every spare moment was spent in returned work to be written out; refusal to accept "I don't know; I forget" reduced the child to despair that led to a dazed stupidity, from which the governess tried to rouse her by throwing books at her or an india-rubber ball kept at hand for the purpose of "waking her up." The shock of this sudden impact to nerves already suffering from overstrain produced tears which the girl could not restrain, so in order to ridicule her into abandoning the habit, which the teacher considered babyish, she made her sit with a mirror in front of her, so that she could see how repulsive she looked when she cried.

Before long the girl's health broke down and she was troubled with asthma, which was not cured, in spite of numerous attempts to so do and experiments with numerous remedies, until the tyrannical teacher had been providentially removed, having received the offer of a post in an important girls' school. This case was an interesting one, since it gives some insight into the pernicious effect that the sadism of a grown-up woman may exert both upon the health as well as the mental welfare of a young girl. This experience, however, had not been the first of the kind in the life of this particular victim. Her memory had already been rendered unreliable by another rather similar traumatic incident in her early childhood, increased by an already strongly developed propensity to doubt, which had been the result of games played with her mother, who tried to sharpen her wits by constantly taking her in or "pretending to cheat" to see how soon the little girl would notice what she was doing (see chapter on Types of Those in Charge of Children), and an interview many years before with her mother, which we may here describe in full as an illustration, will show more clearly than abstract statements how much harm can be done by unthinking persons to children through questioning them unwisely.

When this little girl was quite small, about six years old, perhaps, a sudden gleam of bright spring sunshine disclosed neatly cut initials upon one of the uprights of the banisters leading to the nursery floor. They happened to be those of the child, but also stood for the name of the brother six years older than she, but this was not considered at the time. It was the mother who had noticed them. She called the child into the library, took her upon her knee, and dealt with the situation as follows. It may be now mentioned that this position, which most children enjoy, was connected with mistrust and dislike by this child, because the mother never did so unless a scolding were impending or some visitor were present upon whom she wished to make the impression of a devoted parent. It always annoyed her, however, that the child did not behave as though it were a position she delighted in.

Having settled themselves thus, the mother proceeded as follows :—

"What have you been doing to the banisters upstairs?"

"I don't know—why?"

"Don't say you don't know—that's naughty. When you have done anything wrong, it's better to say so at once, and that you're sorry. Then I should be only too ready to forgive you."

The child looked puzzled, and the mother continued to insist that she must know what she had done, and she *must* say that she was sorry. At last, however, because the child obstinately refused to do so, and the mother was so positive that she was the culprit, she told her about the initials cut in the banisters, and that no one else could have done it, because they were her initials.

"What's initials?" asked the child, which annoyed the mother still more, seeing in the question only a ruse to gain time and a positive sign of guilt and deceit. The mother explained tartly, and told the child it was no use to pretend to be so innocent about it. She *had* done it, and it was no use to try to deny it. Moreover, she would not be so severely punished if only she would own up and say she was sorry. This came as a great shock to the child. Because her mother said she had done this, and because at that time she still believed her mother to be truthful, she was faced with the predicament that she must believe that she had done something wrong and had now forgotten all about it, or she had done it without knowing, like her brother, who walked in his sleep. This worried her considerably, but as a concession to her mother's statement and to get away up to the nursery once more as a haven of peace, she confessed that she had done it, perhaps.

Again the mother scolded her for want of candour in adding that "perhaps," and said how naughty she had been to persist so long in telling the untruth that she did not know anything about it. Just at this juncture, however, the elder sister came into the room, having heard something about the discovery on the stairs. She contributed the startling information that it had been the brother's handiwork with a new penknife in the Christmas holidays, and, of course, the initials were also his. She clinched the argument by saying: "But, Mother, you might have known it was Freddy; Sybil couldn't do anything as neatly as that."

On this occasion the little girl did not resent the implied insult. She was unmistakably relieved to find that she had been right, after all, and that her memory had not played her a trick, although, at the instance of her mother's suggestion and urging, she had almost been induced to believe she remembered carving the letters there. Still her troubles were by no means at an end yet. The mother, rather at a loss how to extricate herself from this awkward situation into which her hastiness and want of discrimination had put her, rounded upon the child once again, "Why, if you knew you had not done it, did you tell me you had?"

Once more the child fell back upon the old excuse, "I don't know," and at last, after a homily upon the sin of prevarication and lying, she was allowed to seek the refuge of the nursery.

We can see from this incident how fear may play tricks with memory; how a child, acting upon the suggestion of an adult, may almost be brought to believe what a moment before she repudiated rightly, and how memory may be injuriously influenced in this way for the future. That child subsequently found it difficult to be sure about things, because the mother constantly acted in ways that countered the little girl's sense of right and wrong. If the little girl believed herself, she was faced with the painful necessity of disbelieving her mother, and feeling that she did not act up to the standard she taught. If the integrity of the mother were to be preserved, the child must falsify or disbelieve her own memory. Because she had been told that it is wicked not to regard one's mother as the dearest and most perfect person on earth, who could not do wrong under any condition whatever, the only possible alternative was to disbelieve her own memory and to doubt that which she really knew to be quite true.

Parents and those in charge of children may thus most dangerously play with young memories. Should they have made a promise, or have been discovered by the child saying or doing something not in keeping with this self-created pedestal of perfection, they may try to escape from the difficult position in which they are now placed by a remark of this kind, "You must have been dreaming; I couldn't have said that," or, "You've made a mistake," all the time knowing that the child is perfectly right.

Children who are taught in this way to falsify memory at command of their parents, or that it is a permissible adult standard to say one thing when you know it is quite untrue,[1] for the sake of politeness or convention, are bound in time to look upon adults as rather less truthful than themselves, or begin to juggle with their own memory until it is utterly unreliable, so that doubt creeps into life to make it almost unbearable.

The obsession to doubt is one which usually may be traced to an early root in childhood, and we often find it inextricably bound up with forgetting and remembering. It thus becomes,

[1] *Psychology of Early Childhood*, p. 241. William Stern.

firstly, a falsification of memory for the sake of making a thing as though it had not happened or had not been said, in order to preserve belief in some beloved person, since to doubt is the only way to escape from believing very unpleasant truths, which must be repudiated at all costs.

We have already seen how doubt sprang up in one little girl's mind concerning herself and her own actions, to exclude the painful necessity of acknowledging her mother to be unjust and untruthful. Another child, a little boy, chose doubt also rather than admit that his mother could herself do that which she had taught him was wrong. It seemed focused upon a moment when in sudden annoyance she had said "Damn," in his early childhood. He tried to believe that he had not heard this, and argued that he must have been mistaken. Consequently he refused to believe or remember many things of the same sort when his mother did not come up to the level of perfection she had set, with the result that the doubt awakened upon this score spread to every other thought that he had, and he would perpetually ask himself: "Is anything true, or am I imagining everything, even myself?"

A second cause of doubt will be the longing for proofs of love, and doubts experienced about the love of one without whose affection the child feels life to be impossible. Rather than believe this love to be diminished, given to another or not so abundant as could be wished, the child will doubt all evidence to the contrary rather than accept the bitter truth, which spreads out like the little cloud which finally covers the child's whole horizon.

A third cause, both of doubt and memory failure, will be found in children of both sexes, because, for one reason or another, they wish they were of the opposite sex from what they happen to be. They will not believe that people have been right in thinking them boys or girls, as the case may be, and continue in the hope that some day the mistake will be discovered and all will be well. This will more often be found in consciousness in the instance of the girl than the boy, but it is by no means uncommon to discover it among a man's *unconscious* wishes, or as a cause for his doubts, just as the refusal to know or to remember things will frequently signify the girl's refusal to recognize that she is not the boy she longs to be.

If her memory, her knowledge of all facts, be weak and
uncertain, neither will it be necessary for this painful circumstance to be remembered, and so it is better to doubt and be
uncertain about everything rather than be obliged to retain
this painful recollection in consciousness. Falsification of
memory will in this way also be brought to bear upon such a
question. We shall find a little girl with a very strong wish
to have been a boy telling someone that when she was born
everybody thought she was a boy, but the fairies stole him
away and left a girl in his place. *She*, therefore, was a changeling.
Some day they would change her round again. And one will
constantly find her changing all sorts of things "round,"
especially her words, to signify the hope that she, too, will be
similarly changed.

We usually find that falsification of memory occurs to fulfil
the demands of a wish at the instance of the pleasure-principle,
and it may often be assisted through the dreams of the
child, which in early life are simply conscious wishes made
visible. The young child, moreover, is quite unable to distinguish between them and reality. Both have the same value
for the child, and for this reason many memories undergo
changes because they have become fused with dreams in some
way related with them. Since dreams are more closely in
accordance with the wishes of the child than the events of
reality, the dream will be superimposed and used to improve
the memory, to make it conform closely more with the wishes.
From being a true record of things as they are, or were, it thus
becomes a picture of things as they should have been, or an
ideal for the future.

In this way, as well as being based upon the child's habit
of connecting the *unknown* with the *known*, we may find the
probable cause of the child's propensity for identifying biblical
or historical scenes with the home, garden, or some familiar
neighbourhood. One child will imagine that Adam and Eve
ate the apple under the ilex-tree on the front lawn, and that
Moses walked down the sloping roof of the potting-shed before
he caught sight of the Golden Calf that was standing on the
chopping-block in the wood-yard. It is quite possible that these
Bible-story phantasies were originally the subject of dreams,
in which the familiar localities were intermingled with the

fabric of the story. In this way, also, the wish to have been a participator in these exciting events was realized, and instead of happening a long time ago and in a country far away, the child literally "brought it home."

The child will do exactly the same with any favourite historical or fairy-tale subjects or persons, and probably at first pictured him or herself as one of the principal actors in the drama, although this part subsequently eludes the memory, especially in the case of the Bible incidents, in order to conform with the requirements of reverence. The locality of the scene, however, is allowed to remain unchanged for all time and shows but another phenomenon of memory, which we will now describe in further detail; this is the *Cover-memory*.

This faculty possessed by memory for retaining one fragment of an incident while the major portion is banished into the unconscious is an important mechanism, and takes place in reference to the affairs of the day just as often as in connection with dreams. These cover-memories, as they are called, are the result of repression. All that is particularly unpleasant or uncomfortable in an event is "forgotten"—that is, excluded—and in its place, as its quite harmless representative, will be left some detail, innocently to enjoy a place in memory, instead of the whole incident, which would not be so agreeable to recollect.

It is extraordinary how many of the isolated, fragmentary souvenirs of childhood belong to this class. We may also call them the scars of our childhood's wounds of pride or ambition, love and hate, which have been repressed otherwise. Occasionally the mists roll back and more details behind the cover-memory will be discerned, which usually entirely change the purport of the fragment that was remembered hitherto. This mist of forgetfulness in which the greater part of our childhood is submerged is known as *Childish Amnesia*, and has been evolved by repression to shield the personality from the remembrance of much that would be painful to retain, or, being retained, would hinder our actions or thoughts from flowing in other channels.

In *Jenseits von Gut und Böse*, Nietzsche writes a striking passage which exactly describes what so often takes place in the human mind in this respect. "I have done that, says my memory," he writes. "I cannot have done that, says my pride, and remains inexorable. Finally, memory gives way."

It is exceedingly rare to find that people have any very extensive recollection of their childhood, especially of the first five or six years, and yet most of them do not seem to think this surprising, nor show any disappointment that they cannot do so. This is but a further proof of the completeness of the action of repression. The forces at whose instance the banishment was carried out in the first place are still in existence to-day. They sternly forbid attempts to lift the curtain which would disclose these ancient sorrows, although, should they now be brought to light, they would no longer seem to us as grievous as in the days of our childhood, since we should now view them from another angle. The emotions which were originally connected with these events would trouble us no more, unless they had been hidden away, surrounded by many emotions, which have remained there undischarged, until they escape when brought to consciousness many years later as fresh and keen as upon the day when the trauma occurred. This discharge of emotion usually brings intense relief to the person who had stored it away without being aware of having done so.

It is very seldom that we have any very definite recollection of the appearance of our relatives when we were very young, but a particular expression once seen, a special garment worn upon an important occasion, may be stamped indelibly in memory, and frequently play the part of cover-memories to something infinitely more important that was said or done by those persons at the same time. These significant factors, however, have become submerged into the amnesia of childhood, and could only be recovered thence after considerable time, patience, and trouble. Yet, although we may not retain any very definite remembrance of what our parents looked like in our extreme youth, we will often, when older, show a marked preference for those who resemble them, even if we should be aware that this is the reason for our choice and friendly feelings towards them.

Memories for places, animals, and possessions follow the same rules as those governing recollections of persons, but we will often find that in different persons memory will be predominantly directed by one sense rather than another. The academic psychologists certainly used to divide memory into two groups, and told us that people had either *visual* or *auditory* memory, which meant that they remembered what they had seen or what they heard. But recent research proves that each of the senses may contribute memories, although in this present stage of civilization we tend to place the supreme accent upon what we see and hear rather than upon the other senses.

In the sections upon Hearing and Speech we have called attention to the immensely high value that the child puts upon words, giving them almost the worth of reality, and the power of creation. Thus we find auditory memory playing the most significant part in the formation of memory, and for the following reasons :—

For those children for whom words or things heard are of prime importance, nothing is true, therefore to be believed or remembered, unless it has been said or, to the visually inclined, seen in "black and white." Following out this condition, unless one admits one's actions in words, or has put one's thoughts into words, even to oneself, the action has not existed; and if it does not exist, it cannot be believed or remembered. Similarly, if one has not seen a statement written in black and white, and if no one has told us about ourselves or our actions—that is to say, our faults—nothing need be thought about them. They also may be excluded from memory. This method will prove of utmost importance to the child as a benefit upon the one hand, but equally as a means of self-torture upon the other. These children may often be found to suffer even in their early childhood from obsessions and pathological doubt. They will evolve certain rituals, and unless these are carried out, the actions they concern will not be held valid, or they will impose conditions with a similar purport upon themselves or others. Such children will require perpetual assurance of love, assurance that they have really carried out certain actions or omitted others; their sense of guilt is exaggerated, and they will suffer from remorse for sins they have never committed, except in thought, and sweep away real misdemeanours by refusal to believe or remember them.

To remember is often to incriminate oneself or another, and the process, so ably described by Nietzsche, occurs in order to preserve one's self-love from collapse. We will thus forget all the bad deeds we have committed and remember our virtuous actions: whereas, in the case of others, we reverse the process—we remember their sins and forget the kindnesses we have received at their hands.

We will also find children who place intense emotional value upon the exact words used by people, remembering them with photographic clarity throughout many years, or reproducing them with startling accuracy should occasion require after lapse of decades, usually to insist upon the keeping of a promise long since forgotten by the other contracting party to prove some present inaccuracy, or to show that the other person has misled them or done them some injury. This photographic remembering usually represents a sign that the child is seeking revenge upon a grown-up person who is felt to be the cause of some great unhappiness, misunderstanding, or injury, and proves the child has been waiting to settle the debt and to demand full price as restitution, as well as to demonstrate that the harm done or the injustice experienced has never been forgotten. At the same time we may see in this character-trait evidence of the influence of some adult who has repudiated promises, who has gone back upon his or her word and may, nevertheless, have laid strict injunctions upon the little one that all promises must be kept, and the truth told under all circumstances. This clear memory of the child in carefully storing actual words also gives evidence of an original deep trust in adults that has subsequently been shattered and an attempt to bring the perfidy of broken promises or untruth home to them.

It is from childish reactions such as these that we may see how characters are developed from the actions of the adults who were in charge of their education. The child who tries to reverse some unwished-for event, to make it as though it had never happened, becomes equally emphatic with regard to the spoken word. The Arab proverb, "There are three things that come not back, the Sped Arrow, the Past Action, and the Spoken Word," tells us the same tale, reiterated by Omar Khayyám in the well-known lines:—

> The Moving Finger writes, and having writ, moves on,
> Nor all thy piety nor wit may lure it back to cancel half a line,
> Nor all thy tears wash out a word of it,

The obsessional child will often work itself into a state bordering on frenzy because of something said or unsaid: "If only someone had or had not said just that," "If only I had not said that," "If only another word had been spoken; if only that could be forgotten, obliterated." But in spite of these wishes it remains seared into the memory, unless it, together with its attendant emotion, is forced down into the Unconscious, leaving to mark the place of its disappearance some ritual of reversal, some cover-memory, symptom, or inhibition, often connected with speech, the omission of certain words or a compulsion to use others.

The idea of guilt will become connected with this idea in the mind of persons, especially of those belonging to a former generation. Sins and their record, which were as unalterable or more so than the spoken word, were inevitably connected with the Great Book which it was believed God would open upon the Day of Judgment, and upon which depended the reward of Heaven or the penalty of Hell. Many children of the past, and no doubt some even in the present, are shadowed by this overhanging dread, and consequently, either consciously or unconsciously, devise methods of self-punishment in order to escape ultimate retribution in the world to come by illness, misfortune, or refusal to participate in any of life's pleasures.

The child who is obsessed with the idea of guilt, with the fear of eternal or even temporal punishment, will frequently be afflicted with a feeling that it must confess all its sins and wrong-doings to parents, worry that it has forgotten to do so or that it has given a false impression, or glossed over its crimes so that it has been forgiven under false pretences, perhaps believes that it may have done wrong unawares, possibly in some dreamy state about which it knows nothing, similar to the idea of the child who was accused of cutting her initials on the banisters. A further explanation of this aspect of the child's feeling of guilt will be given when we come to discuss Childish Bad Habits, but we may be sure of one thing, extreme self-consciousness of sin is the result of teaching, some drastic attempt to make the child feel the burden of sin in early years out of all proportion with the misdeeds of childhood and not compatible with a healthy mental development of the child for the reasons we have given.

Forgetting in emotional crises, the entire absence of memory following a mental shock or physical injury, occurs in childhood as well as in later life. It would seem as though the mind, quite unable to endure increasing cumulative emotional stimulation, or find discharge for its mental pain, suddenly insulates it by interposing a blank between itself and further attack by a varied series of conditions which might be described as merely a dazed condition, or vagueness, while those of deeper intensity are *the fugue*, or actual unconsciousness. During these conditions actions may be carried out and words spoken of which the person has no subsequent recollection, although cases in plenty have been known when the lost events and memory itself have been recovered afterwards by hypnosis and other methods.

The condition known as *fugue*, which often occurs in those children who run away from home or school, will happen in instances of unbearable strain to the boy or girl. One who is intensely unhappy at home or school will disappear, to be found afterwards miles from home or the school, either wandering aimlessly and taken by the police to the police station, to be returned later to the parents, or happily ensconced in the house of relatives, or the home, having, it seems, arrived there miraculously, without knowing how he came, which way he had taken, or how he had known the road to take. An impulse to go away from the place so hated, or the person from whom escape must be made at all cost, should the child feel that it was quite unloved in the present environment and wish to find those who love it, drove it to run blindly on without considering either the consequences of its action or the possibilities of dangers ahead. This state is one in which many child suicides are committed, when an impulse is carried out without consideration or forethought, one idea only being known or realized at that time, which is to get away from the unbearable condition. This subject will receive still further explanation in the chapter upon Children's Games and Phantasies.

The child who realizes that it does perform actions in this way, or one who is given to sleep-walking, which is closely connected with the state known as *fugue*, which we have just described, may become exceedingly alarmed about itself, or be frightened purposely by adults as a method of "breaking it of the habit." This sometimes will happen inadvertently through the child having heard its elders talking of the symptom as one that shows a deranged mind or something of this kind. This fear on the part of the child will then most probably serve to make the condition more frequent, since in all cases it will generally be found to arise from mental worry, overwork, or anxiety connected with home conditions, or difficulties at school which are in need of inquiry and investigation.

For the child to realize that these blanks occur in its mind or memory will be alarming in itself, and cause them to become a bogy of extremely formidable proportions, so that the blank, which was originally a safeguard to protect the mind from some other impression which was untenable, now becomes in itself equally terrifying, since it is so strange and baffling.

A blank, the non-existence of something expected or desired, is in itself alarming to the child. In the same way a child regards a person who *fails* to do or say something pleasant as guilty of having done it an injury. The *absence of the pleasant action* is taken as the *presence of an unpleasant one*, rather than a negative, a blank, a non-performance, and will be reckoned against that person as an adequate cause of dislike. This, most probably, is closely connected with the pain experienced by the infant at the absence of the mother, which is taken as a diminution of her love, a confusion usually occurring between the seen presence and felt love. Freud, in the book mentioned earlier in this chapter, *Hemmung, Symptom und Angst*, shows this first fear of the baby, to be unable to see the mother, the prototype of all subsequent fears. It is, after all, the negative which has produced the fear, an absence of a loved person, rather than a presence of an alarming object which is the cause of the trouble, the lack of the protection, the absence of a surrounding defence from danger, which is the central point of the agony. The child will feel itself a small, isolated unit, when it would prefer to feel a central point surrounded by protection. The blank, the space, is conceived by the infant as a positive unpleasant thing, the equivalent of pain and fear. There is no idea of a negative in the mind of a baby, unless it is represented by this feeling of nothingness.

The child may respond by crying, which would have the

useful purpose of recalling the mother, or suffer from a deeper, silent fear, which itself causes an emotional, dazed condition that acts as the insulation placed between the fear and the self and so produces forgetfulness. This, however, means emotion without discharge. No outlet occurs which may cancel the dazed state, which may therefore continue to increase until it becomes actual unconsciousness caused by fear, akin to the amnesia of the adult, which will follow a serious accident or the condition known as Shock, owing to which it is possible for the people to lose their lives. Death, nevertheless, is a permanent unconsciousness.

The child discovers that it can banish events or unpleasant thoughts by excluding them from mind, and also that it may recall them by thinking and talking of them; that as long as it continues to think or talk of any subject it exists, and, contrarily, it will feel that when the object is not thought of or spoken about, it has gone for ever. In this way the child will often come to believe that words, thoughts, memory, and existence are to some extent identical, certainly that they are interrelated. It will seem that the factor which controls everything is the *word*, whether thought or spoken, and wishes are important that have been put into words, because they are more easily remembered by this means.

Following this logical sequence, the child believes that as long as it remembers things or people in words, it will retain them more concretely than by mere abstract memories. It is as though the child believed that the thought put into definite words could not only recall the memory of the shape, colour, and fragrance of last summer's flowers, but the actual blossoms themselves. It may also transfer this idea to places and persons, toys, or even itself, and question whether they or itself will cease to exist if out of sight, out of mind and memory. It will wonder whether it ceases to exist if or when others leave off thinking of it and loving it, just as when it was small it used to look round to find things that were out of sight, wondering if they had disappeared for ever, or showing that it believed itself invisible when its eyes were closed or its head hidden.

The eyes, the head, thoughts, and existence are readily identified in the child's mind. The eyes are in the head, the gateway to the storehouse of memory, which it locates in its head; and it feels that certainly this is where all the things it thinks about or remembers are. Sometimes we may hear a child pathetically asking people to take some of the thoughts out of its head, because it is too full and ready to burst, should it be suffering from headache or worrying over some problem that it cannot solve. In this connection they will occasionally feel that if they were able to roll their eyes right round in their heads, it would then be possible to look inside and see their own thoughts. It would be like a peep-show, where some of the scenes were pleasant, some of them unpleasant, but all were exciting. These children will find out that they can recall old incidents or scenes by shutting their eyes and, as they term it, "thinking themselves back." This feeling that the sights seen by the eyes may be subjective will gain corroboration from the fact that the child sees visual images that are denied by others, which have already been described in the section on Sight.

The idea of keeping persons or things in one's head or memory, or that while one thinks of others they continue to exist, naturally enough includes the opposite thought. We ourselves only exist as long as others think of us. If people forget us we die. If they die and we exist only in their thoughts, what will then happen to us—shall we die, too? These thoughts are usually precipitated in the child's mind by the death of some near relative, a favourite of whom the child in question may have been. It will prove a serious hindrance to mental development should he or she be already inclined to attach great importance to words, and the creation of objects by words, as well as phantasies connected with the eyes.

Some children will definitely think that the eyes create what they see, or that there is a tiny creature standing inside them on tiptoe peeping out of their eyes. Others believe that they exist in the eyes of other people, having noticed and been particularly interested in the reflection of themselves in the eyes of other people, upon whose lap they were sitting at the time. Should this person die, they wonder what will happen to them. Their image will be extinguished, that is certain—so, too, they fear will be their personality as it exists in the thoughts or opinion of others, especially if this person should die. A mother once, being vexed with her little son, told him that if he continued to be so tiresome or careless she would not think anything of him. Almost in tears, he replied, "Oh, Mummy, I can't bear you not to think *anything* of me," giving one the impression that this would materially affect his personality in some way, or that his existence would be to some extent imperilled by the discontinuance of his mother's thought where he was concerned.

The idea that some part of them ceases to be because somebody thinks less of them becomes translated in the child's mind into the idea that there would be progressively less to think about, they would dwindle in actuality as the thought-image faded away. The reverse idea will also be found. One little girl built up several phantasies of this kind because of a household saying in her family to mean a long time ago, which was, "before you were born or thought of." She took this to mean that the united thoughts of her parents had been responsible for her birth, and that she would continue to exist as long as they continued to think of her. Should she make them angry, they might exclude her from their thoughts, and this would lead to her dissolution. The saying "somebody's thinking about you," connected with a burning sensation in the ears, added to her belief. She felt that the thought of another could make one become aware of oneself in this way, and the becoming aware was equivalent to coming into existence, similar to the child's noticing the objects in a picture when they are pointed out, which was explained in the section on Sight. She had the same idea about God, and believed that He could destroy her by thought or by cessation of thought. This supreme value placed upon thoughts has been called by Ferenczi *omnipotence of thought*, and is akin to the magic practised by primitive peoples by spells, incantations, or death-wishes, which has been found to survive in a great number of children.

The thoughts concerning the child in the mind of the adults around it are of the utmost importance for its development in many ways, but especially for character-formation, as we shall examine more fully in a subsequent chapter on the Growth of Personality. The child will consciously try to live up to the opinion of others, particularly those in authority. If that opinion be good, the child will find encouragement and help in it; should, however, the child feel that little is expected of it, and that little bad, it will strive equally to carry out this expectation, in which case the death or removal from the child's neighbourhood of the person who was expecting small achievements or, worse still, bad behaviour, would be an advantage. It is as well occasionally to inquire of ourselves what our opinion is of the children in our care, and to think seriously whether this may be influencing them dangerously. Whenever we find ourselves saying with confidence, "I knew that would happen—I felt it coming," when a child has done something we consider stupid or naughty, it is time to realize that our thoughts may have a suggestive influence upon the child or our actions may provoke certain behaviour without our being aware of this inevitable result.

In this belief of the child concerning survival through memory or thought we see, not only the child's idea of the concrete value of the word, but one of the roots for the desire for children among many peoples and races, in order that the memory of the fathers may be kept alive through the prayers of their children, especially the sons, and that they may thus live in the thoughts and the words of their descendants.

BOOKS USED IN THE PREPARATION OF THIS CHAPTER.

Hemmung, Symptom und Angst. Sigmund Freud.
Psychopathology of Everyday Life. Trans. Sigmund Freud.
Papers on Psycho-analysis. Dr. Ernest Jones.
Further Contributions to the Theory and Technique of Psycho-analysis.
    Dr. Sandor Ferenczi.
Jenseits von Gut und Böse. Neitzsche.

CHAPTER VI

THE DANGERS OF SUGGESTION

IT is by no means uncommon at the present day to find parents, nurses, teachers—all who have the care of little children—advised to make use of suggestion amongst their training methods—without any particulars being given how this should be carried out, in what cases it may be successful and in which it would be inadvisable, if not dangerous; what are the favourable and unfavourable signs for which to watch, so that we may know whether it is wise to proceed, or still wiser to discontinue, and how it may affect all the persons concerned should it prove injurious, as may easily be possible.

So much suggestion is practised in the daily intercourse of all people without recognition or without studying its results that we are apt to consider conscious suggestion must always have only those results for which we are striving. We have already postulated that the history of child education is largely a record of the various methods from primitive times to the present day by which power can be gained over the child, of making it surrender to our will and wishes, so that our trouble in the process may be minimized. In the scientific use of suggestion, apart from that which is natural and instinctive, and which has always existed in the up-bringing of children, we find a fresh application at work, which we might well call "new lamps for old." The motive of gaining the maximum control with the minimum effort is the same, but the means used, that of up-to-date psychological science in order to gain power over the child, is new. The point that is often overlooked is that it is practised not for the good of the child alone, but also for the sake of our own profit in a great many ways.

The author of that little book *Our Enemy the Child*, Agnes de Lima, with remarkable and unusual perspicacity has laid bare in her title a frequent attitude of the adult towards the younger generation, but one which appears the direct antithesis of the usual sentiments of grown-up persons towards their juniors which generally find utterance in books of this kind.

Among the motives for suggestion which are put forward publicly we seldom, if ever, find that of saving ourselves trouble, and yet, should it be successful, the plan does save the adult a good deal. If merely by the repetition of a few words daily, or by further development of that labour-saving device, teaching the child to use *auto-suggestion*, we can economize infinite time, anxiety, and energy in making the child conform to our opinions and wishes, we can also derive considerable satisfaction from the feeling what wonderful people we are to work such miracles and have children obeying our slightest wish.

We do not often consider, however, that to cultivate the suggestibility of the child, which is usually very great in any case without training, we are once more, only this time deliberately, insisting upon the blind obedience enforced by the last generation, although under a new name. Instead of Conscience being installed as a watchdog in the past, instruction is given to the child in the habit of auto-suggestion, in the service of becoming "better (morally, according to our own standards) every day." This will take the place of *conscience* in carrying out the same function with extraordinary severity or vigour, which in the past was derived from parental oughts and don'ts or the traditional maxims of right and wrong. (See Chapter, "Growth of the Personality.") These suggestions or prohibitions in course of time become incorporated into the Ego, and are believed to be as unchanging and binding as any other law of ancient times. They may also be juggled with by all the arts of forgetting and falsification of memory that can be brought into its service by a child who wishes to evade parental enforcement of discipline of a too high standard before the character can assimilate it, or before any adequate compensatory motive is offered as a counterweight of the sacrifice of pleasure that is inevitable in order to carry out such a process before its time.

In Gertrude Mayo's small volume, *Coué for Children*, we are presented with a most adulatory account of all the benefits that suggestion and auto-suggestion may confer in the education of children, as well as its application for the cure of their bodily and nervous ailments. These apparently are carried out in conjunction with other more traditional remedies which one would suppose contributed a considerable share to the cure, if not the greatest portion. From several hints that are given in the instances quoted in the several chapters, showing results of the method in unskilled hands, one gains some idea of the dangers that may arise from this treatment, especially when carried out by parents and others in the course of education who have had *no* training at all in its application, but, nevertheless, we still find these persons recommended to make use of the method, in spite of obvious disadvantages.

One need not stress the point that in the hands of persons of various temperaments the manner and method of suggestion treatment will of necessity be essentially different, and in some instances might easily degenerate into nagging or bullying from one who cannot bear to be thwarted by a child and who wishes for a rapid way of making the little rebel obedient. The natural tendency to *contra-suggestibility* on the part of some child is seldom taken into consideration, nor the fact that in the case of many it is sufficient to tell them that they must do one thing or refrain from another action to make the one impossible and the other appear the only thing desirable, as well as the only possible course of behaviour.

We do, nevertheless, find this tendency mentioned in Dr. Cameron's contribution to *Health and Psychology of the Child* (Ed. Dr. Sloan Chesser), in connection with advice showing how to make use of it to enable the parent or nurse to gain what is wanted by *tricking* the little one into becoming an obedient child *by mistake*. We are recommended to make our suggestion the reverse of the result we require, so that when the child responds with the habitual opposite or contrary behaviour we gain what we want. One is forced to wonder whether educational methods of this description, based upon trickery, are of much assistance taken on the whole, and especially when we begin to instil a sense of honour as well as an ideal of truthfulness into our children. It is also more than likely that we should be repaid in our own coin for our improbity long before the stage of ethical teaching had been reached. The contrary child is usually an intelligent one, who would quickly see through this unworthy manœuvre on our part and retaliate by unexpected *obedience*. The result in that case being again undesirable, it would be once more corrected, giving the child an opportunity to take advantage of the situation by the retort, "Well, you told me to do it!"

Some children are exceedingly clever in checkmating adults in this way. They will carry out the letter of instructions rather than the spirit, and in such a way as to make the one cancel the other. They will misapply them, with the result that they are soon reduced to absurdity, always with the excuse ready to their lips, "But you told me to do it!" This cannot be denied, although when the particular instruction was given the circumstances were probably entirely different, making the action appropriate in the first case. In these instances we may be almost certain that the child understood only too well the purport of the first or original order, and that the misapplication was as intentional as the attitude of injured innocence which was adopted, usually with sufficient exaggeration to arouse our suspicions. For this same reason, to escape from the responsibility of their deeds or words, children will frequently feign a greater stupidity than is rightly theirs,[1] which includes forgetfulness, since this fortress is almost impregnable, because the adult has no means of ascertaining the veracity of the child's assertion.

We have already pointed out some of the dangers of suggestion in the previous chapter—for example, in the case of the little girl accused by her mother of cutting initials on the stairs, who finally began to think she had done so, in order to comply with the mother, so as to regain her approbation, as well as through the far-reaching power of suggestion, "Mother said so, and whatever she says must be right!" This would be the trend of the child's thoughts. We may also note the effect of the persistent reiteration of the mother's assertion that she had done it, which led the child at last to confess wrong-doing which was not hers and accept what she knew to be untrue because her mother said so.

This used to happen frequently in the nursery long before these days when suggestion is recommended as an educational or therapeutic method. A smaller child who had been a witness or an accomplice in some of the misdeeds of older brothers and

---

[1] "Simulated Foolishness in Hysteria," *Papers on Psycho-analysis*, Dr. Ernest Jones.

sisters, or of a nursemaid, had to be rendered innoxious by some means, or might be dangerous if questioned. The elder ones, therefore, took precautions that no tidings of what the child had done, seen, or heard should reach the ears of authorities, and would either threaten or use the reiterated assertion that it had seen nothing, heard nothing, and done nothing, or if it *thought it had*, it was all a mistake and it had been dreaming. Such an attempt to deal with a child's recollections of what has happened may often have an almost hypnotic effect upon the mind of the child, and is certainly strong suggestion, especially when allied with fear and threats. In time the child will actually believe that what it first thought *was* a mistake and adopts the suggestion absolutely, so that it would be unable to give any clear account of events that otherwise it could have described both easily and accurately, had it been questioned about them, or might even have told this interesting piece of news itself, unasked.

This juggling with the child's memory and its sense of right and wrong, cultivating belief in a positive or negative assertion at will, making the child believe what others say rather than the evidence of its own eyes or knowledge, is the direct aim of suggestion as well as one of its cardinal dangers, whether it be used in the ordinary affairs of daily life or with intention as an educational or curative method.

The child who is trained to react to suggestion will become increasingly suggestible, so that the lightest hint will find response which, should it happen in connection with the person who has been training the child, will be taken as a sign of the pre-eminent success of the method. But it should also be kept in mind that the habit of immediate obedience to suggestion may have equally undesirable consequences. Inadvertent suggestions will have an equally ready response, which may be far from beneficial. Again, a child who has been trained to react so unquestioningly whenever a suggestion be made by anyone who is grown-up will continue to do so, as well as find it exceedingly difficult ever to act upon its own initiative. It will always need a suggestion in order to be able to act at all. We cannot bring up a child to be a reflection of ourselves and at the same time expect it to develop a well-marked and independent personality, because that is the outcome of individuality and a strong character, a pronounced ego-sense that acts upon personal resource and thought-out decisions, which in childhood would frequently be considered evidence of self-will, obstinacy, and contrariness, because in this way the child expresses *itself* rather than another.

The child who is by nature independent and inclined to do battle to retain independence and its own individuality will develop characteristic reactions to the adult who practises suggestion, whether scientifically or not, so that he or she may be deceived as to the success or non-success of the method. One of these will remind us of the famous recantation of Galileo, who, as he arose from his knees after taking oath that his statement was false that the world moved round the sun instead of the sun moving round the earth, which was the accepted view at that time, said in an undertone, "Nevertheless, it does move." The child outwardly accepts the suggestion of the adult, but with a mental reservation that it is right all the same. It will continue to hold its own opinion, although outwardly it may appear to comply with adult authority for the sake of peace and quietness.

This, nevertheless, is a dangerous expedient, and one which it is rash to teach a child, because it is the embryo of that disquieting psychological state known as *Dissociation of Personality*, which shows a cleavage within the personality in order to preserve the Ego on the one hand, and at the same time to conform with the requirements of others. Gradually these split-off portions become more and more remote from one another, playing Box and Cox, so that the person will eventually become entirely baffled when some circumstance forces recognition of the fact that the Self comprises two or more conflicting personalities, often enough contradictory, that know little or nothing about one another's impulses or actions, and produce entirely different behaviour which cannot be predicted nor controlled by the other.

Should such a case of multiple personality be analysed into its original factors, we often find one of the first causes of this dissociation was in order to conform with different standards, those of several influential persons, all of whom had equally to be obeyed, since they represented love and fear, the power of authority or preference, maybe punishment. It shows the impossibility of entire assimilation of outside suggestion taking place, because the Self is too strong to submit to this annihilation or that the demanded sacrifice of the Ego is too great. Again, it may arise because different persons are putting out counter-suggestions at the same time of equal power, which offer no possibility of compromise or harmonious blending. This will occur usually on the side of father and mother in the course of ordinary daily life rather than during intentional therapeutic Suggestion, when the suggestions generally come from one source only, and so are not in open conflict. An exception to this unity in stimulation would occur, however, should some influence of the home environment be in direct opposition to that of the professional exponent. This might happen if one parent or some other member of the household, such as an old nurse, thought that it was all nonsense and it would be found materially to delay the success of the treatment.

The adult may also strive to teach the child to use auto-suggestion, to chant daily, "Every day, I grow better and better," with, one can imagine, from one's intimate knowledge of children and their capacity for juggling with the instructions of adults for their own ends, the most grotesque and undesirable results. The child has an instinctive love and understanding of the principles of magic, a belief that everything which is said *must be true*, so that in this case there would be nothing to prevent the child feeling the daily reiteration of the chant were all that would be necessary to achieve the wished-for result, and that nothing more in the way of action upon his or her part would be necessary.

It reminds us of the child who had been receiving some elementary instruction upon the matter and subsequently managed to break a flower-vase. He was found later on sitting among the fragments, experimenting upon the practical power of suggestion to get himself out of the scrape. First he tried the effect of telling the vase that it was not broken—it was all nonsense. It must stick itself together again and hold in the water and the flowers before mother came back, or she would be angry. When this did not have the desired result, he began to reiterate in a firm voice, "I haven't broken the vase; I have not broken that vase," believing still that he could be able in some way to make the accident as though it had not happened.

The last development was to shift the blame upon an imaginary other person, and then the emphasis of his formula lay thus, "*I* haven't broken the vase," which is yet another construction that can be put upon auto-suggestion of a kind that is by no means valuable for the character-development of the growing child—the denial of personal responsibility.

The child is naturally prone to this method of escaping from difficulties, and will frequently refuse to believe facts which are repugnant, since, were they to be accepted, the child would be obliged to acknowledge itself blameworthy. This method, therefore, finds an all too ready acceptance in the child-mind, and would be especially welcome had it received the sanction of the training adult. We have also mentioned that the use of a formula and the ritual of repetition harmonizes with a large number of the child's natural tendencies and wishes. The paramount wish, of course, is to find a means of obliterating what has already happened, to make it as though it had not occurred, to wipe out all trace of the undesired incident, which Freud describes so clearly in *Hemmung, Symptom und Angst*. The child is always anxious to find ways of making things happen by use of words, or of doing the reverse, to make away with them, fatally ready, since the tendency in children is to stop short at the word—in fact, "to take the word for the deed" in a most literal way. This is a childish propensity, the harmfulness of which cannot be too much emphasized, when we come to consider the dangers of using suggestion or auto-suggestion upon children.

The children who boast and those who lie are themselves making use of the same mechanism to a considerable extent. Many boasters suffer acutely from feelings of inferiority rather than superiority, as one might infer, and for this reason tell wonderful stories of their own cleverness, bravery, or the magnificence of their possessions in order to compensate for the actual deficiency, which they recognize all too poignantly. Upon occasions this may, however, act as *auto-suggestion*, but we usually find that the children would be hindered from carrying the action through in reality, being unable to face the possibility of failing when they came to the test, and so exposing themselves to ridicule or lowering themselves in their own estimation as well as that of others. The form of lying which is pathological, and which will be more fully explained in the chapter upon Phantasy, because it is really a day-dream that is recounted as fact, might in some cases be regarded as successful auto-suggestion in the rare cases when the child afterwards realizes the day-dream in later life. This, however, is extremely rare. Nevertheless, there might be a tendency for enthusiasts of auto-suggestion to claim the credit for instances when the child contrived to carry out some actions beneficial to itself and others in this way. We have to realize that once we have put the power of auto-suggestion into the hands of the child, it may use this means for any end, criminal as well as those that are desired. Many day-dreams, as we shall explain later, are of this type, and enable the child to give vent harmlessly to criminal tendencies which otherwise might cause trouble at some time. It is very seldom, however, that the day-dream breaks through into action. We usually find that it is in itself sufficient gratification for the related tendency or wish to take shape as a day-dream, especially when recounted to another. This sharing of the phantasy, however, is extremely rare, and it is seldom that the day-dream is repeated in the outside world as reality; it will more often take the form of a compensation to balance the gaps left by reality.

Before we leave this subject, one other form of educational suggestion which may also have disastrous consequences may be mentioned, perhaps with advantage. The intention is to spur the child on to greater efforts, to point out the fault, very greatly exaggerated in order that the child may realize how dire is the need for mending its ways. It may even be coupled with a threat, which tries to put before the child what terrible results may be expected should the present course of action be continued, or even insinuate that the child's backwardness borders upon mental deficiency. The boy or girl, nevertheless, may take what is said as a true declaration of the state of affairs, a just assessment of his or her character, talents, or capacities, which it will assume cannot be remedied or altered in any way, and for this reason believes it is no further use to try to do anything about it, but sinks into depression and gloom and gives itself up as hopeless.

To give a few examples of what is meant, but in rather a different way—it is by no means rare to find that children in a family each receive a distinguishing, characteristic label by which they are known, such as the clever one, the artistic one, the pretty daughter, the stupid boy, the good or the naughty one. This label is felt by the child to be inexorable or unchanging as fate. It *must* be lived up to, and this part *must* be played whatever happens. People would show surprise, the child feels, should the reputed brilliant one of the family say something silly, and imagines that the family would call whatever this one said *clever*. The stupid one would not dare to make a joke, even should one occur to him. The unmusical daughter must not compete for musical honours at home; neither can she whose fingers are reputed clumsy take up dressmaking or embroidery, even if she may long to do so. The naughty one also feels that his or her lot is irrevocably cast in advance, and that it is expected that he or she shall be true to the label under all circumstances; also that people would in any case impute mischief to such a one were it discovered, even had it been the work of another, so that he may as well do what is expected of him. For this reason children often feel that it is a great relief to go away from home or to pay visits without other members of the family, because they think these would be on the look out all the time to see whether they lived up to their several reputations or if they behaved differently away from the home environment or with other people.

The suggestion of these labels is as strong as that of names upon children. Many will connect names with their actual or a fancied meaning, or associate them with friends, relations, and the famous persons of history or romance who have borne them, with whom they identify themselves and whose characters they feel bound to copy as closely as possible, believing themselves unable to do otherwise. Surnames which have some definite meaning, such as Good, Wellborn, Hurry, Sharp, Keen, Kind, and Meek, as well as Coward, have all been known to exercise an extraordinary amount of influence upon their owners for good or ill, either rendering them slaves to the virtue implied by the name or anxious to escape from the stigma of one that is not pleasant. The first, however, is by far the more common course of behaviour, except in the case of names like Coward, which generally drive the owner to desperate efforts to prove that it is inappropriate.

Quite well-intentioned parents and teachers may commit grave offence in the character-development of the child in the way of labelling or trying to suggest to a child that its ways want mending or its lack of talent is to be deplored more than is actually the case, in order to produce the effect they wish, when they feel that the efforts made by the child are not equal to those which might be achieved with greater application and perseverance. Unless some fortunate chance allows the child to discover that it has average ability after all, it may continue to act upon these negative suggestions, with the result that it will believe itself incapable of showing or possessing any intelligence, which will form a paralysing obstacle that may continue throughout life and check all success and achievement.

Another equally harmful as well as unwarranted use of amateur suggestion is the habit of those in charge of children of telling them that their actions have had some disastrous effect upon others, which is quite untrue, in order to stop the repetition of undesirable manners or habits of the child. For example, that its rudeness is such that visitors have left the house on account of its bad manners, when their departure was caused in an altogether different way, and they may not even have been aware of any breach of conventional politeness on the part of the child; that another child's constant inattention to its lessons and disobedience to its teacher in not learning and continuing to be so stupid had made the mother ill, when some absolutely independent illness had intervened; that a treat might have been enjoyed by the whole family if only that child had not committed some sin, when the outing in question had been put off because of some entirely different reason.

The adult probably considers that in order to gain obedience, increased efforts, and attention any means may be employed, without pausing to wonder whether evil may result from it in years to come. The future may look after itself, many think, and work upon the principle of "All's fair in love and war," adding to themselves, "*and the bringing up of children.*" They throw their sense of honour and truth to the winds when they adopt such a mischievous course, and yet they are frequently persons who otherwise are conscientious, truthful, and even honourable. We should make a valuable psychological discovery were we able to ascertain why they feel justified under these circumstances in departing from their usual code of truth, uprightness, and integrity, in order to make the child believe something that is entirely false without feeling in any way culpable for behaviour which, under other conditions, or had it been that of another person, they would probably have condemned whole-heartedly.

BOOKS THAT MAY BE READ IN CONNECTION WITH THIS CHAPTER.

Our Enemy the Child. Agnes de Lima.
Self-mastery through Auto-suggestion. Emile Coué.
Coué for Children. Gertrude Mayo.
The Nature of Auto-suggestion. Dr. Ernest Jones. *Brit. Journal. Med. Psychology*. Vol. iii, Part iii. 1923.
Simulated Foolishness in Hysteria. Papers on Psycho-analysis. Dr. Ernest Jones.

CHAPTER VII

CHILDISH BAD HABITS

THERE is a large class of nervous symptoms which appear pre-eminently in childhood to which people usually refer somewhat vaguely as "bad habits." They comprise widely differing manifestations. In this class will be reckoned nail-biting, fidgeting, nose-picking or boring, sleeplessness with bad-dreams or night-terrors, lying, stealing, or more serious types of trouble, enuresis and masturbation.

One may say that in a slight degree all are common if not normal experiences of children at one time or another, but they will usually appear for a time and disappear again in the fortunate cases. Occasionally, however, we find that they become persistent or permanent, in spite of the most strenuous efforts of those in charge of the children "to break them of the habit" by every means they can think of, some brutal, some ingenious, but all equally ineffectual.

How they may be most wisely dealt with is only discovered by an examination of what they stand for in the mind of the child, and why they have arisen, so that they are continued in spite of the most severe pains and penalties. Why adults should feel that it is so essential to prevent them making use of these expressions of their disturbed mental state, while others yet more serious pass unheeded, is, of course, one of the many phenomena of the adult mind and its working in relationship with the younger generation.

Children will frequently have copied some of these habits from the adults around them, who have thought that they are not noticeable, or they may not be aware that they have the same habit as that for which they so deeply censure in the little ones. Should any remark be made by one who has observed both making use of the same practice, the invariable response will be, "I don't think I do that really—not often; it was accidental just then," or, "But that's quite different." Why it should be different as the action of a grown-up person is hard to divine.

Nail-biting is one of the most common nervous symptoms at an early age. It may begin in infancy and continue into old age unremittingly or be merely a passing phase. On the other hand, the old nail-biter who gave up the habit with difficulty may become so afraid of paying any attention to the hands at all, that fingers go untended and unclean. Children's finger sensibility is most acute, and many will develop the habit from trying to remove a rough edge to a nail or a loose fragment of skin that remains after they have been cut hastily or carelessly by an adult. Many will experience great discomfort from having finger-nails cut too short, and the feeling of irritation that will then be produced by touching some surfaces amounts to pain. Another source of the habit is to be found in the early sucking of fingers and thumbs, the aftermath of the pleasure taken in suckling as a baby. We may often encourage a baby to suck its thumb, when waiting for a feed, little guessing that by our suggestion we may be laying the foundation of the perpetual thumb-sucker or nail-biter in the future. The child in this way gains a temporary satisfaction with hallucinatory gratification of its needs. Those whose reaction was sucking or those who used to bite will continue to seek some pleasure from their mouths, but each according to the old habit: yet, instead of biting the fingers, which would be painful, the nail may be chosen, since this is insensitive unless it or the skin around be torn down to the quick.

The discovery in the past that relief of unhappiness caused by hunger and restoration of comfort could be gained, although only in a temporary and hallucinatory manner, will be the cause of the child resorting to the same method later on, when again unhappy, unsatisfied, or embarrassed. If we study the nervous child who sucks its fingers or bites its nails we shall generally find it occur especially at these times. It certainly produces satisfaction of a kind, a feeling of mastery over something in moments of stress, when another more desired action is impossible or from the childish longing to do what has been forbidden.

If we agree that these may be some of the chief causes of nail-biting and consider them in relation to the usual methods that are adopted for curing the habit, are we justified in believing these likely to achieve the wished-for result? That is to say, if we regard the two quite frankly. In the first place, should the motive behind the habit be to find a means of supplying some satisfaction or pleasure which life is not providing, as in infancy the child stilled the pangs of hunger by sucking its fingers, may we assume that to enforce punishment, which often takes the form of a further deprivation, will mend the trouble? And yet we often hear the threat, "If you do that again, you shan't have so-and-so," or "I'll take away your toys." The putting of bitter aloes on the fingers is another attempt of the same description, which aims at destroying the compensation which the child has found, rather than trying to discover why he or she is striving to find gratification for some particular need just then, and what exactly this may be.

We should think of the habit as an attempt to find compensation for deficiency. It may also be provoked through unhappiness caused by humiliation and shame, hence a feeling of inferiority. Once more a favourite method of unthinking people for dealing with the difficulty is to scold the child and try to shame it out of a habit which is already a manifestation of humiliation. This method can, therefore, have no result but to reinforce the feeling and add grounds for the reaction. Constant nagging, constant reminders or taunts that the habit will become ingrained, if it be not so already, that the child will not or does not know when it occurs, which may, indeed, be the case, play a contributory part through suggestion and fix the child's attention continually upon this symptom. It is not allowed to forget the habit, nor the fact that it ought not to give way to it, which frequently increases the obsession. Far better would it be to build up the child's self-confidence than further to undermine it, and still more wise to seek for the cause of the unhappiness or the feeling of humiliation in order to remove that than just to try to stifle the child's own attempt to find a salve for its sorrow by robbing it of that also.

We seldom find that happy, confident, unworried children, who are at peace with their surroundings, fall victims to any of the bad habits we have named. They are all danger signals that something is seriously amiss with the mental health of the child, which needs attending to from the right end, that is to say, the cause, rather than punished. A similar adult reaction would be to rub chicken-pox pustules with caustic to punish the child for having such ugly things upon its body, which offend our æsthetic sense. One more obvious idea may be connected with the finger-nail biting, especially when parents or other adults worry the child to give up the habit on the plea that it causes themselves so much distress to see such hands, and that to please them it must be discontinued. The habit may be abandoned or disappear for a time, but if the parent should afterwards become, to the child's way of thinking, in need of punishment, it may be resumed. It would shed considerable light upon the matter to investigate carefully what has been happening at home for the last few days before the new outbreak, especially when the habit is intermittent rather than constant.

It is by no means infrequent that many of these symptoms have a definite cause in some family event, particularly when the habit is noticed for the first time or suddenly renewed after a latent period. Such causes will often be the birth of another baby, going to school for the first time, or sudden and severe punishment from someone of whom it was not expected. The inciting cause of the symptom should always be sought, because when we hold this clue it will be easier to discover what can be done to give the child an alternative and more satisfactory outlet for the emotion, whatever it may be, for which it is seeking in vain, except in this undesirable expression.

In the case of most of these symptoms we may notice that they have a symbolic value and stand for something besides themselves. Hence they may be called *substitute activities*. They are the only representatives which the child can find to express feelings that have been aroused without being able to discover a more satisfying outlet. In themselves they are not useful socially, nor do they give any real satisfaction to the child, since they are a continual source of strife with those around and frequently only a forerunner of punishment.

Should the condition known as fidgetiness be subjected to close observation, we may often distinguish quite different states which pass under the same name. It may be caused by general restlessness, unrecognized slight chorea, or St. Vitus's dance, which in its true form is usually the sequel or concomitant of rheumatism or a system of compulsive or obsessional actions. All these will naturally have different causes and need various appropriate remedies. General restlessness may arise from a physical cause, pain of some kind, perhaps constant slight toothache, indigestion, constipation, or worry connected with guilt. All of these need full investigation from their own particular angle, but it is always necessary to bear in mind that the physiological as well as the psychological causes may be contributing their share at the same time.

It is just as possible for constipation to arise from any of the psychological causes we mentioned in the chapter upon the Childish Impulses, as for the feeling of guilt to be derived from perpetual toothache, which the child will refrain from mentioning because at some time it may have been threatened with this possible consequence of eating too many sweets. The present pain drives home the meaning of the threat, and for this reason the pain will be disguised to avoid the parental retort, "I told you so," as well as a subsequent visit to the dentist, in which case it would assuredly be regarded in the ligh. of retribution.

We would do well to be very careful how we act with regard to the symptom of pain in little children. If we teach them that it is a sign of wrong-doing, greed, or disobedience in some form (which is not often the case), they will again tend to hide their feelings and will not own to pain, even should it be quite severe. It is doubtful whether this is a wise course. Pain is Nature's warning that something requires attention, that it requires putting right. If the child is taught to look upon pain as a sign of guilt and that any form of remedy is a punishment, it will naturally do its best to deny the pain, because it wishes to escape the punishment of more pain to come, as well as the distress occasioned by the feeling of guilt which will be associated with it.

Doctors may often increase this apprehensiveness quite considerably with their familiar greeting to a juvenile, "Well, young man (or my dear), and what have you been doing?" The question has a sinister ring about it and is alarming, without anything further being said or done, but the inquisition does not stop there as a rule, nor do the consequences. They have yet to begin. Teaching the child stoically to bear pain has also its disadvantages. A neglected tooth will cause more trouble than one filled in time, and an appendix abscess has cost the life of many a young child, because mothers scold when one "makes such a fuss over a tummy-ache," and say that it serves them right for eating too much.

On the other hand, it may also have disadvantages to show the child that it has only to mention "a pain" to become at once the centre of attention, or it may easily be called up directly the child feels in need of a little interest, being bored with the dull routine of everyday life. It is possible to gain some further information about the sources of the restlessness or pain, however, if we watch the little one carefully, although at the same time taking as many precautions as possible not to let it notice that we are doing so. For guidance, we may give a list of the chief points to watch :—

When does it fidget ? At special times, when it is waiting for its turn to be helped to food at table, to be dressed, to go out? Is the reason possibly that it wishes to relieve bowels or bladder and is too shy to ask : it hopes in this way to call the attention of someone to its need and for them to ask if this is so?

Does it happen when any particular persons are present or absent ? Does it want to attract their attention, to be spoken to, and asked what is the matter?

After it is in bed ? Is it warm enough—too warm? Has it a comfortable pillow—tight clothing or "curl rags"—or is it frightened?

At its play, during lessons, in church, or when reading ? If we learn the answer to these questions we will gain some idea of the cause of the trouble, or a part of it. The next important point for our research is to discover *in what way the child fidgets*, which limbs or limb is moved, if there is any special action or grimace which is constantly repeated, as this often determines the difference between the movements of the nervous child with restless movements and those typical of chorea, or St. Vitus's dance, when they are scarcely twice alike, and we never know which set of muscles are to be set in spasmodic action next. (*Common Disorders and Diseases of Childhood*, Dr. G. E. Still).

In chorea there is no part of the body, as a rule, which may be said to be free from these erratic movements. Although they will frequently increase with fatigue or if the child is specially urged to keep still, it is impossible to find in these cases, as in those we have mentioned above, particular times when they occur or any stereotyped actions which will be repeated, nor do we find that certain persons or circumstances will exercise much influence over them. A medical examination of these little patients will generally discover some definite heart trouble and that there is a history of rheumatism, if not rheumatic fever. Perhaps the child will have complained of *growing pains*, without the seriousness of the condition having been realized by the relatives. If so, a doctor's care should be immediately sought should any child in our care develop symptoms such as these. (See also Chapter III, "F. Kinæsthetic Sense.")

Our observation of the fidgety child, however, may present quite another picture. It may be one particular movement that is always presented, a jerk of the head, blinking, a twitch of nose or mouth; that upon occasions the child feels compelled to touch her head or her foot, to walk upon special lines on the pavement, or knock the lamp-posts in passing, like Dr. Johnson. What do we discover as the basis of actions of this description?

It would seem upon investigation that they are the remains, often with their origin forgotten, of some long-ago gesture, grimace, or sign language. Some idea presents itself to the child's mind that it cannot put into words. It is too difficult or vague for verbal expression; the feeling is expressed more directly by the gesture or grimace. It might perhaps be inconvenient or even punishable to say this particular thing to the person who had provoked the idea. For instance, a most usual movement of this kind is a petulant, backward shaking of the head, with the averting or closing of the eyes, sometimes accompanied by a shrug of the shoulders. Such an action might well represent the idea, "Why can't you leave me alone?" or "I don't want to have anything more to do with you." But these words would offend. The purport of the action, however, usually goes unrecognized by those who witness it, and they ascribe it merely to the "fidgets." They seldom imagine it to be the equivalent of verbal annoyance, which might otherwise be shown by the child had it not already learned that it is more expedient not to put ideas of this sort into words. Another proof in favour of this view is that it will usually occur when adults are proving particularly annoying to the child, asking inconvenient questions, not understanding them, or proving importunate in some way.

The blinking habit may have been copied from another. It can also be due to fright or closely allied to the gesture which we have already described, when the girl would "shut her eyes at people who had offended her," implying that she was ignoring them and their existence, and wished them to realize this fact. (Chapter III, "D. Sight.") It is a habit that will be usually soon discarded unless made permanent by too much emphasis, or unless the attitude towards the community which it represents should persist. One occasionally meets it in several varieties during later years : the fluttering blink of the eyelids, which will be used for many reasons, chiefly in times of embarrassment, to attract and interest the stranger or acquaintance, in order to give more time in which to think of something to say or to make people laugh, because it may once in childhood have called forth the remark: "What a funny little person you are." We find the slow, solemn wink that sometimes occurs in men when talking to women, inadvertently, perhaps unconsciously, the reasons for which would only be disclosed by a deep analysis of their unconscious motives, but this is not so likely to appear in childhood. The long-continued closing of the eyes to obliterate unwanted persons, which we will find used by an adult who is talking to children, as though to signify, "You are really so stupid as to be beneath my notice," or in clergymen, when mentioning holy things or at an emotional climax of the sermon, to suggest to their hearers that they are absorbed in ecstasy. In each case it represents a meaning that would be more difficult to put into words, so that the use of the gesture language, with the origin now forgotten or submerged into the unconscious, allows free use of the obsessional action by the person without any feeling of guilt, because he or she would stoutly aver that it has no meaning whatsoever, and is only a habit shared by many others.

Some of these movements are akin to the rituals of the primitive races or of obsessional neurotics, which have already been mentioned, as having the complex function of striving to avert disaster in the future, of making something as though it had never happened in the past or the sign of a death-wish in the present, like the old gestures formerly current to place a person under the spell of the evil eye or avert its curse. We may see the same intention in the religious practice of making the sign of the cross, or in touching wood after boasting: all are equally remnants of an archaic language to counteract danger.

The best cure for these obsessional actions is to discover the cause of the child's negative feeling and to remove the cause, if possible, in order to give a more adequate means of expression to the ideas or the phantasies which they represent. Again, as in the case of other bad habits, they may be a refuge when outside difficulties are pressing hard upon the child, so that it will be wise carefully to review the conditions of life which surround it, and deliberate whether they cannot be readjusted. Should this be done, we will often find the actions entirely disappear, and the child becomes happier as well as more healthy in mind and body.

It is very seldom that one of these habits or symptoms makes an isolated appearance. Usually several are shown at once, and we may find the constellation restlessness, want of sleep, bad dreams, with loss of weight and appetite. It will be the same worry which has caused them all, and the most direct cure will be the correction of the injurious condition in their environment which has evoked them rather than, shall we say, gymnastics to deal with the fidgets and bad posture, sedatives to correct the sleeplessness, cream to increase the weight, and tonics to help the appetite. These measures in themselves will not cure the worry which is at the root of the several symptoms, but the removal of the worry will act more effectually than all the other remedies put together upon the undesirable general condition.

We have already pointed out some of the causes of bad nights, frightening dreams, and night-terrors in Chapter III, in the sections on Sight and Hearing, and suggested that they are due largely to alarming phantasies produced in the minds of little children by sights and sounds that have come to their notice from sharing the sleeping apartment of their parents or an adjoining room, relative to matters connected with married life by no means intended by their elders for the children's participation. Among these will be dreams of engines that make a great noise, that crush and tear people to pieces, swords that pierce, and fighting—terrors innumerable from which the child tries to escape; while dreadful animals or huge men and women, looking angry, with rolling eyes, pursue him or her, will be constant figures in their dreams.

Many of the fairy-tales that are told freely to little children are equally alarming. Red Riding-Hood being eaten by the wolf, Jack the Giant-Killer, and hundreds more, recur to the child mind in the dark, so that children who have similar phantasies of their own will incorporate the whole series to make night-time and the dark a horror that few can imagine, except those who have also suffered from them.

The childish tendency to tell wonderful stories, pathological lies, and to recount adventures which never took place, has been described briefly in Chapter III, "E. Speech," and will be mentioned again in the chapter devoted to Children's Games and Phantasies, since they are the expression of a phantasy which is half-believed as truth by the child, since it is so immensely desired.

In Stealing we may trace several motives at work. One is that of revenge and punishment, already explained as a common tendency in children to balance difficulties caused by the aggression of their parents, but it has also other important roots. Things will be stolen that are wanted and cannot be obtained otherwise, or the articles taken represent something else symbolically, the love of a person, as well as some attribute or possession of this other, because the child feels that by some magic process, if or when this object could be obtained, the possession would somehow transform him into a person who is equally enviable and powerful, or that all would be gained by this one action of taking, which is now felt to be so grievously lacking. There is nearly always a meaning over and above that of the actual stealing of the article, whatever it may be, which gives the deed its obsessional character. Although to the casual observer these bad habits seem nothing more than naughtiness or bad bringing-up, those with a deeper understanding, who realize the seriousness of the condition, reckon them among the manifestations of *obsessional neurosis* that are found in childhood.

Loss of appetite should not technically be regarded as "a bad habit," but, in point of fact, the idiosyncrasies and fancies that some children develop where food is concerned, their likes and dislikes for one article of diet or another, will certainly be considered in this light by a large number of parents and a few doctors, if we may judge by the advice given by some child specialists upon this topic. One reads that punishment, suggestion of the opposite course, or the encouragement of greediness are suitable measures for dealing with the difficult condition that arises when a child persists in adhering to its own point of view concerning dietary. (Dr. H. Cameron, *The Nervous Child; Health and Psychology of the Child.* Ed. Dr. E. Sloan Chesser.)

It is not infrequent that children, without being physically ill, suffer from loss of appetite and temporarily refuse all food or certain kinds of food. Loss of appetite is regarded as one of the classical signs of illness, but it may also appear as an independent symptom. It may even manifest itself in an infant of a few days old, in connection with weaning troubles, which have been described in the section upon Taste, and the infantile impulses, in the section devoted to oral gratification. If this refusal of food should have met with success in these early days, it becomes a model for subsequent behaviour, whenever circumstances confront the child that are so displeasing that they must be avoided at any cost. The refusal of food and temporary loss of appetite will therefore punctuate each conflict between the child and authorities, and one notices, even in infants, that whereas one will continue this resistance until brought almost to death's door by refusal of nourishment, another will give in after a very short and not particularly determined fight.

The habit most certainly alarms adults in charge and often enforces *their* capitulation, so that the child soon discovers how much power may be exerted over the household in this way, be it merely to obtain a favourite pudding or to resolve a more serious domestic problem, such as the restoration of a beloved nurse or any other person whom it misses but sorely needs. The child's refusal of food has also been referred to in this book as a reaction to the symbolic values of food, because it is reminiscent of other substances which it has been taught to regard as unpleasant or arising from a fear of bursting, which may be connected with pregnancy phantasies in early life. (See Chapter XI, "Games and Phantasies.")

In this way fears and phantasies become a cause of the child's refusal of food or loss of appetite as frequently as it is a demonstration of power over the adults of the household. Moreover, the violent reactions to this symptom often seen on the part of the parents will give the child all the attention and excitement that is needed, while punishments and threats will only increase these, plus a feeling of fear and guilt, and so lead to the fixation of the symptom.

Fear and guilt are easily aroused in connection with eating and food because of early oral pleasures which were of such particular moment to the child. It is guilt which will often be responsible for the cyclic nervous vomiting of children, an attempt partially to restore what is felt to have been wrongfully eaten, self-punishment, or a sign of fear. Nausea is one of the typical signs of fear, as it is of apprehensiveness. It may also be symbolic of great repugnance experienced on account of persons or incidents, represented once again in gesture language. "I am sick of this," "My stomach heaves at that person," "It makes me sick," "The position is nauseating." Instances where common usage of words makes a symbolic reference to this physiological process are numberless. A woman known to the writer used habitually to have attacks of migraine with vomiting whenever she was "thoroughly sick of life."

Many children become sick when travelling in a closed conveyance or with their back to the direction in which the vehicle is going. In one such case the cause was as follows. The child learned that the back seat was usually considered the place for children, maids, or other inferior persons, which idea made her sick. If she complained of this feeling and retched, she would be immediately transferred to the other side, where her father and mother or one of the elder ones was sitting, which naturally she preferred.

The travelling in swift closed vehicles seems almost always connected with phantasies that root deeply in the life of the child, and sometimes recall those that represent the pre-natal state, when the child always travelled in a closed conveyance. We do not mean, however, that the child *remembers* this in the same sense as we usually attach to the word, or that it definitely recollects this period and its feelings, but that something in the later movement revives dimly a faint trace in the child's kinæsthetic sense of comfort or discomfort which has already been encountered.

We have now reached the last of the bad habits upon the list with which we started, enuresis and masturbation, and these two are grouped together because they are not only met with frequently in the same children, but may often be caused by one another. We have already referred to them when explaining the importance of the pleasure-principle for the guidance of the infantile life, and relative to the fact that a certain degree of pleasure is experienced from the relief of a distended bladder. But the child often waits too long before attempting to seek a fitting opportunity for relief and the accident occurs. Again, children will discover that the sensation produced by tightly pressing their thighs together when the bladder is full greatly increases the pleasure to be derived in this way, which thus promotes this form of masturbation. It will also happen frequently in the case of children who are too shy to ask to relieve themselves. They will adopt this posture to restrain micturition, possibly because they know that adults will probably notice it and ask them, realizing that it is one of the accepted signs of childish necessity. We will sometimes find that this attitude persists in adults, usually without the persons being in the least aware of what they are doing nor remembering the origin of the attitude, although, should they see a child stand thus, they would immediately jump to the right conclusion. It is a curious fact that it will also be repeated in children as well as in adults in a moment of sudden embarrassment, through the equation, "Wishing to micturate causes me discomfort in body as well as in mind. I could often allay the first by standing in this way, perhaps I can relieve other difficulties by the same means."

Masturbation may frequently be the cause of bed-wetting. The handling of the genitals or their stimulation by other means, such as rubbing against the mattress or bed-clothes, will frequently, in alliance with phantasies which may accompany the action, lead to a flow of urine, which, particularly in little boys, takes the place of the more mature ejaculation that occurs when emotional excitement has been stimulated. We have again found that bed-wetting may occur because children are afraid to get out of bed at night, because of bogies or other fears of the dark. They would rather risk the real experience of the scolding or punishment for the misadventure than the imaginary horrors that lurk in the dim corners of the room or down shadowy passages. Bed-wetting may also occur as the result of dreams, the condition of sleep apparently cancelling the feeling of guilt which would otherwise be experienced on account of this laspe should it take place when the child were awake; great pleasure will often be experienced in such a dream. Occasionally this will be one of the symptoms connected with the *psychogenic epileptiform attack,* which takes place by day or night. It often occurs during illness or other conditions of severe emotional stress, when the child's personality undergoes extremely rapid or progressive regression to an infantile stage when this symptom of incontinence was a usual occurrence. We will find, too, that it is a concomitant of fear, or that it will happen while waiting in suspense for some rather alarming event, which is either known to be imminent or imagined to be a possible or probable sequence of what has just taken place.

We will begin by considering masturbation at its very early stage, in infancy, when the baby first discovers pleasure from touching parts of its body and learns that certain regions provide more agreeable sensations than others. This primarily is a purely sensory experience, and has little associative value in connection with phantasy, nor the more mature emotional and erotic significance which becomes attached to this action in later life.

The adult, seeing the child's hands in the forbidden area, however, takes steps to prevent its reoccurrence and makes the child understand that, pleasurable as this may be, it is a guilty pleasure, and therefore cannot be permitted. This attitude of the adult, nevertheless, not only emphasizes its value to the infant, but lays the foundation of the practice of masturbation as a secret preoccupation, something felt to be eminently wicked but immensely desirable.

When the baby's passion for exploring its own body is waning and its infantile pleasure-seeking in itself is already reaching out to wider regions, the tendency will usually be forgotten among new interests of still greater fascination, unless unwise treatment and punishment should have made it a permanency, or should too intense pleasure derived from it have rendered it a necessity. For other reasons also it may linger on, such as when unsuitable clothing and clumsy napkins have been habitual; or perhaps undue stimulation on the part of adults in attending to washing or toilet operations have called special notice to the sensitivity of this part of the body—all of which disadvantages may easily occur if adults are not upon their guard against the dangers of *too early* and *too great* stimulation of the baby's cutaneous sensations and genital zone.

Usually there will be a pause of a few or even many years after the first period of infantile masturbation has dropped into abeyance, at longest until the commencement of pre-pubertal changes, when growing emotions will revive it; at shortest, perhaps a year or two may pass by, and at three, four, or five it may break out again, when the struggle of the child in the triangular situation of father, mother, and itself is at its height, and it is tossed hither and thither between the feelings of inferiority and its wishes for power. In some cases of severe neurosis and great unhappiness during childhood it may never disappear at all, or even become latent, but remain constant, even if successfully hidden from the eyes of those in authority.

It will occur in both boys and girls, although it is more commonly recognized among the former, as well as dealt with more severely in their case. Many people will notice some form of the practice in use among girls, but appear to remain oblivious of what is really happening, or of its significance, unless they adopt this attitude merely because they do not know how otherwise to act with respect to it. In the case of boys the attitude is different. The usual belief is that it must be checked at any cost, or that the most grave physical conditions will arise as its consequence. Although many parents, schoolmasters, and even some doctors may threaten boys with a horrible fate should the habit be continued, and write pamphlets on the subject with the intent to frighten them out of it, frank research and a more modern attitude towards its actual consequences teach that far more serious psychological results will arise from unwise efforts to check it than those which follow as the physiological sequelæ of the habit. Unless indulged in with extreme frequency, this alone, without fear or guilt derived from threats and inculcated by parental views, is of slight importance. (*Auto-erotic Phenomena in Adolescence*, K. Menzies.)

The cause of such behaviour towards young people on account of this habit probably arises from the adult sadistic tendency and the wish to treat others as they were treated when they were young, but their behaviour does more harm than good, the child frequently becoming ill through their suggestion. He has been told that if he does this he will be ill, perhaps that he will lose all his energy; that people will be able to see what he does by looking at his eyes; that he will become blind or insane. The poor boy is panic-stricken. He feels that his self-control will not be equal to the task or is diminishing; that he is committing the sin against the Holy Ghost; that his brain may be all the time oozing away through the spinal cord with his losses of seminal fluid, when adolescence makes this result practicable. The scare tales that he is told make him feel a victim of abnormal occurrences, should he find that an emission has taken place during sleep, and he becomes terrified to such an extent that he dare not mention his anxiety to anyone, lest he hear that those things he has been warned against are really taking place.

The classical threat for masturbation both in girls and boys is mutilation—in boys that they shall be deprived of the penis, which finds partial or symbolic expression in the favourite medical advice to remedy the habit, namely *circumcision*; in the case of girls, the threat takes the form that the hands will be cut off. This attitude of revenge towards the child, as well as the threats and fear connected with it, will have the most serious and far-reaching results. In the first place, the children who are the victims usually believe that their parents or the doctor will put the threats into practice. The girl's discovery that she apparently lacks an organ that her brother possesses leads her often to jump to the conclusion that the threat has already been carried out and that she is now suffering for past offences. This leads to a feeling of supreme guilt that will increase her sense of inferiority, and she may transfer the original sensation of guilt to all her actions as well as to her whole person, which sums itself up in the belief that she can never excel in anything, she will always be deficient.

At adolescence the appearance of the menstrual flow will reanimate this childish phantasy, and she may strive to hide what is happening because to her mind it is the evidence that she has injured herself in some way and she fears the information that she has only herself to blame, and she is suffering for her past sins in connection with masturbation or some other childish bad habit.

The boy, on the other hand, when he sees the bodily structure of the little girl, and observes that it is different from his own, is filled with similar dread. Here, to him, it appears is someone upon whom the awful penalty has been carried out, and his hurried, frightened glance may discern in the form of the girl's genitals a gaping wound, which increases his own fear that a like fate may overcome himself. His opinion of girls will correspond with his fear. Those upon whom this threat has been carried out must be guilty, valueless, and abhorrent, therefore they should be shunned. He develops numberless phantasies connected with his discovery, magnifying his own possession as an organ of power, that which can accomplish miracles, knows everything, and is a source of magic. He dwells upon ideas of the envy of others on account of it, especially that of girls, and spends much time elaborating theories of the relative unimportance of women because of their lack. He may sometimes phantasy that an important woman, such as his mother, may have retained hers, or given it in exchange for a baby; perhaps that it grows into a baby and afterwards becomes detached. (*Selected Papers* of Karl Abraham. Trans. Hogarth Press.)

The attitude and teaching of the parents is of the utmost significance where all these "bad habits" are concerned. Leniency is the wisest course; over-severity usually fails in its object, as well as frequently causing serious neurotic disturbance or the persistence of the habit in the form of an obsession. We emphasize this significance of the methods used as deterrents, and may learn more about them by a detailed examination. Threats we have already discussed. Punishments may certainly relieve the feelings of the adult who administers them, but they are not beneficial to the victims of the neurosis. If the parents could but rid their minds of the idea of the "bad habit," the *naughtiness* of the child, and replace this with the conception that it is a form of nervous illness, they might be more willing to relinquish the theory of rigorous prevention or cure by violence. In considering it as a nervous symptom, they should once more seek the cause in the child's disappointment with life, a proof that it is seeking the answer to some of life's problems for which at present and unaided it cannot find help nor solution. What it does need is information, not threats; assistance to understand itself, not mere preaching at; that it must practise self-control; sympathy, not scoldings, to teach it shame and guilt. Not until we can take a saner view of the whole matter of these childish bad habits, and be less frightened ourselves of their occurrence in the young, will we be able to deal with them adequately.

For we are afraid! It is fear that makes us threaten, that causes us to use brutality when we should try to understand what is amiss. We lose our heads in these crises of childish outbreaks of emotion, which usually we ourselves have caused, and not knowing what they mean, or whence they come, lay about us with a big stick, as we might do unreasoningly and without consideration at any other crisis that might arise with which we do not know how to deal.

To preach self-control to others, obviously not practising it ourselves in our treatment of them, without offering any good reasons for the practice of self-control, except that it is supposed to be a virtue in itself or presenting alternatives as possible solutions of the difficulty, is to shirk our responsibilities towards the young people in our care. Shame and guilt once established soon spread beyond our control. We cannot undo or remedy the harm that our want of knowledge has produced. It resembles the action of a child who thoughtlessly kills a beautiful butterfly, tears down the blossoming tree, or crushes the singing bird. The deepest remorse cannot replace the life that we have destroyed. But, again, we may follow the example of the reaction of many children in this predicament and revile the thing which we have destroyed for having been so easily crushed and broken. We may wish to fling it away and get rid of it out of sight, because it pleases us no more, since it

only reminds us of what we have done. This is the usual interpretation of the motive of the adult who wants to send away
the neurotic child from home and to banish it from the home
circle. The knowledge of this reason for wanting to get the
child away is hidden in the unconscious mind, and yet we
may observe similar behaviour occurring without disguise in
the child over a toy or pet animal that has been spoilt or hurt.

We destroy energy by crushing these impulses and causing
their repression, which in turn uses up still more energy in its
maintenance, so that the supply available, needed for the
continuance of the affairs of daily life, will be dangerously
curtailed. The fear also aroused in the child by finding that
however much in some cases he or she wishes to abandon the
habit, some impulse that is often a compulsion or obsession
leads on to fresh outbreaks of the symptom, tends still further
to weaken self-control and self-confidence, that develops a
belief in some cases that there is some evil spirit within or
without that cannot be resisted and will drive one on to everlasting damnation.

The symptom itself may be a defence reaction to the stress
of life, a compensation when the outward reality offers nothing
that makes existence worth while, and so pleasure or a feeling
of power must be sought instead within the self to restore the
balance. At later stages, when the habit becomes stronger than
the conscience or ideal self that has been imposed by the
parents, which, in accordance with their instruction, strives
to break free from the old way, but cannot, the following
twisted idea may present itself: "I can stop if I want to do so,
but I don't want to yet. I will go on just once more, and then
stop," which endangers the young person's attitude to reality
and personal values.

Even after these habits have been put aside for a while, we
may often find they will return in a crisis, when life becomes
psychologically impoverished of pleasure and interest, or at
an emotional period for which no other outlet may be found.
Adolescence provides the greatest stimulus for such a reanima-
tion of all or any of these nervous symptoms, for then the
emotional life of the child is undergoing its recapitulatory
period of development, and the old tendencies frequently
reappear. These manifestations at any stage of life in the young

require care, investigation, and a readiness to give sympathy or information. They are best left entirely without threats, punishments, or moral cautionary stories. Wise physiological explanations given by one who is thoroughly conversant with all the facts and pros and cons of the matter, as well as the structure of the body, and suffering from no inhibitions concerning them or discussing them, will often do far more good and be able to clear up a child's real difficulties more than all the other violent or ingenious methods that have yet been invented.

BOOKS THAT MAY BE STUDIED IN CONNECTION WITH THIS CHAPTER.

The Nervous Child. Dr. H. Cameron.
The Auto-erotic Phenomena in Adolescence. K. Menzies.
The Reproduction of Life. A. T. Cokkinis, F.R.C.S. (Eng.), M.B., B.Sc. (Lond.).

CHAPTER VIII

TYPES OF THOSE IN CHARGE OF CHILDREN

ONE of the most common attitudes which we find people adopt with regard to the young child who already shows signs of severe or even slight nervous illness is extreme surprise, as though they could not imagine how this had come about in one so young, as if nervous ailments were the prerogative of those advanced in years or at least arrived at maturity, or that it was comparable to developing measles when no one in the neighbourhood already had the disease from whom it could have been contracted.

In this last idea, however, we come very close to the true state of affairs, because nervous troubles are often the result of the direct or indirect influence of others who are also suffering from them, but frequently in ways which may not be recognized, and least of all by the sufferer. At the present day these troubles are gaining more adequate investigation for the purpose of diagnosis and cure than they have ever been accorded in the past. The result is that the influence which they exert upon other members of the household may now be more accurately ascertained, and steps taken to check the disastrous effect which will operate upon all persons concerned in a cumulative way. Very serious consequences often make it necessary to take such a child to the doctor, who gives some clue as to what is the matter, although frequently not much information is forthcoming, especially as to how this condition has come about.

This is a matter for the specialist rather than the general practitioner, because of several factors. It is such unwelcome news that the illness of the child has been caused by the manifest or incipient neurosis of some other member of the household, that many family doctors would keep silent about it, even should they be aware of this cause of the trouble, for fear of offending the parents.

There is, as a rule, a great antipathy to face the fact that serious nerve trouble is in the family, and that it is necessary to deal with it without delay, lest more grave consequences develop. Many people regard the stigma attaching to nervous trouble as appalling, and look upon it as only slightly less worrying than if actual mental derangement had been diagnosed, or insanity itself. Beside that attitude one finds the extreme opposite, considerable pride taken by many in "being so sensitive" or "so highly strung," as though these conditions were the hall-mark of distinguished ancestry or noble birth. Others, again, appear desirous of being thought peculiar or eccentric and cultivate ways or habits which to an expert could only be considered the manifestations of neurosis. Thus one lady, when paying calls, always asked if the blinds of the room where she was sitting could be lowered, giving as the reason, it was one of her little fads, strong light was so bad for her eyes, adding: "You mustn't think I have anything *wrong* with them, but I want to preserve them, you know." She also wore dark glasses out of doors, although actually there was nothing the matter with her eyes. She was, indeed, proud of the pose, but all the same it was a neurotic symptom. Another will dread cats, and count it as an asset to her social interest that she can detect one of these animals long before it appears in sight. A third may find it impossible to sit in a room with the door closed; while some cannot rest content if it be open.

All these symptoms pass unrecognized by the general public for what they are. They will be counted fads or eccentricities— these and countless others of the same kind. Some, indeed, may remain hidden from strangers and only obtain their outlet upon the children of the family, with the most evil results. It is probably no exaggeration to say that these unrecognized neurotic character-traits may be even more dangerous, where the next generation is concerned, than those which are apprehended at their true value. They will come into operation as influences of up-bringing, proximity, and affect the abnormal reactions of these adults towards the children in their charge, more especially because they are unrecognized as harmful; they may even, some of them, be regarded almost in the light of virtues. In fact, those tendencies which were valued so pre-eminently in former educational methods of childhood— force, the use of shame, fear, and blind obedience—were precisely some of these same manifestations of neurosis finding an outlet where it was possible upon helpless children who could not escape from their clutches. They served, no doubt, as a psychological life-buoy, and prevented those who made use of them as a gratification from suffering from what we call to-day *nervous breakdown*, and later producing the children's failure to respond to the exigencies of life.

The highly-strung, sentimental mother of the past, nearly always a semi-invalid, ruled the entire household from her couch by her tears and nervous headaches. These took place whenever someone had said or done anything of which she did not approve. She may have been called hysterical and dosed with some preparation of valerian, but it was never urged upon her, for the sake of her children and the comfort of the entire family, that she should undergo some radical cure that would get rid of this curse. *Curse* it might well have been from the point of view of the others, but to the woman herself it was the chief weapon in her armoury with which she ruled her household, and with which she would have been as loath to part in those days as her present-day descendant is now with hers.

Again, the father who stormed and raged, thrashed his sons and bullied his daughters, was not considered to be suffering from neurosis. It was thought the right and proper behaviour, the usual way of maintaining discipline in the family and keeping his position as undisputed head of the house.

The governess of the last generation, not having had much education herself as a rule, and feeling perhaps marked inferiority where her own attainments were concerned, and therefore over-anxious that her pupils should do well in order to reflect as much credit as possible upon herself, tried the spur of "shame" upon them. She would constantly tell them how backward they were, how far behind other children they would find themselves should they go to school, and often attained the unwished and unexpected result that they believed her implicitly and felt too much humiliated by her taunts to try to make greater efforts, grasping at last the idea, culled from her incessant reminders to that effect, that they were perhaps mentally deficient, and in that case exertions would be valueless.

Nurses would often try to rule by fear, to threaten and tell bogy tales of what would happen if children were disobedient or got into mischief, all of which were *believed* to the detriment of the child, or found out to be false and *disbelieved*, to the detriment of adult prestige and the child's future lack of faith and confidence in them.

Psychological investigations have shown the harmfulness of these methods and how they arise from unrecognized neurotic tendencies in the adults who have children in their care, and who, without knowing that they are doing so, find an outlet for their unsatisfied childish wishes in this behaviour towards those under them. We have already mentioned some of these adult characteristics where children are concerned, but not exactly from this point of view. The parental attitude and behaviour, typical of the rôle that parents or those *in loco parentis* assume, as soon as these rights and privileges are taken over, are in themselves worth a little consideration, since they provide a foundation upon which we may build further investigations.

This ideal picture of the parent, so zealously preserved, what is it, and where does it come from? It will take many various forms and yet in essentials it remains unchanged, whether the parent is of to-day, yesterday, of a hundred or a thousand years ago. Only the details undergo modification. First in importance comes the love of power and authority, which finds innumerable disguises. This supreme desire for power leads to the feeling that children are a personal possession and takes delight to-day in having a small number of superlative children, or even one super-child, as we might call it; whereas the pride of the past ages was to have progeny infinite as the sands of the sea-shore. Together with this feeling of pride in possession, we shall find that a corresponding sense of mastery is gained. The possessions, that is, the children, must equally own the authority of the possessors. They must submit with blind obedience to whatever command this power dictates. The greater this desire for power, the more submissive will the children be made and the less they will be allowed to develop their own characters.

Another concomitant factor that fits into this picture of parental authority is the feeling that the parent is always right and knows everything. In this case, therefore, children who turn to them for guidance and information will be appreciated, but they must not bring too many inconvenient questions—the answers must be quite easy, and certainly not unknown to the parents—nor those a reply to which is beyond the finite knowledge of human beings, in which some children delight especially for the torture of their elders, when these are quite incapable of saying quite frankly, "I do not know." This reply would, of course, under the circumstances be quite impossible. Self-esteem, personal or parental, could not endure the humiliation of a confession of such magnitude.

Having once constituted this reputation of wisdom and the axiom that parental conduct is always right, it follows that an error on the part of the parents, either in the way of information given, in justice meted out in a family tribunal, or in adult behaviour, must be obliterated in some way or be shown somehow as being quite in order. This requires great adroitness on the part of an adult or extreme gullibility on the children's side to be successful. The parental standard of perfection, however, is an impossible one to maintain indefinitely. Sooner or later, the children discover the clay feet of their idol, and the adult in question will fall from the self-raised pedestal more surely and irrevocably than those who have not worked so hard to establish a reputation for almost divine powers nor set so much store upon it.

The parental attitude, such as we have described it, is, in point of fact, founded upon the traditional patriarchal Deity of the Hebrew Scriptures or any of the other patriarchal theologies that the world has known. With the feeling that the father is the representative of God on earth, that God is the Father in Heaven, the equation is complete. The parent does expect, and often exacts or extorts, reverence and obedience from his children equal to that of human beings towards their God. Should we find the mother exercising the same authority in the absence of the father and instead of him, or in his presence, we may discover in this phenomenon a double identification and assumption of power, both of the male parent and the Deity, which points out the trend of her childish wishes for power, and also, in all probability, to her old desire to have been a boy instead of a girl. In this way she is seeking compensation to make good the injustice which she feels Fate has done her in the matter of her birth.

Let us try to discover the roots of this desire for power and supreme authority. Again we must seek for them in the childhood of the individual, in the unrealized wishes, the desires and impulses which then found no actual fulfilment. These parents, who are so deeply imbued with the idea of the authority of the parent-ideal, the need for instant and unhesitating obedience on the part of the child, are usually those who have copied their own parents in this respect; who, as children, were expected to give blind and unquestioning obedience, to submit all their plans and wishes for parental sanction and surrender them without murmur or regret were they not approved. Ever in their own minds, during this long denial of their own impulses and vain longings to express themselves and gain some immediate gratification for their wish for power, lingered the hope that some day, when their turn came to be a parent, they would then occupy this glorious post of authority; that they in their turn would be the one who answered questions imperiously, with an air of inscrutable wisdom, or delivered judgment so unhesitatingly concerning points of nursery ethics.

The idea that one day their turn would come to be parent, and all that they had found by bitter experience this implied, was the hope that made life possible. Doubtless, when opportunity offered, these children may have tried to wield the authority from which they had suffered long before the day came when they had won the *right* to do so, by being raised to this honourable station by the birth of a child of their own. They may have practised it in advance upon younger brothers and sisters, or schoolmates, who could be made or prevailed upon to fill the position of pseudo-children. All these activities showed the trend of such wishes, bred by seeking compensation to counteract the feeling of inferiority produced by the tyranny of their own parents, a result which manifested itself through the eagerness with which it was sought, the thoroughness with which it was carried out, and the resentment felt against their parents, although it may never in fact have been consciously recognized in the mind of the child, who may all the time have been outwardly submissive and affectionate.

The unmarried school-teacher or nurse who employs a

similar means of instilling discipline and decorum into her charges is reacting to the same stimulus and motive, to attain discharge for her wishes to possess children who can be treated according to this pattern of the past. We may, indeed, often do, find an interesting cleavage in the education methods in one person, showing on the one hand repetition of the parental behaviour in the old home, upon the other a milder course foundedupon the do-as-you-would-be-done-by theory—at once an attempt at a compromise and a scheme of improving upon the old methods; their repudiation and a proof of ever greater superiority. How this distribution may be organized in the same person and at the same time is exceedingly enlightening and will give penetrating insight into the character of the person who carries it out.

We frequently find that a man or woman will treat his or her own children, or pupils, with great severity and maintain a milder attitude towards others, for whose good conduct or ultimate welfare he or she is in no way responsible. Sometimes children who are blood-relations are regarded with leniency, and strictness is reserved for the stranger. These distinctions are in themselves the outcome of peculiar conditions formed by unconscious impulses that arise from the childhood of that person by which compensation and gratification are sought, whilst simultaneously the severity may expunge a certain amount of guilt for over-tenderness, or the over-tenderness cover and be a reaction against unconscious hatred shown by the severity. It may also serve to wipe out guilt connected with this feeling, and yet fulfil the repetition of the strict standard of the personal up-bringing.

JEALOUS PARENTS

When we consider the most conspicuous types of parents whom we have known, besides those whose ideas seem concentrated only upon the exercise of their authority upon their children and making them obedient, we find, perhaps, three main groups—jealous people, over-conscientious people, and sadistic or cruel people, who will show this instinct in many forms of teasing as well as inventing strange punishments for the education of their children or those in their charge.

What of these jealous people, how do they come to be jealous where children are concerned, and how is it shown?

Somebody has wisely said that directly there are three persons in a group, jealousy will creep in. Sometimes the same may be said when the number is confined to two. As soon as a child is born it may become the focus of jealousy from many points of view, and, unless in very exceptional circumstances, it will form part of a group of at least three. We will leave out of consideration at first the child's own reactions as possible consequences or causes of jealousy, because the reactions of the newly-born are of less consequence for the moment than the feelings of those in its environment as manifestations of jealousy.

We will suppose a group around the baby of mother, nurse, and father, which will be quite large enough to show several typical signs of jealousy in adults. At the commencement we may question, as the first point of interest, can a woman be jealous of her own child? Some even may feel inclined utterly to oppose this possibility, because the usual attitude of the mother of a young baby is to identify herself with it completely, feeling it part of herself, which naturally excludes any such feelings. It is possible, nevertheless, for a mother to be jealous of this small creature. The feeling may have been growing during the months preceding birth and increased, no doubt, were there any reason why the woman did not wish for a child, perhaps because it would interfere too much with her pleasure or professional duties, perhaps upon the grounds of financial or housing difficulties. It may sometimes happen that the barrier between herself and being able to look forward to the advent of the child was a psychological inhibition. Some reason arising in her childhood possibly made the whole process of child-bearing repugnant to her, or maybe her self-love was too much centred upon herself and her personal beauty to enable her to make the sacrifice entailed by the birth of the child.

The woman who is intensely self-oriented, or, as it is called in psychological terms, *narcissistic*, resents the loss of beauty previous to the birth of the infant; as well as the fact that the interest and admiration that revolves around the mother of a child must indeed be shared with the baby, rather than received as sole homage from others who cross her path, which was expected and obtained before its birth. These factors will prove ample cause for a mother to feel jealous of her baby, besides any root that may have sprung from her childhood, when in those days she may have been jealous of a baby sister or brother by whom she felt supplanted in the affection of others.

The mother's jealousy of her baby may often be influenced by her preference for boys or girls and her attitude towards her own sex as a child. Again, the capacity to identify with another, or lack of this faculty, will play a large part in her reactions. In some cases her wish to have been a boy may cause her acute jealousy should the first-born be of this sex. Should, however, her feelings be directed towards the acquisition of feminine admiration and advantages, we may find her consciously or unconsciously resenting the intrusion of a little daughter. We often see this unconscious rivalry towards a baby girl manifesting itself in numberless little hostile actions, such as the appropriation of presents of jewellery or other trinkets that are given to the infant, with the excuse, "Of course, she is too young to appreciate them yet. I will give them to her when she is older." This appropriation from the little daughter is typical of the narcissistic woman, who wishes to keep all favours and gifts for herself and has no wish to own a rival. The narcissistic woman in this respect is often cruel, so we will reserve further manifestations of her impulses for the section dealing with the sadistic impulses of mothers, or rather of parents in general.

The mother, however, shows jealousy also where the nurse is concerned, and the nurse is often extremely jealous about the baby from her own point of view. It is a typical attitude of nurses, who occupy themselves with infants or young children, to feel and to represent themselves as the only people who may in any way be trusted to look after them. Doctors, parents, and other nurses are believed to be quite useless, if not positively injurious. They will tell long tales of the numberless babies they have rescued from certain death by their ministrations, when the child was in jeopardy caused by the carelessness or inexperience of these other people, and they will explain how often it has been necessary to instruct mothers how to look after their offspring. They will often grudge another even holding or doing anything for that baby and be careful to point out that the infant cares predominantly for them, always appropriating the first smiles or the early manifestations of recognition and affection. The jealousy between nurse and parents, or that occurring on the part of the nurse when, later on, her charges pass out of her exclusive care to the training of a governess or school, often expresses itself in countless ways which are all too familiar to us, and prove themselves influences which have led to the most serious mental troubles.

The love between nurse and nursling is often extremely strong. The nurse often needs the affection of these children more than she may realize to keep her psychological balance and satisfy her maternal wishes. For this reason she struggles to retain it by working hard to keep her babies always helpless, and thus dependent upon herself, since as babies they will need her alone. As a rule, of course, the nurse loses them entirely when they are grown up, whereas the mother does so only partially.

The jealous appeal for the love of the child and the methods such people use to keep what they feel may be given to or taken by a rival are dangerous. The child, because of the former love felt for this person, becomes bound to her, and correspondingly suffers more acutely from the cruelty of this person, who will not let it go free. At the same time the child may loyally try to respond in a greater measure than it feels, through the wish not to hurt her or from compunction springing from guilt, when it realizes that love has faded from its attitude towards this person now she is no longer so necessary to existence or pleasure as in the past, and that others are now preferred as playmates or confidantes.

Nurses clearly feel that they have the first right to the children, refer to them as "my children," and in some ways arising from this attitude influence them against their parents, or, later, against their teachers for this same reason. On the other hand, in cases where the mother has not particularly cared for a child and left it psychologically neglected and unloved, many nurses have come to the rescue and ministered to that infant body and mind, to the end that both physiologically and psychologically it has been preserved.

One always feels that "Cummy," Robert Louis Stevenson's old nurse, who is honoured in the dedication of one of his books as "my second mother, my first wife,"[1] occupied this position for him. The mother in these cases often becomes a stranger in the nursery, whose advent is resented alike by nurse and child. The child who, when taken downstairs, clamours for the nursery as "home," or is restless when the nurse is out and upon holiday, may frequently be deprived of her presence altogether by the jealousy of the mother, who forgets it was through her initial neglect of the infant that another first adopted it. Still, there are many persons who do not want anything until they observe that it is precious in the sight of another. This factor will always awaken the interest of the jealous man and woman. Hence the object must be acquired forthwith, be it a human being or an article of adornment, in order that they may be equally envied.

In these several ways do we see the child tossed hither and thither among the waves of adult jealousies. Another conflicting current will come from the father, who in reality will often be given much cause to be jealous of this small but powerful rival where he is concerned, which will surely arouse many painful echoes from the past to stimulate hostile feelings in the present. The father most certainly takes up a position in the background when the baby enters the arena. Unconsciously the husband occupies the position of child to the mother-wife; the real baby is the usurper before whom consciously and unconsciously he must abdicate, and the fact that so many women actually do neglect their husbands even more than necessary in favour of the baby still further aggravates the trouble.

Many women, once the baby is in their arms, give to it the bulk of their love and the larger part of their attention and care. The husband is then regarded merely as the universal provider, who is the unwanted third party of the eternal triangle and disturber of the united bliss of mother and child. In these cases it is not to be wondered that the husband goes off to hide his jealousy in golf or dancing, which may or may not arouse fresh animosity on the part of the wife, who, although she does not now so ardently desire his constant society, is

---

[1] *Child's Garden of Verses*, R. L. Stevenson.

nevertheless reluctant to think that he should prefer the company of others to her own.

The child is the innocent cause of all the family strife and jealousy, afterwards paying the penalty by conflict brought about by the reactions caused by parental jealousy towards itself, because parents who are jealous of one another, or on account of one another, seldom remain guiltless of showing some sign of their feelings where the object of their jealousy is concerned. The result is usually some remote or veiled attitude of hostility, sometimes even one that is quite openly aggressive, which will be fed from sources deep in the sadistic impulses of the parent.

The father or mother who asks the child, "Whom do you love best, Daddy or Mummy?" paves the way for mental trouble in the future. It is a question that never should be asked, an evidence of rivalry which is always dangerous in a home. The child, as we explain elsewhere, needs the balance of both parents in harmony for its normal development, and should be allowed to love both, without being encouraged to show favouritism as a means of gaining some advantage or escaping some penalty, which may easily be the next step in parental efforts for supremacy. This question is, of course, always a sign of inter-parental jealousy, the wish to confine the love of the child to the questioner. It shows the desire also to gain some exclusive right to the child's affection or confidence, and will probably show itself with renewed vigour whenever the child is confronted by the possibility of making new friends. This first happens, usually, when it goes to a new school, where new teachers may prove attractive and wean affection from the home which parents wish to reserve entirely for themselves, and again, often still more disastrously, it may interfere with the son's or daughter's happiness when the transference of affection concerns a new partner for life.

As children grow older, we will often see jealous parents hindering their development or thwarting a success through their conscious or unconscious reactions, grudging it should it be attained, and clearly showing by their behaviour that their actions are motivated by jealousy. When this occurs we generally find that the most acute jealousy occurs in the mother over her daughter and with the father about his sons, unless for some particular reason the emotional accent has been reversed.

The child who is brought up thus in an atmosphere of jealousy reacts to it in several ways, most of which will be methods of self-defence, an attempt to serve and please two masters by the usual expedient of hating the one and loving the other. The child who tries to compromise, to struggle against party-feeling, and disguises it for reasons of family policy, is more to be pitied than the one who openly decides in favour of one parent rather than the other; since the ensuing conflict is greater and has more disintegrating consequences upon its character, which thus develops under most inauspicious circumstances. Lying, deceit, and the destructiveness of always trying to please, so as not to lose parental love, will ruin the child's independence and initiative. The efforts of the child, who, feeling bound under all conditions to please, often of necessity striving to satisfy two persons at once, who are requiring different types of behaviour, have some of the most injurious effects that can be met. Yet it is a contingency that is lamentably common in households which contain jealousy, and is the consistent outcome of their jealous requirements, which, after all, are the expression of neurotic tendencies. It is unfortunately an only too common neurotic characteristic to desire evidence of greater affection than that shown to others, and in the case of the attitude towards children will so often show itself in this question mentioned above, and the anxiety to impress upon the child the idea, "If you wish to show your love for me, you will always do what *I* want, and what *I* tell you. You will want to please *me*."

The child learns the lesson and tries to put it into practice at the cost of its mental health.

The jealous parents of to-day were made jealous by unwise management at the advent of another brother or sister or by the favouritism of the parents for one child rather than another, or simply by the imitation of their own parents, so readily are these character-traits handed down from one generation to another, because the child copies those elders who are within the home circle.

It is exceedingly easy to gain the acquiescence of parents to the idea in general that the influence of jealousy in the family is extremely injurious, but correspondingly difficult to gain an acknowledgment from a parent that *he or she is jealous*, that this feeling is actually showing itself in particular ways which will be harmful to the family in that house. The contemplation of a generality is always more pleasant than the recognition of a particular and personal application of an unpleasant realization. Actual experience demonstrates that it is only too true that parents do not like to own to any imperfections in their characters, and strive to maintain the fiction that they are not swayed by feelings that beset other mortals. Why this should be it would be exceedingly interesting to know. "Prophesy unto us smooth things," cried the people of old, and it is still the wish of parents, and for this reason. They usually consider those who bring them different tidings, concerning the origin of their children's nervous troubles, to know nothing at all about them.

THE OVER-CONSCIENTIOUS PARENT

The over-conscientious parent shows us another type of person with neurotic character-traits, and one who occupies a special position for consideration, because this tendency is constantly regarded in the light of a virtue rather than the opposite, so that any suggestion that might shake this belief would seem unlikely to the majority at first view.

How does the over-conscientiousness of a person manifest itself, and by what signs shall such men and women be known? Much fuss, much worry, they will never be content to let well alone. They have morbid fears that they or others have not done their duty, that something has been left undone which will have still more disastrous consequences. Little lapses of conduct will be magnified until they attain the importance of serious crimes, and childish lack of knowledge or want of experience will not be tolerated as the justification or excuse for conduct which does not attain a standard of adult perfection.

Over-consciousness will burden persons with the weight of their own responsibilities and often add to them by taking over those of others, which is a quite unnecessary action. *Ought and ought not* are the Janus-headed God which rules their lives, and they are equally anxious that everyone under their control should bow the knee to the same deity. They become exhausted by punctiliousness, cancelling any benefit which might result from their actions by their methods of carrying them out. They are afflicted by a sense of guilt out of all proportion to the importance of their lapses, real or imaginary, and are never free from self-consciousness and self-esteem for trying to live up to this standard of self-imposed virtue.

Often enough do we trace the origin of this adult character-trait in a reaction-formation to an opposite tendency in childhood, that the natural childish irresponsibility was repressed too young and too severely, so that it was changed into a neurotic and exaggerated version of the reverse manifestation. Nevertheless, it may have always existed in this same form, partly as the outcome of parental severity and undue premium placed upon the characteristic from infancy, because it was the most sure and successful way of securing parental approbation and love, and partly to gain supremacy over less conscientious brothers and sisters, until the tendency developed into an obsession. The most marked characteristics of this type which are apparent in human beings are usually the result of repression, leading to the mechanism we have referred to before as *reaction-formations*. These show the surrender of childish impulses in order to gain or retain love, and concerning which a keen emotional conflict took place. The exaggeration and change into the opposite tendency marks the old scar and shows the attempt to expiate the former feelings of guilt, which may now remain hidden in the unconscious, although marked by the persistent striving after the opposite of the original impulse.

An outstanding characteristic of obsessions is to develop rituals, to attach to special actions a feeling that they must be carried out in some particular fashion so as to avert disaster or in order that the desired result may be attained. Anxiety will be experienced directly any hindrance prevents the correct procedure from being completed. Another characteristic of obsessions which form a large proportion of the over-conscientious person's life and daily activities is that they usually concern trivial events rather than important ones, so that details will be given a greater prominence than the whole affair, which may readily be seen will tend to dislocate the sense of proportion of the next generation.

Cleanliness, tidiness, good manners, proper behaviour, are all matters of superlative importance to these afflicted persons, who wear themselves out as well as others in the struggle to achieve their ideal. Standards once set will be adhered to with unswerving regularity. No extenuating circumstances will be admitted or permitted. No consideration exists of the particular conditions of passing years, nor the changing ways of the world. They retain the same oughts and don'ts in the years of their maturity and independence that were imposed upon them by parental commands and prohibitions when they were under the family roof and jurisdiction. It seems impossible for them to readjust to altered conditions or special requirements, and there will be found more or less repudiation of reality and a clinging to vanished tradition in their vain attempt to hold time stationary both for themselves and their children.

It will not be necessary to point out in detail that the influence of such people as the trainers of youth will be more harmful than beneficial, and yet, until psychology had striven to show that this characteristic is the outcome of neurosis, it was considered a virtue highly to be desired in those to whom the care of children was entrusted. The foremost virtue to be sought in them, one might add, and the priggish children whom they evolved, spoke convincingly for the zeal with which they carried out their task. Priggish children, frightened children, and rebels were three of the nervous types which such early influence threw upon the world. But, then, priggish children were admired by that generation, and so were frightened, repressed children, as long as the symptoms of their neurosis lay along the lines of recognized repression with inhibitions that did not inconvenience adult persons, and fears innumerable that kept them "good" and obedient. It was only the children who were strong enough and independent enough openly to rebel successfully against the regime of the over-conscientious adults that remained mentally healthy, while the parents crossed out their names from the Family Bible or considered that they had joined the ranks of the black sheep of the world.

But, alas! many of these rebels did not rebel successfully. Only too frequently the struggle to gain their freedom would also create a tendency to exaggeration, and we would find the rebellion not confined merely to burdensome parental conditions but transferred to society at large. In the eventuality of the rules that were spurned being not only fussy family injunctions, but social law and order, that would also be kicked aside in the attempt to win personal liberty, this reaction only brought the rebel into conflict with communal justice.

We may then imagine their over-conscientious parents holding up their hands in horror at the reactionary behaviour of some son or daughter, wailing pathetically that they could not imagine how it should have happened when they always tried so hard to teach their children what was right, to set them a good example, and to punish them whenever they deemed it necessary; all for their good and with the best intentions. They took the unsatisfactory conduct of these children as rank ingratitude and never conceived the possibility of their actions being one of the contributory causes of the children's insurrection.

In all probability they always omitted from their calculations the workings of the pleasure-pain theory, the fact that the child will rebel if parental discipline be overstrained and severe education attempted without an adequate pleasure premium. Typical cases where the over-conscientiousness of the parents has been imitated have occurred where the reward offered made the demanded sacrifice appear an equivalent to the burden imposed. Therefore, to do these things meant gain, or, at any rate, the avoidance of guilt and punishment, and to leave others undone meant an easy conscience through adoption of passive obedience, that accepts the parental standard, repudiates personal responsibility, and looks for guidance the whole life long, without accomplishing any personal development except in imitation of the parents. All behaviour otherwise will be reduced to rituals for cancelling wrong-doing, to atone for guilt, or to gain some reward perhaps in the remote future of another world.

Naturally the exaggerated strictness of bygone ideals of religion fostered these sentiments, but their results unfortunately live on in the neurotic persons of to-day, who make it one of their most important life-work activities to educate children. If they have none of their own, and often their tendencies will preclude marriage, they will strive to satisfy their neurotic craving to bring up others in the right way by finding such a mission among the children of others. We may discover them plentifully in educational and welfare circles. The tendency may be utilized socially only too easily and its danger remains undetected, unless it shows itself in some grossly exaggerated form by one who has knowledge and experience of the possibility of over-conscientiousness being, in fact, a form of obsessional neurosis.

THE SADISTIC PARENT

We may find a transitional type between over-conscientious parents and the Sadistic Parent. Often the two are extremely closely interwoven, as sadism forms one of the roots of the former impulse, which will be more easily understood when we reflect upon the close connection between the psychological twins, sadism and masochism. The over-conscientious person is frequently a masochist gladly suffering penalties imposed by another in service of duty. Also because he or she will cause him- or herself endless suffering and glory in it for the same sake of duty, we may also discover sadism turned against itself. At the same time endless pains and penalties will be inflicted upon others, pleasure being taken in so doing, by which process we see the true sadistic impulse at work.

One is fully aware that one runs the risk of incurring heavy censure from parents in pointing out that they and those in charge of children find in their efforts for education most facile methods of gratifying these primitive and sadistic impulses, believing themselves moved solely by the best intentions for the good of the children. We have already referred to some of these methods as well as pointing out a few of the injurious consequences that prove their existence in the character-development of children. But there are other forms besides which have as yet received no explanation, many so subtle in their action that only the suffering of the child, which leaves its mark in the resultant neurosis and its incapacity to face life adequately because of the early training, teaches us how it has been produced.

Children generally take for granted unhappiness caused them by their parents. Seldom do they rebel against it consciously; often they do not seem to love them the less for it, nor seek any redress, yet a compensation will nevertheless be sought and found, usually by means of some unconscious expedient, or a neurotic symptom will make its appearance that serves the purpose of a compromise representing the original impulse of the child that was denied expression as well as a method of avenging itself upon the parent, and acts as a means of self-defence at the same time.

In punishment we have the most direct expression of the adult tendency to cruelty or sadism, and in the choice of punishments we shall find evidence of their personal tendencies as well as proof of acute observation of the child's psychological characteristics, because the most vulnerable spot in its affections or emotions will invariably be chosen upon which to work, in the service of education, according to their point of view.

Punishment has always aimed at a double, if not a triple, purpose. Its manifest reason, nowadays, is to act as a deterrent, and in the interest of this aim much cruelty towards children will be excused. But it also acts as a vicarious restitution for the harm which it is felt the child has done. Therefore that it should be made to expiate by its sufferings the outraged feelings of the adult is an opinion held by many. Thirdly, it is a discharge of the primitive impulse of cruelty, the savage blood-lust that lives on undiminished in the unconscious mind.

We know that in former days the father possessed the right to kill children should they be unwanted, sickly, or rebellious. They might be sold into slavery or disposed of by exposure or indirect methods, should they prove undesirable. We are also aware that from time to time in the world's history, men and women have existed who took a morbid delight in killing or torturing little children. An account of one such distinguished person, Gilles de Rais, has recently been published, compiled from various authentic sources by A. L. Vincent and Clare Binns, with an introduction by M. Hamblin Smith, M.A., M.D., Medical Officer of Birmingham Prison, showing that the sadistic impulse of this once brilliant man was the outcome of neurosis, which had doubtless been caused by a most unfortunate and unhappy childhood which is known to have been his lot.

Nowadays, we are not often shocked by such extensive and spectacular evidence of the sadistic impulse, yet we may find records of it plentifully enough among the proceedings of the Society for the Prevention of Cruelty to Children, but at the same time it may also be frequently seen in the houses of those where it might be unsuspected and where it usually remains undetected, often among the subscribers to the aforesaid Society, without these persons noticing the least connection between their treatment of children who are at their mercy and the cases investigated by the Society.

In the latter case the cruelty is usually psychological rather than physical, which leaves no visible marks upon the child's body, although traces appear that are more lasting upon the mind and character that are not taken into account, however, at present.

A great many punishments still symbolically represent the death penalty, even if they do not directly express it. *Death* is a permanent sending away, a separation from the presence of love of the parents in the eyes of the child. This idea appears frequently in the punishments meted out to quite little children, such as being sent out of the room, up to bed, put in the corner, where they cannot see the rest of the household and where their face is hidden from others. The theme is also constantly represented in the Hebrew Scriptures, namely, that in consequence of the sins of the Children of Israel, God turned His face from them, and they died; were no more seen. If their sins were expiated, God would then uncover His face and give life once more unto His people.

Threats to this effect are still plentiful in the up-bringing of children, from the crude and straightforward "If you do that again, I'll kill you," through the whole gamut of circumlocutions of "Out of my light; I can't bear the sight of you! Get away with you, do! I'll get another child. I'll run away and leave you. I won't love you any more," to "What a cross face! Put it in a bag, so that I can't see it." If a gesture is *an action in little*, as Captain Rattray tells us in his interesting book on *Ashanti*, published some few years ago now, a threat is the echo of an ancient deed of bloodshed and vengeance, which would then have been carried out and to-day survives in the figure of speech. It still expresses the same wish in the mind of the speaker to be revenged upon the other for some misdeed. We are, indeed, justified in questioning emotions hidden behind such words, even if their true import should remain buried in the unconscious mind, whenever a threat of this kind passes the lips of a parent.

The child, moreover, generally recognizes and accepts the unconscious motive of the threatener, and suffers acute fear corresponding to the wish that found expression thus. The fears of the child of to-day, suffered on account of what are often called *imaginary causes*, are for the most part the same as those experienced by the child during past ages on account of events which were then actually possible. Separation from persons to whom the child feels he or she ought to be able to look for love and protection is regarded as an equivalent of death; often far worse, because separation, loss of sight, and loss of love, connected with the idea of loss of contact, are irremediable in the child's mind. Nothing can provide compensation for this calamity, except the finding of a parent-surrogate upon whom the old feelings may be projected and in whom confidence is reposed anew.

These punishments and threats are direct methods of discharge of sadism; still more direct are the corporal punishments which are bound to provide intense gratification for this impulse to the person who inflicts them, as well as pleasure of a sort to their victim, connected with impulse gratification of other erotic zones, which were noted in the section devoted to the explanation of the childish impulses. We constantly see how great must be this satisfaction in the inflicting of corporal punishment for offences great and small from the eager letters that pour into the columns of the Press, opposing any suggestion that it should be abolished, from both parents and school-masters, who declare themselves unwilling to give up the old custom. They will often add that they and their forefathers were flogged at school, so we may conclude that they believe this to provide an excellent reason why they should now continue to do the same, naturally to gain compensation in kind for punishments received by themselves in the past.

Those persons who do not indulge in corporal punishment

may, nevertheless, become very ingenious in devising substitutes that will hurt a child still more in a susceptible part of its mind or affections. A little girl who was devoted to her father was made to go and tell him each evening upon his return from the City whether she had been good or naughty during that day, it being impressed upon her that it would pain him extremely to hear of her wickedness, and it was generally represented to her that she had committed some sin almost daily.

The governess who devised the idea of making the weeping adolescent sit and gaze at her tear-stained face while repeating her imperfectly learned lessons, and jeering at her meanwhile for looking ugly, was giving free rein to her impulse of sadism, trying at the same time to shame her pupil and play upon her impulse of masochism.

The sadistic impulse often finds its discharge in raillery, teasing, games and stories that are always found to frighten the children they are intended to amuse, and yet, in spite of the constancy of this "unexpected" result, it is ignored and persisted in. Fathers and mothers are equally guilty in this respect. Fathers may be more inclined to tease the children openly, play rough games that hurt or frighten them, tell pirate tales, alarming fairy-tales, or blood-thirsty giant stories that send the little ones off to bed with the shivers; but mothers express their cruelty in more subtle ways, such as sharpening their wits on children, playing games that they cannot understand and so always lose, or even cheating and lying to them, taking advantage of their lack of knowledge of the double meaning of words, or their implicit faith in the words and promises of grown-up persons. A few examples may be useful to explain what is meant.

For instance, a little girl's mother, who believed herself a good woman and who was considered a model parent by her acquaintances, was fond of playing games of this description with the child. She would play "Heads I win; tails you lose," with her until, being taken in again and again, the little daughter at last said wearily, "Mummy, you seem to win every time!" "What a silly you are not to have found that out ages ago," was the retort, instead of any explanation of the joke. She would also play a strange counting game in which she began, "I one my mother," the child continuing, "I two my mother," and so on alternately up to eight, the child wondering all the time what it meant. When the little girl said, "I eight my mother," she was severely scolded, presumably in fun, because she was said to have meant either "I *ate* my mother," which was cannibalism and very wicked, or "I 'ate my mother," which was naughty, because in the first place it was bad manners to drop one's aitches, and not to love one's mother was unfilial, forbidden by the Fifth Commandment, and meant that God wouldn't love one either, so that you would go to hell and burn all up when you died.

The child was left in a sad state of mental confusion over this game, more profound than the average adult can realize. She was also emotionally puzzled how to proceed for the best. If she stopped short and refused to have anything to do with this "8" problem, giving as her reason that her mother always turned whatever she said into something that she did not mean, and was wrong, she was told not to be so suspicious, especially of her mother. It would be difficult to find a more refined type of cruelty than this to practise upon a little girl who was outstandingly sensitive, affectionate, and obedient, but the mother would amuse herself for hours in this fashion and had a wonderful repertoire of such games which all ended in the same way. Still this mother was also a keen supporter of the Society for the Prevention of Cruelty to Children, and upon one occasion became most violent in denouncing some person who had recently been convicted of bodily cruelty to a child, adding that no punishment was bad enough for such persons; they ought, if possible, to be made to suffer in the same way. The child, who was present, looked at her mother in amazement, realizing quite well that she was every bit as cruel as those she was denouncing, and longed for the *dénouement* of the fairy-tales, where the cruel stepmother is asked what should be done to a certain person for a certain offence, and is then told that she has pronounced her own doom.

For some strange reason parents, as a rule, do not think that it is necessary to be truthful or honourable where children are concerned. Their usual standards in this respect undergo complete disintegration. They will lie and cheat, or contradict themselves about what has been said upon a former occasion, declaring that the mistake is upon the child's side, and break promises, apparently without the least compunction or a moment's hesitation. They seem to think, by some method of adult reasoning, that a lie is not amiss if told to a child, or to cheat one younger than themselves is not as reprehensible as the same action in regard to an equal. Is it that they do not stand such a good chance of being found out, perhaps? Or do they not value the child's opinion of themselves enough to fear a fall in their estimation, as they might in relation with their fellows, and which then acts as a restraint?

Brought before a tribunal of children, who would judge them according to their merits and not on the principle of parental prestige, or the hypothesis so often insisted upon by the head of the family that a parent can do no wrong, how many would go unconvicted and scathless? Probably very few; nor do many realize how scanty is their sense of honour or truth when dealing with children, what the children really think about it, and how it affects them.

It is, indeed, difficult to instil creeds of kindness, justice, affection for others and altruism, truth, and honour, when we behave so differently towards them. May we be forgiven when we tell them the most transparent lies, perjuring ourselves entirely, adding to our crime by trying to make the child believe that it has been the one to have misheard or misunderstood; that we are really being very kind to it, and acting for its good, when we are really only finding an outlet for our own sadistic impulses and working off feelings of revenge that it or another has provoked, but which for many reasons it would be more difficult to discharge upon another adult than upon our helpless prey, the child.

All this parents do because children are so helpless. They are such easy victims, so confiding, so forgiving. To deceive a child who trusts us, to break faith when we have given our promise, ought to make adults feel guilty, but more often they think themselves rather clever for having been able to score so easily, and that the whole matter is a very good joke.

Other Types of Parents

If these three groups of parents are of the greatest importance in the later development of psychological troubles of children, what of the others, the silly parents, the untidy, the sentimental, even the happy-go-lucky and the wise parents? Silliness will bring its own reward or punishment. First that the child will discover their foolishness sooner or later, whether it remains open and artless or whether a bombastic attempt be made to cover it with a disguise of assumed merit. The child will start by being disappointed with its parents when this truth sinks home; afterwards it may turn and love them again for their simplicity, or despise them for it and go off to find parent-surrogates who are more worthy of its regard. They will not be of very much moment unless their folly makes them try hard to prevent their children rising above their own level, either in intellect or in social or professional work. With the sentimental people, however, we find a different state of affairs.

Sentimental Parents

Sentimental people are frequently those whose own affections have been or are still in a state of starvation, who are urgently seeking some response that will satisfy their pangs of love-hunger. Often, not being attractive to their contemporaries, because they have little to offer by way of equal companionship and are of small intellectual capacity, they will practise a kind of vampirism upon the children who come across their path.

Predominantly they will be parents who are not gaining much affection from their marriage partner, those who have been the victims of sentimentality in childhood and so accustomed to this type of exaggerated love-expression that they do not understand any other variety, or unmarried persons who are pitifully seeking someone to show them affection and upon whom to lavish it; to whom they can be in some way necessary. These people will often show a streak of sadism also running through their other neurotic character-traits, perhaps a tendency to scold or tease a child until it cries, and then lavish caresses or sweetmeats to comfort it. Sometimes the prevailing habit may be to torture it verbally by protestations that they do not love it, or do not think of it when out of sight, so that the child will work itself into an agony of emotion trying to make the adult in question say this is not true. Or the protestations will take another form, and adults will tease the child to obtain from its side pledges of love. These expressions of anxiety on the part of the child concerning affection will salve the wound of the unloved adult. They satisfy the pangs of the sentimental cravings for love, vehemently expressed by someone, no matter whom, and regardless of the sufferings of another if this personal satisfaction can be gained.

Sentimentality may also be adopted as a pose to pass for affection by those who wish to stand well in the eyes of others and to create a good impression. To the children themselves it will naturally come as a surprise that these manifestations take place only in the presence of visitors, and they may even comment upon it, like the little boy who one day asked his mother, "Mummy, why do you stroke my hair and call me darling when ladies come to tea?"

Untidy Parents

Untidy parents may be of two sorts—those who are untidy because they are not afflicted with the neurotic tendency to overtidiness, which we have already described, and those to whom we may refer as pathologically untidy, when, in fact, the untidiness is a revolt against a parental demand for orderliness from them, or because it satisfies some primitive wish to live with all their possessions always in sight.

We often find that small children have a great objection to putting away their toys, because then they can no longer be seen. They disappear, which makes the child apprehensive whether they continue to exist and if they will be found again next time they are wanted. Also the spreading of possessions over the whole room stakes out the claim, as it were, to all ground covered by these articles. This desire to acquire territory as extensive as possible in order to leave no room for others will probably continue to be the underlying motive of their untidiness, although in later life the cause will be forgotten. The wish has been repressed and become unconscious in the adults who show this peculiarity, but it continues unchanged since childhood, when they would annoy their parents in this way.

Generally speaking, however, outward untidiness, be it a

revolt against society and order or a preference for carelessness in appearance or surroundings, will show itself equally in many other mental processes, inaccuracy of thought, slovenliness of diction, bad spelling and the like. The inaccuracy is often a means of self-defence, a protective reaction against correctly remembering or understanding something which is unpleasant. The inhibition where one thing is concerned quickly spreads to others. If accuracy is not too rigid, more latitude is possible in the matter of responsibility, or it may even be possible for untidiness to be adopted as a distinguishing mark, because at one time someone may have commented upon it as a noteworthy trait or thought it amusing. It is, therefore, a way of attracting attention, of gaining a certain notoriety, which does not require much effort.

Happy-go-lucky parents often make an excellent background for children, since they avoid most of the difficulties brought about by those who are obsessed by exalted notions of their own importance as parents and strive to impress their authority; those who are over-conscientious, sadistic, or sentimental. Usually, although they may be lacking in some of the qualities one feels advantageous for the bringing up of children and may throw too much responsibility upon shoulders not yet strong enough to bear them, they will not often indulge in damaging recriminations or stimulate undue feelings of guilt in the child, should the youthful experimenter not be successful. Neither do they err in the important matter of giving the children plenty of space for self-development, ample elbow-room as a tumbling-ground, and they will usually be warm-hearted folks who are ready to pick the child up after a tumble, kiss the place to make it well, and encourage it to try again.

But the wisest of all parents are those who thoughtfully look ahead, while remembering their own childhood, know and understand the minds and impulses of the child, guide it and love it all the while, when it loves them and when it turns from them temporarily to love others, when it makes mistakes, and when it adheres to home-law and follows parental example. Wise are the parents who do not take themselves too seriously, who retain their sense of humour, and, above all, reflect that many other folks are parents too, all of whom are capable of bringing up children better, as well as worse, than themselves; all of them being sometimes less wise and knowing than their children in some matters.

Books which may be Studied in connection with this Chapter.

Mother and Son. C. Gasquoine Hartley.

Psychoanalyse der Weibliche Sexualfunction. Dr. Helene Deutsch.

Cummy's Book. A. Cunningham. Preface and Notes by R. T. Skinner. Chatto & Windus.

Gilles de Rais. A. L. Vincent and Clare Binns.

Child's Guardian. *Proceedings of the Society for the Prevention of Cruelty to Children.*

CHAPTER IX

DAWN OF PERSONALITY

In a lecture given last year before the British Psychological Society in London (March 7, 1927), Professor Jean Piaget, of the University of Neuchâtel and the Institut J.-J. Rousseau, Geneva, stated his views concerning the attitude of the child in earliest infancy, that is, during the first year of life, towards the outside world and itself. They are views which, in the main, are held by all those who have investigated these dim regions of the initial stages of child-life, when definite proofs beyond the evidence supplied by observation cannot be obtained. This, however, is a method that is open to misinterpretation, or even falsification, on account of our own attitude to life, and also towards the particular baby who is the subject of the observation and investigation.

The first conception of the universe held by the average baby, and certainly by those upon whom such investigations are usually carried out, is as a frame for itself, and, in its opinion, the only purpose of all persons is to obey its behests. All objects exist but to be its playthings, is its evident thought. Yet we find those babies brought up in homes where little of the attitude which may be summed up as "baby-worship" is practised, making far fewer demands upon life, showing far less animation and frequently more indifference to their own needs and discomforts. Where these investigations are concerned it is well, from the commencement, to keep in mind the fact that, in the case of the most detailed investigations of infants, the subject has usually been the first child of the investigator, who was probably given every assistance from the outside world to regard itself as a most wonderful being, and the child responded by a warm appreciation of the adulation and ceaseless attention in the ways recorded. The infant, however, who is not made the point around which the household revolves, does not possess this ego-centric character to such a high degree, which seems to demonstrate that it is not an invariable infant characteristic apart from the influence of the behaviour of those around, or entirely independent of the circumstances of environment.

Piaget called attention in this lecture to the fact that the infant awakes from its dream to realize its separate existence through the resistance of others, but before this, Freud postulated that the origin of fear in the infant is this same realization of separation, the feeling of being alone and disunited from the mother by the act of birth.[1] It would have been in accordance with the ego-centric notion of the child had it then been capable of realizing its surroundings to be another human being, connected with itself in some way, to have regarded this other person as its covering, and therefore dependent upon itself and part of itself, rather than itself being part of the larger adult upon whom it was utterly dependent for shelter and subsistence.

Freud and Piaget agree upon these main points of the child's first realization of the outer world, arriving at this conclusion from independent investigation. Those of the one are derived from remnants of infant thought surviving in the mind and actions of the adult, the other from direct observation of one baby, his own first child, in its infancy. They hold that opposition and resistance crystallize the child's conception of itself, through repeated demands for the sacrifice of its narcissism, which, in the first place, appropriated all persons, surroundings, and possessions as outlying portions of itself. In this way we may see upon the one hand that the child's idea of itself in these early stages first undergoes diminution, since it must surrender what was originally but erroneously believed to be part of itself; yet, on the other, it rapidly increases, since it acquires opinions concerning itself, its attributes, potentialities, and values from those around, as well as fresh accretions to its personality through the process of identification with those it loves around, in exchange for what has been given up.

With the growth and development of the child, its thoughts concerning itself become more concrete, if more limited. At first it takes its unity with the world around for granted, subsequently the resistance or opposition of the outer world and the behaviour of others shakes this belief in its own omnipotence.

---

[1] *Hemmung, Symptom und Angst.* 1926. Freud. *Int. Ps.-A. Verlag, Vienna.*

We may watch a desperate struggle on the part of an infant to deal with this disappointment. It may accept the proof of experience and the consequent disappointment, in this way acknowledging its own relation to the outer world and reality, thereby gaining a normal outlook upon life. Nevertheless, it may refuse to accept the proof of experience and struggle to maintain an opinion that *its own wishes are reality*, therefore being compelled finally to replace reality by a phantasy of its own making, which in time becomes an individual reality. That is to say, it creates a phantasy world which completely surrounds itself, separating the person increasingly from the reality of the outside world and that of others. A considerable amount of energy is taken up in the maintenance of this individual reality, and it precludes normal relationships with others. Extreme cases of this refusal of reality will be found in the manifestations of neuroses and psychoses, including especially dementia præcox, as well as in paranoia, where all discrimination between reality, that is, external reality, and individual reality, by which is meant the external world and the phantasy world of the individual, has been lost, or has never been definitely gained. The reason for this has been in some cases that the denial of the primal disappointment occurred too early, the demand was too urgent, or the grief accompanying it was too bitter for assimilation.

Without doubt, were we to make a detailed investigation of individual types, we should find which circumstances, or rather what constellation of special events, led to the original acute disappointment, as well as the chief factor of reality that could not be accepted; probably also that a complete absence of compensation made the acceptance still more impossible. Should these conditions be subjected to minute scrutiny, we may see how careful readjustment in the early training of the infant might possibly have safeguarded the necessary painful transition from primary omnipotence to a limited ego-sense, so as to have lessened the poignancy of the sorrow connected with the acceptance or recognition of reality.

In fact, a baby's training might be made possible without undue insistence upon humiliation and the usual exaggerated demonstration, later on, that it is of little or no importance in the household whatever, as an antidote to the first few years of inordinate spoiling. The sudden contrast and direct contradiction of the two methods leave the child with feelings of confusion or hostility. It will then refuse to consider this altered situation as reality, because its natural bias in favour of the pleasure-principle insists that the earlier state of well-being is correct and the second must be repudiated at all costs, in spite of every proof to the contrary.

When the adults who supervise these first years of infancy and childhood realize what an important part the dawn of the ego-sense may play, we may discover to what extent we may assist most wisely and beneficially in its development, and how this may be accomplished. At present all that we know for certain about it is its negative aspect, how, and in which ways, it becomes damaged and to what extent character-formation may be deflected from the course of development we should wish by mismanagement, early over-severity, ridicule, or prohibition. At present the usual attitude towards a child's realization of the Self, true *self-consciousness*, is that it represents vanity or conceit and shows precocity, and therefore it should be stamped out with all speed. Any realization that it may be useful or necessary for the development of the child's personality, its character, and future prosperity, seems at present outside the comprehension of the adult mind.

Why should this be? What object should the adult have thus to hinder the realization or development of the child's personality, its ego? It appears mainly to be an outcome of unconscious fear of rivalry and the resultant clash of personalities, which might, it is feared, become more emphatic if acknowledged.

From observations that have been already quoted, it may be assumed that the baby's first attitude towards itself and the universe is that they are identical, and that only gradually does it learn to recognize distinguishing marks and boundaries between them, through the resistance of adults in the course of its training. This primary self-feeling or *narcissism*, as it is called, becomes to a very large extent repressed, partly because it has not been successful, and also since it is afterwards found not compatible with the far-reaching demands for sacrifice of baby self-importance in order to retain the love of the adult. This surrender presents serious difficulties for the child, and becomes a question of such cardinal importance that it may be worth while to discuss whether this dual attitude towards the child, which changes so rapidly within the first few years, is necessary or advisable, should we compare the value of results gained with the undesirable consequences which appear.

What, then, may we learn about its undesirable residue in the character of the growing child? Among the recollections of early childhood, gathered through the psycho-analysis of adults as well as children, we find that the cause of a large amount of indecision of character, of failure to undertake the responsibilities of life and grasp the actual value of personal capability, springs from just this source, together with an exaggerated estimate of personal ability, should the second stage, that of curtailment, never have taken place, have been refused, had it been extremely light; or an overwhelming sense of inferiority allied with guilt assails the child, should it have been carried through with vigour.

The first training of the little child is usually attended with exaggerated encouragement. Early attempts at walking, talking and such-like activities are received with praise, so that the baby learns to expect this reward of adulation for each fresh effort or even the repetition of familiar actions. Through the process of repetition this will be regarded as an integral part of its own performance, so that should it be overlooked, omitted in haste or through inadvertence, and when finally it falls into disuse because the novelty of the child's early achievements ceases to be of so much interest to the adults, or because these actions are now taken for granted, the child suffers considerably from disappointment. It will feel either that the adults have changed their loving attitude towards itself or that it has ceased to be so clever as formerly. Consequently it may fancy everything it now does to be wrong, since it does not call forth the accustomed response of exaggerated praise.

In this way the attitude to the Self or the parents may undergo a severe shock, the imprint of which will be shown upon the character in years to come. It may have been caused by the adults thinking that the child was beginning to look for praise too constantly, that it was becoming "spoilt," and therefore it was necessary to deprive it of all gratification of this kind in order to readjust the balance. Even so, this is not altogether a wise proceeding, because psychological starvation is equally injurious. There may also be another reason, however, for this change in the behaviour of the parents. Should another child increase the family, the first-born will suffer in many ways, especially if the accompanying abdication of some baby rights be not managed with special care and forethought. The little child will then, in addition to the other ways in which it feels its kingdom to have been stolen away and its privileges surrendered, be obliged to watch and see or hear another being made the recipient of constant praise and encouragement, which, perhaps, it is beginning to forget was ever bestowed upon itself, of which it may think it is no longer worthy, or because it is not the object of so much love as before. This naturally makes the wound in the child's self-love more tender, and it seeks in vain to find compensation for the trouble. In this case the difficulty is usually further complicated by a hearty dislike of the infant who appears to have been the cause of the change in the parents' attitude towards itself, so that general hostility may be the result, combined with a feeling that whatever it does will be wrong, because the expected and hoped-for assurance formerly gained through lavish praise is no longer forthcoming.

This lack of assurance readily becomes a source of intense diffidence and a sense of inferiority, that of being unappreciated, which will become the more difficult to understand and to bear should the change occur after the child has already enjoyed many years of the former method of over-appreciation.

The normal course of child development shows the child relinquishing the first ego-concentration after a while, and adopting some person or persons, who are necessary to his or her well-being, as objects of affection, whose wishes will be carried out, whose presence is desired, and without whom the baby feels lonely and incomplete. This early transference from the infant's self to mother or nurse is the first step towards social contact and the realization of the existence of persons and objects outside the self. At first, naturally, the child believes that he or she is the only love-object of this dear person, and that no other interest exists for her besides itself. It then becomes a second disappointment or narcissistic wound, as well as an awakening to reality, when the infant learns that it is one of many, and that adult attention has of necessity not one focus point but several. Unless this discovery be utterly refused or struggled against protractedly by the child in the way we have already described, when an unwelcome truth is too suddenly confronted in the early years or insisted upon with too much severity, the resistance offered by the child will be resolved in time. In this case the child will be better able to grasp reality and his or her comparative relationship to others, than if the former infantile self-importance and false values of babyhood had been retained over a longer period or never relinquished until the time came to leave the home circle and meet a fresh standard of the school or the outer world, whose criticism will not be so lenient nor whose praise so lavish as that of the family. This inevitably acts as an unpleasant shock to the child and leads it to believe all those outside the home circle to be most disagreeable people.

In a large proportion of cases we find that the child will feel and express the same opinion about itself as the parent, who has most to do with it, or its nurse. Should there be sharply conflicting views in the household concerning the propriety of its behaviour, we shall then most probably find this same conflict represented in the child's mind concerning itself. The bias, doubtless, will be in favour of the person it loves best or that which is most flattering to its self-love, according to the stage of development already reached, which, of course, naturally increases the difficulty of the child's self-estimation.

The acceptance of the wishes and instructions of another because of love is the best and soundest method of child-training and builds a firm foundation, provided, of course, that the wishes and instructions are in themselves desirable. They will, however, inevitably become transferred to the child and incorporated into its labile character, no matter how freakish and distorted they may be, because the neuroses of the adult are thus only too readily transferred to the extremely impressionable mind of the child at this age.

Through this method of adopting the wishes and standards of the loved adult, the child still contrives to gain its own wishes, since these have now undergone a change and become those of the other person. The child by means of this imitation of the training person has become like the adult, has identified itself with her, and is never tired of imitating her in this way, which, of course, consists mainly of doing what she wishes or as she does. This power of identification on the part of the child is one of the greatest constructive forces of the ego or super-ego development. At the same time, however, it may be the cause of complete bewilderment to the child, should some trait or mannerism, having been faithfully copied and reproduced, fail to achieve praise and bring down a scolding instead, because the adult does not appreciate the imitation.

Before we can advance to the next stage of development, we shall be obliged to retrace our steps slightly in order to make a few fresh additions to the idea of the little child's discovery that other persons in the house are of equal or greater importance than itself, and justly claim a share of the time and attention of the mother. In this way we are brought face to face with the presence of the father in the family, so that it will be necessary to devote some study to the part he plays in the mental development of the child.

Not only shall we be obliged to discuss the attitude of the child to the father, but also that of the father towards the child, of the father where the mother is concerned, as well as the reverse, the mother's conscious and unconscious thoughts towards her husband and her children. In this way we find problems which account for a very high percentage of the mental disturbances of children, especially those who grow up in an inharmonious family where open or even concealed discord exists between the father and mother.

Many parents believe that this may be kept entirely hidden from the children, but from experience it has been discovered that it is impossible to maintain this secrecy where the children are concerned. In spite of all precautions, the children become aware of the strained feeling, or the want of unity between the parents will in itself most adversely affect the children, since it will cause the parents to behave differently towards them. In the first place, when it is impossible for them to find their normal outlet of affection and emotion upon each other, they will probably seek a substitutive outlet upon the children, or upon one of them. Each, perhaps, may try to outbid the other for the love of the children or one child, in order to alienate

that child or all the children from the other. The motive underlying the choice is also important, as well as the particular
form which the discharge of this redirected affection takes.

It is by no means uncommon to find a number of petty
jealousies cluster around a baby, apart from those experienced
by the little creature itself, on account of others who appropriate
the time or attention which to the infant's mind would be
better spent upon itself. These have been referred to in the
preceding chapter, but we may briefly summarize them again
in order to show how they may affect the baby's growth of
personality. Thus, the mother, to whom the baby is a very
precious possession, will scarcely be happy when it is out of her
arms. She feels that no one can look after it or make it as comfortable as herself; but, on the other hand, she may, should she
all her life have played the part of the much indulged infant,
be extremely jealous of the attention now given to the little son
or daughter by others, feeling that she is by far the more
important of the two. The nurse again enters the lists in this
fight for supremacy where the baby is concerned, and feels
convinced that it is upon her that its welfare depends, that
its chief affection belongs to her, and only grudgingly allows
the parents a small share, other people being told firmly that
it is injurious for a baby to have its brain excited by strangers.

The father's part in the early contest for the affections of
the new-comer is not conspicuous, as a rule. We seldom find
him trying to prove himself of the utmost value or importance
where necessary services are concerned. Quite frequently he
goes away to sulk, and feels once more that his nose is out of
joint, as perhaps it may have been in his childhood when
another little sister or brother came to disturb the peace of his
universe. He may be aware of the true origin of his discomfort
or he may not. He will probably consider that it is right and
proper response to "making such a ridiculous fuss about a
baby," and feel justified at going off to play golf with his men
friends or losing himself at his club in the hope of finding a
fellow-sufferer with whom to indulge in mutual sympathy.

It is not altogether rare to find men suffering from some
slight illness or indisposition during the wife's confinement or
directly afterwards, which reminds us of the primitive custom
of the *couvade*, when the father stayed at home in bed to look

after the new-born infant, and to receive the congratulations and gifts of the neighbours, while the mother went back to her work in the fields. Possibly also we may find in this illness an identification with the wife, or even the baby; the hope to capture some interest and sympathy, since so little time or attention is left over for the man of the household at such times in the ordinary course of events, as J. M. Barrie admirably pointed out many years ago in *The Little White Bird.*

The father may be jealous of his wife because she is receiving all the congratulations and is the centre of interest; while certainly he entertains feelings of conscious or unconscious hostility towards the baby, unless he manages to identify with the tiny being, and in this way receive vicariously some of the adulation. This happens most frequently when the child is a much desired son and heir. The father begins to appreciate his little daughter more fully when she is of practical use as a playmate, and later on may become particularly devoted to her, especially if she singles him out for her chief favours, which generally happens before many years have passed, in the normal course of development.

Occasionally we find the mother quite openly acknowledges that she prefers her children to her husband, and notice that he is quite frankly relegated to a second place in her affections and interest after the children are born. He will not be allowed to take a prominent part in bringing them up, except to pay the expenses of nursery upkeep, and may often be told it is not a man's place to interfere with the children; that is the mother's prerogative. The children will soon adopt the same attitude and views corresponding with such expressions of discord as these: "Isn't Father a nuisance"; "It was so nice before he came back"; "He always does spoil everything"; "He's a tease," or "so rough." So in course of time the father learns that he is not wanted in the nursery and has no right to be interested in the bringing up of his own children.

This view, nevertheless, is a mistaken one. Both parents are necessary for a well-balanced psychological development of the child; neither can be excluded without damaging the influence of the parental identifications. Should we now return to the discussion of the child's development through identification, we may see what part the father does play and the result of the harmonious blending of both tendencies at work in the home, as well as the interplay of both aspects of training in the more normal cases. Of course, it is possible to find homes where the father and mother attitudes towards the child, as well as towards life and each other, have become reversed, where the father possesses what are generally regarded as the feminine characteristics and the wife has a decided masculine tendency. This naturally leads to considerable difficulties in the children's development, in the same way that children who are brought up by one parent alone frequently show unusual characteristics in their ego-development, owing to conflicting identifications which are so formed, sometimes from the dual aspect of the character of the same person, without the addition of a second personality to create a balance.

The child, we have already remarked, learns through imitation and is usually encouraged after a time to take as a model the parent of the same sex. This works satisfactorily when they are fairly normal, love each other, and behave towards one another with average kindliness, politeness, and consideration. In such a case the child, anxious to play at being "grown-up," copies them minutely in every respect, and all is as it should be. But this happy state of affairs is by no means always the actual one. Because of the many possibilities of jealousy and its consequences, which have been already described, and since the tendency in some children is always to want more than it is possible to attain, the desire for the unattainable *per se* will be paramount in them, which will cause them to feel that they can never be happy until they attain adult privileges in childhood. They cannot wait to grow up. Sometimes they strive their utmost to gain the whole attention of mother or father, taking the other parent as a rival, who must be excluded at all costs. They will never be satisfied with any substitute compensation, but would rather go without altogether and be miserable than make the best of what may be had.

One of the most frequent wishes of childhood which can never be attained is that of the girl to be a boy. Often she refuses absolutely to accept the fact that she is a girl and cannot by any means change herself or be changed into a boy. The corresponding wish of the boy to be a girl may also be found, but is usually regarded as more uncommon, at least in consciousness.

Both these wishes will be rediscussed in detail in the chapter upon Children's Games and Phantasies. The wish, however, exerts widespread influence upon the mental development of the child. The refusal to accept an unalterable fact certainly affects the grasp of reality in general and tends to make the child identify itself with and copy the parent of the opposite sex rather than its own in order, unconsciously, to achieve its aim by means of this identification. *Unconsciously* the wish remains eternal and the conflict unending. No adequate compensation may be gained except that of identification, unsatisfactory as this may be in many ways.

Hence we shall not find it difficult to recognize in this wish the root of many forms of child neuroses and psychological difficulties, since they arise from wishes which find no gratification or outlet, and particularly those involved in the construction of the ego. The girl who refuses her feminine rôle, who identifies herself with father and brothers, will adopt an almost lover-like tenderness towards her mother, and may become jealous of and hostile against her father on this account, or regard her mother with the same feelings of inferiority as she entertains for herself in the capacity of a girl, accompanied with scorn and hatred, since she feels that her mother was in some way to blame that she was not a boy.

On the other hand, the rather boy-like little girl may be a great favourite with her father. He will make her his pet and share a great many of his hobbies or interests with her on account of the implied flattery of her imitation of himself. She becomes increasingly his companion, until, at last, the mother may become jealous of this alliance and strive to dissolve it. However, although the little girl may do her best to copy father and brothers, her thwarted wishes, nevertheless, cause her to feel the most decided hatred of them, since she knows that they have and are what are denied to herself. Her envy will be such that it may express itself in numerous ways, because her wishes can find no other adequate discharge or compensation.

The normal ego-development of the little girl is often believed to resemble closely that of the boy in its earliest stages, but it is doubtful whether this is possible, since the feelings of both parents differ widely according to their individual psychological make-up, with respect to sons and daughters, which cannot fail to have extensive consequences where the children are concerned. Again, the standard of behaviour required of the girl is still rather different and somewhat more strict than that of the boy, which alters the training of both children from the outset more than is commonly realized. The mother, as a rule, will tend to be more lenient with the son, his actions will be condoned as boyish high spirits or "manly," whereas the same conduct on the girl's part would be considered rough and rude. Of course, at the present day there is not nearly so deep a gulf fixed between the behaviour expected from the girl and allowed from the boy as formerly, but still it cannot be said to have disappeared altogether, especially in the nursery. After all, it is there that these deeply engrained habits are formed, together with the children's reactions to them. Their results are the outcome of the child's feelings of injury on account of the injustice of its parents, and quite small children realize to the full the double standard, which leaves the girl with the disadvantage, while the boy makes use of his advantages to the full.

The mother's influence may be said to predominate in the first stages of the ego-formation of boy and girl, since it plays the chief part in checking the early infantile impulses and changing their course. We have already described this action in some detail, in the section allotted to the impulses, as well as those explaining the influence of the special senses for the child's development and the consequence of inhibitions arising from mismanagement or too hasty and severe pruning of the awakening senses and impulses. The father may also play his part in this phase as supreme authority quoted by the mother, to please whom she urges the child to obey her wishes. He will be made to serve as supreme authority sometimes, at others a nonentity; a sort of bogy; or the source of ultimate justice and retribution should she fail to be able to enforce discipline alone.

This aspect of the father, which we may point out is one usually not ungratifying to paternal vanity, especially to the father of the past generation, portrayed for us so vividly in books such as *Sandford and Merton*; *Father and Son*, by Edmund Gosse; as well as Samuel Butler's *Way of All Flesh*. This struggle for paternal supremacy has had an exceedingly interesting history. It may be traced down the ages from primitive times, through its competition with Mother-Right, which it finally abolished legally, although it has not been able to do so psychologically, in spite of all its efforts. Mother-Right is the natural outcome of the child's first dependence upon the mother, and her essential supremacy where the infant is concerned during the earliest span of life. We may trace the growth of the father's assumption of supreme rights in the Totem Laws, the institution of Puberty Rites, and also in his assumption of power over the life of the new-born child, whether this infant were to be exposed upon some hill-top or brought up. The father possessed jurisdiction over the life of the child, when the practice of abortion and infanticide on the part of the mother was punished with heavy penalties, even if not the forfeit of life itself.

Traditionally the father stands apart from the early training of the child, as the Gods upon Olympus. The modern Daddy in the Nursery, and Clubs for Fathers, run upon the same lines as Mothers' Welfares, are a manifestation of the recent cultural development. What it signifies precisely will be interesting to discover from the psychological point of view. It would seem that it may be the outcome of an unconscious identification of the man with the woman, his wish to be as essential to the early welfare of his children as their mother. If the original unconscious motive of the struggle for paternal supremacy were the jealousy of the father towards the mother, and represented the wish to be of the greater importance in the family, this is but a clearer manifestation of the same wish showing itself in an attitude of solicitude and kindliness rather than the old attitude of authority and severity, which was constructed upon an identification of the father with a paternal and avenging deity.

Several modern books upon the education of young children, written recently by these same well-intentioned fathers, show clearly that they consider themselves the only fit persons to be trusted with such an important affair as the bringing up of the young, and that mothers and nurses by their foolishness influence them most injuriously. (*On Education*, Bertrand Russell.)

However, all the world over, during the first few years of

the child's life the mother attends to them or they are in the hands of women almost exclusively, be they boys or girls. After a certain period, differing widely in various countries, stages of civilization, and times in the world's history, due to different circumstances, although always with the same intention and aim, the boys are separated from their mother and placed under more or less complete male influence and authority. In this action we find the paternal supremacy gaining power. We also find that, together with this actual bodily separation, an accompanying endeavour manifests itself to effect an emotional rupture with the old home ties, especially those which attach the sons to the mother. This is effected by the spatial separation and the presence of male instructors for the outward purpose of education, as well as serving the unconscious and psychological service of the masculine or paternal identification. By this means a new phase of self-love, *secondary narcissism*, will be formed in opposition to the former stage of object-love directed upon the mother, which includes withdrawal from her and the corresponding approach to the father through surrogates, the masters of the school, or the instructors in the primitive tribes, as well as *group identification* and brotherly love between equals in the group, who are all commonly identifying with the group-leader or father. The composite influence of the group forms the model for boys of one set or those who enter a school in the same year or term, among whom we frequently find a bond of friendship springs up which may last for life. This group widens and later includes the whole school, and university, regiment, profession, nation, or race, all of which communities show group-feeling, that is, *extended secondary narcissism* projected from the self upon the group for the exclusion of guilt, which points out that it is not the right thing to do to love oneself, although one *may* feel affection for one's *alter ego*, which is the basis of the team spirit.

A change in attitude regarding former home conditions is commonly met with immediately the little boy leaves home and goes to school. This is another proof of the fresh influence of male authority that asserts itself, with the same result, scorn of the old home ties and the growth of shame felt about acknowledging any dependence upon the mother or the fact that games used to be shared with younger brothers and sisters. We shall also find a relatively violent reaction in favour of the glorification of the schoolboy, schoolboys' games and slang, with a corresponding tendency to ridicule woman's jurisdiction or influence, her capabilities in any direction, but especially as a playmate.

With this fresh stimulus of identification and the construction of secondary narcissism, we find new developments in the ego-structure. These take place rapidly and set themselves the task of remodelling the original *Ego*, which, it is well to remember in this connection, was primarily the result of the mother's teaching and carried out at the instance of her love. Therefore, the paternal administration of the secondary narcissism in the boys' instance which criticizes the mother will also tend to undermine or change her teaching, as well as to some extent destroy the ideal she inculcated. This fresh stage of ego-structure, the characteristic feature of which is criticism or ridicule of the former self, the old ego, has been called the *super-ego*,[1] and is believed to be derived predominantly from paternal influence, which is the logical outcome of the sequence of events here set down. We find this function of the super-ego in great activity during adolescence, and for this reason.

To bring an explanation of the ego-development in the girl level with that of the boy is a rather more difficult and complicated matter. We have seen that fundamentally the baby girl is as much attached to her mother and dependent upon her as the boy, although the feelings of the mother, where she is concerned, are probably slightly different; this is likely to affect her reactions and character-formation from the start. Gradually, however, a change occurs, and we find that she changes her preference, enlists the help of her father, becomes his favourite, and feels the mother to be a hostile rival and an unwanted person who hinders the pleasant companionship between herself and her father. What has caused the little girl to change the direction of her affection thus and to withdraw from her first love—the mother?

A frequent cause of this alteration in the little daughter's emotional attitude is the arrival of a new baby, which is attributed to some change in the mother's affections towards

[1] *The Ego and the Id.* Sigmund Freud. Trans. Hogarth Press.

herself. The child feels that she is no longer as completely the possessor of her mother's love as before, that her mother has taken a new love; therefore she does the same in reply, perhaps also in revenge, hoping possibly to hurt the mother's feelings as much as her own have been hurt. She thereupon adopts the father, who at this time, and for the same reason, may be in need of a companion to take the place of his wife, whom he feels has likewise discarded him for this new-comer. Thus an alliance springs up from fellow-feeling, itself a mutual identification, with the results which have been already described.

We may also bear in mind that there are also two other probable strands in the girl's hostility to her mother—the trauma of birth, weaning, and the training in cleanliness, which she shares with her brother, and the other trauma, which is hers alone, that her mother made her a girl instead of the favoured boy. This calamity is often attributed to the mother, because the little girl knows that she arranges affairs of the kind in her doll family, as well as details concerning choice of eldest or youngest, the favourite and the black sheep. If, therefore, she, as the dolls' mother, settles these matters according to her wishes, why cannot her mother do likewise; and if this has been the case, it must have been a mark of her disfavour that the little girl has come off so badly.

We may ask ourselves, in consideration of the alliance of father and daughter, whether this forms an equivalent to the stage of the boy's development when he passes from the care and influence of the mother to that of the father and other men for the formation of his manly ideal and super-ego. If this be so, one would expect that boys and girls would all grow up with a super-ego of identical structure, and become still more alike at adolescence, instead of showing, as a rule, a sharper differentiation. One might expect in this case that male and female standards, morals and views of right and wrong would be exactly similar, and yet we know that the super-ego of the boy and girl, their codes of behaviour during the pre-pubertal and adolescent years, can be and usually are widely separated, and that it is an exception rather than the rule to find the girl keeping her boyish attitude after the complete feminine super-ego structure has come into being. This is, in fact, impossible, since the condition of the feminine super-ego structure is an identification with the mother. The stage of the *girl's secondary narcissism*, which is connected with the fabric of her super-ego, is essentially different from that of the boy at the present day as formerly, although there is an increasing tendency for them to approach one another. In spite of the fact that a great many changes have indeed taken place in the up-bringing of the modern girl, the standard of conduct that is expected of her has not yet undergone complete revolution.

Upon consideration, it would seem rather that the girl's development possesses a stage more than that of the boy. The original attachment to and dependence upon the mother may be regarded as approximate in both; but the little girl's love and alliance with the father corresponds with the boy's early love for his mother, which becomes dimmed and sinks into the background during what is termed the latency period, which is bounded by the horizon of school-life and masculine companions and interests.

Originally the father's jealousy of the growing sons and their love for the mother led to their separation from the family, the sons being driven away as they grew older and excluded from the old home and the society of the mother. At a more recent date it became the custom to put them in charge of male instructors for puberty initiation, which led to the institution of modern educational systems. So, too, did the mother's jealousy of her maturing daughter's love for her father cause the mother to keep her strictly confined to the house, or in a special hut in the woods during adolescence, busy with household duties and instruction in the arts that were deemed necessary for the education of women. At a later period of the world's development, it became the habit of girls of the upper classes to be sent from home to a convent, into the household of a nobleman or that of the queen, until it was time to dispose of them in marriage. During this time of instruction the daughter again came under feminine influence and learned the manners and customs that appertained to woman's conduct and duties, which became, as in the case of the boy, responsible for her super-ego structure and the development of her secondary narcissism, which probably showed more individual and personal tendencies than that of the boy, because of the effect upon the girl of the severe super-ego criticism on the part of the mother towards the daughter, who is seldom the favourite child and who is frequently regarded in the light of a potential rival.

Hence the girl's final super-ego is usually derived from the mother, or other female persons, teachers, who will take her place, who will attract the girl's admiration and love, and with whom she will identify, although it passes at one time through a distinctly manly phase. The handing down of the female super-ego in this way from mother to daughter will account for the conservative tendencies of women and the idea so prevalent among them in the past that unless they followed in their mother's footsteps they would not be doing right, and the haunting idea, "What would my mother think if she were to see this new fashion or know about our fresh customs?" It also accounts for the handing down of the stricter female code of conduct and behaviour. The prevalence of the unconventional woman of to-day is a modern innovation, predominantly a reaction-formation from the traditional type, which probably reverts to the wish of the unrepressed girl to do exactly what she likes under all circumstances in opposition to the mother and her teaching.

The girl is taught more strictly at the earliest stage of her training, as well as during the later one, that it is her duty primarily to please her parents and people in general afterwards, if it be compatible with the first. She must be obedient and *good*; that, owing to the fact that she is naturally not as welcome in the family as her brother, she must make amends for this misadventure by her own efforts, by her beauty, her charm, her power and willingness to please, otherwise she is of no account and remains nothing but woman, the inferior, whom nobody wants, nor considers, and whom nobody finally selects in marriage from among her companions.

In this way the girl goes through two courses of mother instruction, which comprise the training given to the infant, whom usually the mother does not prefer, unless she should be exceptionally oriented psychologically, so as to prefer her girls to her boys; and one stage of her life under the influence of her father, which represents the attitude of the indulgent parent to his favourite child, equal to that of the mother to her beloved son. But we must bear in mind, relative with this last-mentioned phase, it does not invariably take place. It is much more likely to be missed out in the girl's development, than for the son not to receive the major share of his mother's love and indulgence. Should, however, this middle phase have been unusually prolonged, or if the mother did not have much influence in the household, the paternal influence upon her may continue, so that her super-ego will then tend to be modelled upon that of her father, in which case we should see her with a less severe criticism of herself, with an ideal that allows greater freedom, a less narrow and personal secondary narcissism, readier identification with a group in which she could enter with more whole-hearted enthusiasm than most women can accomplish. She would have thus a better ability for team-work—women tending, as a rule, to insist upon being either the *patroness* or the *drudge* when working with others, especially women, in whom she would still see the reflection of the mother, the autocrat and tyrant, or herself in phantasy, the cinderella, the child, who cannot hold her own where mother or ugly sisters are concerned.

With the years following adolescence, boy and girl usually return to their former loves in preparation for fresh identifications, which lead to the selection of a love-object that shall be the mate, who replaces for them the old love of childhood. The boy seeks someone who will represent the mother-image; the girl rediscovers the father of her middle childhood, frequently a man somewhat older than herself, who will revive her memories of the man she loved so dearly as a child, when she turned from her first attachment to her mother, through the disappointment occasioned by her desertion at the coming of another baby or some comparable disappointment.

Books that may be Studied in connection with this Chapter.

Group Psychology and the Analysis of the Ego. Sigmund Freud.
The Ego and the Id. Sigmund Freud. Hogarth Press.
Totem and Taboo. Sigmund Freud.
Loss of Reality in Neurosis and Psychosis. Sigmund Freud. Coll. Papers.
Narcissism: An Introduction. Sigmund Freud. Coll. Papers. Vols. ii and iv.
Origin and Structure of the Super-Ego. Dr. Ernest Jones. Vol. vii. 3–4.
    Int. J. Ps.-A.
La Première Année de l'Enfant. Prof. Jean Piaget. *Archives de Psychologie.*
    Spring. 1927.

Pedagogue's Commonplace Book. Edith Rowland.
Psycho-analytic Study of the Family. J. C. Flügel.
Origins of Education among Primitive Peoples. W. D. Hambly.
The Child in the Changing Home. Dr. C. W. Kimmins.
The Changing School. P. B. Ballard.
On Education. Bertrand Russell.
Das Mutterrecht. J. J. Bachofen.
Sisyphos. Sigfried Bernfeld.
Stages of Development of the Sense of Reality. Dr. Sandor Ferenczi.
     Trans. Dr. Ernest Jones.
Contributions to Psycho-analysis. Badger.
Father and Son. Edmund Gosse.
Way of All Flesh. Samuel Butler.

CHAPTER X

GROWTH OF PERSONALITY: DEVELOPMENT OF
THE SUPER-EGO: FAMILY BALANCE

In the last chapter some of the attitudes of parents towards
their children have been described, and it was suggested that
many of these characteristic traits of the parents were the outcome of neurotic tendencies that were already developed or
incipient. Some, indeed, were so general as to be regarded as
practically normal behaviour on the part of the parents towards
the children of the household, and yet the investigation of the
nervous troubles of young children shows that these commonly
accepted reactions of adults have been responsible for the
maladjustment of many of the second generation.

A word that is frequently used in connection with the nervous
or mental adjustment of persons to their environment is *balance*.
We say that they are *well-balanced* or lacking in this, meaning
by the first expression that there is no exaggerated emphasis
to be found through which one impulse or tendency dominates
the life of that person to the exclusion of all others, signifying
that at some time this aspect of life became a cardinal point of
defence or an overwhelming interest, which has been constantly maintained, as though the person still expected attack
or a preponderant pleasure-premium from this direction.

Reinforcement of tissue in animal life proves the need for
psychological defence or protection against external friction.
We may see a similar mechanism appearing in the nervous
symptoms of children, when they mass their resources to with-
stand pressure put upon them from outside forces in one
direction or another; sometimes the exaggeration occurs owing
to constant stimulation of this impulse by parental reactions,
either through encouragement or the negative process of
prohibition.

When we talk about family balance, we mean usually the
equilibrium maintained by the emotional reactions of the
father and mother towards each other and towards the children,

since research has shown that maladjusted children are usually the result of training in homes where the family balance has been by no means normal or that the child or children in the family have been used, unconsciously no doubt, in the struggle to restore the individual equilibrium of the adults, or to act as a compensation for lack of opportunity for emotional discharge, from which the parents are suffering, in ways that jeopardize the mental health of the children.

It is again a question of family balance that parents and children should live together upon terms of amity; yet it is by no means infrequent that one finds frank hostility between members of the household, that two or more camps are formed and an ever-present internecine strife causes reactions which will tend to increase rather than diminish it. We may often see this state of affairs working in emotional cycles. Frequently it will arise from jealousy. The father and mother may be jealous of one another where the affection of the children is concerned, or they may be in a state of friction one with another. This being the case, they may either consciously or unconsciously provide stimuli to which the child reacts in a way which causes the parents to feel justified in taking steps to punish it, or act in some way that the desired result is gained —at least in that it relieves the pent-up feelings of the adult.

This process may often be watched in the child also, frequently following directly upon the sequence of events just described. In this echo, however, the children tell us, or we observe, that when feeling sore or angry at having been scolded or punished by an adult, upon whom direct retaliation is out of the question, they find relief by issuing commands to toys, animals, or even taking trees, stones, and paper figures as their substitutes. When the orders are disobeyed or ignored, they beat or otherwise punish the offender, which relieves the emotional tension and makes the children feel friends all round once more. This happens also when the child itself has been punished and makes friends again with the parent, who has experienced a similar relief of emotional tension from the punishment of the child.

It may, perhaps, not be superfluous to note in this connection that acts of mischief on the part of the child, or destruction of property belonging to another member of the family, which are considered wanton and beyond adult comprehension, and for which the little ones are often believed to be lacking in intelligence or suffering from "moral imbecility," may in some children regularly occur immediately following some aggressive action on the part of an adult or the denial of a child's dear wish. In this incomprehensible action, therefore, we may recognize an attempt on the part of the child to punish the adult for the conduct which has been suffered. It is, in fact, often a close imitation of the adult behaviour. The adult in temper will throw away some toy belonging to the child that has been left about or played with against orders. Shortly afterwards the child purposely, or even *accidentally*, breaks some treasure belonging to the same person. This brings fresh parental retribution upon the child, and the parent once again stands in need of punishment. This motive and imitation has in many cases been found the incentive for acts of violence and destructiveness on the part of young children, but it is exceedingly difficult to discover this sequence of events, because in listening to the narrative of the child's misdeeds it is practically impossible to discover what incident or action on the side of the parents immediately provoked it, especially when the parent concerned on this occasion is also giving the history of the child's symptoms.

Parents always seem to consider that the child must passively accept all and every description of behaviour from them, that it should always remain good-tempered, unmoved and loving, in spite of scoldings, blows, or the confiscation or destruction of toys and other treasured possessions belonging to it. This is one of the great difficulties in dealing with the nervous symptoms of young people, that are fundamentally defence-reactions to the aggressions of parents. They require the symptoms removed, the child made good, passive, doll-like, so that they may continue to use it for the discharge of their emotions without any inconvenient response from the child. In many cases, when one knows the true history of what has preceded the actions of the child, we find that they are not inappropriate neurotic reactions as much as an attempt at ordinary normal self-defence. To deal with this situation adequately and provide a proper cure would be the restoration or establishment of fair-play towards the child, so that it does not need to exert itself to resist this kind of hostility nor demands

which should not be made to one who has not perfect freedom
to refuse them openly.

In this question of fair-play between parents and children
we find the kernel of much trouble. We have already pointed
out ways in which it may be expressed in the teasing and
cheating of children, ostensibly in fun, through telling them
lies and pretending that misunderstanding has occurred on the
part of the child to cover some error of the adult. We find the
same conduct occurring in the common adult reaction, where
the growing knowledge and observation of the child may leave
them in some respects possessed of inferior wisdom. To satisfy
the parental ideal, the balance must always tip in favour of
themselves. If a child in the garden hears the first cuckoo,
parents will say it was a boy down the lane. If *they* first hear the
voice of this spring visitor, then the child must certainly believe
them, and will be allowed to hear it afterwards or at the same
time. But first must come the ritual of parental permission
and calling the child's attention to the fact, "My child, there
is the cuckoo; do you hear it?"

Is this jealousy? It would seem so, but the child is supposed
not to resent the parental disbelief. Should it, however, react
by not giving tidings another year of the first cuckoo or swallow,
nor about primroses found in the wood, unless one can be
brought home in proof, parents will often complain that the
child is uncommunicative; that it keeps all its doings to itself,
forgetting the inhibiting influence of former belittlement of the
child's observation and achievements.

We see this refusal to give the child his or her due growing
with the child's development, and in many instances it will
irrevocably tend to pile still higher the barrier between parents
and children, as well as to destroy the family balance. It is
not always, however, that the parental attitude of hostility,
due to the jealousy of one generation for another, shows itself
in such frank expressions. The present-day familiar reactions
of allowing children to do as they please, to refuse to give them
any direction, which is often the same as *support*, may, in fact,
be a disguised form of ill-feeling and the outcome of the idea:
"If you won't do as I say, go to destruction your own way; I
wash my hands of you!" As a violent reaction to the former
over-severity of parents of the past generation, responsibility

is disavowed, the difficulty is evaded by a negative course of refusing to give the children help or guidance in case they should afterwards be blamed for playing the part of "heavy parent."

These evasions and escapes from responsibility on the part of parents are a dangerous background for the bringing up of children and should be carefully distinguished from the un-neurotic happy-go-lucky parents who were described in the last chapter. To the superficial observer they may seem closely connected, even identical, but if the cause of the behaviour were investigated, it would probably be found to spring from widely separated, fundamental characteristics.

Too much and too little may be expected from children by those who have not remembered enough of their own early days to be able to calculate how the world seemed to them long ago, and exactly what they could or could not do at certain ages—when a difficulty lured them on to overcome it, and when it seemed too hard and must be left alone. Memory may be a guide to some extent, but it is by no means infallible, because each child's attitude to difficulties varies so widely that it is misleading to expect all others to feel about things as we did ourselves; moreover, it is, of course, quite possible for us to add phantasy to our memories of childhood, by which they may be very much distorted.

This is, indeed, a frequent pitfall to the grown-up person. They will often tell the most wonderful tales of their own infant adventures and prowess, to which wise children listen with patience and tolerance, using the same proverbial pinch of salt that they learn to take with other fairy-tales and stories of adventure that concern unknown people. Parents who are really very clever and capable, however, certainly have an inhibiting effect upon their children. Either they have not the patience to watch their children bungling over things that are so easy to them, and do them instead, so that the child is never allowed any opportunity to learn, or they will laugh at their lack of proficiency, and in this way frighten the child into inactivity by the discrepancy between their own brilliant per-formance and the child's lack of skill, so that the latter is afraid to start because the handicap appears too hopelessly vast.

Such a difficulty will be found in the reactions of only

children brought up among adults or when a late-comer in the family finds brothers and sisters already proficient in all the common abilities of daily life. A child will often learn more quickly from those a little older than itself, who are not so skilful as grown-up persons, because in that case it will not be so conspicuous by its clumsiness nor laughed at for failure.

We have already considered one aspect of the problem of family balance, where the child's development was the main issue, when we were discussing the growth of personality and the influence of identification for the construction of the ego and the super-ego. It is impossible for these chapters not to overlap somewhat in content, nor to repeat themselves at times in discussing the causative factors of character-formation, whether healthy or neurotic, because the various aspects of the influence of persons in the environment, together with their causes, play such an important part. Formerly we have pointed out that the attitude of the parents towards one another cannot be disguised should the relations between them be strained, and that the harmony of the home is a deciding factor for the psychological well-being of the children. Lack of harmony immediately upsets this home balance, and its derivative influence will be seen in the treatment of the children, because parents will frequently not only seek a compensatory discharge of emotion upon the children, but find gratification for their impulses directed upon the marriage partner through the children in ways that we have already briefly sketched. For this reason we may see a husband or wife setting out to seek one child's affection in order to thwart or undermine the authority of the other parent; perhaps showing hostility to another because it may be the favourite of the mother or bear some close resemblance to the marriage partner, who is also a rival and has become unpopular due to some psychological or actual reason. The factor of the mother's preference for her children outweighing that for her husband and the injurious consequences of her reactions dependent upon this basis must also be kept in mind.

The reactions of parents to the only child will naturally be different from their behaviour when the family consists of several children. In the case of the only child, we may sometimes find keen rivalry on the side of the parents, bidding for the preference of the child. In the case of several children, the other aspect comes to the fore: the children compete among themselves for the preference of one parent or the other. The question of family balance, the relative importance of the two parents in the house, and the position accorded to the child, whether it is an only child, the eldest, middle or youngest, if it is a favourite or the family scapegoat, will all play their part in the development of character, the formation of ego and super-ego, and in the growth of personality. Let us, then, for a while consider the question afresh from this aspect and try to discover what general characteristics will be found arising from these causes.

The only child has a peculiar attitude towards life, to adults, towards contemporaries and its juniors. Adults will be regarded often with affection, as beings from whom constant service is expected and to whom little need be given in return. The important necessity of pleasing, which will be so prominent in the not particularly favoured child among several, is not conspicuous, because its position in respect of this problem is assured; its faith in its own supremacy has never been shaken by the advent of a rival in the family. We may see for this reason that the only child builds up its ego with confidence, finding rivals only in the triangular situation of the Œdipus Conflict and the rivalry of the parents, which is different to the trouble and conflict that arises when rivalry comes simultaneously from many sources. Difficulties arise chiefly when it steps out of the charmed circle of the home to meet others to whom it is an object of indifference. The regard of these persons must be won by pleasing them. This is an idea that has never before been a serious necessity to this child, and it does not know how to deal with it. It believes that its position in the outside world will be the same as that at home, that it will always meet with preference, that others will be set aside in order that it may remain without rivals, whose rights and perhaps greater capabilities must be taken into full account.

Where contemporaries are concerned, it is also at a loss to know how to act. Usually the only child finds it difficult to take the place of one among many. It prefers to be continually the only one, who gains the entire attention of those older than itself, and it will generally be unpopular with other children of like age. The young are no respecters of persons, and are inclined to make fun of its unchildlike ways and speech, likes and dislikes, because children have a tendency to resent the intrusion of such into their midst, because of their usual attitude of superiority, criticism, and sometimes fault-finding, copied from the adults who have been their companions.

Nevertheless, these children who like their elders and shun or are shunned by their contemporaries will often be found in the society of younger children in no way connected with the family, who usually return their affection. These little ones will give the only child an opportunity to identify itself with the grown-up persons in whose society it lives, and it may derive great pleasure from looking after them in this fashion. There will be no rivalry and no bitterness concerning these juniors, since they have not been instrumental in supplanting itself in the affection of its parents, as would have been the case had they been little brothers and sisters. The elder child, looking after its own small relations, often reacts towards them with some degree of conscious or unconscious hostility on this account, and even when it is kept carefully hidden away, the grudge still remains, that these little ones have been the cause of its own dethronement.

The only child remains with full rights undisputed. All eldest children have, of course, been only children for a time, and to a certain extent possess the same characteristics, but all show this difference, that the blow has fallen, the rival has come, and to a certain degree they have been deprived of some of the love of their parents and some of their own power. Part remains to them, nevertheless—those rights and that power which fall to the share of the first-born—which is clearly recognized by children even when they are still young. A little girl of six, known to the writer, who was one day deploring the fact that everyone made more fuss of the baby than anyone else (meaning herself), and that her brother had a great many advantages not possessed by the rest of them, added with pride that was largely compensatory, in any case she was the eldest, and whatever happened that could not be taken away from her.

The eldest child, however, needs compensations. In many families she finds her lot a hard one and parents would do well to consider whether they do not give too much responsibility to the eldest in making her answerable for so much of the care of the younger ones. It may be that they are burdening her with too many anxieties for which she is not yet ready, and draining her childhood of its rightful freedom from problems concerning the conduct of others, as well as making her censorious and prejudicing others where she is concerned, or, on the other hand, making her through habit and expectation the slave and servant of all.

Thus we find the position of the children in the family influenced by their early training from the parents, their commands and prohibitions, which will usually be the reflection of their own childhood, either similar to that which was expected of them or, as a reaction-formation, the direct opposite. The eldest may be treated, as we have already said, like a supplementary nursemaid, the burden-bearer, the errand-runner, who must give up all her personal pleasures and wishes to wait upon the little ones and amuse them, or she may make herself a mother-surrogate, armed with power and authority, who insists that all her juniors shall wait upon her and refuses to carry messages except for her elders.

This may readily be seen to be of vast importance for the character-development of the child. It appears to have come into being through the early training of the parents and the ways in which they worked upon the child's feelings of love and guilt impulses to achieve their end. It occurs pre-eminently when the eldest child is a girl, because it is very seldom that a boy is expected to wait upon others, or actually help where the babies are concerned. As a rule, he plays with them only when he wishes to do so.

When we consider the attitude of younger brothers and sisters towards this eldest, we often find that she may be adopted as a friendly mother, an intermediary between themselves and the more remote parents, as the devout will regard their saints, or her authority will be thoroughly resented, especially should she be inclined to be "bossy," because, although children consider that real adults have a right to order them about, they feel that authority should not be exercised by one of themselves.

The parents' attitude towards the eldest is often a peculiar one and depends largely upon the difference in age between this child and the others. The advent of the eldest may provoke many conflicting feelings. It may, as we have already pointed out, be welcomed unhesitatingly. It may, on the contrary, be regarded as a disturber of the peace and the happy *solitude à deux*. Should there be a considerable number of years between the birth of this first child and those of later children, she will probably be taken as the confidant of the parents when the others arrive, and step into a position of parental understudy. Consequently she or he in some cases may become isolated midway between the two. In reality, this is a very lonely position, because the younger children, who may be more nearly the same age, tend to play together and group themselves so that the eldest will be excluded from their games. The grouping of children in a family is of great significance, and to understand why it should have occurred in any special way would be to disclose the psychological undercurrents and tendencies of the whole family, their unconscious loves and hatreds, as well as the attitude of each to the other.

If we leave the affairs of the eldest child for a while and consider the characteristics of the second, we often find that extreme jealousy may be seen not only on the part of the elder, which is a reaction that is now generally accepted, but that the second baby in course of time, when the presence of the elder is fully realized, becomes thoroughly jealous or envious of the first-born, constantly turning over in its infant mind the problem—Why did that one get there first; did the parents love it best and so make it the elder? The special jealousy that is experienced when the children are boy and girl, and which is the elder of these, will give rise to innumerable phantasies, which are attempts on the part of the child to formulate some satisfactory reason why this should have happened. The question of comparative age, like the problem of difference of sex, is one that the child cannot solve, but for ever seeks to find some method of being able to control or alter, and upon which it can gain little or no information from outside sources.

Many children, dissatisfied with one or other of these unalterable facts, will construct wonderful phantasies concerning reasons for the causes of things and invent strange rituals for being able to change anything "the other way round," to reverse things, with the intention that could they but discover how to alter things in general, they could then readjust these matters in particular in a way more satisfactory to themselves. Such children will usually develop very strong views about being given their choice, neither do they like to have anything arranged for them without being consulted, since this acts as a compensation for their primary loss of choice in the essentials of life. The children whose predominant sorrow it is not to be the elder or eldest will often have great difficulty in learning to tell the time or in solving any arithmetical problem, because numbers and age, figures and the number of children before and after them in the family, are of such great emotional consequence in their minds. To one little girl, who would have much liked to discover a means of catching up an elder sister in age and height, learning to tell the time was a severe problem, because to her this difficulty was always before her upon the face of the clock. A little one with stumpy legs was trying to catch up a tall, long-legged sister, who always ran away too fast and wouldn't wait. Her chief interest, as well as the only thing she tried to find out about the question of time and the clock, was when and how both hands came together, which was a natural wish in her case, and it absorbed her whole attention in this problem.

The second child, for a time at least, will enjoy some of the advantages of being the baby of the family. It is the favourite for a time because it is the youngest, a love right which comes next in importance to being the eldest. It is one of the especial positions in the family, and one which is too well-recognized as a vantage-point to need detailed description until we examine some of its less well-recognized aspects later on. But it may be that the second child is called upon to abdicate this proud standing when another baby adds a third to the family group. What, then, will occur to the grouping of the children, and how will this change in position affect their character-formation and reactions?

Character-development takes place through being moulded by all such factors. The consequences of relative position in the family will be reflected in each member of the family. Some mark is usually made upon the character of each by the advent of another brother or sister, that would be plainly discernible, were the psychological construction of the children's mental life to be investigated.

With the arrival of the third child, the grouping of the family may arrange itself thus : the eldest may become the companion of one or other of the parents, and the two younger ones become fast friends, should the dethroned baby manage to deal with the disappointment and love the little new-comer, or we may find that because both children have now suffered the same deprivation, the first and second will make common cause and leave the baby to possess the mother undisputed, having nothing at all to do with it, and become fast friends. Yet another alliance is possible. The second child feels sadly displeased and cannot readjust to these changed circumstances : instead of finding any compensation with other people in the world around, and because, too, the elder child may also adopt the baby as its special protégé, it will retreat within itself, sore and angry with everybody. It will have nothing to do with them, and feels that the only person who has not betrayed it, to whom it can still turn for sympathy and solace, is itself. This gives peculiar characteristics of the ego-development, and will often be the cause of a stronger realization of the personality of *myself*, which shall be described at length elsewhere.

This type of ego-structure consequently takes on somewhat of the nature of a double personality, one aspect being the protecting mother, who loves the helpless and otherwise deserted infant, and the other the abandoned baby, both of whom are now contained in the person of the same child, who feels that he or she must act both parts. If this withdrawal into the self takes place on the part of the second child, we will often, at the same time, find the alliance, already mentioned, springing up between the eldest—who has by now found consolation for former feelings of desertion when the second was born— and the new baby, who will be tenderly mothered. This may also show a belated, unconscious revenge upon the second child for having been the cause of the first desertion. It would be necessary, nevertheless, to observe each case most minutely in order to determine the correct sequence of these apparently concurrent events; whether the friendship between the eldest and youngest caused the second child to go away to play this solitary part or if this precipitated the action of the elder child. Should, however, the second child feel deserted by the former playmate as well as by the mother, we may be certain that it will prove an additional factor in the extreme unhappiness of the younger one, who feels totally alone for this reason and deserted upon all sides.

It will now be a middle child, and as such has a peculiar and not particularly enviable position in the family. None of the influential positions fall to its lot, unless it should happen to be the only girl in a family of boys, or the only boy among a number of sisters, which would, of course, make all the difference to its status. But as the middle child it has neither the advantages of the eldest nor of the baby. The first turn or first choice never falls to its lot, whichever end of the family the count commences, which the child may observe only too sadly. Another childish hardship is the handing down of clothes and toys which elder ones have outgrown, of which they are tired, or that are spoilt or damaged in some way. The feeling arising from this custom is usually that nothing belongs personally to them, that everything has already been possessed or damaged in some way by others. There is always the suggestion of having only second-hand possessions, being a second-best or a second choice, in this taking over things that others have ceased to want, which is apt to make the child sad and disappointed with life.

An interesting development of this early taking possession of spoilt or broken things only, and those that were no longer wanted by others, was that it formed one of the roots which led one girl to take up the profession of a sick-nurse. These injured, hurt people were her property, as surely as were the broken toys bequeathed to her by elder brothers and sisters which in her childhood she would carry off into her corner of the nursery and try to mend. She would fondle the dead rats and birds, smoothing and putting in order their blood-stained fur or ruffled feathers, before consigning them to neat little graves, in the hope that they would come up again in some other form, like the unwanted plants or the left-over bedding stuff the gardener used to give her for her little plot. The great longing of this child was to have something of her very own. If anyone gave her a present and said that it was for her, she would immediately ask, "To do as I like with?" which was a telling comment upon the family habit of putting toys or other possessions away, or allowing the others to have them first until they were spoilt, when she was then allowed to enter into her own. Often they would be given as a present.

This child was a middle one, and stood between the Scylla and Charybdis of those older than herself and a baby, who was permitted to claim any of her most cherished possessions and destroy them, which the little girl was supposed to endure with perfect equanimity because this other was delicate. Another grievance was that after vainly trying to discover some occupation, hobby, or game of which the elder children had not taken possession, and then rejoicing in having it as her own without copying the others (to be a copy-cat was a crime in that family, where the elder ones and herself were concerned), the younger one would be immediately helped by the parents or the nurse to imitate her, or she would be made to surrender the prize that she had found to the baby, who wanted it to break in pieces.

All these childish feelings may seem trifling to grown-up persons who look on, but they are enough to make a child very unhappy and appear to the young mind as gross instances of parental injustice. When the middle one has learned to accept the fact that the elder ones, because of their superiority in age, are allowed privileges it cannot yet have, but must wait to possess, the fact that the baby is permitted to share the stage of development without waiting is considered "too bad."

Bedtime is a focus of much childish grief on the part of the middle one, due to the adult habit of only recognizing two groups in the family, *the big ones* and *the little ones*, the middle one when convenient being classed first with the one, then with the other. Bedtime becomes of prime importance in cases when it falls to the lot of the middle one to be put in the second category and sent to bed with the baby, which will be most keenly resented as a blow to its dignity and self-respect.

These middle children, on account of being classed sometimes with those older than themselves, when their performance must of necessity fall short, or again with the babies, when they will easily excel, experience a serious difficulty in forming any correct estimate of the true standard of their personal efficiency. We may find undue humility about some things and an exaggerated pride taken in others that are not in themselves so creditable in children of their age, or still more when they grow up.

Ego-development is made less stable and the establishment of the super-ego criticism uncertain, becoming first lax, then severely censorious on account of this early training. There will always be the tendency to identify either with those whose capacity is far in advance of their own, and suffer disappointment when achievement falls short of expectancy, or to prefer the society of those whom they can easily outstrip, because the ego, on the one hand, seeks compensation for those ways in which the child feels inferior, while the super-ego structure imposes severe censure for not being able to equal those who are older and have had greater experience in any particular form of activity or learning.

Contemporaries will prove as great a stumbling-block to the middle child as to the eldest. The relation to those older and those younger will be understood to some degree, and will follow the same pattern of the reactions that have been established in childhood; but exactly what attitude should be observed to equals is always so baffling to this middle one that they will usually be avoided or ignored. A frequent idea respecting itself may be summed up in the old saying, "Neither fish, flesh, nor fowl, nor good red-herring."

Of course, the middle one has also gone through the stage of being the baby for a period long or short. The termination of this section of life may be seen relinquished with regret or hailed with delight, at least consciously. To the child, to whom this idea of being "the baby" is concerned with that of inferiority brought home by older brothers and sisters who adopt this attitude as a compensation for their own dethronement in the past, it will become at first a matter for rejoicing to be the baby no longer, but it will be equally determined to keep this baby duly in its place as its own inferior, which theory becomes greatly upset if the parents insist upon raising the baby to the same status as itself and allowing it to share carefully guarded privileges, such as they are, without waiting to earn them by growing up.

In order to maintain the family balance, parents need to keep in mind this childish sense of justice, and to remember how much importance it will attach to its own status in the family, and that of the other children. They will cheerfully put up with a great deal, if they feel that they are justly treated and that others besides themselves are obliged to conform to strict regulations of family discipline. For this reason most children resent favouritism shown by so many parents, except the favourite, although sometimes all will combine to make one of the baby. Usually the baby accepts this position without hesitation as a right, and vociferously demands concessions from all should they not be instantly forthcoming. This aspect of the baby's character is familiar, and accepted; but there is another point of view often held by the youngest in the family that is not given so much consideration or publicity, and which results in typical and clearly marked characteristics of a peculiar sort, which make subsequent life not particularly easy for this youngest, nor for those who come in contact with such a one.

The attitude is chiefly a reaction against the spoiling it has received or is receiving, a direct refusal consciously to recognize it as an advantage, and an attempt to cancel it by the assertion that it is distasteful, unwanted, and oppressive, a sign of the overbearing behaviour of its elders that merely emphasizes their superiority and the child's inferiority. Favours will be accepted grudgingly, but will nevertheless be taken for granted. New acquaintances will be regarded in a friendly manner, but only if they show an outstanding preference for the other, as well as signs of being ready for service. Usually, however, they will be considered disappointing before long, and later they are generally dropped, because they are felt not to come up to expectations or because they are supposed to have changed and are not so attractive or kind as formerly. New occupations, especially those of others known personally to them or of relations, are eagerly taken up. They will be learned quickly; and the learner soon feels that he or she can carry out the newly acquired craft or study as well if not better than the teacher or friend, and that in this way they will compel the attention of the public. The interest wanes very quickly; the public attention is found not to be attracted so easily as anticipated, or that it cannot be kept, and a fresh attempt will be made to excel in some other direction, with the same series of reactions towards those with whom the work is carried out or from whom the subject is learned.

Here we find the reverse side of what the middle child

found so disappointing, that the baby tried to imitate whatever he or she had striven to do, and was helped in the attempt so that it might seem to achieve a better result than the child who had originally tried. If this one then took up some fresh hobby, the baby once more came hot in pursuit upon this trial of imitation.

It is possible for this youngest to feel exceedingly jealous of the proficiency of those older than itself and strive by way of compensation to rival first one and then the other, to attract the praise and attention of all adults and gain their help to equal the ability of these other brothers and sisters. When praise ceases, they lose all interest in the work for itself. The desire is to learn to become as proficient as the others, or to appear so, to attract attention, and as soon as the novelty wears off to change to another form of employment or to fresh friends, giving as the excuse that the latter have treated them badly, the work is unprofitable or limited in progressive interest.

We may see by the instances we have quoted how much importance for the foundation of character lies in the position of the child in the family, and its later reactions towards the events and persons it encounters will be regulated after the same pattern. Another aspect of this same problem will be met should we watch carefully to see how the accent of favouritism falls upon the children from the parents or other close relations—in particular, the grandparents. It has been found through recent psycho-analytical research connected with the development of the individual child, as well as in ethnological research, that in past ages to grandparents or one particular uncle were given distinctive rights and privileges connected with the education of the children of the tribe.[1] The fact that the child knows that it is the favourite of a certain person will generally contribute largely to the tendency of the child to identify with the same person, especially should it have been named after the other and led to believe that material inheritance is to be expected from the same source. Common superstition has connected the appearance of certain character-traits or illnesses with the third generation, and should the grandparent be already dead, it is frequently believed that the

[1] *The Psychoanalytic Study of the Family*, J. C. Flügel.

spirit of the ancestor will be revived in the infant next born into the family. We will find a full explanation of the ancient belief of this *reversal of generations*, as it has been called, as well as its survival in popular superstition and the phantasies of little children as well as those suffering from neuroses, in an illuminating paper by Dr. Ernest Jones, among those on Education and Child Study, in his book, *Papers on Psycho-analysis*. In children the phantasy is connected with the childish idea that the adult begins to "grow down again" after reaching a maximum height and becomes once more a baby, having noticed that grandparents are often old and bent. The phantasy will be mentioned again in our next chapter.

Where the favouritism of an adult for a child is concerned, however, the determination is also a matter of importance and will frequently have nothing at all to do with the child itself, although in some cases it may spring from the fact that the child may have shown some particular fancy for this person, or may be the only one who dared to face some tyrannical old grandmother, which may have pleased the old lady. Other-wise we may see causes such as these apparently being the basis for the adult preference: a real or imaginary likeness, in name or in some characteristic, either to the adult in question or to some person intimately connected with this relative, or to some person much beloved by them. Sometimes the motive of favouritism may be an identification connected with narcissism on the part of the elder person, and through which the child is made to fit into some phantasy, usually partly unconscious, of gaining eternal life or at least a prolongation of life by this means. It will often occur in the case of an unmarried, childless aunt or uncle in connection with a godchild, who will take the place of personal offspring.

The favourite child will derive some benefit and perhaps also not a little psychological injury by the occupation of this envied position. It will usually become the object of intense rivalry on the part of its brothers and sisters. The marks traceable therefrom in the character-formation and the attitude of mind of this favoured child will be especially discernible in its feelings towards others in relation with itself. It will always take its own superiority for granted, believing that in some way it is more excellent than others and *merits* this position of pre-eminence, which we have already shown is seldom the case, and is due rather to past associations in the thoughts of the adult than the personal achievements or charm of the child, or it may have been purely accidental.

The most injurious situation in the family which a child may occupy, however, is to feel itself the *scapegoat* or the *black-sheep of the family*. Not only may it in consequence of the suggestion derived from the label set itself to live up to the reputation, but unconsciously it will react to the paralysing influence of the negative feelings shown by those around, by death-wishes towards itself or others, and adopt an attitude of hatred in exchange for the active or passive persecution which often takes place under such circumstances. Not only do the parents treat this child as the scapegoat, the butt of every caustic jest, the victim who gets scolded from all sides for every bit of mischief that occurs in the household, the real perpetrator of which cannot be discovered, but they often encourage the other children to join them in their sport, or, at any rate, do not attempt to check them from following their own cruel example. It may be clearly seen that it is parental sadism which provokes this behaviour, that provides such direct discharge for the tendency, and perhaps acts as a means to preventing scolding or punishing a favourite child, who may have been the actual culprit, through transferring the blame upon one who is unloved. It is also possible that this child may either bear some resemblance to an aspect of themselves which they dislike but cannot satisfactorily deal with, or to some other person towards whom their dislike, fear or hatred could never find expression in earlier days.

Usually such a child becomes moody, self-concentrated in self-defence, revengeful, or suffers from melancholy, depression, and night-terrors. It may also be suicidal or physically delicate. Only in very rare cases does it set itself to achieve some distinction in later life, to force the family to acknowledge its real worth, as an attempt to humiliate them in return for their former treatment, although this will be the common subject of its day-dreams and phantasies. This child will become the weaver of many phantasies, and life becomes a secret, imaginary affair, carefully hidden from the knowledge of its persecutors of daily life for fear of ridicule, and, by way of compensation, the need for which is imperative, a magic country is sometimes invented, where it may escape in mind whenever its oppressors drive it too hard in the encounters of daily life.

To many it may seem impossible that such happenings could take place in a family with parental sanction, or that the parents themselves might even take part in such treatment of one of their own children; but, in point of fact, it has been discovered only too often to have been the case. It is also possible for this persecution to be carried out in the presence of parents and other adults, who either do not notice what is going on or are oblivious of its harmful consequences. They may believe that it is only fun, and that the child is foolishly sensitive to react in this way to a little teasing, so that the best cure is to laugh it out of it, which they will proceed to do, with the best intentions and the worst results.

Parents and other adults in charge of children can be surprisingly blind to events which have their unconscious sanction or to behaviour of their own, as we have already frequently pointed out. They do not realize that teasing is a form of cruelty, and a mean form, because it is also a lie, since it pretends to have no special purport, when actually it is motivated all the while with the express purpose to hurt the child in such a way that it can neither escape nor retaliate.

Children in the family are keenly aware of the parental attitude to themselves as well as towards others. The neurotic child will frequently bewail the fact that nobody loves it, an observation that the parents make, too, but fondly believe that they have hidden the truth from the child. The parental attitude towards boys and girls of the family will be certain to colour the feelings of each one towards the other, and also where their own sex is a matter of consideration. If the girls are made to feel unwanted and that boys only are desirable; are required to wait upon their brothers and are put in the background, while everyone and everything is sacrificed to enable the boys to receive the best of everything, as well as an expensive education, while they go without all that makes life attractive, or even necessaries, it will affect the boys as well as their sisters. Should the reverse take place and be the predominant attitude of the parents, we shall find a correspondingly different orientation on the part of the children. Yet both of these exaggerated preferences show an equal want of balance on the part of adults in charge that is going to dislocate the psychological equilibrium of the children.

Boys and girls in themselves are neither inferior nor superior to one another, except as the result of some neurotic reasoning on the part of the person who holds this theory. Both are equally necessary to fulfil their several functions in the world and should not be compared one with another in the family in this way. Justice and equality of upbringing are as necessary for the one as for the other, but the tendencies and unconscious phantasies of adults will materially affect the minds of children at an exceedingly early age in this respect, which will have grave consequences and injure the character-formation of the child utterly, in ways to which we have already referred in other chapters.

The dual feelings of superiority and inferiority, with their inseparable connection with the results and causes of Guilt, will work havoc with the mental development of the child. The axiom once established, "Because I am a girl, therefore I can never excel," will become a hindrance for life, unless some most unusual occurrence or special form of treatment be taken in hand to reverse it. "Because I am a boy, I can do as I like," will make the boy take for granted that all women will allow him to do so, and feel deeply injured when this does not happen. The counter-expression of feelings derived from a difference in the parental attitude and early training, "Because I am a girl, therefore I need never do anything unpleasant; I can always find a man to do that," and "If only I were a girl, I need never do any work," will be of equal danger to adequate adjustment of life that produces happiness and a minimum of friction with the outer world.

All these matters are concerns of family balance, the attitude of the parents towards the children and towards each other. What the real thoughts of the children are towards their parents is usually most carefully screened from the closest observation. A hint may be dropped here and there, some information is gathered sometimes by a remark made almost inadvertently by the child, or when it thinks no one is paying particular attention. Children have a wonderful capacity for discerning the unconscious motives, impulses, and wishes of their parents, of reading their thoughts which they would be inclined not to acknowledge to themselves even if they were aware of them; but children seldom divulge these matters, and are particularly silent concerning them at the time, although they may confide them in one whom they believe safe not to give them away, years afterwards, partly from loyalty, partly from guilt. They have been taught, especially in the past, that to criticize one's parents was forbidden by implication in the Fifth Commandment; but there is another still deeper root of their silence, which is the pain that is associated with finding out that they are not perfect, which will be accentuated when the acknowledgment is made in words and to another that the parents have failed to come up to expectations and have proved a disappointment. We are left to gather by inference the child's attitude towards those that are most near and most dear to it from material supplied by its health or its neurosis, its day-dreams, games, and phantasies.

BOOKS WHICH MAY BE STUDIED IN CONNECTION WITH THIS CHAPTER.

Love in Children and its Aberrations. Oscar Pfister. Trans. George Allen & Unwin.
The Young Delinquent. Cyril Burt.
Mental Abnormality and Deficiency, and Introduction to the Study of Mental Health, by Prof. Sidney L. Pressey, Ph.D., and Luella C. Pressey, Ph.D.
Vom "Mittleren" Kinder. *Imago.* 1921. Vol. ii. Heft i. Dr. H. Hug-Hellmuth.
Significance of the Grandfather for the Fate of the Individual and The Phantasy of the Reversal of Generations. Papers on Education and Child Study. Papers on Psycho-analysis, Dr. E. Jones.

CHAPTER XI

CHILDREN'S GAMES AND PHANTASIES

WHEN we come to consider the importance of games and make-believe in the life of the young, we find that they provide a key to the child's mental activities, as well as an index of developing personality. At first glance this may seem a statement too sweeping to be justified, but should we analyse the significance of these means of mental expression and ascertain the exact part played by them, including the source from whence they spring, it may then be found possible to understand that this is true, and therefore change our opinion as to its temerity.

It is now generally accepted that all children, with very few exceptions, play games of some kind, and that it is rare to meet those who do not love make-believe in some form or other. Those who are conspicuous, because they do not play, are some of the lowest grades of the mentally deficient, in whom we should not expect to find the characteristic signs of mental activity, which gives us valuable evidence for the truth of our first statement. We frequently find, nevertheless, that children in whom a faculty for make-believe is very highly developed may, certainly when they reach the later stages of childhood, keep their ideas most carefully hidden and are by no means willing to communicate any details about them, especially to those whom they feel are asking out of curiosity, who are going to criticize, or, still worse, may constantly refer to them afterwards as a joke or relate them to strangers. Other reasons why this secrecy should be observed we will explain later in connection with their origin and purpose. Still, the fact that games are played in secret may mislead casual observers into thinking that the children do not make use of this expression of thought.

Among this group of childish mental activities must also be placed the phantasy, so like the other two, games and make-believe in some ways, so unlike them in others, with this great distinction, that, whereas the former are characteristic of early childhood, when both will generally be practised quite openly, they become of less importance later on, and usually fall out of use entirely. Their place will be taken by the phantasy, which increases in importance in correspondence with the diminution of the original forms. Although ideas that run through all these stages remain unchanged, different phases of development show various means of expression to which distinguishing names have been given. The phantasy continues to be of value throughout the whole of mature life and may be clearly traced, recurring at times of stress, whenever the need for this solace is required, to balance adverse circumstances arising from the outside world of reality, since the compensation thus provided seems in many ways necessary for the maintenance or restoration of mental balance.

If we accept games and make-believe as the earliest manifestation of this compensatory activity, we will see that they all contain the same fundamental ideas from which the later phantasies are woven; indeed, they are created out of the same materials, from the same source, almost by the same process, but have one main distinguishing peculiarity. They represent that form of the phantasy which can be shared with others in our childhood, and about which we do not mind anyone knowing. They may continue to show this characteristic until we have discovered that others are likely to abuse our confidence. But a difference is apparent in the child's later behaviour towards the true phantasy. This attitude then becomes extended to the closely related day-dream and night-dream that are based upon phantasy material. These are most carefully hidden from others and are not shared, being, with very few exceptions, jealously guarded as the private and personal property of their owner, not only when we are young, but also as adult men and women.

There is also another distinction which is not without certain significance. The language, we may say *the form*, in which they are expressed is different. At first the idea is put into *action*, given outward and visible form. It is there for all to see, and upon it others may put their own construction, or none at all, resembling in this way the child's rituals disguising the death-wish and its obsessional actions. The phantasy, however, may also exist in words or thoughts alone and may be treasured thus as a valued possession, which would be lost if shared with another, or should another know anything about it. Children often feel that the told phantasy is lost to them, because it has ceased to be locked up inviolate in their own mind. It has then gone and can never be regained, which, of course, does not come into consideration in the case of the games and make-believe of the earlier stages.

Another reason for the difference between these two manifestations of the same mental phenomenon is that the games have often originated from adults, who may have taught them to the children, and frequently join them in this play, thus sharing them with the little ones, whereas the phantasies which are kept so secret are, as a rule, the versions and variations of the game which the child has evolved for itself and to which some element of things *forbidden* has crept in. Guilt is present in some form, or there would be no such need for secrecy. The child's first expression in action is almost entirely automatic, imitation of the grown-up person, as in games of *peep-bo* and like diversions. The thought is represented by the action, probably action comes first and thought afterwards, and there is no intermediate stage where one thing is sought to take the place of another idea, which is one of the disguises of the phantasy in later life, where usually everything is altered just a little or may be most elaborately symbolic.

We have said that the child's first games and make-believe need not be hidden, because they are the result of instruction and imitation of their elders, who would naturally approve of their own inventions. But quite often they will show disapproval when the child begins to make individual variations in the parental themes, working into them some of its own peculiar interests, which the adults have perhaps carefully and purposely excluded from the first version, and which they will remorselessly continue to remove as soon as they appear. The child may appear to turn them out in compliance with the wishes of its elders, but makes of them a *private phantasy* of its own, and afterwards experiences greater pleasure on account of them, because they were points of especial interest to itself in the first instance and were repressed by the discipline of training adults. The child most certainly does not strive to hide anything until it has been taught shame and guilt through adult prohibition, as well as their censure and disgust.

The hiding that the child learns in peep-bo will not be taken in this light, unless some definite alteration in the idea of the game has been made or the mother has already practised taking away and hiding the child's toys as a punishment for wrong-doing, or refusing to look at the baby itself when it has been naughty. In that case the idea of peep-bo would become the alternating symbolism of good and naughty, with the guilt expunged by the return of the mother, who by her deed declared all to be right once more. The mother, however, will not have given the baby any impresssion that the game of peep-bo should not be played, and babies already make a careful and hair-splitting distinction founded upon the difference between what is guilty and what is not—that is, which actions are permissible and which are forbidden. The complex emotion Guilt thus becomes attached to certain actions: how, we do not altogether know, but it is generally because something has been said, done, or implied that has given the idea to the child.

The change from the open game to the secret, treasured phantasy is affected by the operation of this factor Guilt, as we shall investigate later. Only upon very rare occasions, when some accidental occurrence, a common sorrow or difficulty, has shown two persons that the same phantasy is possessed by both, will it sometimes be shared, to their great mutual benefit, because *Guilt shared is*, like sorrow, *guilt halved.* (A sorrow shared is a sorrow halved.) It is seldom confided in anyone else, however, or to a third person, unless, perhaps, many years afterwards, when it has ceased to be of such significance, and then only to a most intimate friend, whose approval will be taken for granted. (*Gemeinsame Tagträume*, Dr. Hanns Sachs.)

It may happen that a further development of the childish phantasy may find its way through to reality in later life as a hostile, even criminal tendency, in illness or insanity. Sometimes it will be given back to the world as a beneficent gift, shorn of a few of its earlier ego-centric characteristics, and clothed with a beautiful disguise, as a work of creative art, a poem, or some other literary production, drama, painting, sculpture, or music. It is possible, then, that the author may not fully realize that in this way material is being reanimated which was contained in embryo in the phantasies of childhood, that the chief figure around which the artistic work circles is still the Self, but in some changed form, the ideal or chosen figure, represented as fulfilling the desired moment. Others, who participate in the production as onlookers, readers, or audience, also derive an outlet for the same phantasy, which is hidden within themselves, equally without recognition of the fact, yet their emphatic praise or stringent blame will point to its existence.

Friends and relatives will show their entire lack of knowledge of the artist's essential phantasies by remaining oblivious of the identity of this transformed self; nor will they recognize the expression of the personal phantasy, which they must already have encountered in numberless forms as it changed and developed during the various phases of life, since however, carefully the child or the adult may try to hide a prevailing phantasy in its entirety, some clues will usually be found upon the surface which will tell much to others who know their meaning or who are in sympathy with their owners.

If, then, all these manifestations are but the expressions of the same material and spring from a similar source, what is this material and whence the dynamic force that creates such energy? These are naturally questions which confront us at first glance and appear to be as important as the reason why their later stages should be kept so carefully guarded from prying eyes.

In the course of this book we have already given hints concerning the importance of the phantasy in human life as a source of ideas and activities, suggesting that it is one of the products of the unconscious mind, where the ungratified wishes and unfulfilled desires of our childhood continue to exist. It has already been mentioned that wishes and impulses which fail to gain their gratification and are discouraged by parental prohibitions suffer repression, and remain thus outlawed through becoming surcharged with shame and guilt. In this way they are banished from the conscious mind and the rest of our mental activities for insubordination, but from their exile are ever seeking some means of slipping back again, either in alliance with some other idea, which has not yet suffered the same fate on account of its evil company, or in a disguise by which it may elude the usually vigilant guard upon the threshold of consciousness, the Censorship, that is always ready to turn away suspects when recognized.

The game, the make-believe, the phantasy, and the day- or night-dream are all representative examples of this same process, wishes striving to gain their desired gratification. In this sequence we may trace the growth of repression in childhood, with its dangerous aftermath, when the phantasy may cease to be recognized at its true worth. It will then fail to be realized as *unreality*, and may be taken progressively for *reality*, a condition which is to be found in the psychoses, with their manifestations of delusions, hallucinations, and fugue, when the day-dream or phantasy is given the full value of reality and the real world becomes a shadow. However, we have already mentioned that the phantasy may show another aspect, which has a healing and reinstating power to lead back the personality to the world of fellow-creatures and social service, in the work of art.

One of the most interesting discoveries that have been made relative to these phantasies that make their appearance at different stages of the child's mental development is that they usually correspond, even to the most minute details, with myths and legends of primitive races, just as games[1] of children frequently repeat their activities, hunting, use of the bow and arrow, wigwam building, as well as their drawings; modelling, and attempts at arts and crafts, ornament and design, again represent those early specimens, which may be seen in the ethnological departments of our museums. The study of genetic psychology has shown us how the mental activities of the individual recapitulate the development of the various races of mankind. Psycho-analysis demonstrates through the study of the history of human phantasy the close connection of this form of mental process with human behaviour, not only now, but in the past, by the comparison of the various forms in which it may appear in normal as well as abnormal conditions. We may also discover how they have come into existence, and why they may be of the greatest service of mankind as a means

[1] *The Play of Man*, Karl Groos. Heinemann.

of restoring mental balance, on the one hand, or of destroying it should they, through over-development and the counter-current of the outside world offering too hard conditions, finally take the place of this repugnant reality, and so lead the dreamer away entirely into the realm of shadows which we call insanity.

We have already suggested that through play, games, and make-believe the child shows us the trend of its mental activities. Those children who are very backward, whom we call imbecile, whose minds are as yet in the vegetive condition of the very young infant, will not play at all, or merely in the same fashion as a babe of a few months old, and in this way we may use the play faculty as a sign of the development of the child mind. The newly-born infant does not play. We see this capacity gradually awakening, especially during the latter half of the first year. At first it will show signs of "playing" with a small bright or moving object, its own fingers or toes, trying to catch them. It is evidently interested most deeply in the brightness or the movement of the object under observation. By and by, we may watch the appearance of the first game of make-believe, *peep-bo*, which has all the characteristics of both game and phantasy. Although at this exceedingly early stage there is no very clear distinction between the individual conscious and unconscious mind of the baby, we must not forget that there are certain racial inheritances in the human mind, representing cultural repressions of impulses, that are due to the use of fear and guilt that have been inculcated from ancient times which will find relief by this means.

In the game of peep-bo we find an alleviation of the most primitive fear of babyhood, as well as one of its first wishes. In this method we may observe two important functions of make-believe and phantasy at work, the attempt (1) to gain information or to resolve problems, as well as (2) to derive a gratification of wishes. The baby's first fear comes into existence when left alone, if it should wake, or realize when awake that no one is there upon whom it may rely for consolation or succour, therefore a realization of its helplessness. Biologically, this situation is always one of possible danger to the infant, and in the past ages it was of very real danger. The infant's immediate reaction is to cry, which will have the useful result of calling some special person and serve to guide this one or some other to the place where the baby is, as well as to intimate that help is needed. It also has the effect of releasing the emotion connected with the fear and giving it free discharge, which is valuable in itself.

Freud has shown that the game of peep-bo is an attempt on the part of the mother or nurse, although one that has been unconscious rather than consciously thought out, of giving the baby experience and knowledge of her alternating going away and returning, to teach the infant that her disappearance does not necessarily mean that she or the baby is lost (separated) for ever, but that reunion may be expected and watched for (*Hemmung, Symptom und Angst*, Sigm. Freud). The baby's wish may be seen in the expectancy with which the handkerchief covering the mother's face is regarded, the eagerness with which the child will expedite her return by pulling it away. Joy in acquiring the wish and relief of the original fear is only too evident when her face is once more seen. The baby may cry at first as soon as the loved face is out of sight, showing the fear in immediate operation, but presently it will enjoy this stage also, because it has now learned to anticipate return, so that it then forms a preparatory pleasure in the chain of expectation leading to the final pleasure of regaining her later on. This phantasy concerning the absence and return of the mother and the lost baby may be traced in many forms during the life of most persons, both boys and girls, sometimes persisting into maturity. It is one of the basic phantasies from which others spring, and one which gives rise to many fears on the part of the child, connected with adult threats and punishments. The phantasies descended from it concern the self and others, life as well as death, which to the child mind is but going away without return. Some children begin to wonder when things disappear whether they have ever existed, or only in their thoughts—that is, if they have been always subjective.

The life of the primitive infant was precarious without doubt. Upon the march of migratory tribes, the mother with several little children to carry and scanty food to give them would often be obliged to leave one asleep in the bushes to die of exposure. This is the theme of several well-known fairy-tales, such as *Hansel and Gretel*. The mother of to-day uses the same threat: "If you are not good, I will run away and leave you"; "I'll send you away—give you to the dustman." The sending upstairs of a naughty child, or putting it in the corner, contains the same idea, hiding the face, absence, which was originally the death of the offender, a cause surely for the child's fear and made particularly emphatic through religious teaching, where the same idea is presented, that God hides His face from the wicked, with the result that they die.

Gradually out of the peep-bo phantasy emerges an idea concerning the differentiation of the self and others. The baby sees the mother. Sometimes the mother changes her technique and shows the little one its own face in the mirror, making it play with its own reflection, which at first is the source of the greatest interest and wonder. Primarily the baby does not realize the phenomenon of reflection, and thinks it is another baby. It may love it and try to kiss this baby face, or be jealous to see another baby in the arms of its mother. It will look from the reflection of the mother to the real mother standing behind and evidently try to understand why she should be in two places at once, and why there are two mothers and two babies just alike.

One little girl who used to be very unhappy when left in her perambulator in the garden was made contented through hanging a little mirror at the other end. She would then laugh and quarrel with this reflection of herself for hours, until one day she happened to ask: "Who's that pretty little girl?" and was laughed at by those of whom the inquiry had been made. This caused her the greatest humiliation, to think that she had called herself "pretty," which shows us that guilt had already been impressed upon this child for such a natural tendency as to admire something that was pretty, even when it happened to be herself. It also shows the trend of instruction that the self must be regarded in a different way and with a different standard to that which one adopts towards others. Later on, the child developed phantasies, which were kept most secret, of being a beautiful princess, beloved of her father, who would never want to marry anyone, because she would want to keep all her beauty to herself. That is, of course, she would not allow anyone to look at her and derive pleasure from her beauty, just as she had been forbidden to admire it herself. She was punishing others in the same way as she had been punished herself.

Because the child was not allowed to admire herself, this did not mean that she ceased to think about herself. Gradually she thought more and more about the identity of *I* and *myself*. "Who is myself?" she would ask herself. "I can talk to myself, but you can't hear me. Is the looking-glass me, myself, or my shadow?" Her favourite rhyme became:

> As I walks by myself, I talks to myself,
> And I says to myself, says I,
> You must care for yourself, and beware of yourself,
> For nobody cares for I.

This phantasy was developed still further because just before her fifth birthday her mother had a new baby, which, she felt, left her entirely to her own resources. In fact, it was probably this event which emphasized in her mind the need to "take care of yourself, for nobody cares for I," since it now seemed that the mother only loved the little brother, and so she played mother to herself, which, as we have explained, is sometimes the typical consolation of the middle child deserted by its playmates. The lost mother and the abandoned baby may here be seen in a second stage of phantasy instead of the original game of peep-bo.

Many of the *Self-phantasies* may spring from this source, the reflection, seeing, and a play upon the words, Eye and I. The child will also become confused by different words which denote itself. Thus it will have its own name, a most important possession for the child, a nickname, the prerogative of father and mother, maybe one that it uses for itself. It will also be called "you" and has to learn to call itself "I," and speak about itself as *me* or *myself*. Here are a collection of perplexing problems. It is no wonder that little children find a good way out of the difficulty by referring to themselves at first by name. So that when asked, "Whom does this belong to?" the child replies, "That's Polly's," or "Who's that?" "It's Polly," when she has advanced far enough to recognize herself when she looks into the glass and sees the little girl there.

The child who is suffering from confusion of ideas arising from the words I and Eye will attempt to solve the difficulty by the creation of self and seeing phantasies. Many children, as did the ancients in years gone by, imagine the self as a miniature human being, standing inside themselves and peeping out of their eyes. The children of to-day who sit on their mother's lap and see the reflection of themselves in her eyes, a miniature human being, sometimes wonder if she has caught and imprisoned them there, or if that is another baby waiting to be born. Perhaps this is where the unborn babies live? Half-frightened, the child steals a glance down at its own body, to make sure that it is still there and free, because once again it does not understand how it can be in two places at once. This fear of being possessed by another is connected with that fear felt by some children and many primitive races for the camera, and the idea of having their likeness "taken." They believe they are going to be taken away, shut up in that box, and that others will then have power over them.

If the ego-sense of the child is strongly developed in early childhood, it may even be frightened by the possession exercised upon them by the parents, and in this connection may become really alarmed should they overhear any remark about their parents' opinion of themselves containing the words, "in their eyes." They may also link this up with their fear of being eaten or swallowed, which we will describe presently. Still, if they are somehow in the head, the only possible entrance must have been through the mouth, to their way of thinking. The quite young child also seems able to grasp the significance of absorption of the child's *personality* by the adult, and struggles against it most vigorously, as though fighting for its life, as well as the existence of its ego.

Existing in anyone's eyes or to be the apple of somebody's eye seems equally dangerous to these children, but a question of difficulty arises in their mind related to this: does one continue to exist if these eyes are shut, if that person goes away or dies? The child, as we know, has a great antipathy to shut eyes, and always tries to prise them open whenever a sleeping adult is found.

This is the converse of the child's thoughts concerning itself and its power of creation by seeing. As long as it looks at persons or objects, they still exist; when its own eyes are shut, they vanish. This phantasy has been already mentioned in the section on

Sight. The child finds objective and subjective control of vision an exceedingly difficult problem to grasp, and when we take into consideration the child's propensity for visual imagery[1] and its absolute belief in the creations of phantasy we will understand how hard it must be to draw a distinction between them. Only as the years go by, each usually contributing to the child's experience of these differences between things that exist in some external form and about which others will deny, will the boundary-lines between various mental processes be found and the game of make-believe will come to be prefaced by the formula, "Let's pretend," which is usually a verbal concession to the regulations imposed by adults, who are worried in case the child's idea of truth may become a little lax through games of this description.

The young child does not consciously "pretend" in its games of imagination, as a rule. The deficiencies of reality are automatically supplied by the phantasy without explanations to itself or others, such as the grown-up person might require. Again, *the wish* is paramount. If we want a horse to ride, a sofa, chair, or even our own legs will serve just as well; imagination amply fulfills our wishes. If we want a play-companion and are tired of always being alone, we may have one also, a part of ourselves, linked, no doubt, with the little person in the mirror, the echo and the shadow.

The *Play-companion* is a distinctive feature in the day-dreams of the child who is lonely and who, having much time to think, is beginning to give deep consideration, often without realizing it, to the problem of the personality and the self. Not only does this phantasy child supply the wish for a friend, a twin, but has also to play the part of the double, the *alter ego*. Sometimes it may be the self who is naughty, and does things which the developing ego and super-ego of the child is learning not to do, through identification with the instructor. It may also be an impossibly good person, a super-ego itself, or a conscience, who goes about to protect the child from wrong-doing or temptation, doubtless incorporating the guardian-angel idea of parental teaching. This, however, we may consider an almost pathological second-self, a too highly developed super-ego

[1] "The Infantile Psyche, with Special Reference to Visual Projection," Dr. David Forsyth. *Br. J. of Psychol.* 1921.

for the comfort and health of the child. The mischievous double who in phantasy gets into all the scrapes envied but not ventured upon is actually a far safer companion.

Little children frequently do not try to disguise the existence of their play-companions. When this appears at an early stage of development, about three years old or so, they will talk about her or him quite freely, have a name ready-bestowed and spend time and trouble in inventing a family history and description of the house where he or she lives, and know all about the brothers and sisters. Frequently these will be found to be closely modelled upon the child's own, which gives another clue that this little playmate is a part of the self and yet a form of phantasy which is still a game. When the "double" phantasy appears in the older child, it takes on the secretive characteristic of the real phantasy, and the boy or girl keeps this imaginary friend and their doings together safely hidden from the knowledge of the rest.

The child, like the primitive peoples, will invent phantasies as an attempt to procure information, to construct possible theories in order to unravel problems that offer no other solution. The second self who possesses the bad qualities and does the naughty things is the child's commentary upon this difficulty, "How is it that I seem so different upon different days? I don't feel like the same person." This is what the child is expressing, not in words, as the adult would do, but when it invents the naughty playmate or when it develops the habit of being various real persons upon different days of the week. One day, if we inquire, we will find a Mrs. Smith, a mother of eight; another day, we meet Buffalo Bill; on a third, it is Tinker Bell or Puck; or again, we may hear a dog's friendly yap answer our query, or a bear may hug us when we say "good morning." The child realizes, even more clearly than many grown-up persons, how we incorporate in our personality both male and female elements, that we possess not only the good and the bad person, but the animal characteristics, and those of fairy and spirit, witch and demon. A whole galaxy of beings representative of different stages of cultural belief, each with its own appropriate wishes and impulses struggling for expression and fulfilment, may be seen in the games and make-believe of children.

This shows us the value of the game for little children, how it may give them the possibility of harmlessly discharging primitive emotions and finding gratification for wishes, which in our present-day stage of existence might be hard to obtain otherwise. The child who cannot thus give expression to phantasy in the made-up game or feels that make-believe is *silly* is probably accepting the standard of some adult who has also been hindered from gaining satisfaction for primitive wishes in childhood by the operation of the repressing factor of guilt. In this case a substitute form of discharge has probably been found in the austere training of children, depriving them of pleasure, or causing other neurotic symptoms. Not allowing children to play as they wish and forbidding them this outlet of make-believe would usually be a sign in itself that might well arouse the gravest suspicion in anyone who observed it.

We shall find that the consecutive stages of the game, make-believe or phantasy follow the line of ego and super-ego development, from the vogue of peep-bo and the lost child, the double-self, shown in the play-companion, through all the complicated changes of the Œdipus Conflict, which include the Hero Phantasies. Many of these will at first be concerned with the desire of the love for the mother alone and the wish to get rid of the father, who is regarded as a tyrant. Then we shall find the hero, during the Latency Period, as a leader, sometimes in the games at school, at others in phantasy and day-dreams, when marvellous feats outside the boundary of reality are given satisfaction in imaginary fulfilment. In the game stage of this leader phantasy we shall see in quite little children the tendency to "boss" or be "bossed," to rebel or be a faithful follower, which has already been founded by the child's attitude to the parents in the first instance.

Children who have not much imagination, or, shall we call it, power of phantasy, prefer playing with toys, balls, bricks, etc., but these toys always remain just themselves; and so do the little people who play with them. If bricks are built up, they are put one on top of another, and nothing more; often they will be made into a faithful copy of the picture on the lid. They do not form part of a phantasy or a basis for make-believe. They are never the home of Jack the Giant-Killer, nor the cottage of the Three Little Pigs. They are bricks and remain bricks.

They never, whatever happens, turn into cakes, precious jewels found in Aladdin's cave, or rowing-boats. Yet the little matter-of-fact builder in later life may become a famous architect or contractor and construct huge, solid factories or giant hotels; and the other type, the imaginative builder, creates a modern version of one of the ancient gothic cathedrals or fan-vaulting like that in Henry VII's Chapel at Westminster; while the phantasy builder will go on piling up his phantasies all his life long and never get beyond the production of castles in Spain.

Only or lonely children will always be the greatest weavers of phantasy. They play the most wonderful games of imagination by themselves, taking now this part, now that, never at a loss how to fill out the tale of many persons necessary to the continuation. Others are seldom requisitioned, especially adults, to help in the game, except one favoured one, perhaps, who can be relied upon to observe the unwritten rules of the great game of make-believe. These are those which are used by most:

Never to say, This is impossible; it couldn't happen. It's only a game. You can't do that. We mustn't say that; Mother wouldn't like it

Always to behave as if everything were real, and anything that is to be said must come through the voice of one of the characters in the game and be in keeping with the part.

Never to make comments upon how funny anybody looks, or what a difference between the play-self and the real-self.

Never to refer to the game again once it is over, nor before strangers especially.

Because adults seldom remember to keep these rules, or because they do not know them, children generally prefer to play with other children. They know from experience that grown-up people cannot be trusted, and have forgotten how to play even if they once knew how, which, of course, is very largely true. Adults are too self-conscious to get away from the idea that they are playing, pretending to be So-and-so, rather than feeling it. If they felt themselves the person or thing they were supposed to be, they would not constantly have to stop and ask what they were to do next or what they must say. This always annoys or disappoints the child, but it is quite within the rules of the game for the child to give a running commentary upon what everyone does, with stage directions thrown in by the way, in the guise of the leader, a magician, or the mother of an unruly family, which shows another important factor at work. The child will be several persons at once, or quickly alternating, and the rest are expected to know immediately that the change has taken place and who the person is whom now she or he has become. Not only does the child take several parts, but it is also stage-manager, scene-shifter, and director of everything, giving one the impression of the ancient miracle-plays. The child can change how he or she likes, and, if preferred, suddenly play the part previously allotted to another actor, so that characters are freely interchangeable or merge like the persons in a dream. For the same reason, the dreamer often has a sudden fancy to take another part, because it has for the moment become the most important, and the phantasy-maker must always be found in the chief rôle, like the dreamer.

Working upon the basis of games and phantasies being founded upon wishes, we shall find children readjusting things they do not like in reality by alterations in their make-believe or day-dreams. In this way we may often find a criticism of the home and the parents, which might never be gained other-wise, since the child is too loyal to complain to another about these private matters, however uncomfortable home conditions may be. Parents, of course, have not the slightest compunction about complaining of their children, and never think it necessary to be loyal to them.

A favourite game of nearly all children is to pretend to be grown-up. The cup is full if an understanding adult, who can play properly, can come and take the part of a child, who will then be systematically bullied. The adult is thus shown an ironical picture of how adults appear to children. This idea usually calls up the phantasy of changing places with the grown-ups and the reversal of generations. (See last chapter, p. 333.) The child's idea will be that one gets older and older, and larger and larger, until one reaches a maximum point and stops. Then one returns back again slowly the way one has come and retraces the steps to childhood, with the possibility of becoming the baby of one's own child. This is a particularly favourite phantasy of little girls. So also is the topsy-turvy idea, the finding of a country where everything is reversed, where the boys are dressed like girls and the girls like boys.

In that country, if you want to be very polite, you put out your tongue and turn your back on others. Yes means no and no means yes. The children look after the grown-ups, and the grown-ups have to do everything they are told. It is easy to see how a phantasy of this description may spring up out of the unattainable wishes of a child.

We find in the little boy phantasies of going to battle, and after a gigantic slaughter only the hero is left alive. The hero of every day-dream or phantasy is always the creator of it; and here comes in the supreme difficulty of the game that is founded upon such phantasies, because everyone wants to be the hero and there can only be one. Force, cajolery, or the natural self-abnegation of some children (or have they already learned that to take a second place is their only chance of being included in the game of the others?) make some ready to play the part of the faithful ally, the second in command, the wonderful servant, without whom the master would be in sore straits. Sometimes in the game founded upon fairy-tales this will be an animal, a horse or hound. In reality this figure is the mother or nurse in disguise, the person who is always there, but in the background, to rescue the hero from any predicament, self-effacing until needed, and ready to give endless praise to the hero, "to kiss the place and make it well," after a tumble to body or pride.

Gradually, as the child grows older, he or she will become selfconscious about these games and phantasies. Those who are allowed to participate in them become fewer; those who may watch are still more limited; and at last we find the individual isolated, alone with the game or make-believe, which presently changes into mental phantasy, an idea only, which no other shares, watches, or even knows about. This is because the conception of the self has grown and now includes the idea of individual shame and guilt. This feeling inhibits the capacity to give publicity to the phantasy, because there is always a fear of ridicule or blame from those who witness it or become acquainted with it in any way. The chief wishes that are contained in these phantasies are to be strong, to overcome rivals and do wonderful things, or, for the same reason, to be beautiful and marry the fairy prince or the princess, and so we hide these wishes away and indulge our thoughts about them in private.

The Hero Myths have been the best beloved of every race, and through the process of identification each boy has played the part of all these giants of antiquity. The less Reality has had to offer the growing boy or girl in the form of deeds of daring, prowess or ability, the more eagerly sought will be the phantasy in which these results may be attained. Attempts will be made to counteract the deficiency by the invention of exciting day-dreams, to read about courage and endurance in the adventure story, to see them on the "pictures." Cinema films take full advantage, perhaps unknowingly, of the propensity of the human being to make and enjoy phantasies by means of identification, and for this reason we find the stories upon which film-plays are based follow over and over again the well-worn lines of the most ancient and popular phantasies.

The hero phantasy is always well represented in some way in every programme, whether the hero shown be Cowboy or Eskimo (Nanook), Ben Hur, Charlie Chaplin, or Harold Lloyd. All these in their own way have an opportunity for adventure or mischief which others might long to carry out, but which dare not be put into action by those who look on. Another factor which we find running through the phantasy, in whatever form it appears, is that in spite of all tribulations heaped upon the hero by jealous rivals or cruel enemies, finally, by dint of brilliant feats of courage or strategy, the hero manages alone to triumph victoriously. Sometimes this result is achieved by wonderful endurance or even simplicity or stupidity, so there is hope for all. The jealous rivals generally fall into their own trap, and the cruel enemies are defeated and punished. Frequently these are to be divided roughly into two main groups, the old oppressors, in whom we may find the enemy of our boyhood, in disguise, the hated father, in distinction to the loved or ideal father, who is often represented in the phantasy as an adopted benefactor. The oppressor, the hated father, is brought to account and his evil plans turned against himself, as are likewise those of the rival brothers, the contemporary enemies.

It is always the desire of children to be able to turn the tables. The second class of oppressors, the malicious enemies or rivals, are usually contemporaries of the hero, in whom we will find the brothers or schoolmates of the young hero, over whom he would so dearly like to triumph, to gain some prize, his own honour and glory, the admiration of the mother, and, at a later stage of development, the girl of his choice.

This is the outline of the phantasy which we find endlessly repeated in a thousand forms, reflecting the wishes of the boy in every stage of civilization or development. Wherever the scene is laid, in whatever country or period of history, its appeal is sure, so closely does the phantasy adhere to type throughout the ages. The hero and the *wonder-child* are but two aspects of the same idea. The first may be the favourite form for the boy, whose ideal is set upon physical achievements, not always because actual strength of body gives stimulus to the wish, but often for the opposite reasons. Delicacy may deny any physical satisfaction in reality and make the phantasy gratification more imperative for the balance of self-feeling, to fulfil the un-attained wish, which in this case would be one that is fully conscious, because the phantasy may satisfy conscious wishes just as completely as those that are unconscious. In children, of course, they will often coincide.

The wonder-child phantasy would be chosen by the child with artistic aspirations or by one who feels that destiny has pointed the way to fame in some miraculous life, that of a Napoleon or Mussolini, perhaps a genius of some sort, or, in a girl, a Joan of Arc. The wonder-child phantasy is frequently found in the girl. So, of course, may be that of the hero; but in the girl who wants to be a boy, if she attains her wish through this phantasy, it will still remain a boy's phantasy whatever the actual sex of the person in whom it may happen to appear.

Both types show the theme of dissatisfaction with the home and parents. These heroes or wonder-children usually leave home in the phantasy. Sometimes they are driven away by cruel parents, who beat or otherwise molest them, and go out into the world to seek their fortune. It will occasionally be imagined that the home which is left is not the real home of the children, but that of foster-parents, with whom they have lived since infancy, or that they were stolen away by gipsies. They wander on, lost or abandoned (the original phantasy once again), for some time, and at last, cold, starving, and almost exhausted, **are** found by some kind person, man or woman, (the ideal father- or mother-figure), who offers to adopt them, bring them up as an only and beloved child, and develop their wonderful talent, which is generally the same as that possessed by the new parent substitute. If the persons who were left, in the first instance, were foster-parents, then these second kindly people may be discovered to be the real parents of the children, who have been longing for them all the time, and are represented as being not only far more clever and wealthy than the others, often of noble or royal birth. The details of the phantasy will show the special features of the boy's or girl's wishes and the goal of the artistic ambition. This negative attitude towards the parents, however, gives us but another proof of what children may really think about them.

Girls' phantasies show some special characteristics. At certain stages of their development they will be in many cases identical with those of the boy, because their wish is to have been a boy. In spite of this wish, nevertheless, there is often an accompanying hint that she does still want to be a girl who is playing at being a boy, a masquerade theme, with the inevitable *dénouement* sooner or later, and the reservation that she will be able to derive, if need be, some advantage from her girlhood, the love and perhaps homage, which the romantic princess expects from her male subjects and admirers at whatever age and period of history it may be, and however much she may believe at other times her only wish is to be a boy.

If the boy is always and essentially the hero, and, although at times unrecognized and persecuted, he finally achieves his triumph, the girl is always in phantasy the beloved princess; and in spite of the fact that she may have to serve in the kitchen as Cinderella, or on the hill-side as a Goose-girl, and be the drudge of the Ugly Sisters, she eventually marries the fairy prince, although he may be disguised as a toad until the magic of her love sets him free.

The phantasy is a magic carpet that bears us safely from the donjon of darkest reality to a warmer, brighter country, where the self may find some healing compensation. But it must be able to bring us back again, once more able to bend our backs to the burden of daily life. The existence of phantasies shows us that the children who make use of them are needing both a means of escape and solace; and if we discover that this be so, it should make us review the conditions of their lives, to see from what point the oppression and darkness is coming, rather than laugh at them for being so fanciful or tease them for being silly and romantic.

The girl, too, in her phantasy will often wander off to seek the ideal parents, father or mother, according to whether she retain her original love for the mother, as when an infant, whether she has already transferred her love to the father, primarily as the little girl or secondarily after or during adolescence, when perhaps the youthful father-lover will be sought or the father-figure, the older man, whom she may feel she wishes to solace and console. This rôle of loving daughter, who is also wife, is seen in many phantasies. Sometimes it will be varied, and we see the devoted daughter unable in reality to tear herself away from the father to go to the lover. The phantasy element appearing in real life always makes a difficulty in the love-affairs of man or woman. Wagner repeats the father-daughter situation with several variations in his operas. In the *Flying Dutchman* the father is doubled in Senta's father and his friend, the Flying Dutchman, to save whom from his curse Senta first marries and then sacrifices herself. Sieglinde, wedded to the old and savage Hunding, is taken away by Siegmund, who is also her brother (which is frequently a favourite motif in the phantasy, the love of brother and sister, the brother in this case representing partly the brother and partly the young father). Wotan and Brunhilde show another father and daughter problem, and the latter, because she displeases her stepmother, is enchanted by her father, doomed to sleep on her rock, to become the wife of the first hero who breaks through the fiery circle with which she is surrounded. This is Siegfried, who comes and wins her, but loses her again through the curse of the gold or, according to an older tradition, treachery of another woman. Isolde is torn with love between old King Mark and the young lover Tristan; while Eva, in the *Meistersinger von Nüremberg*, is wooed and won by Walther, although she is loved profoundly by Hans Sachs, who has known her from childhood and looks upon her almost with the devotion of a father.

The idea of marrying the father, taking care of him, or having him all to herself, and at the same time sending the mother away for a long holiday, is found in quite little girls as well as those approaching adolescence. The mother in the girl's phantasy often plays the same rôle as the father in that of the boy, and carries the negative feeling, which the daughter may find it difficult to discharge in reality. For this reason an imaginary, rather sinister, persecuting female figure is invented, resembling the elderly woman who oppressed Sarah Crewe, which has been a favourite story of countless little girls in the past, who were also voracious readers of *Quechy*, *Melbourne House*, and others of the same type, in which the martyr and beating phantasies were equally prominent. The *Daisy Chain* and the *Heir of Redcliffe* present the phantasy of the girl who actually takes the mother's place and looks after her father, finding it difficult to break away from this childish wish-fulfilment when the more mature phantasy figure of the lover comes upon the stage.

The rescue theme in the phantasy is another that may appear in many forms. We find the young hero or heroine rescuing parent figures, rendering them assistance, which earns their infinite gratitude and sometimes also reforms them for life. It will also serve as a turning of the tables and provide a solution to the problem, that the child is supposed to owe the parents a debt of deepest gratitude, even for life, by putting the parent under a counter-obligation, again for life itself. By this means the debt will be cancelled. As well as putting the parents under an obligation, which is a way of humiliating them, it also shows a disguised death-wish; but at the last moment, after the intention has been made clear, a reprieve is granted and the child becomes the rescuer. Yet a further sign of negative feeling is shown when it is stated in the phantasy that the character of the person who has had this narrow escape from death undergoes a complete change, and all the wicked deeds that have been committed are deplored. Sometimes the person is also fancied to make restitution by forfeiting lands or wealth in favour of the rescuer. This tells, once again, how much the parents are considered to be in need of reformation and what is thought to be their besetting sin, because the imagined punishment would most probably be arranged to hit them in their most vulnerable part.

The rescue theme changes as the child nears the age of

adolescence. The boy then rescues a girl instead of father or mother, and eventually marries her. The girl saves the boy from some terrible peril and gives herself to him afterwards, or allows herself to be rescued with a similar result, like Andromeda and the Monster of ancient myth. The rescue may lead on to a medical or moral phase, and the saving will then take place in the operating theatre or by the hospital nurse, during the career of a social worker, or on a mission field. Afterwards, this phantasy becomes an ambition upon which the life-work is based. In this way we may learn how the phantasy may lead on to the choice of a profession or career. One chosen in this way will generally be successful because a similar satisfaction will be found in it to that derived from the day-dream, plus the factor of social sanction. We have said that guilt and fear lead to hiding the phantasy; the disguise of wishes in this form adds to the idea that perhaps after all it is the adventures of another or purely imaginary person with whom one is occupied rather than those of the self. But in the profession it finds a form where gratification may once more be made public and enjoyed in the company of others.

Similar satisfaction will be found in the phantasy which reaches the transformation of social service by incorporation in a work of art. The applause of others gives evidence that they, too, have struggled with the same wishes; that they, through watching the play, reading the book, gazing at the picture or sculpture, have found a corresponding discharge of pent-up emotion. Their praise bears witness to this and salves the old wound of the creator of the artistic production, which was originally made in childhood through some wish that then could gain no fulfilment, but consequently drove the artist to seek a goal for his ambition which would also serve as an outlet to the phantasy in whatever way best discharged the impulses of his or her unconscious mind.

This may be the course followed by some of the more normal Ego and Œdipus phantasies, but there are many others that may be termed pathological, which are usually found in the children and adults who tend to develop neuroses and are allied to other difficulties, which we will now describe briefly. We may often notice that these phantasies, which have been already explained, may advance from their simple and normal forms and take on pathological symptoms. For instance, the suffering hero and the afflicted heroine phantasies may increase in severity, until they become the serious condition known as the persecution mania; the wandering from home, or foster-parent phantasy, may actually be put into practice, which is the fugue, a form of mental trouble that is unfortunately only too familiar; and the play-companion mechanism, when a part of the personality is represented as another entirely different person, may become permanent in that form of serious mental derangement known as multiple personality.

The difference between the harmless phantasy and the dangerous one is mainly one of degree. The same phantasy may be found in those whom we call normal people as also in the insane, but the former will know that it is not really true; that it is only an emanation of his or her imagination, although at times it may seem *almost* true. In the case of the insane person, however, the phantasy has broken through the bonds of reality and appeared in the daily life, so that it has now a greater significance and power than real life, which becomes proportionately shadowy and unreal. This is a serious peril for children. They find that reality offers them so little by way of compensation for its hardships and is poor in supplying the kind of satisfaction their impulses require, whereas these may be obtained both readily and easily through the phantasy or day-dream. In this case there is always the possible danger that they may drift farther from unpleasant reality and become more occupied with the pleasant phantasy which fulfils their dearest wishes, so that the phantasy world at last entirely replaces reality, a condition that represents insanity in some form or another. In children this is usually dementia præcox.

In these cases we shall often find a typical form of day-dream which represents the desire to escape from unpleasant circumstances. It will often be accompanied by significant actions on the part of the child. The boy or girl, as the case may be, actually goes to hide whilst the day-dream is in progress. He will find an unused dog-kennel, the shelf of a cupboard in an attic, or an old chest, and lie there curled up, frequently in the position of the unborn infant, which shows the desire to return to this state of bliss, when no troubles could assail the unbroken peace from the outside world. Those phantasies we are about to quote belonged to a little boy, who believed nobody loved him and who was intensely unhappy for this reason. The mother fancied that he had ceased to care about her and was also sad about it, but consoled herself with lavishing a double portion of affection upon a new-comer to the family, a little daughter. Her chief trouble seemed to be that she had ceased to be the essential person for her son, but it was clear that he was no longer of any particular moment to her since the arrival of the baby. She said that the little boy always seemed so far away, *up in the clouds*, or *in a brown study*, and "looked at you as though you were not there"; also he never heard what was said to him.

The favourite hiding-place of this child was the top shelf of a store cupboard. There he would curl himself up and cover himself with newspapers that were up there too. He used to hear them calling him and stayed quiet as a mouse. He generally crept away there after his mother had been cross with him. One day he wrote the following story. "There were four little girls who went away to live up in the clouds, instead of their home, the Palace, because the Queen was often very cross." This phantasy elaborated their adventures for several days. One of the girls found a kind mother-bird who adopted her and fed her on her own eggs, one each day, after she had left all the others because she wanted to live alone. Finally the Queen set out to look for them and brought them back to fairyland. When the story was complete, the little boy added the illuminating remark that his mother always said he was "up in the clouds," when they spoke to him and he did not answer. He also saw the connection between the little girls going away to play in the clouds, when the Queen was cross, and himself retreating for the same reason to the store cupboard. The reason why these fairy children were *girls* was probably because the little boy noticed that the mother preferred his sister to himself, and so made these quadruplicates of himself *girls* in order to win back his mother's affection. It may also have contained the suggestion that he would like that little sister to go back to the clouds and stay there, as before. The Queen in the phantasy, especially of children, nearly always represents the mother, as does the King the father.

The curled-up attitude of the child and the habit of creeping away into a little hiding-place is significant for two reasons mentioned above. It will be found in countless forms, but always shows the same desire to escape from the world of reality and find the original state of solace before birth, where no outside worries could pierce one's calm and every wish was automatically gratified. Some children develop this particular phantasy still further. They will find a summer-house, a hole in a tree, some odd corner away from curious eyes, which they will call their house, and go there in times of stress and misunderstanding. Perhaps the refuge will be purely mental and take the form of an imaginary island, a phantasy kingdom, occupied by this child alone, with hundreds of tiny subjects, over whom it reigns in solitary splendour and the greatest tyranny. The island is once more a representation of the unborn condition, and the devotion of the subjects and the sheltering seas which surround the island home a picture of the mother's body.

Such a retreat as this from the world and outside reality takes place in the state already explained, dementia præcox, when the phantasy or *individual reality* absorbs the personality to a varying extent, so that contact with outside events and other people is more or less destroyed. (*Loss of Reality in Neuroses and Psychoses*, Sigm. Freud. Collected Papers, vol. iv.)

The Fear Phantasies, which contain, as their kernel, the phobias seen in later life, are equally destructive for the child's personality. The world becomes peopled with monsters, who can kill and eat the child whole, swallow it or destroy it in some way, as well as maim it for life. The eating phantasy is a very common one. It is primarily connected with the children for whom the oral zone played an important part, who may have been biters themselves, whose parents used to play biting games with them, or took a delight in frightening the child by pretending to gobble it up. Later on, it will join forces with night-terrors and bad dreams, in which wild beasts take the place of the parent, make them flee from their hungry jaws. We have already suggested that many of these fears of children will be aroused by observing incidents related to the intimate married life of their parents they are not intended to know anything about, and it has usually been found that they become connected in the child's mind with the doings of animals and deeds of savagery.

These Eating Phantasies may lead to various symptoms connected with eating, likes and dislikes of special foods, or to loss of appetite that may arise from a belief that babies come from food, and that if too much is eaten of certain things, one may grow inside them. This is a widely-spread idea among children as well as in some primitive races. It is met once again in fairy-tales that the child develops from something eaten; that it eats its way out of the mother, or is passed from her after the manner of the excretions.

Being swallowed by a monster, therefore, is an attempt to solve the dual problem of life and death. Where did we come from? Whither do we go? Out of a hole somewhere, and we are put into another hole when we die. The child first grasps the idea from observation that it is possible for a baby to be inside the mother, but the next difficulty is, how did it get out? And the last of all, how did it get in?

A little simple explanation of the true facts of these problems usually dispels the trouble and restores the appetite, but allowed to continue, we may often find the most serious gastric troubles, fears of being buried alive, of being in rooms with the doors shut, of going in lifts, or any small spaces, *claustrophobia*, in fact, and maybe also fears of the dark, because when you were inside the animal's body it would be very dark and dirty, after it had swallowed you.

Phantasies of hatred and revenge may often take the place of simple death-wishes, directed against others in the child's environment, or against the self, to punish them for wrongs which it feels have been done towards it. Long phantasies of suicide, or killing others slowly by torture, being so destroyed itself, and the effects this may have upon parents or school-teachers, whose misunderstanding and sympathy have been felt to be lacking, will be evolved. The child derives much sad pleasure and consolation from picturing their sorrow and remorse, as well as arranging with the utmost care exactly how many wreaths would be placed upon the grave, who would send them, what inscription will be written on them and selecting a touching epitaph for the tombstone. It is said that those who plan suicide seldom carry it through. Still, each year there are a certain number of child suicides and accidental deaths, which lead one to suspect that their cause had been an unconscious death-wish carried out against the Self, to put an end to the life which was proving such a bitter disappointment. (*Über den Selbstmord insbesondere den Schüler-selbstmord*, Freud, Adler, and others. 1910.)

Death-wishes may often lead to the child developing the fear that others are going to kill him in revenge. He believes that they will think as he does himself, and consequently the fear of death frequently shows that in this child's mind lies deeply buried the wish to get rid of somebody, so that, one rival or enemy being removed, somebody else may love him the more. This generally occurs in the boy with reference to the father and mother; the father being the rival, the death-wishes are directed against him and death is expected from him. At the same time the love and protection of the mother against the father is most earnestly sought. Were only the father away from the home, the boy feels that he could then enjoy the love and indulgence of the mother unhindered and unimpeded. One remarks sometimes that a phantasy will exist in a boy, whose father is dead, that somehow or another an early death-wish or some action on his part had brought about this result, for which the boy suffers the most profound unconscious guilt. This belief frequently provokes grave neurotic symptoms, or even physical illness, as a means of self-punishment and expiation to atone for the patricide. The boy often feels that he is under a nameless curse that can never be dispelled, and which brings his dearest wishes to disaster.

One is sometimes led to wonder, from the history of cases respecting these death-wishes of a child against one parent and the desire of love from the other, when it is inordinately strong, whether one of the inciting causes is not a difference of opinion on the part of the parents where the son's upbringing is concerned, or that they are not particularly happy together. Some lack of harmony generally shows itself sooner or later both in the proofs of the child's symptoms as well as the words of the parents themselves. One often suspects that in some cases the mother may prefer her son to her husband and also wish to direct all his love to herself. There is frequently a quite marked correspondence between the phantasies of persons in the family who are closely connected by affection, as Abraham pointed out in the article published in the *Internationale Zeitschrift für Psychoanalyse*. ("Coincident Phantasies in Mother and Son," *International Journal for Psycho-analysis*. Trans. Jan. 1926.)

If this be true, we may find that the Œdipus Conflict, which is the name given to this triangular struggle in the family, taken from the ancient legend of Œdipus Rex, draws a large percentage of its dynamic force from the sources within *the parents, as well as those arising from the child*. It may well be that the father may actually cherish hostile wishes against the son, even should they be unconscious; and the mother, like Jocasta of old, prefers the love of the young son to the companionship of the old father, and would gladly put the one in place of the other.

Not only do we find the tendency to suicide arising from phantasies of revenge and disappointment, with some slight alterations in the orientation of the phantasies, but these may seek actual expression in reality instead of remaining in the world of make-believe, and show themselves in what is known as the *criminal tendencies*. Those which are most familiar to us in childhood are stealing (kleptomania), assault, destruction, arson, and, perhaps, pathological lying. The principal motives of stealing have been described already in a previous chapter, as the attempt to punish the person from whom the article is taken or whose possessions are destroyed; to gain possession of some article which represents symbolically something that is envied, the possible identification with a magpie, eagle, or some robber animal, or to be like the mother and own a baby all to oneself. Destruction generally means that someone has to be punished, or if the article cannot be stolen and possessed, it will then be destroyed so that no one else can have it. ("Case of Kleptomania in a Child of Ten Years," *International Journal of Psycho-analysis*, Mary Chadwick. July 1925.) The foundations of arson are too complicated to discuss in this general description.

It is by no means unknown that even small children will assault babies or those smaller than themselves, with the clear intention of hurting them. The motive is jealousy, the hope to get rid of the rival and to return to those peaceful days before this new-comer spoilt life for the little sufferer. One little boy, found about to hit the baby upon the head with a croquet mallet, was told that he might have killed his little sister had he carried out his plan; to which he replied gruffly, obviously disappointed that he had been frustrated, "I only wish I had."

Minor injuries, some of them appearing as accidental, will often be due to this same cause. The most intense guilt may often survive throughout life connected with some childish actions of this kind, or arising from a death-wish, never actually put into practice, but nevertheless clearly felt upon the part of the elder child, and made still more poignant because, owing to some totally different cause, this baby may subsequently have died. The child feels the death has been the result of these wishes and that it has for this reason been guilty of murder. ("The Psycho-analysis of an Early Case of Paranoid Dementia," Dr. David Forsyth, M.D., D.Sc., F.R.C.P. *Proceedings of the Royal Society of Medicine.* July 1920.)

A curious symptom may occasionally arise due to this same feeling on the part of the child towards a younger one, which is evidently a case of a phantasy breaking through into reality. Often after the birth of a baby in the family, an elder brother or sister becomes intensely destructive, especially concentrating these efforts upon throwing china or crockery out of the window, as did Goethe under similar circumstances. ("Eine Kindheitserinnerung aus 'Dichtung und Wahrheit,' " Sigm. Freud. *Imago.* V. 1917-19). Upon investigation, we find that the china thrown out of the window takes the place of the hated baby, and the throwing out, the idea of treating it like rubbish and getting rid of it, or to return it whence it came, to throw it back into heaven. The law of gravity, however, frustrates the intentions, but the young child is not very clear why things always fall down and never up, nor why they do not stay up for long even when one throws them up. To the child mind destruction is often thwarted construction, and may show the wish to have a baby itself or to create one. Then, if not, it will destroy that which has been already created by another. As an example of the tendency, we may take the inexpert builder of houses of cards, who cannot construct them satisfactorily, but who takes infinite delight in getting another to do so, and then knocks them over. The child in destroying something feels that it has proved itself stronger than this thing; in some way also stronger than the person who has made it, and has in this way gained a mastery over them both.

Crime, in whatever form it appears, is, after all, the attempt to put phantasy into practice, living it in the real world instead of make-believe. To play at pirates, cowboys, bandits, is harmless enough,but to lead a real marauding band of fellow-schoolboys to the wholesale robbing of fruit-stalls, orchards, or a bank would bring these heroes into conflict with the law. This has been a matter which has been brought forward in censure of the film, that it is supposed to *create criminal tendencies* in the minds of little children. When we come to investigate this matter from the psychological point of view, however, this statement does not seem to be entirely correct. It does not "create" these tendencies, nor the phantasies; it may awaken them from a temporary slumber, sometimes not even that. They are already present in some form, or to some extent in practically all children, and usually find their safe discharge in day-dreams. But the fact that this same phantasy is presented by the film in such an alluring light, and that the hero is shown to be such a magnificent fellow, will lead the child to wish to identify still more closely with the hero-actor of unreality. No real consequences are shown, none of the inevitable results that attend criminal actions are made plain, only some improbable sequence of events that are romantic, sentimental, and clearly wish-fulfilments. The most grave indictment that can be made against film representation for children is that it presents the phantasy arranged as reality, fiction masquerading as fact, exaggerated, speeded up, with all difficulties, all unpleasantnessess, smoothed away entirely, or, if shown, just in order to be magically dispelled.

If the fairy-tale and its wishing-cap were bad for children because it taught them to rely upon magic or miracles instead of their own efforts, the cinema is equally injurious, because it has the same fault. It presents an untrue view of life, a dream-world, which will not help children to learn about reality and things as they are. Even Nature Films, and those especially arranged for the instruction of the young, show the same error. The study of nature should essentially teach the child patience, expectancy covering long stretches of time, and that the development of plants, animals, and birds is a gradual proceeding. We cannot teach a child satisfactorily about natural development, when we demonstrate this with a form of presentation which gives an entirely distorted idea of natural processes, an impression that they are rapid and that everything happens in the twinkling of an eye.

The production of the unreal element in the real world is attempted by many who are striving to live in these phantasies. Not only may this be seen taking place in those where make-believe breaks through in criminal tendencies, but also in those who clothe their wishes and the struggle to attain them in the guise of illness. Many phantasies may unfortunately find their realization in this way. The search for fresh parents, who are kinder than the old, may be realized in those who are more lenient or demonstratively loving to a sick child than to the more robust members of the family; or it may be that the new parents will be found in doctors and nurses in hospital. The sick child gains more attention and concessions than the one who is well. The mother's lap will once more become his throne, and he may control the rest of the household from that vantage-ground. The domination of the sick person is a secondary gain that only illness provides for many persons. The family may already have supplied the pattern in some other generation from which the child will faithfully copy.

The doctor game that is so much beloved by little children will show many purposes. In the first place, identification with this most important of grown-up persons, who knows everything, may do anything, and who may never be disobeyed, not even by another grown-up person, is essentially one to be envied and emulated. This phantasy also proves the truth of what we have already tried to point out, that the attempt to acquire information is one of the cardinal objects of the games and phantasies of childhood. The relation between this desire for knowledge and the phantasy will be the attempt to solve the problem by this means, to find a convincing proof, or that some onlooker may supply the right information by correcting the wrong interpretation which the game presents. Children will often take advantage of the adult readiness to correct others by deliberately making a false statement, which they know to be wrong, because they realize that

AA

someone will then be more certain to contradict this misstatement than to answer a direct question.

Knowledge concerning the origin of babies and other physiological matters, especially outward differences in bodily structure of boys and girls that are usually, even now, withheld from little children, is sought through the doctor game, by means of the examination of one child by the other in the respective parts of doctor and patient in this nursery drama. We have already mentioned that old threats of punishment by mutilation for forbidden handling of the genitals will produce fear in little children, aroused especially in the boy by the sight of the little girl. The fear arouses doubt in him and he wishes to make sure that the evidence of his eyes is correct or incorrect, as the case may be, whether he really sees here one upon whom this awful punishment has been carried out, while the girl wishes to make sure how it is that the boy has something which she lacks. In order to try to explain these riddles and to allay their fears the children will try to solve many theories, which they clothe in phantasy form to show how these things have taken place, that are often wonderfully similar to the myths of the ancients. To this group has been given the name of Castration Phantasies.

The doctor game of little children will serve many other functions besides that of trying to unravel these problems. It combines with the rescue phantasy in many cases, the doctor becoming the rescuer and the patient the rescued. As time goes on, this doctor game may be repeated in the real life of these children when they are grown-up, the erstwhile patient resuming the part of patient in reality and still finding it an intense gratification to be the object of experiment and investigation, as well as a focus of medical interest. With this intention, although it may not always be a conspicuous wish, he or she will go from doctor to doctor and from one hospital to another, repeating the favourite doctor game of the past. ("Doktorspiel, Kranksein und Arztberuf," Dr. Ernst Simmel. *Internationale Zeitschrift für Psychoanalyse*, vol. xii. Heft. 3, 1926.) The later development of the child who sought knowledge actively will probably be that of scientific research of some kind, even if not actually that of medicine. The connection between this desire to acquire knowledge and the later adoption of a professional career of research is close, as might well be supposed.

The desire on the part of little children to examine themselves and each other is closely allied with the phantasies related to curiosity concerning seeing and with a considerable guilt conflict; it may frequently lead to cases amongst children which will be considered instances of "sexual or indecent assault," when they are probably only putting their phantasy into practice and making some experiment to solve the problems which worry them. The dynamic for such actions may also be derived from incidents in the lives of the parents, which the children at some time may have witnessed, without anyone having thought of the possibility of this factor having any effect upon the minds and impulses of the children in later life.

It is also remarkable how frequently the phantasy of having been assaulted or seduced in childhood will exist in children, and persist into adult life, when it is not at all probable to have been actually true. The origin is often found to be in whippings administered to girls by their father and to boys by their mother, at which time some voluptuous sensations were experienced. This is one of the reasons why it is now advocated that this form of punishment is unwise in childhood. However, these things may actually occur in early days as well as in phantasy. We should be prepared to receive them with recognition of what they are: not criminal actions in the usual sense of the word, but serious neurotic symptoms. These require treatment as such and not punishment alone, which only relieves the outraged feelings of those who have discovered them.

In the service of the desire to know whence babies come, many individual theories are invented by the child, besides those conventional ones which are produced for its benefit by adults. One child imagined a magic balloon filled with tiny ones, which became bigger. When these were large enough they were taken out and others grew in their place. Another little boy thought the tongue grew into a baby; a third that they lived in the eyes: one could see them there when one looked in; that they grew from the breasts, boys from one, girls from the other; that calves came from excrement one saw in the fields. If one kissed one's pillow and wished very hard one would find a baby under it in the morning, or that the two parents, thinking of the baby they would like to have, produced it; which theory was elaborated by one little girl from the saying of her family, meaning a long while ago, "before you were born or thought of." She was always disappointed that they had not thought of her as a boy, and not a girl, being quite convinced that this mistake was due to some error or want of due precaution on their part; that they had been careless and had not given the matter enough thought.

The little girl will often have phantasies of finding a baby that she may adopt as her own, which is easily understood; but many are surprised to hear that the same phantasy is shared by the small boy, although it may be fleeting and quickly withdrawn, because it will meet with certain ridicule. The usual desire is for a manikin that they can take about with them, which recalls the attempt of the mediæval alchemists to produce the Homunculus. This wish will find its substitute usually in the wish to keep small pet animals and allow them to breed. It is frequently an intense grief to little boys to learn that they will not be able to produce a baby unaided, and they feel envious of the girl for what they believe is her greater advantage. This wish for direct production on the part of the boy may often lead to phantasies of creation by magic, upon the basis of the conjurer's production of the rabbit from the hat, as well as symbolically in the composition of music, sculpture, creation by words, literature, or through the excretions. Nietszche quite plainly speaks of himself as the parturient woman with his thoughts (books) as his offspring, in *Jenseits von Gut und Böse,* and we find the same idea consciously or unconsciously amongst many authors.

This outlet of the phantasy in creation through words shows how the phantasy may form a bridge from the secret production to one which is put to public service. One by-path, however, leads off from this highway and takes the form of that curious phenomenon, pathological lying, which is now becoming more readily recognized and accepted in its true position, a central point midway between the normal phantasy and the abnormal condition of delusion and hallucination, the phantastic literary production and the well-told experience of actual daily life occurrences—that is to say, anecdote.

We have mentioned before that pathological lying was a species of day-dream that has been put into narrative form. In this way it stands half-way between the phantasy and the literary work that takes the form of an autobiography. It has no preface, which leads the hearer, however, to suspect that it is a specimen of desired fiction rather than fact; and it is to be wondered occasionally if, after many repetitions of the same story, or when it has been continued for a long time, it does not appear almost true to the teller: almost, but still not quite. The temptation to astonish the audience, to be wonderful and envied, supplies the chief motive power, besides that of making the adventure true in as far as words have their own creative value. The telling of the tale makes that adventure real for the moment, just as to the child the game and the make-believe are almost true at the time; still, when it is not being acted, the child knows well enough that it is only play.

Some of the romances that arise in *pseudologia phantastica*, as it is called, may continue for years. An elaborate tale may be told by a schoolgirl of adventures at a sea-side resort in the holidays, of attentions paid her by a boy staying at the same hotel. Later, she may produce a photograph, which she had signed and upon which she has added an inscription of devotion, but one which she has procured in some other way. She will write letters to herself, purporting to come from this admirer, send herself flowers as from him, and make the other girls thoroughly jealous of her good fortune. Presently the tales come to an abrupt end. Tired of the make-believe romance, or perhaps having met some real man, with whom she has fallen in love, she may artistically find some tragic end for her phantasy lover, or own to having taken in her girl friends.

All these conditions which play with the person's grip of reality show a highly developed capacity for phantasy-making. They will, however, all have the possibility of becoming serious and pathological, so that when one finds a child who seems becoming increasingly absorbed in any one particular day-dream or series of phantasies, it is wiser that they should be investigated by someone who has made a special study of such manifestations, than merely considered of no particular importance and that the child will grow out of them. They may be leading fast to serious nervous trouble for the little one. There is also another step which it would be wise to take in the matter, and that is to give serious consideration to the external conditions of this child's life and its relationships with other people; to ascertain whether the burden of life, which makes this form of escape necessary, cannot be lightened in some way, so as to give it a more sure happiness than obtaining it only in thought.

The game and the phantasy are a delight to the child, but we do not want them to be the only blossoms which its starved soul can enjoy—every child should have a right to expect a few real flowers; neither are all phantasies happy ones by all means—grief and uncertainty, fear and despair, often figure in them too.

Yet it would not be entirely correct to gather that it is only the children who are intensely unhappy who have phantasies. Happy children have them, too; but the eagerness and emotion which attends them in the unhappy child will show a like comparison between a normally hungry child eating a bun and the ravenous speed with which one that is famished will do so. No one could confuse the phantasy-making of an emotionally starved child with that of the one who evolves them for the sheer joy of using the creative faculty of phantasy.

Books which may be Consulted in connection with this Chapter.

Gemeinsame Tagträume. Dr. Hanns Sachs.
Hemmung, Symptom und Angst. Sigmund Freud.
Eine Kindheitserinnerung aus "Dichtung und Wahrheit." Sigmund Freud. *Imago.* V. 1917-19.
The Play of Man. Karl Groos.
The Place of Play in Education. M. Jane Reaney, D.Sc.
Myth of the Birth of the Hero. Dr. Otto Rank. Mental Monograph Series.
Über den Selbstmord, insbesondere den Schüler-Selbstmord. Freud, Adler, and others.
Case of Kleptomania in a Child of Ten Years. Mary Chadwick. *Int. J. Ps.-A.* July 1925.
The Psycho-analysis of an Early Case of Paranoid Dementia. David Forsyth, M.D., D.Sc., F.R.C.P. *Proc. Royal Society of Medicine.* July 1920.
Doktorspiel, Kranksein und Arztberuf. Ernst Simmel. *Int. Zeit. für Psa.* vol. xii. 3. 1926.
Über die Pathologische Lüge. Dr. Helene Deutsch. *Int. Zeit. für Psa.* 1922.
Coincident Phantasies in Mother and Son. Karl Abraham. *Int. J. Ps.-A.* January 1926.

CHAPTER XII

BOTH SIDES OF THE ŒDIPUS CONFLICT

IT is about twenty-eight years ago now since the importance of the emotional conflict between parents and children was first demonstrated as the foundation of many nervous and educational troubles that may be found in children and young persons.

This factor was then postulated by Freud in his book, *Traumdeutung*, published in Vienna in 1900, and translated by Dr. Brill, of New York, in 1913. Here we read as follows (p. 221):

According to my experience, which is now large, parents play a leading part in the infantile psychology of all later neurotics, and falling in love with one member of the parental couple and hatred of the other help to make up that fateful sum of material furnished by the psychic impulses which has been formed during the infantile period, and which is of such great importance for the symptoms appearing in the later neurosis. But I do not think that psycho-neurotics are here sharply distinguished from normal human beings, in that they are capable of creating something absolutely new and peculiar to themselves. It is far more probable, as is shown by occasional observation upon normal children, that in their loving or hostile wishes towards their parents psychoneurotics only show in exaggerated form feelings which are present less distinctly and less intensely in the minds of most children. Antiquity has furnished us with legendary material to confirm this fact, and the deep and universal effectiveness of these legends can only be explained by granting a similar universal applicability to the above-mentioned assumption in infantile psychology.

I refer to the legend of King Œdipus and the drama of the same name by Sophocles. Œdipus, the son of Laius, King of Thebes, and of Jocasta, *is exposed while a suckling*, because an oracle has informed the father that his son, who is still unborn, will be his murderer.

The result of this statement was to awaken considerable excitement, not to say consternation, as well as opposition and horror, on the part of the medical profession, educationists, and parents, together with such laity as eventually became acquainted with the content of the passage. Although the evidence of observation must have presented adequate corroboration of the statement to all these persons, they joined forces in refusing it at first, but afterwards acted upon the same pattern as the neurotic, who, when convinced about the truth of an interpretation to one of his symptoms, first denies and then accepts it, saying he has known this always, it is nothing fresh, and that it was his own idea all through. In this way we find the same information repeated in countless books upon the troubles of childhood that have appeared since the *Traumdeutung*. They deal with the conflict between parent and child; they state also the significance it has for the subsequent life of the child, with the disastrous consequences it may cause, but they present it as their own theory or discovery, either ignoring entirely the part played by Freud as pioneer in the first instance, or adding that in part Freud may be right, although they believe *he* overdrives its significance. This reaction, however, if we give it the analytical interpretation it deserves, corresponding with the Œdipus Complex, i.e. the attitude and behaviour of the sons towards the father, is but further evidence of the hostility of the sons and their desire to kill or banish the father in order to take possession of his belongings. Freud is slain figuratively by means of their repudiation of his part in the discovery of this important factor in the ætiology of childhood's difficulties and of neurosis, but his possessions— the knowledge gained through it—are appropriated and made to appear their own lawful property.

In spite of the inauspicious reception first accorded the theory, Freud continued to develop it, and showed more insistently than before the influence it exerts upon the early years of childhood in a short but most valuable work that emphasized the significance of infantile tendencies for later life, *Three Contributions to the Theory of Sex*, 1905, which afterwards appeared in the Nervous and Mental Monograph Series, published in Washington. The years, however, when Freud worked alone in the field of this research were drawing to a close. The discoveries were beginning to attract other keen young men of science, who were sufficiently adventurous and broad-minded to be anxious for information that would help the elucidation of problems that hitherto remained unsolved. At first a small group only, they sought Freud in Vienna to learn all he had then to teach. Some of them still remain the most loyal and devoted adherents of the Freudian teaching; some have been separated from the work by death; others have seceded for reasons of their own. One of these, at first a most ardent disciple, who broke away early from the Psychoanalytic Society, took up this subject of the Œdipus Complex, as it has been called, with the greatest alacrity, and in 1909 wrote an important paper on the subject, published first in the journal devoted to the young science, and afterwards in a small book, *Die Bedeutung des Vaters für das Schicksal des Einzelmen* (The Significance of the Father for the Development of the Individual). This was Dr. C. G. Jung, of Zurich. A few years later, he had rebelled against the father and developed his own theories derived from Psycho-analysis, under the name of Analytical Psychology.

At the commencement of this paper, in the quotation from Freud's own introduction of the subject, the theory of the conflict is disclosed. Quite simply he constructs for us a situation which is common enough in many families with which we are acquainted personally, as well as a malign influence that has wrecked the lives of persons with whom we have come into contact professionally. Although the idea seemed strange and perhaps repugnant when first encountered in 1900 or thereabouts, we have subsequently met it reiterated so often that the strangeness has been worn down and the repugnance is not so deep as heretofore. Called by other names, and disassociated from that given by its discoverer, it is received almost universally at the present among the people who concern themselves with psycho-therapeutics or the application of psychology to the education of children.

We find the term Œdipus Complex exploited in all directions, on the Magazine page of our evening papers, in Woman's Fashion Journals, sometimes correctly, frequently as a mere catchword, used because it has a certain modern flavour and may still be expected to arrest the attention. Its full significance, however, is seldom realized, and particularly true is this concerning its double-sidedness, that part of the Complex that affects the parents themselves, which is the outcome of their neurosis, and endangers them as much as its influence hinders the development of the children upon whom it reacts.

Usually we find the accent of the Œdipus Conflict laid upon

the child. The description given is the love of the child for one parent and the hatred for the other. But by far the larger part of child behaviour is not unstimulated action arising from the infant alone, but *reactions* to adult stimulations, which we have attempted to show in the previous chapters of this book. If we turn once again to read the account of the Œdipus legend in the *Traumdeutung* given on the first page of this chapter, we find that the trouble began long before the birth of the child who was to be the victim of the tragedy. The nucleus of the drama was the jealousy of the father and the manifestation of his fear, following a prediction by the Oracle that his life should be taken by his son. This leads him to order the exposure of the son shortly after birth. The first decisive step is the attempt of the father to slay the son, not the rebellion of the jealous sons, which is frequently supposed to be the prime factor. In this case the father has actually given the son cause for hatred in this attempt upon his life. The love of the mother is given to the son afterwards as a reward for services, and is not recorded in the original version as the result of seeking by the son. Nor is this the case in the experience of the individual male child of to-day—the mother gives herself to him, loves and tends him with devotion, often consciously or unconsciously prefers him to her husband, for reasons some of which have been already enumerated, whereas others will follow in due course.

The child, therefore, is still the victim of parental emotions in the Œdipus Conflict that is seen at the present day, as was Œdipus in the tragedy by Sophocles, and to-day we are still inclined to blame the child for his part in the affair more than the parents, whose actions in the first place have set the stage.

It is curious how the fear of death on the part of the father and the theme of the exposed and helpless infant, the earliest representation of the fear of death on the part of the child, are two points from which the drama unfolds. The woman appears as the life-giving protector throughout: first Jocasta the mother, then the wife of the herdsman, who adopts him, and finally the return to Jocasta the wife, by whom children are born to Œdipus and in whom his life is continued after his own sacrifice for the welfare of his people. This is familiar. Freud in his recent important work, which we have already quoted so frequently, *Hemmung, Symptom und Angst*, shows that the helplessness of the infant is the beginning of fear, and that fear is closely connected with the other significant factor Guilt, which plays such an important part in the Œdipus Complex; another chief fear in childhood is that of the child for the father on account of castration. This is frequently ascribed to the inversion of the child's death-wishes experienced towards the father, relative to jealousy concerning the mother. The father's inciting behaviour in the original story of the Œdipus tragedy of old, and its later version of the Œdipus Complex of to-day, is usually passed over without the significance of this factor being shown. The child's fear of the father is usually represented as an imaginary or fictitious fear, arising from jealousy on the part of the son, together with primordial guilt experienced by the child on account of his love for his mother, the relic of ancient taboos, whereby the incestuous love of mother and son was punished by death.

Possibly the reason for this attitude is that those who have described and explained the state of affairs found in the Œdipus situation have themselves been men and fathers, who naturally would see the situation from this angle, or those who followed closely the same line of argument. The other side, however, was presented at the last Psycho-analytic Congress at Innsbrück, September 1927, in a paper on the Fear of Death, when attention was drawn to this factor of the influence of the father's behaviour, where children were concerned, in respect to the constellation of ideas—The Fear of Death; Helplessness; Fear and Guilt. ("Notes upon the Fear of Death," Mary Chadwick, to appear in the *International Journal of Psycho-analysis*.)

The typical inciting causes of the Œdipus Complex have been described at length in the previous chapters of this book. The tiny boy desires his mother and her attentions only, viewing with disfavour, even hostility, any who come between them or cause diminution in the tender bond. The mother, on her side, returns the love and cherishes the idea that her son requires her alone. She wishes to be of first importance to this child and frequently neglects her husband or other children on this account, consequently fixating the boy to her, so that any inclination on his part to seek other friends, or, later still, a wife, meets with her disapproval, and sometimes leads to a nervous breakdown on the part of the mother.

In this way many a woman who is not deeply in love with her husband actually takes the son for a love-object, and treats him in such a manner as to put him in the place of a rival to the father, allowing the child to occupy his father's place by her side at night during his absence, bathing with him and keeping him in a condition of constant emotional excitement. This may be unwitting—to satisfy the craving for love which is not gratified by the husband, or to annoy him, but sometimes it may also occur by way of identification. This woman has wished to be a boy, and now loves in the son a representation of her own desire.

The father's attitude to the boy under these conditions has also been described. He will be jealous; he may try by spoiling the child to alienate his affections from his mother or tease and bully the little boy, allowing his hatred to appear in a direct form, which will incur the child's hatred and fear in reply. It is seldom that no trace of these characteristics of the Œdipus Conflict is found in any family, although in some they may be very slight and achieve normal resolution in the later stages of development.

The building-up of the ego and super-ego of the individual from tendencies adopted from the mother and father respectively have been explained at some length in the chapters devoted to the Development and Growth of Personality, as well as the characteristic reactions of both boy and girl children to disappointment in love offered by either parent.

The Œdipus Conflict undergoes many stages and constantly shows fresh developments. Each child, having suffered a love disappointment from one parent, will feel neglected and helpless, quickly turning to the other in the hope that compensation may be found. In this way we may frequently discover the inception of an inversion. The son, having undergone some trauma on account of the mother, sets himself to win the tenderness and affection of the father, which tends to develop his feminine traits. He wishes the father to love him as though he were a little daughter. He tries to please him—a characteristic not seen in the usual course of the Œdipus situation, when the love of the mother is taken for granted and received as a right, to obtain which there is no need for the son to exert himself to please her or in order to maintain the continuance of her love. In the inversion, however, we find this development of the feminine attitude and the wish to please partly an identification with the mother, whom the child feels has abandoned himself. This may often lead to a homosexual tendency in the boy of a passive, feminine kind, and he will be popular with his schoolmasters and the elder boys, with perhaps dangerous results.

Should this second attempt to obtain the exclusive love of one parent again fail, the child will be thrown back entirely upon himself. He will try to incorporate the parental solicitude of both parents in his own person, feel that he alone can be relied upon to look after himself, which leads to independence and success unless carried to extreme, in which case it may make the boy grow up suspicious and unable to learn or put himself under the guidance of another for any purpose whatever.

The attitude of the child at home will be repeated in a series of events of later life, principally schooldays and the opening of a business or professional career. Hostility felt for the father will be transferred to the schoolmaster, university professors or tutors—all authorities, in fact; a state of affairs which has been familiarized by constant explanation in books upon Modern Psychology founded more or less directly upon Freud's teaching.

These repetitions, however, may by their over-emphasis declare themselves the symptoms of neurosis based upon the original Œdipus Conflict of the child, arising from a more than usual craving for love on the part of the child, undue tenderness and the keeping of the son too closely at her side by the mother, or jealousy leading to open expression of hostility on the part of the father. Unless these factors have been unusually highly developed, the Œdipus Conflict should wear itself out by degrees. In an article, now included in the Collected Works of Freud, he describes *The Passing of the Œdipus Complex* as the gradual lessening of this emotionally-toned stage of development due to two factors : the boy relinquishes the mother through fear of the father or to save himself the pain of constant feelings of guilt connected with his illicit attachment to her, and also because he becomes his father through identification, which naturally cancels the hostility that he has previously entertained for him. This stage corresponds very nearly with that which has been called for some considerable time the *Latency Period*, mentioned in the chapter on Games and Phantasies, and extends over the early school-life of the boy, when school interests and the companionship of contemporaries obtain paramount interest.

That this latency period does not exist, or is scarcely noticeable when the Œdipus Conflict is causing some form of early neurosis, has been pointed out by Anna Freud in her book *Kinderanalyse*, and by Melanie Klein, who has tried to show very early influences for the development of the Œdipus Complex in the child's reactions to weaning and contemporary parental troubles, in a paper read at the Innsbrück Conference, and since published in the *Zeitschrift für Psychoanalyse*, 1928. In this case it will continue to maintain the struggle without intermission. Otherwise the latency period exists until the years preceding puberty and its characteristic disturbances show a revival of the former Œdipus Conflict, an attempt to secure the manifest love of the mother, either in the person of the mother herself or in some mother substitute or Imago, together with marked hostility of the father and his surrogates, frequently an exaggerated impatience connected with authority or attempts at parental restraint.

At maturity the resolved Œdipus Conflict allows the son finally to break away from home and parental fixation, to choose a wife of suitable emotional temperament and age, that in due course sets in motion the family cycle anew, with a fresh series of representations of the old drama.

The harmful results, however, which may follow the unresolved Œdipus Conflict, from whatever source this may have arisen, will often discover the son continuing to live unmarried with his mother or another female relative, maintaining a markedly childish attitude to life, together with emotional dependence upon her, or, should he marry, he may seek as his wife a woman of mature age, who will represent his mother.

This is the love side of the picture; upon the other, nevertheless, we may find the hatred and hostility to the father repeated in the man's attitude towards every older man with whom he comes in contact or with authorities. Thus we may find the criminal, the neurotic, with grave symptoms, showing belief in parental persecution, fear of the police, or of organized plotting. Many artists show in their work phantasies derived from the Œdipus situation, the triangular tragedy of which forms the kernel of such a large percentage of literature or drama, as well as other forms of art. The transitions of these various stages of the Œdipus Phantasies and their connection with the day- and night-dreams of average individuals has already been discussed at some length in the previous chapter.

The girl's side of the Œdipus Complex is a very difficult one to trace. Freud assures us that it is modelled closely upon that of the boy, yet it contains greater complexities, but he does not make it clear upon all points, nor explain it anywhere as fully as that of the boy, showing in what actual ways it influences her full development.

Starting at the earliest phase of childhood, that of infancy, it is to be assumed that the girl baby does not receive exactly the same amount of love and attention as that devoted to the boy, because of unconscious emotional factors on the part of the mother, for reasons which have been already given. On this account the Oral Fixation of the girl does not appear so deep as that of the boy, which probably arises from the fact that the mother herself does not experience equal pleasure in feeding her daughter as her son, unless her personal orientation happens to be inverted, with the consequence that her preference is in this unusual direction. In this case we shall find throughout in the development of this family the girls will be regarded as the favourites, and the son, or sons, will be treated as the scapegoat, which generally gives a homosexual trend to the subsequent love-life of the children, the girl's chief love remaining with the mother that directs the antithetical hatred to the father, as her rival where the mother is concerned, and leads the brothers to seek the companionship of the father. This state of affairs, of course, will be accentuated by the fact that the mother's tendency of preference for her daughters points to her own homosexuality, which would hinder her own normal attitude towards her husband keeping the family balance of love proportions.

The girl, however, also is generally brought up with different standards, such as have been already described, and the *duty to please* is early made incumbent upon her. As we pointed out in the case of the boy in this present chapter, he does not feel this necessity to the same extent as his sister, because it has not been taught to him from an early age. He takes for granted that those in his environment will be pleased with him without any efforts on his part to cause the happy condition. Should he find that his actions do not please those around him, he will hate them, leave them, or perhaps regret it; but it never seems to occur to him that it is necessary to change his ways in order to keep or gain the affection of these dissatisfied people. If they do not like him as he is, he will go away to find others who do so.

In all probability the origin of this tendency is the household in which the little boy grows up. It is usually full of women who are inclined to spoil the little fellow and are flattered when he turns to one of them for comfort and love, having fallen out with another. The girl, on the contrary, finds all equally insistent upon her learning to please them, and only one father who may be lenient and spoil her. Should she fail to please him for any reason there is usually no other male relative at hand to whom she may transfer her slighted affections.

The girl will eventually sacrifice her own wishes in order to keep the love of her parents, feeling that should she fail to do so, the loss of their love and protection will make life unbearable, if not actually hazardous. In ancient times, of course, the girl who displeased her parents was in a more dangerous plight even than the boy. She was always more or less kept on sufferance, so that she might be useful or of value in marriage. If her nature was not pleasing, her worth would be diminished in proportion, and this would react upon the treatment she received at home.

For this reason we will often find an important symptom in woman's neurosis being an anxiety to please. They will do anything in order to keep the love of those who are of most significance to them, and the loss of this love will often be felt an equivalent of life itself. It is to be deplored that parents make this factor of pleasing so insistent in the education of the girl, because, although it may appear to be an effective method, it may have interwoven with it injurious results in later life, when the feelings first experienced in connection with the parents are repeated during school-days and mature life, especially in their relations with the marriage-partner.

The usual course of the girl's development has been already explained. She turns from her baby fixation to the mother in due course, sometimes as early as weaning, when this trauma has been made particularly severe for her, or when another baby absorbs the attention of the mother, and transfers her affection to the father. This again undergoes a latency period comparable with that of the boy, which is increased should she also go away from home and spend several years of the formative period of life in the companionship of schoolmates and mistresses, all of whom are of the same sex as herself, some of whom among the latter may entertain conscious or unconscious feelings of hostility towards men, which is often the case among professional women.

The influence of the mistresses at the particular school attended by the girl thus require the most searching attention, since through the law of identification especially she will adopt any emotional bias or other peculiarities they possess. In any case the Latency Period represents a homosexual phase followed by adolescence, when we find her veering round once more and becoming attracted by her father and his friends, or those of her brothers.

This, however, may not always be inevitable. Her wish to have been a boy will greatly influence the Œdipus situation, showing itself clearly in its emotional impulses. Again, in the case of the little girl who wants to be a boy, we shall find the chief love-object to be the mother, with her hostility directed against the father, until the stage is reached when she also identifies with him and becomes not his rival but his smaller double and inseparable companion. Freud has pointed out, in an illuminating paper upon *Paranoia, Jealousy, and Homosexuality*, now translated among his Collected Papers, that former rivals may become firm allies in order to abolish the pain felt by the younger rival, who otherwise cannot deal with the situation.

The girl who loves her mother in the same way as a boy and identifies herself strongly with her father is going to find many difficulties in life as maturity approaches. She will want to find some occupation closely resembling that of men, which is not difficult at the present, and will not like to busy herself with domestic affairs. Her choice of friends will also reflect the same tendencies. She will try to be accepted by boys or other men upon an equal footing, and is ready to be resentful should they attempt to regard her as a girl or want to flirt and make love to her. Instead of receiving this kind of affection she will want to bestow it upon others, often preferring the society of women or choosing to live with another woman upon terms of the warmest intimacy.

We have endeavoured throughout this book to show the importance of parental behaviour for the reactions of the children, but in no other direction does this factor assume such heavy proportions as in the question of the Œdipus Conflict. Parents will—unconsciously, it is true—in many cases sway their children by their own preferences, dislikes, or jealousies, and fear the future rivalry of the child when maturity is reached. Like King Laius of Thebes, the father wishes to dispose of the son or make him ineffectual as a rival in love or professional career, because it seems a future possibility that he may be supplanted (slain). The mother also, although often unconsciously, hinders the development of a pretty daughter, in case she may rival her and detract from her own charms, when they are already on the wane.

In this way the parental side of the Œdipus Complex needs attentive study, especially when it is surmised that children are suffering from symptoms which are usually attributed to it. It will then be necessary to review the actions of the parents, taking into consideration what they may be doing, or what they have done which has produced this effect. It is for reasons such as these that it seems justified to believe the Œdipus Conflict to be double-sided, with the parental aspect as much in need of curative treatment as that of the children.

BOOKS TO BE READ IN CONJUNCTION WITH THE PRECEDING CHAPTER.

The Interpretation of Dreams. Sigmund Freud. 1900. Trans. 1913.
Psychopathology of Everyday Life. Sigmund Freud. 1904.
Three Contributions to the Theory of Sex. Sigmund Freud. 1905.
Introductory Lectures. 1915–16. Sigmund Freud.
Collected Papers. Sigmund Freud. Esp. Analysis of Phobia of Five-Year-
    Old Boy; A Child is Being Beaten; Passing of the Œdipus Complex.
Group Psychology and the Analysis of the Ego. Sigmund Freud.

The Ego and the Id. Sigmund Freud.
Das Inzest-Motiv in Dichtung und Saga. Otto Rank.
Die Bedeutung des Vaters für das Schicksal des Einzelnen. C. G. Jung.
Psychology of the Unconscious. C. G. Jung.
Papers on Psycho-analysis. Ernest Jones.
Essays in Applied Psycho-analysis. Ernest Jones. Esp. Hamlet.
Einführung in die Technik der Kinderanalyse. Anna Freud. *Int. Ps-A.*
  Verlag. Vienna.
Frühstadien des Œdipuskonfliktes. Melanie Klein. *Int. Zeit. für Psa.*
  1928. 1.
Die Erste Entwicklung der weiblichen Sexualität. Ernest Jones. *Int. Zeit.*
  für Psa. 1928. 1.
Notes Upon the Fear of Death. Mary Chadwick. *Int. J. Ps-A.*

ADOLESCENCE

Where there is Life, there is Growth.

THE important subject of Adolescence has been chosen for a brief last chapter to this book for a special reason, although the real subject of discussion has been mainly the early development of the child. Not only is Adolescence a phase of life of which some of the most important details are often unknown, misknown, or to a great extent overlooked, but because it is a focus-point in existence where the past and the future overlap with the present, where the child and the man or woman may be seen simultaneously, as though two exposures had been made upon the same plate or film.

To many psychologists it has become certain that Adolescence forms a second stage in life, a *recapitulation*, where all the characteristics of childhood are repeated, although perhaps with a somewhat different setting and often outside the family circle instead of within it, when the old loves and hatreds, the old jealousies and sorrows, even sometimes the old illnesses of childhood, will recur. To many this idea of repetition may make a strong appeal, representing the idea of a second chance, but unfortunately this is not often the case in reality, because the law of repetition usually means repeating our behaviour in almost every detail, as we acted in the first place, given similar circumstances, and it is more difficult than we think to break away from the old pattern. We are apt to construct our lives upon patterns, which continually show this tendency to repeat. Let us explain further. Close study of child psychology has led those who have conducted careful research to believe that the original complete pattern is constructed in the first five years, and that by the end of this time we may see the child's character showing distinct form. His or her reactions to given conditions become more definite, we can almost predict what a child will do under certain circumstances, and observe first his ego and then the super-ego incorporating the characteristics of loved ones, who have been taken as examples for identification. Then at the end of the first five years—sometimes this may be delayed until the sixth or seventh, or put forward by the same amount of time—we find a change taking place in the child. The sharp outlines of childish individuality will become blurred, childish good-looks will fade a little, and it may happen that those who showed promise of great intelligence at the beginning will prove rather disappointing to parents or teachers when this second period of development sets in, unless its significance is understood.

Several years are now taken up with interests of school-life, playmates, teachers, and lessons, taking the child away from the family circle; these pass and again we find another change taking place. Characteristics which were strongly marked in earlier years thrust themselves with boldness into the forefront, and thus we find adolescence and the few years preceding it a time of exaggeration. It is this exaggeration which makes many people afraid of the adolescent and most certainly the adolescent apprehensive of older persons, fearing their adverse criticism.

Let us see if we can understand why this should be the case. Why, indeed, the exaggeration should be so marked, and then why it alarms the onlooker as well as those who are struggling with its deep waters. To many people it may appear ridiculous to question this at all. They have taken it for granted, but these are the persons who, for some reason, have left off saying *why* to the riddles of the universe, probably because of some problem for which in their childhood or adolescence they could not find any answer. It is a sign, nevertheless, that our interest is beginning to shrink, that we are getting "old," or that we are afraid of what we may find. When we leave off asking questions, we leave off learning.

Adolescent exaggeration is largely due to the fact of cumulative personality. Self-consciousness in its real sense, that is consciousness of the self or ego, impresses the adolescent afresh to a high degree, and he or she wishes the people around to be equally impressed with this individuality. Finding that the rest of the world does not respond readily, the adolescent exaggerates, in the same way that many shout to compel attention, for the pleasure to be derived from doing things to a superlative degree, or because of the pleasant muscular vibrations which such movements occasion. This will continue until the novelty wears off and the new experience has provided all it can by way of new sensations. The adolescent claims a place among people who count, refuses any longer to be passed over as a person of no consequence, a child, and so becomes aggressive and morose in turns, over-emotional, excited and sentimental, when different attempts to win attention fail.

It is now thought that the psychological changes that are typical of adolescence may precede the physical manifestations by some few years. Curious emotional states, those which we have already described, and the reverse, extreme shyness, diffidence, fear of strangers, or even unaccustomed reserve with close relatives, make us suddenly aware that the child we knew is slipping away from us. Those looking on will shake their heads and make some remark about the child's age and leave it at that. Seldom do they think very deeply what this remark signifies, or question exactly the connection and the condition which they ascribe to this cause, or why the age should account for such strange phenomena. They do not often face the problem seriously or honestly, and especially with the child, should he or she ask for help in order to understand this changing self, which is so perplexing. Again mysterious hints and veiled allusions. Some will be inclined to feel that we, too, may be indulging an adolescent craving for exaggeration, because their own intimate circle may have cast aside the shackles of early Victorian prudery, or because they themselves received the inestimable benefit of wise and loving instruction and understanding at this critical time.

The reason why we emphasize this point so strongly is because there are actually so many persons, men and women, whose life has been heavily handicapped by lack of understanding. It is no private phantasy that this is so, but an opinion that has been built up from experience of a great number of persons, whose daily work is to investigate illness of this kind and who discover that a goodly company of those who later on have broken down with some definite nervous trouble, who have fought hard in the face of great odds, and, all honour to them, won through, as well as those who, while escaping actual neurosis, are inhibited in some way and prevented from enjoying life to the full because of injurious influences in childhood. This experience has been gained not only from cases of men and women, but also of adolescents, and those during the years preceding it, who have undergone psychological treatment and through it have been enabled to continue their lives without these grave handicaps.

The adolescent is peculiarly at the mercy of adults around, and frequently we find these treating their juniors with surprising lack of sympathy and even harshness on principle. We read in books of advice on this topic that "their whims should not be indulged, nor their sentimentality encouraged. They should constantly be urged to be up and doing, kept always employed, and made to take an active part in games and sport, all tendencies to consider themselves not strong being dealt with very summarily." No suggestions are made how the adolescent may be helped to use the superfluous emotions, which are a conspicuous factor, nor are ways suggested of giving outlets to the heavy surcharge of phantasy that surges up at this time in creative work of some kind, art, writing, or some hand-work, for which the adolescent shows some inclination. The mental growth is not taken into consideration, nor that it is necessary to help this side of the girl or boy as well as to find outlets for this physical energy. The fatigue of the body leading to physical exhaustion is by no means a satisfactory way of dealing with the psychological and emotional impulses that are needing exercise, and is only a way of escaping the real issues.

Now advice such as may generally be found in booklets and which is frequently given in the treatises prepared for those in charge of adolescents shows that those who give it or follow it have not taken into consideration the many-sided conditions of adolescence. They are forgetting what is happening at this period and that bodily and mental energy are being spread out to cover fresh activities ; also that the mind will now be obliged to assimilate these bodily changes and keep pace with them. In these new conditions they will find the echoes of old childish things and must incorporate them with new functions and startling emotions. Our common-sense should make us realize that a dynamo which has originally run only one set of engines *would* and *must* need carefully readjusting before it can run a second set without detriment either to old or new. So with the human apparatus, which at puberty is leaving the more machine-like stage it has just been through in the Latency Period, as it is called.

But in spite of these facts, human dynamic energy is expected not to flag one iota throughout the change from childhood to maturity, from child system to adult system. It must be kept at high pressure all the time by adult supervision, if necessary.

We are again forced to ask, why are adults so heartless and wanting in understanding when the young need so much sympathy? Do they not remember the doubts and misgivings they went through at this time? Let us go back to the remote past and perhaps we may find there some explanation, because in the habits of to-day we often find some trace remaining from the rituals of our savage ancestors which throws light upon the underlying motive, since the primitive people did not consider it necessary to disguise their intentions, nor, indeed, to pretend to themselves that their wishes were different from what they were.

Unconsciously, the adult harbours very mixed feelings where the next generation is concerned. "Actions speak louder than words" is a proverb we were taught in the nursery, but, of course, the adults only meant it to apply to the misdeeds of the children, and it never occurred to them that these same little ones might apply their axiom to the actions of "grown-ups " and judge them by the same standard.

Initiation rites and puberty rituals are to be found among nearly all primitive races. Frequently both boys and girls are subjected to them, but in some tribes the boys only. They were usually mainly connected with religious ceremonies, of which Confirmation is doubtless a modern survival, but were also allied to various kinds of instruction. They included symbolic rites in which some form of bodily mutilation or the infliction of severe pain was carried out to prove whether the boy or girl were worthy to take his or her place as a member of the tribe, sometimes instruction embodied the myths of the gods, tribal legends, and even, in the case of the girls, information concerning birth-control, but more frequently this knowledge, together with the necessary herbs and other drugs, was placed in the bride's hands by her mother at marriage. Therefore our ideas at the present day on this subject may not be so new as we are often inclined to believe.

But to return to the Puberty Rites. Boys, besides enduring tortures, were often submitted to a symbolic rebirth ceremony, which was supposed to sever their former childish tie to the mother and make them members of the Men's Hut, until they left it at marriage. The marriage or totem restrictions, the taboos, would then be taught them, and they were warned about the severe punishments which their infringement would bring upon offenders. They received instruction in hunting, fishing, and warfare, often not being looked upon as a man until they had slain a member of some hostile tribe or an old woman. They would then be considered ready for a mate, whom it was usually necessary to seek from a different tribe, marriage within the same clan being usually forbidden under Totem regulations. During the Puberty Rites the candidates occupied separate huts far away from the village, fasted, and were generally tormented and frightened by adult members of the tribe. This was supposed to be good for them and make them manly.

The girls were separated from the family hut at the first sign of menstruation and also carried off to some remote camp in the forest by certain old women of the tribe. They were also made to undergo bodily mutilation, and instruction was given them concerning ritual dances. The section which included religion as taught to the boys would be omitted in the case of the girls, because women were carefully excluded from these matters among the primitive races, since it was believed that they had no souls. Probably in place of first importance among the instructions would be placed those which concerned regulations regarding menstruation, which were very strict, and the beliefs current in the tribe with respect to childbirth, pregnancy, and abortion.

The attitude of primitive peoples relative to menstruation is interesting as well as enlightening, respecting the present-day attitude towards it, because much of the old superstition connected with the menstrual flow survives consciously or unconsciously to this day. In ancient times they would say that the women had been bitten by some wild beast at night or that a devil had assaulted her. She would be held unclean for the duration of the period and must touch nothing belonging to men or she would rob them of their virility. Shunned by men and considered a creature to be avoided as a personal danger in those days, the feeling may still survive to some extent in the loathing many women feel for themselves at this time and the attitude of men respecting the menstruating woman. It is by no means uncommon to find men who think of it as "women's disease," or that it is a sign of the impurity of the inside of their bodies. The unpleasant odour affects them particularly, as it does little children, who connect it with bad people and witches.

At the present day there is a tendency to ignore or deny any changes that occur in physical or psychological well-being during menstruation, which, on one hand, may be due to reaction against the old horror of women at this time, and partly the modern attitude that a woman is by no means a weaker vessel than a man. Many women, especially those belonging to the medical profession, will not admit any diminution of vigour or mental balance at this time, because to do so would be a tacit confession of inferiority and confirm the suggestion that it is a hindrance to their profession. So it happens that our girls have to suffer because of the prejudices of their elders.

But we were speaking of the harshness often shown to the adolescent girl being possibly a far-off echo of the cruel Puberty Rites, when she was deliberately made to suffer by the old women of the tribe, who considered it good for her. Then the old women made no secret of inflicting pain upon the younger folk. They do so still, but in more subtle ways. Why? Probably because fundamentally they are still jealous of the young, who have so many more years and chances before them, for whom usually death is not so close.

What is the effect upon the girl of her first menstruation? we may now ask. Even nowadays she may often encounter it unprepared, and receive a shock thereby which will influence the rest of her life. She, like her primitive ancestors, does not understand what has happened, and frequently imagines that she has in some way injured herself, or has contracted some horrible disease. She may attempt to hide it or, driven to this expedient, ask someone about it. What does she receive by way of explanation or consolation? Little enough. Only too often we hear of girls who are told, "That is the beastly side of life"; "That is what women have to put up with. You may expect that every month." Nothing further, no solace, no pointing out that although it may have its attendant inconveniences, it is the sign and seal of her womanhood; in itself nothing to be ashamed of, a mark of maturity, a hope that one day she may bring a wonderful new life into the world. Put this way, and at the same time greeted by her fellow-women and received with all signs of welcome and honour by them, taught to regard it as a sign of pride and no humiliation, we should no longer see the tremendous discrepancy between the usual girl's attitude and the general feelings of joy with which the boy hails the marks of his approaching manhood. We often find that shame and horror which were experienced at the onset of menstruation will be continued throughout life, appearing sometimes as acute physical pain suffered at these times or still more frequently mental distress, tension, and extreme depression for a few days before, at the time itself, or afterwards. Those people who experience the least discomfort or mental derangement are generally found to be those who were either wisely prepared or received it, as we have already mentioned above, as a sign of maturity.

Two themes arise calling for special comment and warning from what has already been pointed out. Should anything be said to a girl beforehand by way of preparation, great care will be necessary to choose what is best suited to the individual temperament with which we are dealing, because in some cases, when the warning of what will happen someday is couched in vague or alarming terms, it will leave the girl with fears for the future or distinct anxiety about growing up and facing this awful event before her. Again, in the manner in which the adult explains matters to the growing girl, we gain an impression of the adult character. The person who herself has regarded that side of life as horrible will doubtless pass on her opinion, possibly without being aware what she is doing or to what extent she is poisoning the girl's mind.

This contrast emphasizes still more forcefully the boy's

elation at the onset of his maturity, and makes the breach between the boy's and the girl's outlook upon growing-up more noticeable, so that it becomes almost impossible for the woman to understand the adolescent boy or for the man to comprehend the reactions of the girl. Actually women are often lamentably ignorant about the actual changes that take place in the boy and make the common mistake of believing what can be seen or heard, the downy upper-lip and a breaking voice, to be the only developments. To some, again, this may appear a gross exaggeration and utter nonsense, but, nevertheless, one has often found this state of affairs existing among both married and unmarried women, those with children of their own and those in charge of young people belonging to others. One mother to whom recently we explained these changes in her growing boy was amazed and thought her son ought to be told too. This would probably have been quite unnecessary, because he had been at school for some years. She thought he did not know because he had not mentioned the matter to her. So many parents and others make the grave mistake of assuming that young people never think about anything without speaking to them about it. Adults do not realize that to bring up children not to mention intimate personal matters to them in their childhood will not teach them to be confidential or communicative later on. We cannot have it both ways.

Whereas we find the greatest shock occurring in girls at the unexpected onset of puberty, in boys the reverse is most often the case. The delay of what they expect and look forward to fills them with the greatest alarm and foreboding. Then it is that they wonder what they can have done to produce this awful catastrophe, and once again out of the past comes the haunting menace of threats or evil consequences for the habit of masturbation, which has been held up to them so often before, but in vague terms. They now feel that it is coming true, and that they are condemned to life-long punishment and the horror of being different from their fellows.

Boys probably have more difficult problems to face at puberty than girls, and once again it is the elders who, through lack of knowledge or recollection of their own experiences, make the conditions doubly hard. Any discussion of this new phase of life amongst the young people themselves would and is regarded with abhorrence by grown-up people. They preach "purity" and self-control to the boy and girl in veiled terms, in tracts of which it is probable they do not understand the meaning unless they are already expert in the knowledge of those things about which such remote hints are given. The whole matter is so carefully disguised that only the grisly threats, in which there is little truth from the physical standpoint, force themselves into stark prominence, but which, for this reason, work the more havoc upon the psychological side. One very seldom finds a woman who will own up quite frankly that she does not know anything. On the surface of things one would assume she might conclude that boys go through developmental changes which correspond to those they know about in girls from their own experience. Married women are the most culpable, and should make sure of information of this sort before they need it for the bringing up of their sons. Spinsters are usually still more vague about these things, as one would suppose, but that does not prevent them from being full of theories of what people ought to do, and confident that no young people can have any feelings or emotions which are more difficult to deal with than they have in their own later middle age, following their repressed childhood and stifled adolescence, and may even go about the country lecturing the young on the virtue of self-control and purity, spreading repression and fears.

Nurses, teachers, and those who have the care of young people ought to make it part of their business to know as much as possible about these bodily functions, to become familiar with them, so that they can regard the boy's problems from the frank point of view of the boy and not only that of the spinster well advanced in years, as so many of us are who teach and preach about such matters. Spinsters are in a difficult position and often fall between two stools, sentimental ignorance or shocked ignorance, both of which result from lack of understanding and often arise from the fact that at some time in their lives they would have liked to have been boys instead of girls, which bitter disappointment has warped their outlook upon life and their attitude to boys especially. It is no uncommon thing for them to deny the truth of this statement at first hearing, yet it does not prove that it is incorrect, but, on the other hand, many will openly acknowledge its truth.

We may also be brought to wonder whether one of the motives of this conspiracy of silence can have been the desire to make the truth appear less real. We will try to answer this last question briefly for the present, because it has already been mentioned so often in previous chapters. The small child believes that he can make himself disappear or other people vanish by the simple expedient of closing his eyes. We all know the familiar expressions, "closing one's eyes to a thing" and "binding oneself to the truth." They mean that at all costs we are determined not to see or recognize something; if we do not see this thing it may be non-existent. Again, the child is a firm believer in the magic of words. He calls "Mummy," and his mother comes. Toys that he asks for have a way of appearing before his eyes, so that he readily confuses the use of words with some magic power of production, which, of course, is further endorsed by the practices of the conjurer.

The saying, "Speak of the Devil and he will appear," proves a similar belief in the magic properties of speech. Following this line of argument, it is no difficult thing to perceive we believe nothing is there unless we admit that we see it, and should we persist in denying that it exists. A small child said one day, when shown a picture of a Royal Mail Steamer, "Letters do not go in ships." He was asked how he thought they got over the sea, and promptly replied: "They don't go over the sea." Again asked why he thought that, and shown a letter that had come from South Africa, his answer was: "Because I never seed 'em."

Many of us are like that little boy; unless we have personal experience of anything, we will not believe in its existence. With Doubting Thomas, we need the evidence of our eyes. The difference increases when we are dealing with emotional values. We cannot see what others feel or experience the emotions of others. A few more characteristics of the little boy just mentioned will explain why this should be so, because his remark was typical of his general tendency. He cannot bear anyone to have anything which he has not got, and will protest that he has a larger toy at home than another child when it appears with something he has never possessed, or that his mother is going to buy him one to-morrow. He is the only person who matters in his own eyes, and he has not yet learnt that things exist on the other side of his horizon. Therefore he cannot or will not admit that things exist which he has never seen. This refusal to believe that anything is greater than ourselves or more important, and exists outside our own possession or knowledge, may develop into the serious mental derangement known as megalomania, or omnipotence, and is allied to the philosophic concept that nothing exists outside our own consciousness. It is actually a denial of unpleasant reality, the *reality of others*, and the firm holding of one's own beliefs in opposition to the opinion of others or in spite of proofs of their falsity.

This is one of the main difficulties which prevent adults from understanding children and adolescents, and these younger people from comprehending adults. Neither do the boys and girls understand themselves, their new emotions and sensations. At one and the same time they feel shy and reserved about them, but would like a confidant with whom to discuss such matters and from whom to receive some explanation of the things which puzzle them. If they could feel sure of meeting sympathy and not endless advice, or perhaps only instructions which are almost impossible to carry out, such as not to think about themselves and their feelings. Much of what is meant by "improper conversation" taking place between young people may be genuine searching after knowledge to straighten out these problems for themselves, the children feeling only too truly that the parents cannot help them. Fathers do not realize the feelings and mental experiences of a daughter at puberty any more accurately than the mother about the mental conflicts which usually attend the dawning manhood of her son. The spinster is usually thoroughly alarmed at the whole subject and pretends that it doesn't matter, that people are making a lot of fuss about nothing, and that a great many feelings are imputed to young people that they never experienced when they were young and about which they never troubled themselves.

Adults often wish to keep children from growing up, and, in the opinion of many, knowledge is a sign of growing-up, getting wiser and older, therefore to withhold knowledge prevents this taking place and keeps the children in mental swaddling-clothes. But out of past ignorance and chaos a new, cleaner sanity is slowly emerging. A more scientific and honest spirit is emerging that embodies the wish to know and the wish to help.

These difficulties of childhood and adolescence, with many closely allied topics, constantly come under discussion nowadays, as well as psychological problems of all kinds, because the public is now thoroughly aroused to the importance and interest of the subject, and those in charge of children's education or welfare work should be prepared to meet calls for help on these subjects. It is most earnestly to be hoped that these new ideas may soon filter through into general knowledge, and that the day is not far distant when people may know at least as much about their minds and psychological needs as about the health of the body, the diet and cleanliness necessary to keep in health, and not to consider that to think about ourselves from this point of view is morbid introspection.

BOOKS WHICH MAY BE STUDIED IN CONNECTION WITH THIS CHAPTER.

Juvenile and Adolescent Delinquency. M. Hamblin Smith. July 1923. Article in *The Child*.
Some Problems of Adolescence. Ernest Jones. *Br. J. of Psychol*. General Section. July 1922.
The Adolescent Girl. Winifred Richmond, Ph.D.
Pubertätsriten den Wilden. Dr. Theodor Reik. *Problems der Religionspsychologie*.

INDEX

GEORGE ALLEN & UNWIN LTD.
LONDON: 40 MUSEUM STREET, W.C.1
CAPE TOWN: 73 ST. GEORGE'S STREET
SYDNEY, N.S.W.: WYNYARD SQUARE
WELLINGTON, N.Z.: 4 WILLIS STREET

For Product Safety Concerns and Information please contact our EU
representative GPSR@taylorandfrancis.com
Taylor & Francis Verlag GmbH, Kaufingerstraße 24, 80331 München, Germany